P9-DDG-130

HIDDEN®

Baja

HIDDEN®

Baja

Including Tijuana, Ensenada, Mulegé, La Paz and Los Cabos

Richard Harris

FIFTH EDITION

Ulysses Press®

BERKELEY, CALIFORNIA

Text Copyright © 1998, 2000, 2002, 2004, 2007 Richard Harris.
Maps and Illustrations Copyright © 1998, 2000, 2002, 2004, 2007
Ulysses Press. All rights reserved, including the right to reproduce this book or portions thereof in any form whatsoever, except for use by a reviewer in connection with a review.

Published by:
ULYSSES PRESS
P.O. Box 3440
Berkeley, CA 94703
www.ulyssespress.com

ISSN 1529-658X
ISBN10: 1-56975-577-9
ISBN13: 1-56975-577-8

Printed in the United States by Bang Printing

10 9 8 7 6 5

MANAGING EDITOR: Claire Chun
PROJECT DIRECTOR: Elyce Petker
COPY EDITOR: Lee Micheaux
EDITORIAL ASSOCIATES: Lauren Harrison, Emma Silvers
TYPESETTERS: Lisa Kester, Judith Metzener
CARTOGRAPHY: XNR Productions, Pease Press
HIDDEN BOOKS DESIGN: Sarah Levin
FRONT COVER PHOTOGRAPHY: couple on beach in Cabo San Lucas
    ©Bruce Herman and surfer ©Guillermo Aldana; both courtesy
    of the Mexico Tourism Board
ILLUSTRATOR: Doug McCarthy
INDEXER: Sayre Van Young

Distributed by Publishers Group West

HIDDEN is a federally registered trademark
of BookPack, Inc.

Ulysses Press 🐢 is a federally registered
trademark of BookPack, Inc.

The author and publisher have made every effort to ensure the
accuracy of information contained in *Hidden Baja*, but can accept
no liability for any loss, injury or inconvenience sustained by
any traveler as a result of information or advice contained in this
guide.

Write to us!

If in your travels you discover a spot that captures the spirit of Baja, or if you live in the region and have a favorite place to share, or if you just feel like expressing your views, write to us and we'll pass your note along to the author.

We can't guarantee that the author will add your personal find to the next edition, but if the writer does use the suggestion, we'll acknowledge you in the credits and send you a free copy of the new edition.

ULYSSES PRESS
P.O. Box 3440
Berkeley, CA 94703
E-mail: readermail@ulyssespress.com

What's Hidden?

At different points throughout this book, you'll find special listings marked with this symbol:

◄ HIDDEN

This means that you have come upon a place off the beaten tourist track, a spot that will carry you a step closer to the local people and natural environment of Baja.

The goal of this guide is to lead you beyond the realm of everyday tourist facilities. While we include traditional sightseeing listings and popular attractions, we also offer alternative sights and adventure activities. Instead of filling this guide with reviews of standard hotels and chain restaurants, we concentrate on one-of-a-kind places and locally owned establishments.

Our authors seek out locales that are popular with residents but usually overlooked by visitors. Some are more hidden than others (and are marked accordingly), but all the listings in this book are intended to help you discover the true nature of Baja and put you on the path of adventure.

Contents

Maps

OUTDOOR ADVENTURE SYMBOLS

The following symbols accompany national, state and regional park listings, as well as beach descriptions throughout the text.

▲	Camping	🏄	Surfing
🥾	Hiking	⛵	Windsurfing
🚲	Biking	🛶	Canoeing or Kayaking
🐎	Horseback Riding	🚤	Boating
🏊	Swimming	🛥	Boat Ramps
🤿	Snorkeling or Scuba Diving	🎣	Fishing

ONE

The Other California

Sitting in the shade of a 30-foot-tall *cardón* cactus on a rocky hilltop, you can look out across a turquoise-blue bay so clear that golden tropical fish can be seen dancing beneath the surface. Vultures drift in lazy circles overhead, pelicans skim the water, and cormorants dive for fish from high in the sky. A pod of dolphins leaps along the surface of the bay in joyful abandon, and far off in the distance a whale spouts, looking like a geyser on a drifting desert island. Palms line the gracefully curving beach of sugary sand and thatched-roof shelter where you've made camp for the night—and maybe the next week or so. A Oaxacan vendor comes by, selling drinking water, fresh fruit and colorful handwoven blankets. It's the way you imagine a South Pacific tropical paradise would be—except for one thing. You can drive there. You don't even need a passport.

This is one aspect of the Baja peninsula, a scantily populated wilderness that is startling in its immensity. Much of the wild interior has been set aside as national parks, biosphere reserves and other protected areas. Here you will discover majestic mountain peaks, cool forests, and some of the most dramatic desert scenery on earth, studded with volcanoes and alive with giant cactuses and strange species—elephant trees, incense trees, boojum trees—found nowhere else on earth. You'll visit exotic port cities and graceful old colonial towns built around centuries-old mission churches. You may linger in laid-back fishing villages or bask on the beaches at world-class resort areas.

A road trip from the U.S. border to Los Cabos and back—just over 2000 miles—has all the elements of a once-in-a-lifetime adventure. But the fact is, once bitten by the Baja bug, most people return year after year. There are seemingly endless "hidden" places to explore, and with the gradual improvement of many secondary roads, more such places become accessible to motorists each year. Read on and start planning your own journey of discovery in Baja.

▼▼▼▼▼▼▼▼▼▼▼

Where to Go

Only one main highway runs the length of the Baja peninsula, so you'd think trip planning would be a snap. But as you'll discover in later chapters of this book, the best Baja adventures can be found on side trips from the main highway by back road or boat. Where you decide to spend most of your time will depend on the season, the duration of your trip and the outdoor activities you enjoy most.

Most travelers from the West Coast cross the **U.S.–Mexican border** at one of two ports of entry in Tijuana, a large city that also attracts many daytrippers with its duty-free shopping, raunchy nightlife and bullfights. Some travelers avoid Tijuana traffic by crossing at the hidden-away border town of Tecate. Mexicali, the capital city of Baja California, is a reasonable border-crossing choice for anybody headed for San Felipe, though overindustrialization has created traffic congestion on its main thouroughfares. The truly "hidden" border crossing for Baja is Algodones, near the California/Arizona line; motorists who cross there will still have to drive through the outskirts of Mexicali before heading south.

◆◆◆◆◆◆◆◆◆◆◆◆◆◆◆◆◆◆◆

Summer is prime time for sportfishing— the warm seas attract marlin, sailfish and other big game fish in large numbers.

Northern Baja is a study in contrasts. An hour's drive south of Tijuana on the Baja Highway, the sprawling city of Ensenada offers shopping and sightseeing possibilities along with plenty of traditional Mexican seaport charm. The coastline and mild, sometimes misty climate resemble San Diego's. At the opposite extreme, San Felipe on the Sea of Cortez, a fishing village turned RVers' paradise, is surrounded by the driest desert in Baja. San Quintín, south of Ensenada, hardly looks like it belongs in Baja: Irrigation has transformed the coastal plain into a rich agricultural zone. Some of the best Pacific beaches lie south of San Quintín, but the area's most spectacular attraction is Parque Nacional Sierra de San Pedro Mártir, with its cool alpine forests and Baja's highest mountain peaks.

As you enter **central Baja**, you suddenly find yourself in the vast, mainly uninhabited Desierto Central. The Baja Highway takes you through the surreal heart of the Cataviña boulder field—all huge cactuses, bizarre trees and rocks the size of houses. Rocky side roads lead to old mission ruins and far older cave paintings. Toward the south end of the desert, a paved side road takes you to Bahía de los Angeles on the Sea of Cortez. This quintessential gringo enclave has great fishing and sea kayaking.

If you decline to take this turnoff and continue south on the main highway, you'll reach the Pacific Coast at Guerrero Negro soon after crossing into Baja California Sur. This rather bleak company town (nearly everybody works at the nearby salt mines) has emerged as a major ecotourism center thanks to the gray

Text continued on page 6.

Baja

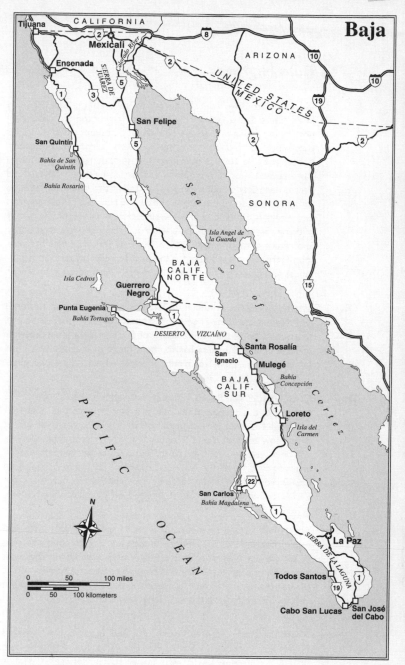

CALIFORNIA

Tijuana

Mexicali

Ensenada

SIERRA DE JUÁREZ

San Felipe

San Quintín

Bahía de San Quintín

Bahía Rosario

ARIZONA

UNITED STATES

MEXICO

SONORA

Sea

Isla Angel de la Guarda

BAJA CALIF. NORTE

Isla Cedros

Guerrero Negro

Punta Eugenia

Bahía Tortugas

DESIERTO   VIZCAÍNO

San Ignacio

Santa Rosalía

Mulegé

Bahía Concepción

BAJA CALIF. SUR

Loreto

Isla del Carmen

of

Cortez

P A C I F I C   O C E A N

San Carlos

Bahía Magdalena

N

SIERRA DE LA LAGUNA

La Paz

Todos Santos

Cabo San Lucas

San José del Cabo

0   50   100 miles

0   50   100 kilometers

The Baja Highway

It's possible to drive from the border to the tip of the Baja Peninsula in 24 hours flat, stopping only for military checkpoints and seeing nothing but a blur of roadside cactuses and boojum trees. In fact, it's surprisingly common to encounter Southern Californians pretending to race the Baja 1000 as they make teeth-gnashing, wild-eyed three-day-weekend runs to Los Cabos and back jangled on caffeine and Tecate beer. Stay out of their way. I've found that the ideal duration for a road trip down the length of Baja and back is a little more than two weeks. (Of course, many snowbirds take much longer; the danger of doing so is that you may experience an irresistible urge to go native and return home months later to find that someone else has your job.) Here's my tested plan for the best basic Baja experience (distances and times are from the last previous destination in boldface):

Day 1   Upon crossing the border into **Tijuana**, stop to buy car insurance and then hit the highway south to **Ensenada** (190 km./2–3 hours). En route, stop at the fishing village of Popotla for a great sidewalk seafood dinner. Ensenada has the best range of lodgings you'll find for several days, as well as plenty of places to stock up on supplies.

Day 2   Continue south on Route 1 through farmlands and small towns. The highlight of this section of the road is a side trip into the mountains of Parque Nacional Sierra San Pedro Mártir, but I suggest you pass it by for now and visit it on the return trip, when the cool pine forests will be a welcome contrast to the desert that lies farther south. If instead you drive all the way to **Cataviña** (322 km./5–6 hours) on Day 2, you'll have plenty of time to explore the beauty of the Desierto Central in the cool sunset and early morning hours.

If it's whale-calving season, you'll want to spend at least a day and two nights—and perhaps more—in the salty, spartan company town of **Guerrero Negro** (278 km./4–5 hours), situated on the most accessible of Baja's legendary whale-watching lagoons. At other times of year, the area is a great birdwatching destination where you can rest up before tackling the next long desert crossing.

Cross the stark Desierto Vizcaíno to **San Ignacio** (140 km./2–3 hours) and continue to **Santa Rosalía** (73 km./1–2 hours), both unique, picturesque towns with limited tourist services. Continue down the coast to **Mulegé** (63 km./1 hour), a gringo-friendly little "Margaritaville" where you'll finally feel like you've arrived in the Mexican tropics. If your dream vacation includes sea kayaking, this is one of the best places in Baja to do it. It's also the departure point for all-day whale-watching expeditions to wild and remote Laguna San Ignacio on the Pacific Coast.

Spend a long day driving down the seacoast, over the mountains, through farm country and across another long stretch of desert to **La Paz** (483 km./6–8 hours), a vibrant Mexican capital where you'll find a welcome assortment of comfortable lodgings and first-rate restaurants at prices far lower than those that await you in Los Cabos. There are pretty pocket beaches east of the city and great sea kayaking and scuba diving around Isla Espiritu Santo.

Pick out your personal piece of paradise along the 333-kilometer loop trip from La Paz to the tip of the peninsula and back. There's a wide range of spots to choose from: the rustic sport fishing and windsurfing resorts around **Los Barriles** (103 km./2 hours) to the cafés, galleries and gentrified colonial charm of **San José del Cabo** (80 km./1–2 hrs) and the cruise-ship port and mega-resort ambience of **Cabo San Lucas** (30 km./45 min.) to the laid-back artists' and surfers' haven of **Todos Santos** (67 km./1 hour).

From **La Paz**, begin retracing your route northward. Stop for the night in the romantic colonial town of **Loreto** (346 km./5–6 hours). The next day, continue to **Guerrero Negro** (406 km./6–7 hours), and on the third day go on to **San Quintín** (413 km./6–7 hours).

Day 15 Pack a picnic and spend the day in the evergreen forests and alpine meadows of **Parque Nacional Sierra San Pedro Mártir**, reached via an unpaved side road that turns off the highway north of San Quintín. When you return to the highway, you're just four hours from the border. However, since crossing the border can mean waiting in line for several more hours, the preferable plan is to rest up in Ensenada before returning to *los Estados Unidos*.

Of course, as you'll find when you read further in *Hidden Baja*, this itinerary takes in only the high points along the main highway. Let this serve as your introduction to "the other California" with the understanding that just about everyone who visits Baja once comes back for more.

whales that return to nearby Scammon's Lagoon each winter to calve and breed. Beyond Guerrero Negro, the vast Desierto Vizcaíno sprawls across the widest part of the peninsula. A long backroad journey will take you to a remote stretch of the Pacific coast, where huge colonies of sea lions and elephant seals inhabit the offshore islands.

Palm trees appear as **southern Baja** begins. Following the Baja Highway through landlocked San Ignacio, the starting point for whale-watching expeditions to the pristine Bahía San Ignacio, you'll hit the Sea of Cortez coast at Santa Rosalía, a strangely un-Mexican town founded by European copper miners.

My favorite part of Baja lies south of Santa Rosalía, on the Sea of Cortez, near the hidden refuges of Mulegé and Loreto. Along the highway between the two towns, the beaches of Bahía Concepción have palm trees, sea shells, tropical fish, big cactuses, crystalline turquoise water and creamy sand that slides through your fingers like sugar. Snorkeling the bay or gliding across it in a kayak, you could easily decide never to return to civilization at all (though you'd change your mind when summer arrived). Beyond Loreto, the Baja Highway begins another long desert crossing, which you can break into manageable segments by taking a side excursion to San Carlos on Bahía Magdalena, the southernmost of Baja's famous gray-whale calving bays.

The **Cape region** of Baja California Sur begins with La Paz, the state capital, a small, laid-back city on a lovely harbor. Though sightseeing attractions are few, you won't notice their absence as you explore the cheerful city streets and the exquisite nearby beaches. From there, it's on to bustling Los Cabos, as San José del Cabo and Cabo San Lucas have come to be known. This mega-resort vacation zone on the very tip of the peninsula is Baja's epicenter of mainstream tourism, where beaching, boating and deep-sea fishing attract more visitors than all other Baja destinations south of Ensenada combined. Being surrounded by the industrial-strength tourism of Los Cabos can quickly become a lot like having bees live in your head, but "hidden" getaways are nearby. Perhaps the best is Todos Santos, an emerging artist community that boasts legendary surfing beaches. It's one starting point for hiking and horseback trips into the Sierra la Laguna, an isolated and unique natural area.

When to Go

SEASONS

There is no wrong time to go to Baja. Peak tourist seasons are May through September on the Pacific coast and Christmas week through early April on the Sea of Cortez. As the growing hordes of snowbirds and whale watchers who head down the peninsula in January, February and March will not hesitate to caution you, some winter days can make you wish you'd brought your parka, especially along the windblasted Pacific coast. More often than not, however, the winter climate is mild, with temperatures in Ensenada running about the same as in San Diego and those in Los Cabos about 15 degrees warmer. Deep snow can render the high sierra inaccessible.

Spring offers an ideal climate for travel on the Baja Highway. It's not too hot for desert hiking, and after a wet winter, you'll see incomparable displays of desert wildflowers. Off-season rates prevail everywhere. The only downside to a spring trip is that the water off both coasts is still too cool for comfortable swimming or snorkeling.

Summer is relentlessly humid and hot on the Sea of Cortez; the Pacific coast can be more inviting. Desert areas are unbearable by day but may cool down by 40 degrees at night; on the Sea of Cortez, temperatures typically reach well above 100 degrees and stay there, day and night, for weeks on end. Water temperatures in the Sea of Cortez are nearly as high as air temperatures. Tropical storms called *chubascos* can pummel the coast without warning. The summer climate is extremely humid, and this is the only time of year when you'll encounter mosquitoes.

Autumn means warm water, moderate temperatures, low room rates and—in September and October—unpredictable weather patterns. Many sporting events, from huge bicycle races with thousands of contestants to the legendary Baja 1000 car and motorcycle races, take place at this time of year. Early December marks the beginning of snowbird season, when RV campers begin arriving in droves.

CALENDAR OF EVENTS

Early January Not many events take place in January, though the snowbird season is at its peak. **El Día de los Santos Reyes**, January 6, marks the end of the Christmas holiday season. It is on this day, not Christmas Day, that Mexicans feast and exchange gifts.

JANUARY

Late January Puerto San Carlos celebrates the cetaceans of Bahía Magdalena with the **Festival de la Ballena Gris** (Gray Whale Festival).

During February In Ensenada, San Felipe and La Paz, **Carnaval** (the Latin Mardi Gras) is celebrated with five days of parades, fireworks, costumes and dancing in the streets. Monday of Carnaval week is "henpecked husbands' day," when men are allowed 23 hours to indulge every desire—at their own risk.

FEBRUARY

Early February On February 2, La Paz and many villages mark what they consider the end of winter with music, dancing and processions of **Candelaria** (Candlemas).

Late February   Sports car racers compete in the **Mexicali Grand Prix**. Todos Santos holds its annual **Festival del Arte**, the biggest arts-and-crafts festival in this artists' colony.

MARCH

Early March   The desert around San Felipe provides the course for extreme off-road racing in the **Score San Felipe 250**, a scaled-down version of the famous Baja 1000.

Late March   Over **Spring Break**, traditionally the third and fourth weeks of March, college students from all over the western United States descend on Baja. The San Felipe area is hit hardest; Rosarito, Ensenada and Los Cabos are also packed with student bodies. The **Fiestas Patronales de San José del Cabo**, honoring San José del Cabo's patron saint, falls right in the middle of Spring Break.

APRIL

During April   Holy Week (**Semana Santa**), the week before Easter, is not as crowded in Baja as elsewhere in Mexico. But many people visit relatives on the "mainland," and many businesses shut down from Wednesday through Sunday. San Felipe hosts a series of beach-style sporting events through the month, including the **Posada del Mar Aerobics Meet**, the **San Felipe Triathlon**, and the **Beach Volleyball Slam Festival**. Around the same time, 10,000 cyclists participate in the semiannual **Rosarito to Ensenada Bicycle Race**, and the **Newport-Ensenada Yacht Race** draws so many boaters that it claims to be the world's largest regatta.

Early April   On the first weekend in April, San José del Cabo and Cabo San Lucas host the **Concurso Señorita Piel Dorada**, one of the world's largest bikini competitions.

Late April   What better place to recover from the month's fitness events than at the **Tijuana Pizza Festival**? Farther south, La Paz is the setting for the **Baja California Sur Kayak Regatta**.

MAY

Early May   The **Fiestas de la Fundación de La Paz**, during the first week of May, offers everything from street processions to off-road racing. **Cinco de Mayo**, a major holiday all over Mexico, is observed in most Baja communities. The streets of Cabo San Lucas are the scene of the annual **Fireman's Chili Cookoff Festival**, which also features dancing, entertainment and a pie-eating contest.

Late May   Vaqueros (Mexican cowboys) come from all over Baja and northern Mexico to compete for prizes in the **Tecate Rodeo**.

JUNE

Early June   The biggest happening of the month is **Día de la Armada** (Navy Day), when Mexican naval bases stage military boat processions for the people of nearby coastal towns. Ensenada holds its annual **Paella Festival**.

Late June   The Mexico International Volleyball Tournament, the world's largest volleyball event, attracts more than 2000 players to Playa Estero south of Ensenada.

During July   July 11 marks the **Anniversary of Tijuana**, founded in 1899. The fiesta lasts all month; it's sure to be especially crazy in 1999. Baja's economic development, from factories to farming cooperatives, is the focus of **Expo Ensenada**. Binge on mollusks at the **Clam Festival** in San Quintín.

During August   Tecate's **La Pamplonada** is patterned after the Running of the Bulls in Pamplona, Spain, and every bit as dangerous. The event is followed by the **Guadalupe Valley Wine Festival** in the vineyard country around Tecate. The **Feria de Tijuana** features entertainment, carnival rides and livestock shows at Agua Caliente racetrack from mid-August to mid-September.

Early September   The **Fiesta de Santa Rosalía** is colorfully celebrated in both Santa Rosalía and Mulegé. A few days later, Loreto's **Día de la Virgen de Loreto** climaxes with a spectacular street procession.

Mid-September   Many Baja towns celebrate Mexico's **Independence Day**, September 16, with fireworks and festivities. In Mexicali and La Paz, the observance lasts for two days and includes an array of cultural events. Both Santa Rosalía and Todos Santos observe their **Fiestas Patronales** (Founder's Day) with street celebrations. You can join the **Baja Sea Turtle Rescue** in Cabo San Lucas.

During October   El **Día de la Raza** (The Day of the Race, referring to mestizos) is celebrated in place of Columbus Day. In Los Cabos, why not check out the **Tequila and Mariachi Festival?**

Late October   The **Mexicali-San Felipe Sports Weekend** features a Mexicali-San Felipe Bicycle Ride (55 miles or 125 miles), a San Felipe Mountain Bike Ride (10 miles or 20 miles) and a Mexicali-San Felipe Five-Person Running Relay. Around the same time, the 50-mile **Rosarito-Ensenada Bicycle Race** draws even more participants than the same race held in the springtime; cyclists have numbered around 16,000 in recent years. Cabo San Lucas honors its patron saint with the **Fiesta de San Lucas** on October 18.

Early November   El **Día de los Muertos**, or Day of the Dead— actually two days, November 1 and 2—is generally a quiet, stay-at-home time in Baja; most businesses close. Soon afterward, San Felipe's biggest party of the year, the **Shrimp Festival**, fills three days with music, dancing, seafood and beach fun.

Mid-November   Granddaddy of backroad Baja races, the **Baja 1000** follows different routes in different years, alternating between the traditional 1000-mile Ensenada–La Paz race (a Baja institution long before the highway was paved) and a 1000-kilometer circuit of Baja California Norte. The race has four divisions—motorcycles, dune buggies, stock cars and four-wheel-drive trucks.

DECEMBER   **Early December**   San Felipe stages a **Snowbird Welcome Fiesta** in observance of the annual mass migration of RVers to its beaches.

▼▼▼▼▼▼▼▼▼▼▼
Before You Go

VISITORS CENTERS

The **Secretaría de Turismo de México** (SECTUR) maintains tourism offices in Tijuana (Sor Juana Inés de la Cruz No. 12914; phone/fax 664-681-9893; e-mail cortesdh@yahoo.com) and La Paz (Carretera al Norte, Km. 5.5; 612-124-0100, fax 612-124-0722; e-mail turismo@gbcs.gob.mx). SECTUR operates tourist information offices in Ensenada, San Felipe, Tecate, Tijuana and San José del Cabo; their locations and phone numbers are listed in the "Addresses & Phone Numbers" sections at the end of each chapter of this book, beginning with Chapter Four.

Some Baja cities and towns have tourist offices operated by a municipal **Comite de Turismo y Convenciones** (COTUCO). They also appear in the "Addresses & Phone Numbers" sections.

Among the most valuable travel information sources is **Baja Life**, a slick, colorful magazine that covers topics from fishing and wildlife watching to new resort hotels and Mexican property taxes. ~ Baja Communications Group, P.O. Box 4917, Laguna Beach, CA 92652; 949-376-2252, fax 949-376-7575; www.baja life.com. Also helpful is the biweekly newspaper-format *Baja Times*, which lists current events and includes how-to information of interest to gringo travelers and residents alike, available at all resorts and many restaurants and sightseeing attractions (P.O. Box 430145, San Diego, CA 92143; 661-612-1738, fax 661-612-0028; www.bajatimes.com).

Several California-based travel clubs rank among the best sources of up-to-date information on road conditions, weather, fuel availability, fishing and such. They also offer discount rates for hotels, restaurants, RV parks, kayaking and sportfishing trips, books and maps; member discounts on Mexican car and boat insurance can save you more than the price of membership (in the $30- to $40-a-year range). Leading travel clubs include **Vagabundos del Mar RV, Boat and Travel Club** (190 Main Street, Rio Vista, CA 94571; 707-374-5511, 800-474-2252, fax 707-374-6843; www.vagabundos.com) and **Discover Baja Travel Club** (3089 Clairemont Drive, Suite A-2, San Diego, CA 92117; 619-

275-4225, 800-727-2252, fax 619-275-1836; www.discover baja.com).

Flying to Los Cabos? Keep your packing simple. A camera plus whatever else you can fit in your daypack or weekender will be fine, as long as it includes a wad of cash or a major credit card. Bring a bathing suit or buy one there. A T-shirt, shorts, athletic shoes and a shady hat, along with a pair of long pants or a skirt for café evenings in San José, are sufficient. Dressing up is unheard of even in the best restaurants. More than one change of clothes may be superfluous, since many hotels in all price ranges offer overnight laundry service. If you're going in the winter, take a sweater or light jacket. You can rent sports equipment when you get there. If you plan to explore the desert and sierra, at minimum you'll need hiking boots, a canteen and a bandanna that you can wet down to keep cool.

PACKING

> Travelers with preteen youngsters would do well to try a test excursion to San Felipe to learn how their kids cope with long hours on the road and few diversions, before committing to drive the length of Baja.

If you're driving, the situation is different. No matter how small your vehicle, you should be equipped to camp at least part of the time. In many areas, the camping beaches are more appealing than the hotels. In a passenger car, a tent, sleeping bags and other basic gear may take up a lot of trunk space, making it wise to limit your material possessions almost as much as if you were flying. Cooking gear is good to have along. More important for motorists who plan to explore beyond the paved main highways is safety and repair gear. This should include a first-aid kit, a flashlight, motor oil, transmission fluid and brake fluid, tire inflation cans, replacement V-belts, hoses and fuel line. And be sure to bring a toolkit that's adequate to replace these bits and pieces.

As your packing list grows, keep in mind that if you pack a car too tight, it will "explode." After a couple of days' beach camping, the prospect of fitting all that stuff back into the car may look so daunting that you may be forced to remain at the beach for the rest of the winter.

Obviously, with a large motor home the situation is different. One of the biggest joys of RV travel is the materialistic satisfaction of taking along every possession you could conceivably want. Before your trip, you can spend weeks thinking up hypotheticals like, "OK, suppose we're on this idyllic tropical beach and there are all these coconuts around that would be perfect for making a Thai fish curry. Better take the electric wok, huh?"

There are only a few places in Baja where hotel and motel rooms outnumber campsites. The 120-kilometer stretch of road between Rosarito and Ensenada, all within an hour's drive of the

LODGING

U.S. border, boasts an abundance of stylish beach resort hotels, as well as motels with more moderate rates across the highway from the beach.

From there all the way to La Paz, a distance of 1400 kilometers, lodgings of any description are few and far between. Most towns along the way have just one or two motels. As the state capital of Baja California Sur and a main port for travelers arriving from the Mexican mainland, La Paz hosts more business travelers and politicians than tourists. There are plenty of good hotels across the street from the beach and waterfront promenade that run along the Bahía de La Paz, and rates are among the lowest in Baja.

Los Cabos—the towns of Cabo San Lucas and San José del Cabo and the luxury resort developments that line the 30-kilometer stretch of divided highway between the two towns—has the most plentiful and most expensive accommodations in Baja. Even there, however, rooms are available at lower rates if you know where to look.

Budget-minded travelers can save by visiting during the off-season, which is different in various regions of Baja. Ensenada's off-season runs from October through April; rates drop by about 20 percent during these months. Hotels in the area are packed to capacity on weekends but empty out during the week, so there is often a discount on Sunday through Thursday nights. In Los Cabos, rates are highest from Christmas week through early April, and lowest from September to early December. Less dependent on tourism, La Paz hotels have no high or low season. In all beach resort areas, rooms that face away from the water cost less than those with sea views, and motels across the highway cost less than those with beachfront locations. Another way to economize is by reserving a room with a kitchen.

To help you decide on a place to stay, I've described the accommodations not only by area and amenities, but also accord-

FLOATING ROOM RATES

Room rate categories are necessarily approximate because of fluctuating currency exchange rates. International resort hotels that merit four or five stars in the Mexican government's hotel rating system are allowed to set their rates in U.S. dollars as protection against possible peso devaluations. Lesser hotels—generally, those that fall into the budget and moderate categories—set their rates in pesos and are subject to federal price controls, so during Mexico's recurring periods of economic instability, lower-priced lodgings tend to become absurdly cheap in dollars, while the expensive places cost as much as ever.

ing to price. Rate categories listed are for two adults during the high season. *Budget* hotels are generally less than $40 a night for two people. The rooms will be clean and basic, lacking such luxuries as air conditioning and in-room telephones. All hotels listed in this book do have private baths. *Moderate*-priced hotels, at $40 to $80 a night, provide larger rooms and plusher furnishings. They generally have air conditioning and satellite TV and may have phones. At a *deluxe* accommodation you can expect to spend $80 to $125 for a double. These places are generally large beach resorts with spacious rooms, balconies overlooking the sea, and guest amenities that include swimming pools. With rare exceptions, only in Los Cabos will you encounter *ultra-deluxe* hotels where rooms begin at $125 a night for double occupancy. These world-class resorts have spectacular locations and every imaginable amenity, including tennis courts, landscaped grounds and sometimes golf courses. Guest accommodations, whether spacious, semi-divided rooms or full suites, will be stylishly decorated and enjoy exceptional sea views.

DINING

Within a particular chapter, the restaurants are categorized geographically. Restaurants listed offer lunch and dinner unless otherwise noted. Each restaurant entry describes the establishment's cuisine and ambience along with a price category—budget, moderate, deluxe or ultra-deluxe. *Budget* eateries usually cost $7 or less for dinner entrées; *moderate* restaurants range from $7 to $12 at dinner and offer pleasant decor and a broader menu than budget restaurants; *deluxe* establishments tab their entrées between $12 and $25 and feature sophisticated cuisines and personalized service; and *ultra-deluxe* restaurants are generally priced above $25. Restaurants add a 15 percent IVA (sales tax), and some resorts add a 15 percent service charge on top of that. Some restaurants also add a tip (*propina*) to your check automatically, so inquire before you leave a tip too. Prices given are necessarily approximate because of fluctuating currency exchange rates.

Besides modest indoor restaurants, the budget category includes roadside stands that sell tamales, fish tacos and whole fried fish to motorists on the go, as well as *comedores,* open-air fast-food places where the cook prepares your food while you watch, and you eat it at a nearby picnic table. The food is good at these places, and the prices are great.

Some travelers shun food stands and *comedores* for fear of contracting "Montezuma's revenge." Mexicans, too, believe that gringos will get sick if they eat local food because their digestive systems are not accustomed to it. The truth is, travelers in Baja today rarely get the dread distress in the lower tract. As in the United States, food sellers are licensed and subject to government inspection, and health regulations are strictly enforced in areas that depend on tourism.

As for restaurants, you don't have to be in Ensenada or Los Cabos to find great food. RVers spread the word quickly, and memorable meals tend to wait at the end of long desert crossings. Some of the finest dining in Baja is found in unexpected places like San Quintín, Guerrero Negro and Santa Rosalía.

HEALTH & SAFETY

Medical Emergencies Visits to doctors are relatively inexpensive, and hotels can usually recommend English-speaking physicians. Contact your health insurance carrier before you leave to find out the extent of your coverage while abroad.

For serious medical emergencies, Mexican health care does not measure up to U.S. standards. Mexico has about half as many doctors per capita as the United States. For true emergencies, a San Diego–based service called **Critical Air Medicine** provides air ambulance service to anywhere in Mexico 24 hours a day, every day of the year. ~ Toll-free from Mexico, 95-800-010-0268 or collect 858-010-0268. One little-known option is **SkyMed International Insurance,** a membership program that guarantees "flying emergency room" evacuation to the United States, as well as assistance in returning family members, vehicles and pets, for a very reasonable annual fee. ~ 4425 North Saddlebag Trail, Scottsdale, AZ 85251; 480-946-5188, 800-475-9633 from the U.S. or 001-866-805-9624 from Mexico; www.skymed.com, e-mail info@skymed.com.

Full-service hospital facilities in Baja are: in Mexicali, **Hospital Civil** on Calle del Hospital ~ 686-557-3700; and **Hospital Almater** on Avenida Francisco I. Madero ~ 686-553-4015, e-mail hospital@almater.com; in Ensenada, **Hospital General** on Avenida Reforma at Fraccionmento Bahía ~ 646-172-4500. There's also **Hospital Velmar** at Calle Arenas 151 ~ 646-173-4500; in La Paz, **Hospital Salvatierra** on Calle Bravo at Ortiz de Domínguez ~ 612-122-1496, 612-122-1596; and in San José del Cabo, **Hospital General** on Calle Doblado at Avenida Márquez de León ~ 624-142-3713.

Other towns have public health clinics staffed by nurses, and major tourist towns have English-speaking doctors in private practice. Most areas have local *Cruz Roja* (Mexican Red Cross) contacts who can quickly arrange helicopter ambulance service for serious medical emergencies.

Prescription Drugs Make sure that your health insurance policy provides coverage outside the U.S. Most do; Medicaid does not. Hospital Las Américas in Ensenada is set up to bill most U.S. health insurance companies directly; in all other hospitals, you must pay at the time of treatment and seek insurance reimbursement later. If you require medication, you'll want to bring a suf-

ficient supply for your whole stay in Mexico, since not all prescription drugs are readily available south of the border. Don't
throw away your empty prescription vials, ◆◆◆◆◆◆◆◆◆◆◆◆◆◆◆◆◆◆◆◆◆◆
though. Many popular pharmaceuticals are sold

Many Mexicans swear by
garlic as the best prevention for *turista*. Juice of
the *lima* (Mexican lime)
is also a traditional
preventative for
stomach problems.

over the counter at *much* lower prices in Mexican
farmacias, but U.S. law is currently interpreted as
prohibiting the importation of pharmaceuticals
bought in Mexico, even if you have a prescription. As
a practical matter, though, if they are in vials showing
that a U.S. doctor prescribed them, it's difficult to de-
termine whether they were actually bought in Mexico.

AIDS   AIDS (SIDA in Spanish) is a growing problem in
Mexico's urban areas. According to public health agencies,
40,000 Mexicans—or about .04 of one percent of the population—are presently infected with the HIV virus, though independent experts believe this figure is unrealistically low. The situation is said to be worse in Tijuana than in most parts of the
country, mainly because heroin use (which is said to be respon-
sible for most transmission of the virus in Mexico) is higher in
border areas, and because political differences between Mexico's
federal government and Baja California's state and local govern-
ments have led to funding cuts for AIDS clinics in Tijuana.

At present, anti-AIDS drugs are hard to get in Mexico, and official efforts to control the disease are limited to advertising cam-
paigns urging the use of condoms. (Until recently, condom use,
like other birth control methods, was officially discouraged in
this Catholic country.)

For health updates on areas you're visiting, contact the **Centers for Disease Control.** ~ 404-639-3311, 877-394-8747; www.
cdc.go/travel/camerica.htm. For current AIDS information from
the Mexican government, contact the **Consejo Nacional para la
Previsión y Control del SIDA** (CONASIDA), 525-207-4077 or toll-
free within Mexico 800-712-0886; www.ssa.gob.mx/conasida,
e-mail conasida@prodigy.net.mx.

Diarrhea   The illness most people encounter is diarrhea, euphe-
mized as *turista* or "Montezuma's revenge," caused by food and
drink carrying unfamiliar strains of bacteria. A bout can range
from a 24-hour case of mild cramps to an all-out attack with several days of fever, chills and vomiting, followed by a lousy feeling that lingers on for weeks. I have suffered both kinds, and they
are truly no fun. But not everybody who visits Mexico gets sick.
Those who stay healthy use the best defense: prevention.

Avoid drinking tap water or ice made from tap water (commonly used in restaurants—ask!), and don't brush your teeth
with it. Ask if your hotel has *agua purificada* (purified water).
These days, virtually every food store in even the smallest towns
sells Evian or another international name-brand bottled water.

Nevertheless, it can't hurt to bring along a small bottle of water purification tablets just in case.

Eat with discretion. Consume only thick-skinned fruits that you peel yourself, such as oranges and bananas, and vegetables that are cooked through. Nuts with shells, such as peanuts and coconuts, are pretty safe bets too. Avoid milk products; unpasteurized milk is sometimes served in Mexico. Steer clear of garden salads. Even if the produce was rinsed in purified water, it may have been fertilized (in the fields) with human waste, a common practice in some parts of Mexico.

Raw seafood—especially ceviche—is also renowned for causing *turista*. But it tastes so good. Be aware of the risks and decide for yourself what chances you're willing to take. In fact, there's a risk of diarrhea any time you eat meat, seafood, peeled fruit used in drinks or candies on which flies may have taken their siestas. However, a lot of the food from stalls is delicious and very well prepared. If the facilities look clean and the food is hot off the grill, it's probably ok. Be the judge and take your chances.

Take it easy the first few days, especially with the more piquant varieties of Mexican food. If you sock your system with spicy food and heavy liquor right away, your stomach may seek revenge. Eating jalapeño chicken followed by quesadillas and enchiladas chased by tequila slammers is asking for mucho trouble.

Many people believe in preventive medicine. Some take a slug of Pepto-Bismol before every meal (effective enough, though it has the peculiar side effect of turning your tongue and stool black); others, a shot of tequila, believing it will extinguish any threatening organisms. The antibiotic Doxycyclin is commonly prescribed as a preventative, although it causes sensitivity to the sun—not a good situation in the tropics.

If you take all the necessary precautions and still get hit with *turista*, several remedies are available. Lomotil, the stopper-upper, is not a cure; it's a morphine derivative that induces a kind of intestinal paralysis. Use sparingly. Stop the dosage as soon as symptoms disappear. The same is true of Paregoric, Kaopectate, Kaomycin, Imodium AD and Pepto-Bismol, which help keep the cramps down. Diodoquin, Mexaform, Streptomagnum and Donamycin are stronger over-the-counter cures available in Mexican drugstores. For diarrhea with a fever, you can take Septra or Bactrim if you are not allergic to sulfa drugs. But remember that prolonged use of any antibiotic is not good for your immune system and can make you more susceptible to other tropical diseases.

Manzanilla (chamomile) tea, popular in Mexico, soothes the stomach and often works wonders. *Yerba buena* (peppermint) tea is also soothing. Papaya restores the digestive tract. Light, easy-to-digest foods like toast and soup keep up your strength. Lots of nonalcoholic liquids—any kind—prevent dehydration. Carbonated water with juice of a *lima* is another popular stomach soother.

Rest and relaxation will help your body heal faster than if you run around sick and wear yourself down. The symptoms should pass within 24 hours or so. A case of *turista* seems to have an immunizing effect—any subsequent bouts you may have will be less severe, and eventually your body will adjust to the foreign water. If you spend a month or more in Mexico and Central America, you may find that you have similar problems with the water back home when you first return—just like Mexican tourists, who suffer from *turista* when they visit the United States.

In rare cases, diarrhea may be a symptom of a more serious illness like amebic dysentery or cholera. See a doctor if the diarrhea persists beyond three days, if your stool is bloody or foamy, or if you have a high fever.

Illegal Drugs   Mexicans, by and large, do not accept the slightest blame for drug abuse in the United States. Ballads called *narcocorridos*, about the bold exploits of drug smugglers are among the most popular kinds of recorded music in Mexico today. Mexicans see narcotics use in their own country as a public health problem and narcotrafficking as a risky route to riches.

> Be forewarned that the legal system in Mexico presumes the accused guilty until proven innocent. Foreigners are not allowed bail or a trial by jury and can be kept in jail for up to 13 months before trial.

The U.S. government pays Mexico and other Latin American countries a lot of money to enforce drug laws, and marijuana, cocaine and heroin, though imported to the U.S. through Mexico, are highly illegal here. Possessing, using or exporting any of them can land you in jail, where getting out can take a lot of time and money. Prison sentences for possession may run from 7 to 15 years, and there is no parole or other early-release program.

Firearms   The real problem, from the Mexican point of view, is guns, not drugs. With a few minor exceptions, firearms and ammunition are as illegal in Mexico as heroin is in the United States. This has been the law since soon after the Mexican Revolution, when disarming the populace was an essential step toward a stable government, and for generations it has kept the rate of violent crime much lower than in the United States. But in the past few years, under the influence of the drug trade and American action movies, guns have been flooding from Southern California through Tijuana, most of them bound for the Mexican mainland. Political unrest in states such as Chiapas and Guerrero has heightened government concern about gunrunning to a fever pitch. Officials complain that the United States is not doing enough to halt the flow of guns across the border. Most Mexicans believe that guns—not drugs—threaten to destroy the fabric of their society. Don't even consider traveling in Mexico with a gun in your possession. The risk is high, and penalties are extreme.

Crime   Travelers from the United States often have a mistaken notion of Mexico as a dangerous place peopled by bandits, leftist guerrillas, brutal or corrupt police, torturers and midnight death squads. This impression has been heightened recently by reports of skyrocketing crime rates in Mexico City—more than a thousand miles away from Tijuana. Evil forces do exist along the border, of course, but as foreign tourists we almost never encounter them. Once you get 20 miles south of the border, though you may be surprised to find yourself feeling more at ease in Baja than you do at home. The reason is simple: the crime rate is lower here than in the United States.

The fact is, traveling in Baja today is probably at least as safe as strolling the streets of your own hometown. Thanks to tough laws, the only people who own handguns in Mexico are gangsters and terrorists whom travelers will never meet. Images of *bandidos* are left over from a century ago and have no more present-day substance than the idea of wild Indians on the warpath in the American West.

You may not know that Latin Americans often have the same kind of anxiety about visiting the United States, believing it to be dominated by organized crime and filled with shootings, racial prejudice and promiscuity, a stereotype that comes from American movies and TV. But this notion was confirmed in 1994 when the leading candidate for the Mexican presidency was shot and killed during a speech in Tijuana on the U.S. border—with a gun the assassin had just bought in the United States.

In the past, the most likely way visitors have gotten in trouble in Tijuana was with the local police, whose corruption was legendary. The Mexican federal government probably would not have become very concerned about cops' scamming tourists for bribes, but in recent years the police fell under the control of drug-smuggling organizations. One of incoming President Felipe Calderón's first acts upon taking office in January 2007 was to disarm the entire 2300-member Tijuana police force. At the same time, he sent some 3000 soldiers and federal agents to patrol the city. As this book goes to press, it is too soon to tell whether this drastic move will end corruption in Tijuana or merely federalize it.

When choosing a hotel, make sure it's in a safe part of town, preferably one that's frequented by travelers. All hotels recommended in this book are located in safe neighborhoods. As a general rule, downtown areas where there is a lot of activity after dark are safer than outlying neighborhoods of the city. Don't tempt fate by wandering around dark back streets late at night. If you're camping out, avoid lonely roadside stops or isolated beaches unless you're with a group. Stay away from drug deals. In short, exercise the same caution you would use at home. Observe these common-sense precautions and feel fortunate that you are not in New York City, where, unlike in Mexico, every petty criminal carries a gun.

TRAVELING WITH CHILDREN

Baja is an ideal vacation destination for family camping adventures. It lets kids and parents experience a vast, strange desert wilderness between idyllic beaches, and it provides a low-stress introduction to foreign travel. Virtually all restaurants, hotels and campgrounds are comfortable with kids. Campgrounds often provide opportunities for "gringitos" to meet Mexican kids their own age.

The biggest drawback to traveling with kids in Baja is the long-distance driving. In a land where you can drive through desert for many hours without passing a single house, there may be no acceptable answer to "When are we gonna get there?" Some kids also have problems with the lack of roadside restrooms. Which leads us to another drawback: Parenthood can be nerve-wracking in a land where the common wildlife includes scorpions, tarantulas, rattlesnakes, stingrays, jellyfish and sharks, and where almost every plant has sharp thorns. Obviously, it's important to educate the kids about these hazards and how to avoid them. While you're at it, why not commit yourself to practicing the delicate art of not worrying. This is, after all, an adventure. Oh, yes . . . and pack a complete first-aid kit just in case. Full-service hospital facilities in Baja are: in Mexicali, **Hospital Civil** on Calle del Hospital ~ 686-557-3700; and **Hospital Almater** on Avenida Francisco I. Madero ~ 686-553-4015, e-mail hospital@almater. com; in Ensenada, **Hospital General** on Avenida Reforma at Fraccionmento Bahía ~ 646-172-4500. There's also **Hospital Velmar** at Calle Arenas 151 ~ 646-173-4500; in La Paz, **Hospital Salvatierra** on Calle Bravo at Ortiz de Domínguez ~ 612-122-1496, 612-122-1596; and in San José del Cabo, **Hospital General** on Calle Doblado at Avenida Márquez de León ~ 624-142-3713.

> Planning the trip with your kids stimulates their imagination. Books about travel, beaches, whales and deserts help prepare even a two-year-old for an adventure. So do CDs and DVDs designed to introduce young children to Spanish.

TRAVELING WITH PETS

Technically, if you want to bring a pet with you to Mexico, you need an International Health Certificate for Dogs and Cats (Form 77-043) signed by a U.S. veterinarian verifying that the animal is in good health, as well as a separate certificate stating that the animal has been immunized against distemper and rabies within the last three years. Both are supposedly required by U.S. Customs when you re-enter the United States. Mexico theoretically requires a visa for animals, which must be obtained in advance at a Mexican consulate in the region of the United States where you live. You need to show the International Health Certificate and pay a small fee.

In practice, so many RVers and campers travel with dogs that authorities on both sides of the border pay no attention to them. In extensive travels throughout Baja with my dog, Oso, who is big enough so that it's hard not to notice him, I have never once been asked to produce his paperwork. Of course, a current rabies vaccination is especially important in Baja, where a combination of infected rodents and stray dogs makes the disease more prevalent than in the United States.

Mexican law prohibits domestic animals, including dogs, in hotel and motel rooms. Mexican dogs, like pigs and turkeys, are allowed to roam loose—but only outdoors. Beaches and campgrounds, however, have no leash laws. Local dogs often form a welcoming committee to give campers' dogs a guided tour of the neighborhood.

WOMEN TRAVELING ALONE

Although sexual assaults and other crimes of violence by local residents against women tourists are relatively rare in Baja, unwanted sexual advances can be a nuisance for some gringas. Torn between the rising tide of feminism in Latin America and the old code of machismo, Mexican men often behave unpredictably toward North American and European women. There is a widespread belief, born of countless Hollywood sex-and-violence flicks, that many gringa women are wildly promiscuous. Anything a gringa does that a Mexican woman would not do may be seen by some men as provocative. This includes hitchhiking, drinking alone in a cantina, and, to a certain extent, simply traveling alone.

Many North American and European women (as well as many Mexican women) travel independently by temporarily joining up with other women travelers.

Mexican women often travel on trains and buses without a male companion, but they bring their children. Perhaps as a consequence of this strange attitude, many Mexican men turn into strutting, drooling idiots in the presence of a woman with blonde hair.

I have made a point over the years of interviewing women who are seasoned Mexico travelers about this subject. One gringa in her thirties, who has dark hair and speaks fluent Spanish, says she finds Mexico a comfortable place for women traveling alone: "To avoid problems, dress modestly," she suggests. "Flirting—or forwardness that may be mistaken for flirting—can attract more attention than you expect. But Mexican people are very friendly and like to flirt in a joking way that's not intended to be taken seriously. A light attitude goes a long way. Women travelers in small towns and villages are in a better position to meet local women, who may not speak to foreign men at all but will often invite a gringa to meet their children or see their kitchens."

The best way to obviate harassment is to travel with companions. Two or more women, or a woman traveling with children, will almost never be harassed.

GAY & LESBIAN TRAVELERS

Mexico's Catholic, family-oriented society is far behind the United States and Canada in coming to terms with its own gay and lesbian community. This is not to suggest that homosexuality is any less common in Mexico than anywhere else, just that the closet door is still closed, though the knob may be turning.

Puerto Vallarta, on the Mexican mainland 250 miles down the coast from Los Cabos, has emerged as a major international gay zone in the past few years, and there is no apparent reason that the same could not happen in Los Cabos or some more secluded spot like Todos Santos or Loreto. So far, though, it has not.

Today, Baja has several gay nightclubs—in Tijuana, Ensenada and La Paz. Only a handful of gay bed and breakfasts or beach resorts are to be found on the peninsula. Information on gay-friendly accommodations, cafés and clubs in Tijuana and Ensenada is available on the badly out-of-date **GayMART** website (www.gaymart.com). Up-to-date information on gay lodgings in La Paz, Loreto and Todos Santos is available at www.purpleroofs.com/mexico/bajasur.html. Los Cabos has only one gay bar, and if there are any gay lodgings, they are well hidden indeed.

The good news is that Baja residents have long since given up being shocked by anything gringo tourists do, creating at least a grudging tolerance. Public displays of affection are ok on out-of-town beaches but not in hotel lobbies. You are likely to encounter gay and lesbian couples and groups camping on many beaches, especially in the Bahía Concepción and Todos Santos areas.

Information on organized gay and lesbian tours worldwide is available at **Now Voyager**. ~ 4406 18th Street, San Francisco, CA 94114; 415-626-1169, 800-255-6951; www.nowvoyager.com.

SENIOR TRAVELERS

Look behind the steering wheel of any monster motor home, travel-trailer-hauling truck, fishing boat or Baja bug and chances are better than even that you'll find a senior citizen. Many retired Americans and Canadians make their homes in Baja (though only the most diehard fishing fanatics stay during the sweltering summer), and many others migrate down the snowbird trail in motor homes for the winter season. Active seniors will find opportunities to meet like-minded new friends daily, and the English-language periodicals feature articles of special interest to retirees.

You can also join escorted tours, leaving the planning to others. **Elderhostel** provides week-long programs on the natural history and culture of Baja four times a year during the winter months for seniors ages 60 and up. ~ 11 Avenue de Lafayette, Boston, MA 02111; 877-426-8056; www.elderhostel.org.

The only real drawback to Baja travel for seniors is the absence of medical facilities in many areas. (See "Health & Safety" above for information on hospital facilities in Baja.) Be extra careful about health matters. Bring any medications you use, along with the prescriptions. Consider carrying a medical record with you—including your current medical status, medical history and your doctor's name, phone number and address. If possible, include a summary of your medical status and history translated into Spanish. Find out whether your health insurance covers you south of the border. Medicaid does not, and many private health insurance policies require special riders for temporary coverage abroad.

DISABLED TRAVELERS   Mexican society has traditionally been insensitive to the needs of physically challenged people; they are viewed as burdens imposed on their families as divine punishment and are often reduced to begging. So far, this attitude has shown few if any signs of changing. Mexico has no regulations equivalent to the Americans with Disabilities Act. Newer resort hotels, found mostly in Los Cabos, are designed to accommodate disabled visitors. In most other areas, the physically challenged are likely to encounter more challenges than they might wish.

PASSPORTS & VISAS   U.S. and Canadian citizens do not need a visa to enter Baja, but if you travel south of Ensenada you are now required to stop and purchase a multientry tourist card, which allows you to come and go repeatedly. The card is good for six months and costs 225 pesos (about US$20) per person. Vacationers going to San Felipe do not need a tourist card since, like Tijuana and Ensenada, San Felipe is part of the "border zone," which has free immigration; business travelers need multientry visas, though.

You can get a blank tourist card before you leave from a Mexican consulate or a travel agent, but the card still needs to be validated when you stop at the Migración station on the highway south of Ensenada—if it's open, which it hardly ever is. If you don't have an opportunity to get your tourist card stamped, in the rare event that you actually need to show it to somebody, your passport alone will usually serve just as well.

Although technically Americans and Canadians don't need passports to enter Mexico, those traveling by plane or ship *do* need passports to reenter the United States (including Canadian visitors who change planes in the U.S.), so you can't board a plane or cruise ship without having a passport in hand. As of January 2008 this requirement will also apply to motorists, bus passengers and anyone else entering Mexico by land. A United States passport, only available to U.S. citizens, costs from $82 to $97 and is valid for 10 years. To get one, you must appear in person, with proof of citizenship (certified birth certificate or naturalization papers or an expired passport, plus a photo ID) at any of the 7000 offices around the U.S. that are authorized to accept passport applications, including many post offices, libraries, courthouses and other government facilities. To find the nearest office, consult the official government website passport.unitedstates.org. Allow at least six weeks for processing of your passport application. (In an emergency, you can get a passport in two weeks, but you have to appear in person at one of 14 Passport Agency offices in or near major U.S. cities.) Every U.S. citizen traveling abroad, including infants, must have their own passport. Travelers from countries other than the United States or Canada must have valid passports.

If you don't have a tourist card (e.g., if you travel from San Felipe to the main highway via the backroads) and you are asked for one at a military checkpoint, they will issue you one there. (To keep it simple, just say you lost it.)

MEXICAN CUSTOMS

The state of Baja California (though not Baja California Sur) is a free-trade zone, exempt from the high protective tariffs that Mexico imposes on imports in the rest of the country. Mexicans go through customs when they travel from Baja to the "mainland." Travelers, whether Mexican or gringo, rarely even have occasion to talk to a customs agent when they cross the border from the United States into Baja. Once in Baja, however, motorists don't get far without experiencing the first of the guns-and-drugs roadblocks that symbolize the mounting border tension between Mexico and the United States.

Most marijuana, cocaine and heroin imported into the United States today comes across the border from Mexico. The U.S. government considered this a major international relations problem even before March 1997, when the chief of Mexican drug enforcement was exposed for accepting drug cartel bribes. The United States Congress threatened to cut off economic aid to Mexico, and to demonstrate that his country was doing its part to stem the flow of drugs, then-president of Mexico Ernesto Zedillo shifted the responsibility for narcotics interdiction to the army. Today, there is an army checkpoint at every main road junction in Baja California Norte. (They are rare in Baja California Sur.) They briefly search every vehicle that passes, especially those with U.S. license plates.

Hand-lettered signs explain in Spanish that the checkpoints are "for the safety of your entire family." The soldiers, most of them 18 or 19 years old, are courteous, usually bored, and often curious about what gringos carry along on vacation. Their mission is to create the appearance of cooperation in the War on Drugs, not to cause tourists any real problems. They do not solicit or accept bribes. They do not use dope-sniffing dogs. One word of warning, though: never drive through an army checkpoint without stopping, or you'll have a jeepload of irate soldiers with assault weapons in hot pursuit.

U.S. CUSTOMS

When you return to the United States, customs is a different story. The uniformed agent who checks you out as you cross the California border is trained to prevent illegal drugs, not to mention switchblade knives, Cuban cigars and firecrackers, from entering the United States. The problem is, border crossings between Southern California and Baja California Norte are among the busiest in the world. As this book goes to press, U.S. border security is tighter than it has ever been, and delays of several hours are typical at Tijuana's border crossings. Many vehicles are diverted into "secondary inspection areas," where agents thoroughly search the vehicle and sometimes the driver and passengers. Drug-sniffing dogs are often used. Customs agents say that the driver's attitude and demeanor, not appearance, are the main factors determining who gets searched. Agents are most likely to search carloads of teens or college students and vehicles carrying individuals who appear to be Middle Eastern or Latino.

MONEY MATTERS

Currency The official currency of Baja is the Mexican peso. In Baja California and in all major towns of Baja California Sur, however, almost every business accepts United States currency as readily as pesos. Plagued by runaway inflation in the aftermath of the 1994 peso devaluation, many Mexican entrepreneurs believe a horde of dollars at home is safer than pesos in a bank, and taking payment in U.S. currency makes it simple.

Businesses customarily make change for U.S. dollars in U.S. bills and coins, and for pesos in pesos. The cash savings from spending pesos instead of dollars is minor, but the first time you ask, "*¿Y en pesos, cuánto vale?*"—"And in pesos, what's it worth?"—you'll instantly feel less like a tourist and more like a traveler.

While Mexican currency is easy to figure out, coins are another matter. There are nine different denominations, and sorting them out can be tricky. It pays to sit down one evening and study the various coins. Those worth less than a peso are made from aluminum and range from the tiny silver-colored centavo to the large, gold-hued 50-centavo piece. Coins worth from one to five pesos are heavier and two-toned, with nickel around the outside and a brass plug in the center. They are not very different in size. The largest-denomination coins—10 and 20 pesos—are slightly larger than the others, with brass around a nickel plug. Don't judge coins by their size alone. A 5-peso coin is smaller (though heavier) than a 50-centavo coin worth one-tenth as much. Take care not to minimize coins when leaving a tip or giving alms. A 20-peso coin may be only the size of a U.S. quarter, but it's worth more than $2.

> When you pay in dollars, be sure to ask for change in pesos; that way you can pay in pesos next time.

The peso sign is identical to the dollar sign except that it has one vertical line through it instead of two. Prices in pesos are usually followed by a dash ("$10—" means ten pesos) instead of decimals ("$1.25" means a dollar and a quarter). Many places mark their prices in dollars; when in doubt, ask. To avoid confusion, many stores and restaurants indicates prices as "USD" (U.S. dollars) or "pesos."

Changing Money   The exchange rate restaurants and stores use when translating their prices into dollars is rounded down to the next lowest half-peso. For instance, if the official exchange rate is 11.50 pesos to the dollar, most places figure it based on 11.10 to 11.25 and make an extra profit of a few cents on each dollar you spend. It's a small price to pay to avoid standing in a long, slow line at the bank or searching for a *casa de cambio*.

Credit Cards   MasterCard, Visa and some other major credit cards are as widely accepted in most parts of Baja as they are in the United States. They do not work in remote places where there are no telephones. Credit card transactions often take longer in small towns, where it is common practice for merchants to call their bank, which in turn calls the credit card company for authorization. A bank charge of 7 percent is assessed on credit card transactions, and some hotels assess additional charges.

Wiring Money   If you need a financial transfusion while on the road, transfers can be made via Western Union (*usually* taking one day) or via any big bank at home through one of its Mexican affiliates (which can take up to five working days). Check before you leave home to see whether your bank offers this service. Mexican grocery stores and telephone shops in many U.S. cities have services that wire funds to Mexico for free (as with currency exchange, their profit comes from the exchange rate), designed to enable Mexican workers in the U.S. to send money home; but you need an account in a Mexican bank for them to send it to. For most gringo travelers, the easiest way to transfer money from the United States is to have a friend deposit the funds into your stateside bank account; they'll need your account number. You can then get pesos from any ATM machine in Mexico, usually within 24 hours.

Tipping   Tip expectations are lower in Mexico than in the United States and Europe. In Mexico, it is not customary to tip taxi drivers. In restaurants, the standard tip is ten percent of the food and beverage total, *not* including the tax. Other usual tip amounts are: helpful kids—one peso apiece; street performers—two pesos; and bellhops or skycaps—ten pesos total (*not* per bag).

ELECTRIC VOLTAGE   Electric outlets use currents of 110 volts, 60 cycles, the same as in the United States and Canada. To use appliances made for other electrical systems, you need a transformer or adapter.

WEIGHTS & MEASURES   Baja is officially on the metric system, like all of Mexico, but the same bicultural attitude that applies to currency and language goes for weights and measures as well. You're equally likely to find measurements expressed in kilometers or miles, meters or feet, pounds or kilograms, liters or gallons. Throughout this book I use kilometers for all road distances because the highways are marked with kilometer signs. Trail mileages and other geographic distances that don't refer to roads are given in miles because they are easier for most gringos to visualize.

Temperatures are always given in Celsius. To convert from Celsius to Fahrenheit, multiply times 9, divide by 5 and add 32. For example, 18°C—the average temperature in Loreto in January—equals $[(18 \times 9)/5] + 32$, or $(162/5) + 32$, or $32.4 + 32$, or about 64°F. If you don't have a pocket calculator along (you should), just remember that 0°C is 32°F and that each Celsius degree is roughly two fahrenheit degrees. Here are some other useful conversion equations:

- 1 mile *(milla)* = 1.6 kilometers *(kilometros)*. 1 kilometer = $3/5$ mile.
- 1 foot *(pie)* = .03 meter *(metro)*. 1 meter = $3\frac{1}{3}$ feet
- 1 pound *(libra)* = 0.45 kilogram (kilo). 1 kilo = $2\frac{1}{5}$ pounds.
- 1 gallon *(galón)* = 3.8 liters *(litros)*. 1 liter = about one quart.

COMMUNI-CATIONS   **Mail**   Mail from Baja to the United States is quite reliable and generally takes less than two weeks to reach its destination. If you want to mail goods to the United States, you may send items of less than $50 value duty-free to a given address (but not your own) as often as every 24 hours. Mark the parcel "Unsolicited Gift—Value under $50" and enclose a sales receipt to prove it.

While on the road, you can receive mail at the main post office of any city via *Lista de Correos* (similar to General Delivery in the United States). Use this address format: [Your Name], Lista de Correos, [City Name], [State—"BC" or "BCS"], Mexico. The post office holds Lista de Correos mail for only ten days, then returns it to the sender. The post office will charge you a small fee, and you will need identification to pick up your mail.

Telephones   Calling into Mexico can be a frustrating experience, but recent changes have made the process easier. To call a number in Mexico, dial 011 (international code), 52 (country code), then the three-digit area code, followed by the seven-digit local number. Mexican phone listings in *Hidden Baja* include the area code, which you don't need to dial when calling locally.

> The more away-from-it-all towns in Baja, including the "gringo villages" of Puertecitos and Bahía de los Angeles, have no phone service.

Mexico deregulated its telephone system in the early 1990s, allowing private corporations to go into competition with Telmex, the national phone company, and share the cost of new microwave transmitters and fiberoptic telephone cables. For many small towns in Baja, this has meant getting telephone service for the first time. For city dwellers, it has meant reduced rates and shorter waiting lists for installation. For travelers, however, it means an array of options for phoning home—with widely varying costs.

By far the most common are the ones with no dial or number, just a big sign that reads, "Call the USA—credit card or collect." They are located at almost every campground, hotel lobby, restaurant, grocery store and gas station on the peninsula. Such convenience costs a lot, though—as much as $10 a minute!

Many hotels that have telephones in the rooms add a surcharge to your bill for each long-distance call you make, including calling-card, collect and toll-free calls. This practice is especially common at big resort hotels, where the surcharge is often several dollars a call.

Casetas de larga distancia, which were the main means of calling the United States until a few years ago, are still common in midsize towns along the highway in Baja today. Most major towns have someplace—a photocopy and fax service, a currency exchange, a bus station, a pharmacy or even a video store—where you can use the phone to call home while they time you with a stopwatch. After the call, you pay them in cash. It may take some exploration to locate one of these places, because they are not always in the parts of town where tourists go. Compared to the easy-to-find phones, the cost is much lower—about $1.30 a minute.

One economical option is to buy a prepaid long-distance card that works in pay phones marked Ladatel (which stands for Larga Distancia Automática). Many stores sell the cards, including RV parks that cater to "snowbirds." The cost of calling the United States varies with destination and time of day but is usually under a dollar a minute.

Calling-card calls using your United States carrier are somewhat more expensive than Ladatel calls, but you don't have to pay for them until the phone bill arrives. For AT&T access from Baja, the number is 001-800-462-4240. The access number for Sprint and PacBell is 001-800-462-4240. You still need a Ladatel card to call from a Ladatel phone, but if you use the card only to connect with your U.S. long-distance carrier, it is not debited and you can use it to phone home over and over again.

Many internet cafés now offer internet-based long-distance phone service at rates much lower than the phone companies, usually 30 to 50 cents a minute for calls anywhere in the world.

For placing unassisted calls, here are some key numbers to remember. Long-distance operator: 91; international operator (English-speaking): 98; prefixes for dialing direct to the United States, Canada and Europe: 95 (station to station) and 96 (person to person).

In Baja, it seems that all the locals have a cellular phone, so it's hardly fair that your own cell phone won't work there—even when you're waiting in line a few feet south of the border. Some cell phone service providers can make advance arrangements to activate your phone for use in Mexico. Otherwise, you'll see dozens of cell phone stores along the highway and on city streets. You can buy or rent a prepaid cell phone there, or if your cell phone is unlocked (ask your service provider about this) you can get a prepaid SIM chip—a postage-stamp-size microchip that slides into your phone and connects you to the local phone company—that works in Mexico. This way, you don't have to buy a new phone or put down a large deposit on a rental. Be careful to keep your old chip, as you'll need to put it back in when you return to the United States. Some international cell phone companies, such as Satellite Phone Store (1945 17th Street, Sarasota, FL 34234, 941-955-1020; www.satellitephonestore.com) rent phones with U.S. phone numbers, making the cost of calls between Mexico and the U.S. much lower. Cell phone coverage is

PLEASE, MR. POSTMAN

Some gringo communities and campgrounds in Baja have their own "U.S. Mail" drops. Whoever is heading back to the United States for any reason takes responsibility for carrying accumulated mail north and dropping it in the first mailbox they come to after crossing the border. Most of the time, this method gets letters to U.S. destinations faster than the Mexican post office does, even though they may sit for days before somebody comes along to carry it north. (Actually, the same is true of letters mailed in a Mexican post office, where a certain quantity of international mail must accumulate before it can be processed, which accounts for much of the slowness.)

spotty in Baja. You can expect your cell phone to work in all border areas south to Ensenada, in the San Felipe and San Quintín areas, between Ciudad Insurgentes and Ciudad Constitución, and everywhere south of La Paz. Do not expect your cell phone to work in the deserts of central Baja.

Faxes Because mail was slow and long-distance phone calls were expensive, faxing became the primary mode of business communication in Mexico even before it caught on in the United States. Most hotels and many other businesses can send and receive faxes for you. Larger towns also have storefront fax services. They used to be the least expensive way to send a message home and be sure that it will get there before you do, though e-mail has now pretty much replaced faxes for this purpose.

E-mail Just about all populated areas of Baja have internet cafés where you can rent computers by the hour. Even places like Bahía de los Angeles, which didn't even have telephones until a couple of years ago, now have such cafés. In fact, any vacant commercial building is likely to be turned into an internet shop at least temporarily until another tenant can be found. Rates are surprisingly low. A half-hour of computer time costs about the same as one minute of long-distance phone time on Ladatel, making this by far the most economical way to stay in touch with the world back home (provided that your contacts have e-mail). High-speed internet hasn't reached Baja yet, so at this writing all public computers use frustratingly slow telephone modems, which are fine for e-mail but can take a tediously long time to send photographs. Sometimes, though not as often as you might expect, you may get a computer with a Spanish-language keyboard, on which many punctuation marks and symbols are in different places. If so, be sure to ask what the keystroke sequence is for @—it doesn't appear on the keyboard, and you'll never find it on your own.

Most visitors travel by road and enjoy the flexibility of going where they want for as long as they want. It is possible to reach some Baja destinations by plane or boat, though the choice of destinations is limited.

Transportation

GETTING TO BAJA

AIR There are only a few places where airliners land. The most straightforward plan is to catch a jet to Los Cabos, then rent a car and explore from there. **United, Mexicana** and **Alaska Airlines** offer daily flights from Los Angeles, with connections from other U.S. cities.

Aeroméxico and **Aero California** offer flights to La Paz from Tijuana, Hermosillo, Mazatlán, Guadalajara and other Mexican cities. Aero California also has a flight from Los Angeles to La Paz, as do Delta and Alaska Airways.

The most "hidden" spot in Baja that can be reached by commercial jet, the 300-year-old colonial town of Loreto, is served by Aero California, Delta, Alaska Airways and US Airways flights from Los Angeles, with connections from San Diego and Phoenix. Air fares to Loreto are much lower than to La Paz or Los Cabos.

The border cities of Tijuana and Mexicali are served by **Air L.A.** from Los Angeles and **Noroeste** from Las Vegas, Phoenix, Tucson, El Paso and cities of northwestern Mexico.

SEA   Several cruise lines operate weekly trips from Los Angeles to Baja ports. **Royal Caribbean**, with the largest and most luxurious ships, takes seven-day cruises down the Baja coast on the ship *Vision of the Seas*, putting in for a day at Cabo San Lucas and continuing to Mazatlán and Puerto Vallarta on the mainland coast before returning to L.A. Lower-priced three- and four-night cruises aboard the *Monarch of the Sea* go to Ensenada, stopping on Catalina Island for a day en route. ~ 888-313-8883.

Unless you're on your honeymoon, and maybe even then, the big drawback to cruise ship travel is that sailing schedules leave little time to explore ports of call beyond a few blocks of "cruise-ship-approved" galleries and shops. Shipboard luxury is the essence of most cruise experiences, and ports of call are almost incidental. Many passengers never disembark until the end of the cruise. Amenities on the ships—swimming pools, fine dining, showrooms, casinos—rival those of land-based resorts, and the all-inclusive accommodations are priced in the same range per night as the better Los Cabos resorts. Ticket prices vary widely depending on the time of year and on whether you take an inside (windowless) or outside (with portholes) cabin. Discounts and other little-known deals abound, so it's best to enlist the help of a travel agent who specializes in cruises; most of them emphasize this specialty in their Yellow Pages listings.

Travelers can combine a road trip with an all-day or all-night cruise across the Sea of Cortez by entering Mexico on the mainland and taking the ferry from Guaymas to Santa Rosalía or from Mazatlán to La Paz. The ferries are inexpensive for walk-on passengers but rather expensive for motor vehicles, and bringing your car across the border into mainland Mexico involves official inconveniences, described in the next section, that can be avoided by crossing directly into Baja from California.

DRIVING   The Baja Highway—Mexican Route 1, officially called the Carretera Peninsular—extends a distance of 1730 kilometers, or about 1060 miles, from Tijuana to Los Cabos. Other highways go to San Felipe in the northeast and Todos Santos in the southwest, but most Baja destinations are along Route 1 or on unpaved side roads off the main highway.

For driving in Mexico, you'll need a valid U.S., Canadian or international driver's license and Mexican auto insurance. To get that, you need your driver's license and proof of ownership—a current registration certificate or title. Auto insurance policies issued in the United States are not valid in Mexico. An uninsured accident is a crime under Mexican law, which presumes the defendant guilty until proven innocent. This means that if you don't have liability insurance and you are involved in an accident that causes property damage, your vehicle will be impounded until you pay the damage and a fine. If any person is injured in the accident, you will go to jail. Motor vehicle liability insurance costs about $3 a day, with slightly lower weekly and monthly rates. Collision/comprehensive insurance is also available but not required, and many Mexican insurance agencies sell prepaid legal insurance, entitling you to a Mexican lawyer if you get in trouble any time of day or night. At a flat fee of $50, the advisability of buying this coverage depends on how much trouble you're planning to get into.

Some travelers coming from Arizona and points east cross the border at Nogales, drive south on Route 15 to Guaymas, and take the ferry across to Santa Rosalía. This short cut saves about 1250 kilometers over driving to Tijuana and then south. The one-way cost of taking a vehicle on the ferry ranges from about $100 for passenger cars to more than $300 for motor homes. If you choose this option, however, you must comply with the much stricter requirements for taking a vehicle into mainland Mexico. You need a tourist card and a car permit—a window sticker plus a special stamp on the owner or driver's tourist card. Get them at the customs and immigration port of entry on the highway south of Nogales. Here, too, you need proof of vehicle

ROAD RULES

When driving in Baja, bear in mind that Mexican driving rules are sometimes different from those in the United States. This is especially true of turn signals. A left-turn signal can mean three different things: if the vehicle is slowing down, it means "left turn" as in the United States; more commonly, if a vehicle ahead of you is not slowing down, and there's no obvious place to turn left, then a left-turn signal means "OK to pass"; when an oncoming vehicle flashes you a left-turn signal, it's a greeting. Mexicans never flash their headlights as a greeting; an oncoming vehicle flashing its headlights means that there's not enough room to pass. When an oncoming vehicle flashes its emergency lights, it's a warning of a road hazard ahead such as an accident scene or animals on the road.

ownership. If the title shows a lien against the vehicle or if it is registered in another person's name or a company name, you need a notarized letter from the lienholder or owner authorizing you to take the vehicle to Mexico for a specified time. The owner or driver who has the car permit stamp on his or her tourist card must be in the car whenever it is being driven.

Strict regulations designed to stanch the flow of stolen cars from the United States to Mexico are in force. Anyone bringing a motor vehicle into mainland Mexico (but not Baja) must carry with them a major credit card in the same name that appears on the vehicle registration; Mexican Customs will place a charge of US$16.90 on the card. A vehicle owner without a credit card will be required to post a cash bond in the amount of US$800 guaranteeing that he or she will return with the vehicle to the United States—through the same border crossing. These rules have been changed frequently over the past few years. To check on the present requirements for bringing a vehicle into Mexico, contact a Mexican consulate in the United States or the **U.S. Embassy** in Mexico City. ~ Paseo de la Reforma No. 305, 60500 Mexico, D.F.; 5-211-0042. Remember, none of these formalities apply to driving a car into Baja from California, but you must go through all the same red tape if you take your vehicle on the ferry between Baja and the Mexican mainland.

> More U.S. motorists drive the Baja Highway than any other road outside the United States.

RENTING A CAR   Tijuana, Ensenada, Loreto, La Paz and Los Cabos all have car rental agencies. Rates are lower in Tijuana than in other destinations farther south. International agencies such as Avis and Hertz offer lower rates than most local outfits. You cannot normally rent a car in the United States and take it into Mexico, though some RV rental places will make special arrangements allowing you to take a motor home across the border, especially if you are traveling with a caravan.

A valid U.S., Canadian or international driver's license is required to operate a vehicle in Baja. Some car rental companies require that visitors from places other than the U.S. or Canada present both a driver's license from their own country and an international license.

When renting a car, the person who signs the contract must be over 25 and have a valid major credit card. You must take out Mexican liability insurance with a $1000 deductible. Collision/ comprehensive insurance is optional, and expensive; this kind of protection is good to have on Baja roads, but check first to find out whether you need it. Many credit cards provide the same coverage when a rental is charged to the card. Your personal insurance policy may also provide for rental cars, or you can often add a rider clause providing for rental coverage for much less than paying the rental agency's insurance rates.

Car rental rates fluctuate with the season. Slack tourist seasons mean good deals. Three-day, weekly and monthly rates are almost always cheaper than daily rentals. Cars with standard shifts are generally less than automatics. Compacts are more economical than larger sedans and vans. In Baja, Volkswagen Beetles are by far the most affordable rental cars. Membership in such groups as the American Automobile Association or the American Association of Retired Persons entitles you to a discount at most international car rental agencies.

Four-wheel-drive vehicles are available at premium rates from some agencies. Most resort destinations have places that rent sport vehicles such as ATVs, motorcycles, dune buggies or jeeps.

CARAVANS Caravans of a dozen to fifty or more camping vans, travel trailers or motor homes are such a common sight on the roads of Baja that you're sure to encounter several (except in the heat of summer, when boaters organize caravans). Organizers make campground arrangements ahead of time, and a caravan may fill the whole campground to capacity for a night or two before moving on. Caravanning means RVers tour with the same like-minded people for the whole trip instead of meeting new friends at each campground, and traveling together guarantees help in case of mechanical or medical problems. It is a great solution for people who lack confidence about traveling in a foreign country on their own.

Various kinds of groups organize Baja caravans. Travel clubs charge for membership and provide up-to-date travel information, discounts and low-cost insurance. Most Baja travel clubs also organize caravan tours for members; others provide information on commercial caravan tours and members' cooperative trips. Major Baja travel clubs include **Vagabundos del Mar RV, Boat and Travel** (190 Main Street, Rio Vista, CA 94571; 707-374-5511, 800-474-2252, fax 707-374-6843; www.vagabundos.com) and **Discover Baja Travel Club** (3089 Clairemont Drive, Suite A-2, San Diego, CA 92117; 619-275-4225, 800-727-2252, fax 619-275-1836; www.discoverbaja.com).

Independent tour operators also organize Baja caravans using your RV or theirs. **American RV Rentals**, for instance, owns its own fleet of motor homes, which caravan participants rent as part of the tour price—a great option if you want to experience the ultimate RV adventure but don't own one (yet). ~ 1866 West 6th Street, Corona, CA; 909-520-9940, fax 909-520-8491; e-mail info2americanrvrentals.com. Or look on the internet for the nearest location of the nationwide motor home rental agency **CruiseAmerica**. ~ www.cruiseamerica.com.

Other Baja caravans are offered through national motor clubs, West coast car and motor-home clubs, and owner's groups such as Winnebago and Airstream.

To rent a motor home and take the trip on your own, contact **El Monte RV**, the only major RV rental firm that lets you take the vehicle to Baja California Sur as well as Baja California Norte. There are many locations in the San Diego, Los Angeles and San Francisco areas, as well as a few others scattered around the West, but considering the high fuel cost of motor homes, it usually makes the most sense to fly or drive to San Diego and rent from the location closest to the border, in Santee, from which the Tecate border crossing is easily reached. ~ 8665 Mission Gorge Road, Santee; 619-449-1513, fax 619-562-9507; www.elmonterv.com. When considering this option, though, bear in mind that driving the Baja Highway in a wide vehicle such as a motor home can be a hair-raising experience because the highway is narrow and, in places, edgy, and it is used by many large trucks. Add the problems of managing Tijuana traffic and parking in downtown Ensenada, and motor home travel can make driving the Baja Highway highly stressful unless you're an experienced RV driver.

TWO

The Land
and Outdoor Adventures

Baja is a paradise for campers, kayakers and off-roaders. The varied terrain makes it possible to experience all kinds of outdoor adventures. One day you may hike up a secluded canyon with palm trees and waterfalls; the next, you may surf the big waves of the Pacific or snorkel the still waters of a shallow bay on the Sea of Cortez, camping on a gracefully curving beach with only seabirds for company.

In this chapter, we'll take a look at the environments of Baja, its unique and often bizarre plant life, the animals, birds and fish that inhabit its vast wilderness, and the outdoor skills involved in exploring the region. This is no comprehensive study of desert survival; I'm simply sharing my own observations in the hope that it will enhance your Baja experience as well.

GEOLOGY

Baja is the creation of the same slow, ponderous geological movement that causes California's earthquakes today. You could say that the peninsula is the part of California that has already fallen off into the Pacific.

Both Californias began to form more than 200 million years ago, when the North American continent separated from Africa and drifted westward, creating the Atlantic Ocean. Like a cruise liner running aground, the western edge of the continental plate pushed its way over the hard rock crust that supports the Pacific Ocean floor, crushing it down into the earth's superheated interior. As the continent grated and ground its way across the ocean crust, it scraped granite and sediments into a ridge more than 1200 miles long, forming the foundation for the Sierra Nevada. The oceanic crust buckled under the pressure, cracking into huge slabs of rock called batholiths that slanted upward from west to east, then plunged straight down on the east side in jagged, fractured escarpments. The massive geological collision also ruptured veins of magma deep in the earth, and volcanoes began erupting all along the Pacific coast. This geological turmoil continued for more than 100 million years, spanning the age of dinosaurs from dawn to extinction.

The earth fell silent. The two mountain ranges—one on the mainland and the other on the island—slowly eroded. Mountain streams carried sand, soil and sediment down to the sea until it completely filled the trench that separated the island from the mainland, creating Alta California's central valley and merging Baja with the mainland. The new land blossomed into a lush subtropical eden where prehistoric mammals grazed. The quiet lasted for 30 million years.

But deep in the earth, pressure was building up from the inexorable westward drift of the continental plate. Something had to give. About 30 million years ago, the Pacific Plate started grinding northward along a crack—which developed into the San Andreas Fault. The land from around present-day Puerto Vallarta to beyond San Francisco started slipping very slowly up the coast. Over 30 million years, the California coast and Baja have moved some 450 miles north along the San Andreas Fault (called the Sea of Cortez Rift when it's underwater). Along the way, the Baja peninsula has peeled away from the mainland to create the Sea of Cortez, one of the most recently formed seas on the planet.

Sixteen million years ago, the climate changed drastically. Rainfall all but ceased, creating a drought without end in the interior and west of the major mountain ranges. Then, as now, rain and snow fell on the highest ranges, Sierra Juárez, Sierra San Pedro Mártir and Sierra de la Laguna, but the water evaporated or soaked into the earth before reaching the lowlands. Over millions of years, vast quantities of fresh water accumulated in aquifers, or underground lakes, beneath parts of the desert, where they remained hidden until the mid-20th century.

Today, the Baja peninsula is about as wide as the sea that separates it from mainland Mexico. It continues to slip north at about an inch a year, grinding its way up the San Andreas Fault, resulting in California earthquakes. Volcanic activity has also continued into recent times. Franciscan priests were there to witness the last eruption of Volcán Las Tres Vírgenes, in the Vizcaíno northwest of Santa Rosalía, in 1746. Tres Vírgenes and possibly other volcanos on Baja are dormant but not extinct.

FLORA　　The Desierto Central, Baja's most magical desert, displays the most remarkable profusion of plant life on the peninsula. Almost all the cactuses, agaves and trees found in other desert areas of Baja are here too, along with strange species that exist nowhere else on earth.

The plant that particularly gives the central desert landscape its surreal quality is the *cirio*—"candle" in Spanish. Cirio trees are shaped like giant upside-down carrots, sometimes twisted into whiplike curves, reaching heights of up to 60 feet. Their trunks are covered with thousands of tiny, twiglike branches that sprout leaves after rainy spells. Spring rains also bring out crowns of white flowers on the tips of the trees. Cirios are of no known use to man: They cannot be burned as firewood or cut into boards or posts for construction. They produce nothing edible. They are protected by the Mexican government as an endangered species. A gringo botanist exploring Baja in 1922 burdened the cirio with the whimsical name "boojum tree" after an imaginary species mentioned in Lewis Carroll's *The Hunting of the Snark*; the name is still in common use among North Americans in Baja.

Country people chop down the woody skeletons of dead *cardones* for use as firewood.

The *ocatillo* grows from the Mojave Desert of Nevada and Arizona south along the eastern side of Baja. The ocatillo has slender, polelike, thorny branches that grow in bursts ten feet tall. A relative of the cirio, it sprouts leaves along its branches after rainy spells and flies sprigs of flamingo-pink blossoms like banners from the branches' tips in April. Another species of ocatillo, found in the south between La Paz and Los Cabos, looks the same except that its branches grow from a central trunk, not directly from the ground.

Also unique to Baja is the "elephant tree," called *copalquín* by Mexicans. Its thick, twisted trunk and branches contrast the tufts of tiny twigs that burst from the branches and sprout leaves after rare rainy spells, when it may bloom with tiny pink flowers.

A second species of elephant tree, the *torote blanco*, looks almost like the *copalquín,* as its white, papery bark peels away, it is yellow instead of green underneath. A smaller relative, the incense tree or *torote colorado* is most common south of San Felipe; it exudes a fragrant oil and smells like incense when burned. Another common desert tree that is leafless except after rain, the *palo verde* has a green trunk and branches and can blossom in a profusion of tiny yellow flowers in April. An unrelated species, the *palo blanco* is a straight, slender tree with smooth white bark that grows in dense thickets near seasonal water holes.

The *cardón*, found in abundance through most desert areas of Baja, is the world's largest cactus. It is similar in appearance to the saguaro of Arizona but larger, reaching 40 feet with trunks up to eight feet around. Forests of these tree-sized cactuses are called *cardonals*. Another unique Baja cactus, the creeping devil or galloping cactus, sends out long, wavy branches in every direction. As they grow longer, they eventually touch the ground and put out roots, so that over decades the plants "creep" across the ground from one root system to the next. A single plant can cover an area thirty feet across with an impenetrable tangle of sharp-spined branches that provide protection for small animals and birds. Known to Mexicans as the *pitahaya agria*, this cactus produces a sour but edible fruit. Despite appearances, the creeping devil is closely related to the organ pipe cactus, or *pitahaya dulce,* whose sweet fruit was a staple of Baja's original Indian inhabitants and is considered a delicacy today. The *nopal*, or prickly pear cactus, also produces a tasty fruit, and its leaves are often sliced into strips, cooked and served as a vegetable. Other common cactuses of the Baja peninsula, which also grow in the deserts of the southwestern United States, include the barrel cactus, the jumping cholla, the teddy bear cholla, the candelabra cactus and the old man cactus.

Several species of desert plant have bursts of swordlike leaves with sharp points. Some are yuccas, and others, with wider, thicker leaves, are agaves. Besides the ground-hugging common yucca, sometimes called Spanish bayonet, another yucca that is abundant in some areas is the *datillo*, which grows on a trunk, looks much like the Joshua tree of California, and reaches heights of 20 feet. The most striking agave is the century plant, or *maguey*, whose English name comes from the popular myth that the plant lives for a hundred years, then blooms once and dies. The plants' normal life span is more like 40 years, but the blooming-and-dying part is true. Century plants store growth energy for all those years, then pour it forth in a flowering, branching once-in-a-lifetime stalk taller than a man.

Many colorful wildflowers are native to the Baja deserts. Although they are termed "annuals" (as opposed to perennials), their seeds can lie dormant in the desert sand, awaiting a rainy spell, for twenty years or more. When rains do come—generally

BAJA'S FRUITS AND VEGETABLES

Virtually all agricultural crops come from somewhere else. Three hundred years ago, missionaries brought *las tres hermanas*—corn, beans and squash, the three staple foods of Mexican Indians before the Spanish arrived—and taught their converts how to farm. The missionaries also introduced olive trees and grapevines; olive oil and wine were shipped back to mainland Mexico, where their sale helped to support the missions. Today the major agricultural crop is wheat, grown in vast fields in Baja's northern hills and coastal plain. Most crops are grown for export to the U.S. market and are more familiar to shoppers in American supermarkets than in Mexican produce markets. Asparagus, strawberries and onions are regional specialties.

in the spring in Baja California and the summer in Baja California Sur—the desert blooms into a carpet of brilliant blossoms.

In the Sierra Juárez and Sierra San Pedro Mártir, juniper, piñon and oak cover vast expanses of rolling foothills and canyonlands. At higher altitudes that accumulate snow in winter, tall evergreen species including bishop pine, lodgepole pine and sugar pine, and white fir form majestic forests that look more like the Colorado Rockies than like most people's idea of Baja. Aspen trees grow in isolated stands amid the evergreens. The Sierra San Pedro Mártir also boasts a unique tree species, the San Pedro Mártir cypress. Columbines, lupines, Indian paintbrush and other mountain wildflowers bloom in early summer.

The mountain vegetation of the Sierra la Laguna, in southern Baja California Sur between La Paz and Los Cabos, is even more remarkable. Desert plants (large cactuses and datillo), mountain trees (oaks and pines), tropical coastal vegetation (palms and madroña trees) and extravagant displays of wildflowers grow side by side in his unique subtropical mountain Eden. Almost unknown (though it is only 45 miles from Cabo San Lucas), the Sierra la Laguna's unique ecosystem is not protected by law, only by its remoteness: it can only be reached by an overnight backpacking trek on rugged foot trails. It is the most endangered environment in Baja today. Water from the sierra's lakes, including the one for which it was named, has been diverted to Los Cabos, reducing evaporation, cloud buildup and rainfall in the mountains, so the luxuriant flora is gradually drying and withering as the arid desert below gradually advances up the slopes of the sierra. As environmentalists lobby urgently for Sierra la Laguna to be granted national park status, other powers want to see the sierra opened up to cattle grazing.

The San Ignacio and Mulegé rivers and other sources of fresh water support an oasis-like ecosystem made up of cottonwoods, willows, tamarisk and palm trees. The tamarisk, or salt cedar, an Asian ornamental bush, was originally introduced to Mexico and California to help stabilize river banks. It thrived and soon ran wild throughout the region's riparian ecosystems. Unfortunately, tamarisks kill off other plants by lowering the water table and increasing the salt content of the soil around them. They grow in impassable thickets along river banks and around waterholes, reaching heights of 25 feet, and cannot be burned or otherwise gotten rid of. At least tamarisks are pretty, with their long, plumelike lavender blossoms and their delicate lacework of leaves that resemble juniper needles at first glance but turn golden in the fall.

The palm trees most commonly seen in southern Baja are date palms, a species introduced by missionaries in the 1700s.

They, too, prospered in Baja's hot, sunny climate and spread into the wild. It is estimated that more than 80,000 wild date palms grow on the peninsula today, along with lesser numbers of coconut palms. The palm trees that are native to Baja are California fan palms and blue fan palms, whose pointed leaves radiate in flat spreads from long stems. Fan palm fronds are the preferred material for making palapa thatched roofs.

Subtropical vegetation does not stop at the water's edge. Many varieties of seaweed grow in the shallow waters off both shores of the peninsula. Largest of these is giant kelp, which grows along the Pacific coast in thick underwater tangles, providing shelter for young fish and many other kinds of sea life. When bunches of kelp break loose in rough seas and wash ashore, they make unsightly, smelly piles of rotting vegetation that flies love.

FAUNA   Baja is one of the world's major whale-watching destinations. The center of attention is the astonishing number of gray whales that gather each winter in three Pacific coast bays—Scammon's Lagoon (Laguna Ojo de Liebre), Laguna San Ignacio (Bahía de Ballenas) and Bahía Magdalena. All three are shallow, protected bays where water evaporates so rapidly that thick, snow-white crusts of sea salt crystallize along their shores; the salt content of the water is much higher than in the open ocean.

A *panga* ride among thousands of gray whales is certainly one of the most remarkable experiences Baja has to offer, but veteran whale watchers know that these waters have an even bigger thrill in store. The Pacific Ocean off Los Cabos and Todos Santos, and the Sea of Cortez as far north as Bahía de los Angeles (especially around Loreto and the islands of Monserrate, Santa Catalina and Santa Cruz), are among the world's best places to observe blue whales, the earth's largest living creatures. Reaching lengths of 100 feet and weighing up to 180 tons, the giant beasts are three times the size of gray whales. Their blowholes can spray plumes of water up to 25 feet in the air. Despite their bulk, they are the fastest of all whales, swimming at up to 30 miles an hour. These leviathans once numbered about 250,000 and inhabited all the world's oceans; they were hunted nearly to extinction between 1909, when steam power first made whaling ships fast enough to catch them, and 1966, when hunting blue whales was outlawed worldwide. At that time, scientists believed that the whales were technically extinct—too few in number to find mates and reproduce. In the northern Pacific, including Baja, blue whales have made a much stronger recovery than in other oceans, although they still rank among the most endangered mammals. They now number an estimated 2500.

Gentle Giants
off the Baja Coast

Gray whales spend the spring and summer months in the Bering Sea off the coast of Alaska, where they feast on huge quantities of tiny organisms called lobster krill and plankton. In November, the female whales migrate southward in small groups, hugging the Pacific coast of Alaska, British Columbia, Washington, Oregon, California, Baja California and Baja California Sur to reach Laguna Ojo de Liebre (Scammon's Lagoon), Laguna San Ignacio and Bahía Magdalena—salty, protected lagoons where the water's buoyancy makes birthing whale calves easier. The calving takes place in January and February. At the same time, the males are making their way down the coast. Arriving at the calving lagoons, they breed with females who are not nursing newborn calves. The males' subtropical vacation is brief. They begin their northward migration on the first day of spring, and all are gone from the lagoons by April 1.

The gray-whale calving grounds were discovered in 1857 by American whaling captain Charles Melville Scammon, and within two years the whales were completely annihilated in Laguna Ojo de Liebre, which forever after would be known as Scammon's Lagoon. By 1900, no whales could be found along the entire Pacific coast, and by 1937, after a generation without whaling in the lagoons, they still numbered fewer than 100. Their numbers began to recover quickly only after 1972, when an international treaty abolished whaling in the open Pacific Ocean. In 1996, the whale population reached 20,000, the estimated number before Scammon's arrival.

Migrating whales can be seen all along Baja's Pacific coast, traveling about four knots per hour and swimming past at an average rate of one every two minutes during peak migration times. They usually travel in small family groups called pods. Male gray whales sometimes venture into the southern part of the Sea of Cortez, joining other whale species that frequent those waters.

Binoculars are better than telescopes for spotting whales. Watch for a cloud of spray above the water. One of these spouts is made when a whale exhales air through its blowhole.

Other whales that frequent the Sea of Cortez include humpbacks, orcas, dwarf sperm whales, fin whales, Bryde's whales and shortfin pilot whales. Dolphins including the common, bottlenose and Pacific white-sided varieties as well as the endangered Gulf of California harbor porpoise—are also seen in the Sea of Cortez. In the Loreto area and at Bahía Concepción, boaters and beach campers might see as many as 100 dolphins gliding and leaping along the surface.

Seals and sea lions also live in the waters of the Pacific coast of Baja. The most common are harbor seals, California sea lions and huge, grotesque elephant seals. More exotic species include the Guadalupe fur seal, a threatened species. The largest seal and sea elephant rookeries are located on the hard-to-reach ocean side of Isla Cedros, west of Guerrero Negro. Travelers who don't have their own yachts find the seal colony on offshore rocks near Santa Rosalía and the sea lion colony off Land's End at Cabo San Lucas easier to reach.

Another marine mammal sometimes mistaken for a seal is the southern sea otter, the largest member of the weasel family, which reaches four to five feet in length. The otters were hunted to the brink of extinction in the mid-1800s. In 1874, the U.S. state of California passed the world's first endangered-species law to protect sea otters north of the border, and fur hunters moved their operations to the waters off Baja, where the otters were completely exterminated. A century later, after they were placed under worldwide protection, the otters began to reappear along Baja's Pacific coast.

Endangered species of sea turtle found on Baja beaches include the hawksbill, leatherback, green, loggerhead and olive ridley. The southern Pacific coast and the entire coast of the Sea of Cortez, especially the Bahía de los Angeles area, have been turtle breeding grounds. Local people would go there to gather turtle eggs, which were considered a delicacy, and fishermen would

SHELL OUT

People in Baja are familiar with the consequences of extinction. Once they could choose to spend their time diving for oysters instead of fishing. These made good eating, and there was always a chance that one would contain a pearl like the ones that originally lured Cortés to the peninsula more than four centuries ago. With the invention of diving suits in the 1870s, La Paz quickly became the world's largest source of pearls, but an unidentified mollusk disease struck the oyster beds of La Paz in 1936, and by 1941 the entire oyster population of the Sea of Cortez had been wiped out. Clams, scallops, mussels, crabs and lobsters continue to thrive along both coasts.

catch adult turtles for food. As the coastal population of Baja grew, overgathering of eggs and overfishing drastically reduced the number of turtles in Baja waters. A Japanese fishing fleet finished the job, killing all the turtles in Bahía de los Angeles to process and ship back to Japan, where the meat has traditionally been prized as a sushi ingredient. The government banned the killing of sea turtles and the taking of eggs in 1990, and Japan signed an international treaty the following year prohibiting the importation of turtle products. A research station has been set up at Bahía de los Angeles to study the best way to restore the wild sea turtles of the Sea of Cortez.

Many fish, large and small, live in Baja waters. On the Pacific side, ocean currents cause an upwelling of deep-sea water to the surface along the coast, carrying with it game fish such as marlin and sailfish. The big fish often round the tip of the peninsula to take refuge in the calmer, more sheltered waters of the Sea of Cortez. Sharks, mostly of the small and not-very-threatening variety, infest Sea of Cortez waters and keep them as clean as piscine vultures would. The most spectacular fish of the shallow waters off Baja shores, the manta ray, or devil fish, measures an awesome 20 feet or more across, weighs up to two tons and can leap from the water, gliding and landing with a dramatic *splat*. Smaller species include the bat ray, the mobula, the guitarfish, the butterfly ray and the dangerous stingray.

Largest among the seabirds that inhabit the Baja coast, the California brown pelican (Mexicans know it as *pelicano gris,* or gray pelican) nests in large colonies on many islands both in the Sea of Cortez and along the Pacific coast. The pelicans eat fish, which they scoop from the water using their long, pouched beaks. They often fly in formation just inches above the water surface, but can also dive from heights of up to 200 feet and snatch fish with deadly accuracy. They gather wherever fishermen are to grab discarded trash fish and entrails. Other common seabirds of the Baja coast include seagulls, terns, boobies, cormorants and frigate birds.

The most common large wading bird of the peninsula is the graceful, solitary great blue heron, found any place where there is calm, shallow water, salt or fresh. The heron hunts by stepping so slowly through ankle-deep water that it appears motionless, then shooting its S-shaped neck forward faster than the eye can follow to snap up a fish, crab or frog. Concentrating on its quest for food, a heron may appear completely oblivious to the din of fishing boats, motor homes and soccer players that come within a few feet of it. Great blue herons sometimes live inland near springs, rivers and intermittent waterholes, where they feed on snakes, insects, rodents and smaller birds. Other wading birds often seen in Baja include white herons, green herons, ibis, spoonbills, storks and four kinds of egret, as well as sandpipers and godwits.

Ospreys, or sea eagles, live along both coasts of Baja, especially around protected Pacific coast bays such as Scammon's Lagoon, where they nest on telephone poles along the main street. These large raptors circle over the lagoon at heights of about 100 feet until they spot a fish near the surface, then dive and snatch it in their talons. During the spring nesting season, both male and female bring back whole fish to rip into strips and feed to their ravenous offspring.

The forbidding Baja interior also provides habitat for many animal species, but most of them are rarely seen. Burrowing mammals such as prairie dogs, ground squirrels and jackrabbits live underground during the day to avoid the brutally hot sun and emerge in the morning and evening hours. Coyotes, which prey on the rodents, are also nocturnal. Intelligent and curious, they can sometimes be spotted around sunset observing campers from a discreet distance.

Wild burros are a common sight in Baja California Sur. They often stand placidly by the side of the highway watching the occasional vehicle speed by. They are the descendants of beasts of burden who proved to have better desert survival skills than their masters. Wild burros have been roaming Baja for at least 200 years, yet they have not developed a noticeable fear of humans. Locals sometimes catch them and domesticate them. More often, they are used for breeding, since wild sires are believed to produce offspring that are stronger and better adapted to the harsh Baja environment. Ranchers let their female burros loose with the wild burro herds to round up later when they are pregnant.

Pronghorn antelope are occasionally seen grazing on high, open plains. Once abundant, they were hunted to the brink of extinction. Today, the Baja pronghorn is listed as an endangered species in Mexico, and it is illegal to kill one. Their numbers are increasing, but they now graze in remote areas far from roads.

Deer abound in the northern Baja sierras. You're likely to see them in the high country of Parque Nacional San Pedro Mártir, where they are protected from human hunters and less vulnerable to attack by their other major predator, the mountain lion, which stalks the dense scrub oak woodlands in the foothills of the sierras. The most common denizens of the foothills are *javelinas*, or peccaries, piglike animals that root in packs and can be dangerous to hikers. Other wildlife of the sierra includes squirrels, skunks, raccoons, and the occasional bear.

Twenty species of birds of prey patrol the skies of Baja. Besides the osprey, they include golden eagles, peregrine falcons, hawks, harriers and owls. Turkey vultures, known in Mexico as *zopilotes,* are the most commonly seen large birds in the Baja interior. They are the size of eagles but soar with their wings in a V instead of straight out and have small, bald, red heads. They are everywhere in Baja, sunning themselves in groups of a dozen or so on giant cactuses, gliding in lazy circles overhead, huddling around road kill. The unique power of the vulture is its natural immunity to botulism, salmonella and other poisonous bacteria, allowing it to eat the most disgusting things. In the southern part of the peninsula, they are joined in their scavenging by *caracaras*. The head of this big tropical carrion eater looks much larger because of its sweeping black and white feather crest—like a vulture with a bad toupee.

Although turkey vultures are far from endangered as a species, they are protected under Mexican law because of their vital role in keeping the desert clean.

Many songbirds, including meadowlarks, orioles and blackbirds, migrate to the deserts of Baja in the winter. Perhaps the most common desert bird is the cactus wren, a brownish bird with a spotted breast. It builds its nest in a tall cactus and feeds on insects and worms. White-winged doves, another common desert bird, nest near springs and waterholes; people have survived in the desert by following the doves to water. Other common desert birds include roadrunners, mockingbirds, ravens and ladderback woodpeckers.

The most conspicuous mountain birds are several species of jays, including the piñon jay, which is sky-blue and robin-sized with no crest, the Gray's jay or camp robber, and the Stellar's jay with its long black crest. Other common mountain birds include flycatchers, juncos, nuthatches and woodpeckers. More than two dozen hummingbird species migrate to Baja in the winter. Some, such as the black-chinned hummingbird and rufous hummingbird, are found throughout the northern sierra; many more species gravitate to Baja California Sur's lush Sierra la Laguna.

Outdoor Adventures

With its magnificent beaches, bays and national parks, Baja is a wonderland for campers and water sports enthusiasts. Adventures of every description await, from whale-watching excursions to canyon hikes to all-day desert excursions on rugged, unpaved four-wheel-drive tracks or horse trails. The Pacific coast boasts some of the world's great surfing beaches, such as those on the Islas de Todos Santos near Ensenada, and near the towns of San Quintín and Todos Santos.

Mexican boating restrictions are generally at least as strict as those in the United States. Authorities recently prohibited sea kayaking among the whales in Magdalena Bay and Scammon's Lagoon, putting an end to one truly unique Baja experience. Today, most sea kayaking is done on the Sea of Cortez side of the peninsula, especially in spring and fall. While kayaking is feasible anywhere along the east coast, the most popular area (and the one where most rental kayaks and guided trips are available) is south of Mulegé at Bahía Concepción, where curious dolphins often approach kayakers and whales can sometimes be seen in the distance.

A permit is also required for kayaking at Loreto National Marine Park, which includes the waters off Loreto and Playa Nopoló as well as Isla Coronado, Isla del Carmen and other off-shore islands. The permit can be obtained through local outfitters.

FISHING   Deep-sea fishing in the waters off Baja is some of the best in the world. Cabo San Lucas is renowned for sailfish, swordfish, blue marlin and white marlin. Japanese and domestic overfishing with drift nets exterminated billfish in the Sea of Cortez during the 1970s, but their numbers are recovering; today sailfish and marlin are often caught around La Paz and Loreto and as far north as San Felipe. Commercial fishing is prohibited in much of the Sea of Cortez, and tourist sport fishing is being promoted as more environmentally friendly and profitable than catching fish for market. Though it is not legally required, boat operators and federal officials urge catch-and-release sport fishing.

On the Pacific side, Ensenada's charter fishing boats go out in search of yellowtail and tuna. Other Pacific coast game fish include albacore, barracuda and bonito. Local fishermen along both coasts catch sharks for food, and it is easy to arrange a shark-fishing trip. In most settlements along the Sea of Cortez, independent fishermen who own *pangas*—long, open wooden motorboats that ride low in the water like rowboats—prefer taking gringos out for a day of sport fishing over going out to catch fish for the local restaurants: It pays better.

Deep-sea fishing is a pricey sport, since charter boats capable of handling a billfish cost several hundred dollars a day. Surf fishing offers more affordable angling thrills, especially in the Los Cabos area, where roosterfish feed close to shore. These big, silver fish reach 65 pounds, and since they live in the surf, they are powerful swimmers skilled in using the breaking waves and undertows to their advantage, giving them a reputation as formidable fighting fish. They are edible but not very good. The idea is to battle the fish for 20 to 30 minutes, land it, have your picture snapped with your catch, and release it into the surf before it gasps its last.

The best months for fishing on either Baja coast are mid-June to mid-November, peaking in September when water temperatures are warmest. Big fish are still caught sometimes in January and February, but much less often.

On a boat from which anyone is fishing, every passenger—children included—must have a Mexican sportfishing license. The licenses cost between $15 and $30 each, depending on their duration and the size of the boat. Snorkelers and scuba divers also need the license for spearfishing. A license is required for fishing in streams, rivers and lakes, but not for surf fishing from the beach or rocks without a boat. The easiest way to get one is to contact the California office of the **Secretaría de Pesca Mexicana**. ~ 2550 5th Avenue, Suite 101, San Diego, CA 92103-6622; 619-233-6956. There are also Secretaría de Pesca offices in many of Baja's major coastal towns, and fishing outfitters along the Tijuana border and in all tourist areas sell fishing licenses.

OCEAN SAFETY

The waters of Baja invite swimming, boating, scuba diving, fishing, kayaking, surfing and other recreational activities. Whether you're out for a short swim, a day of angling for roosterfish or a sea trek in a kayak, it is prudent to be aware of the ocean's risks. Baja's Pacific coast gets big waves and high winds, especially during the winter and spring, while the more sheltered Sea of Cortez coast usually has a gentler surf. Enter the water on the Pacific side with extreme caution. There may be overpowering waves and, in some places, treacherous undertows.

In summer, except during rare but devastating tropical storms, waves in the Pacific subside until they can't be ridden on a surfboard, and the Sea of Cortez becomes as flat as glass. The major hazards are from marine life. If you step on a sea urchin, soaking the affected area in very hot water for 15 to 90 minutes will draw the toxin out. Another remedy is to apply undiluted vinegar, ammonia or even urine. The same remedies work equally well with jellyfish stings. If these preliminary treatments don't work, consult a doctor.

Although the sea was overfished to the point of sterility 20 years ago, smaller native fish are returning in large enough numbers to attract billfish.

A far more painful injury, and one that always calls for medical treatment, can be inflicted by the poisonous tail spine of a stingray. These creatures are not aggressive and prefer to bask peacefully on shallow, sandy sea floors. They will strike if a bather kneels or steps down on them directly, so when walking in shallow water, shuffle your feet in a way that will send stingrays scooting off to safety.

DESERT SAFETY

The heat of the desert can be fatal if you are stranded without sufficient water. A well-acclimatized human adult needs at least one gallon of water a day to survive in the Baja desert. Motorists are wise to stock up on all the water they have room for; buy five or more gallon jugs of drinking water at a time, and replenish whenever your supply falls to less than two jugs per person. Salt tablets cause water retention and can help prevent dehydration and heat exhaustion. Beer and other alcoholic beverages are not a substitute for water. In fact, alcohol increases your body's rate of water loss.

Rattlesnakes, tarantulas and scorpions are found in all parts of Baja except the high mountains. All three are poisonous and can be deadly in rare instances, but none is aggressive toward humans. They can tell that you are too big to eat and will only bite or sting in self-defense, so the best way to avoid bites is to make a lot of noise while hiking in the desert and be alert to avoid putting your hands or feet where you can't see them. Most scorpion stings and spider bites happen at night from rolling over on a poisonous insect while sleeping. If you are tent camping, be sure to keep the tent zipped shut whenever it is set up to prevent insects from entering. Scorpions sometimes live in the thatch roofs of camping palapas and drop down on sleeping campers in the night, so it's a good idea to thrash the roof with a stick as you're moving in to shake loose any lurkers. Finally, whether you're camping or sleeping in hotels, it is prudent to avoid unpleasant surprises by shaking your shoes or boots out before putting them on in the morning.

In the event of a bite, get to the nearest medical clinic as fast as possible. Like bumblebee stings, tarantula bites are rarely fatal except to small children and people with heart problems, insect bite allergies or other medical conditions, but they are quite painful. Rattlesnake bites are rarely life-threatening. The snakes can control how much venom they release from the poison sacs behind their fangs, and when striking in self-defense they tend to inject a low dose or even none at all. Unfortunately, there is no way to be sure until the poison takes effect, so don't wait—head for the nearest town and medical help. Scorpions cannot control their poison dosages as snakes can, and some are lethal while others are merely painful. Take no chances; seek medical treatment immediately. Some people carry snakebite kits in their emergency survival gear, even though doctors disagree on the advisability of using them. If you slice open a snakebite wound and suck the poison out, the risk of infection may be greater than the risk of death from the venom, and the person who sucks the venom out can become poisoned in the process.

CAMPING   Whether you camp in a tent, in a van, under a shell on a pickup truck or in a motor home the size of a city bus, you'll find Baja a camper's paradise. Hundreds of beach campgrounds along both coasts are operated by individuals or rural collectives called *ejidos*. The campgrounds' amenities vary widely. A top-of-the-line RV park has "full hookups"—water, electric and sewage—and sometimes television cables. Level concrete pads are provided for motor homes, and campsites may be suitable for tenting. Parks often have a swimming pool and restaurant and may be protected by a high wall and a guarded gate. Designed for long-term "snowbirds," these places can take much of the fun out of on-the-road camping. Per-night prices typically run about $25 in season. Most of these places are found in or near major towns, including Ensenada, San Felipe, Loreto and Los Cabos.

Mid-range private campgrounds have central restrooms with flush toilets and showers, sometimes hot. Sites are usually on or near the beach; the packed sand is suitable for tents and RVs; they'll have sheltered picnic tables and (often) fireplaces. They typically have electric hookups and a sewage dumping station. These places are not walled, but the owners live on the premises. Sites cost $10 to $12 a night in season.

A third category of beach campgrounds, often run by *ejidos*, has only the most primitive facilities. Sites usually have a palapa, or palm-thatched shelter, for shade, and that's about it. There may be fiberglass portable restrooms or makeshift outhouses nailed together out of scrap lumber. The good news is that they are located on many of Baja's most magnificent beaches, and the cost is minimal—typically $5 or less per night. There is no security and no real crime problem either.

Finally, many remote beaches can be reached via unpaved side roads, some of which may require four-wheel-drive. Unofficial tent and truck camping areas have evolved in many of the most beautiful spots. Camping is unrestricted and free away from developed areas. It's up to you to bring your own water, food and shelter, to dig your own latrine and to haul away your own trash. Camping is also allowed on all offshore islands that have suitable beaches.

Away from the coast, just about the only campgrounds are in the national parks—Parque Nacional Constitución de 1857, Parque Nacional Sierra San Pedro Mártir, Cataviña in the Desierto Central Natural Area and San Ignacio on the southern edge of El Vizcaíno Biosphere Reserve.

For the casual vacationer, hiking will consist of long walks on seemingly endless beaches and short desert walks on four-wheel-drive roads near the main highway. The difficulty of carrying enough water to meet your needs in the sunbaked desert prevents long-distance trekking in most areas.

HIKING

The best hiking and backpacking possibilities are found in two mountainous areas of the interior. Parque Nacional Sierra San Pedro Mártir has an extensive, though poorly marked, network of alpine hiking trails starting from the road to the Mexican National Observatory; 10,000-foot Picacho del Diablo can be climbed either from this approach or from Diablo Canyon on the San Felipe side of the mountains. Even more spectacular—and even harder to get to—is the Sierra de la Laguna, an area of lush mountains north of Los Cabos in the rugged interior of the lower peninsula.

THREE

History and Culture

 THE INDIANS In the remote canyons of the Desierto Central, under huge rock overhangs, murals in burnt sienna and black depict deer, mountain lions, desert bighorn sheep—and the people who originally inhabited the Baja peninsula. Experts think the giant paintings were made over a thousand-year period from A.D. 500 to A.D. 1500, but little is known for certain about their meaning or about the people who made them, who are called simply "the Painters"; their relationship (if any) to the Cochimí people, who lived in the area when the Spanish landed but had no apparent artistic tradition, is a topic for endless academic argument. When 18th-century Spanish missionaries asked the Cochimí about the cave art, they claimed the murals had been painted long ago by an extinct race of giants. Today, the Cochimí no longer exist, and it is unlikely that the mystery of the paintings will ever be definitively solved.

Here's what anthropologists do know about the ancient people of Baja. A single arrowhead found recently in the vastness of the Desierto Central is of a type used 12,000 years ago to hunt mammoths and giant bison. The first people to set foot in Baja may have followed big game animals as they moved south ahead of the creeping glaciers that marked the onset of the last Ice Age. Stone tools and other artifacts found throughout the peninsula show that people lived there by 8000 B.C. Ancient clamshell middens 20 feet high remain as evidence that fishing villages existed along the Pacific coast as early as 6000 B.C. We know nothing of the relationship, if any, between the people of the coast and whoever made the cave paintings in the remote canyons of the interior. They wore little or no clothing, and their possessions were minimal. They lived softly on the fragile land and left few clues for modern scientists.

Millennia passed. When the first Europeans arrived, they found the Baja peninsula populated by an estimated 50,000 nomadic Indians who traveled in small bands. They were skilled hunters, and some scratched out small cornfields in the mountains; for the most part, though, they lived by harvesting shellfish from the sea and plants from the desert.

The Indians were separated into more than a dozen language groups. Major among them were the Pericú people in what is now the Los Cabos area, the Guaycuro in the region of La Paz and Loreto, the Cochimí in the central desert, and the Yumano in the mountains of northern Baja. The four groups were divided by ancient hostilities. Deadly raids and ambushes were commonplace along the fringes of their territories. The violence claimed so many lives that adult women outnumbered adult men by a wide margin, and it was usual for a husband to have several wives. Clans, the central unit of Indian society in Baja, were essentially polygamous extended families.

At the time of European contact, none of the four groups had tribal leadership. All were guided by shamans, who lived in remote locations and practiced herbal medicine and magic. An enigmatic account by one early missionary reports that the Guaycuro worshiped an entity known as "the man who came from the sky."

THE EXPLORERS   Spanish conquistadors first came to Baja as a result of the rivalry between two would-be rulers of colonial Mexico, Hernán Cortés and Nuño de Guzmán. Cortés, the discoverer of Mexico in 1519, had conquered the Aztec capital of Tenochtitlán in 1522, demolishing the ancient city and rebuilding it as Mexico City. Cortés then set out on a 20-month expedition to Honduras. In his absence from Mexico City, his enemies spread false news of his death and seized his property. Upon his return, Cortés was arrested and taken back to Spain to stand trial on false charges that had been made to stop him from reclaiming his property.

While Cortés awaited trial, the King of Spain appointed an *audencia*, or tribunal, to govern Mexico temporarily until the court case was resolved. But one after another, the members of the audencia died mysteriously, leaving Guzmán, a former slave trader and the most despised villain in Mexican colonial history, notorious for corruption and cruelty to Indians, as the de facto dictator. His rule lasted less than a year before he outraged his subjects by physically attacking the Bishop of New Spain during church services. On the Bishop's complaint, the King of Spain sent a new audencia to relieve Guzmán of his post. Hearing that they were on their way, Guzmán decided to get out of town before they arrived. He mounted a private army and set forth to conquer the west. In a brutal campaign of terror, he swept through Michoacán, Jalisco, Nayarít and Sonora, massacring the local Indians wherever he went. Guzmán's reign as warlord instilled in the Indians of western Mexico such hatred of the Spanish that for more than a century afterward, no one who traveled overland in the region returned alive.

Meanwhile, acquitted of the charges against him, Cortés returned to Mexico to reclaim his place as the rightful governor; but the king had other ideas. He decided that henceforth the colony would be ruled by a viceroy—a surrogate for the king himself. Cortés lacked the noble lineage to qualify as viceroy of the land he had conquered. Instead, the king sent him to Cuernavaca, where he built a castle and reigned as the Marquis of Oaxaca, with dominion over the southern territories all the way to Guatemala, but had few responsibilities and no real power.

All the metal fittings, rigging and other components for building a ship were transported 400 miles over the mountains from Veracruz on the Gulf of Mexico to Cortés' early-16th-century shipyard (located near modern-day Zihuatanejo).

With excess time on his hands, Cortés decided to outfit an expedition in hopes of parlaying his personal fortune into a new empire. His plan was to explore the unknown west coast of North America in search of a navigable passage between the Atlantic and the Pacific. He established a shipyard near modern-day Zihuatanejo to build vessels for this expedition.

Cortés did not go along on the early expeditions, though he financed them. The first ship, commanded by Cortés' cousin Diego Hurtado, set out in 1532, but encountered pirates led by Nuño de Guzmán near the mouth of the Sea of Cortez. The ship was seized, and the crewmen were either executed or put ashore at the mercy of hostile Indians.

The following year, Cortés sent out a second exploration party in the newly built ship *Concepción*, for which the magnificent Bahía de Concepción would later be named. This expedition, too, was doomed. The captain was murdered by mutineers led by the ship's pilot, Fortún Jiménez, who made the first Spanish landfall on the Baja peninsula in 1534. The mutineers had little opportunity to bask in the glory of their accomplishment. While refilling their water casks at a spring near what is now La Paz, they were attacked by Indians. According to Mexican legend, the Indians were enraged when the Spanish tried to rape their women. Jiménez and the crew members who had accompanied him ashore were killed. The men who had stayed aboard ship escaped, but lack of fresh water forced them to land on the opposite shore of the Sea of Cortez, where Guzmán's soldiers captured them and their ship. A single survivor escaped and eventually journeyed on foot down the west coast to Cortés' port with the first report of a huge "island" where pearls were found in abundance.

Spanish exploration of the Americas in the 1500s was characterized by the notion that human imagination was divinely inspired, and therefore, every place that was described in a legend, novel or epic poem must actually exist. Visionary tales of golden cities in the wilderness sent conquistadors off in futile quests for such nonexistent empires as El Dorado, Quivira and Cibola. A popular Spanish novel of the time, *Las Sergas de Esplandián* by Garcí Ordóñez de Montalvo, mentioned "an island on the right hand of the Indies very near the terrestrial Paradise, peopled by black women among whom there was not a single man . . . . Their island was the most impregnable in the world with its cliffs and headlands and rocky coasts. Their weapons were all of gold, because in all the island there was no metal except gold." The fictitious island was named California after its ruler, Califia, queen of the Amazons. As reports began to filter back of a huge island off the North American west coast, Cortés and others easily convinced themselves that they had found the fabled California.

Enthusiastic over the prospect of treasure, Cortés decided to finance a third expedition. This time, he decided to lead it himself and confront his nemesis, Guzmán. He set off with three ships, 500 soldiers and sailors, 37 families and 130 horses, planning to establish a permanent colony on the shore of Bahía de la Paz. He never met Guzmán, who, hearing the news that Cortés was on the way with a sizable army, fled across the rugged Sierra Madre to the Gulf of Mexico, where he was arrested by the viceroy's soldiers.

Cortés built Santa Cruz, a sturdy little village with stone houses and a church, at the site of present-day Pichilingue near La Paz. There he found the remains of the mutineer Jiménez and his unfortunate followers. He also found a handful of the pearls that he was seeking. But he did not find the Amazon warrior women or their gold. Burdened with too many soldiers and too few farmers, plagued by drought, storms, and disease, Santa Cruz never became self-sufficient, and after two years Cortés and his colonists abandoned it and returned to Mexico.

Obsessed with the hope of redeeming his failure by discovering an Atlantic-Pacific passage, Cortés applied to the viceroy for permission to organize a fourth journey of exploration to California. When permission was denied, he went ahead and invested the remainder of his fortune in an illegal 1539 expedition, sending two ships up the Pacific coast under the command of Francisco de Ulloa. The ships traced and mapped both the mainland and Baja shores of the Sea of Cortez. Then, having determined that Baja was not an island, they rounded the tip of the peninsula and continued up the Pacific coast. When they reached Isla Cedros, an island off the tip of Baja's Vizcaíno Peninsula, Ulloa dispatched the smaller of his ships southward to report his discoveries to Cortés, while he continued north in his other ship. Ulloa was never heard from again. His fate and those of his crew and ship remain unknown to this day.

Destitute but for the money from selling the surviving ship, Cortés returned to Spain, where he died five years later at 63. The sea that separated Baja from the mainland was named in his honor—the Mar de Cortés. Centuries later, after Mexico gained its independence from Spain, history would be revised to paint Cortés as a villain, and the name of the sea would be officially changed to the Golfo de California, but Mexicans still prefer the more evocative name Sea of Cortez.

Viceroy Mendoza commissioned one more sea exploration of the west coast two years after the Ulloa voyage. Unlike his predecessors, Portuguese-born sea captain Juan Rodriguez Cabrillo bypassed the Sea of Cortez and, after stopping to replenish the expedition's water supply at what is now Cabo San Lucas, sailed up the coast to Isla Cedros and the Bahía de Todos Santos. Cabrillo and his crew went on to anchor at the sites of present-day San Diego, Catalina Island and Santa Monica. While exploring the Channel Islands off Santa Barbara, he slipped, fell from a cliff and died from his injuries, but not before claiming the entire Pacific coast of North America in the name of the King of Spain.

Cabrillo's pilot, Bartolomé Ferrelo, continued the mission, sailing as far north as Oregon before returning to Mexico. Unfortunately, he brought back no treasure, and Cabrillo's and Ferrelo's discoveries were dismissed as insignificant. There would be no more Spanish expeditions up the Pacific coast for more than 50 years. Instead, the viceroy would turn his attention to developing trade with Asia, and this enterprise would eventually lead to the colonization of Baja.

THE MANILA GALLEONS Centrally located on the Pacific Rim, the Philippines had been a hub for trade between the merchants of China, Japan, Indonesia, Malaya, Indochina and India for centuries. Ferdinand Magellan had reached the Philippines in 1521 and claimed the islands for Spain. Soon afterward he died there, fighting alongside his new ally, the Rajah of the Philippine city of Cebu, against the rajah's enemies. Magellan's fatal heroism earned Spain an alliance with the rulers of the Philippines that would endure for centuries.

If Spain could establish commerce with the Philippines, it would break Portugal's monopoly on the lucrative spice trade in Europe. From the new port of Acapulco on Mexico's southern coast, Spanish ships could easily ride the prevailing winds and ocean currents across the Pacific Ocean to the Philippine Islands in about three months. The problem was getting back. After several failed attempts, a 1542 Spanish expedition led by Ruy López de Villalobos made the crossing from Acapulco, but he could not find a return route and finally surrendered his ship and crew to the Portuguese.

The return route was not found until 1564, when Miguel López de Legazpi navigated far northward to the latitudes of Japan.
Westerly winds and the North Pacific current carried him back
across the ocean to California, where it was an easy matter to
follow the Baja coastline south to Acapulco. Instead of three or
four months, this circuitous return route took at least seven
months and often as much as a year, but the rewards were awesome.

The Philippine trade, which soon shifted from Cebu to the
more accessible port of Manila, proved to be one of the biggest
coups of the Mercantilist era. Instead of carrying silver from the
mines of Mexico back to the king's treasury in Spain, merchants
shipped the silver to the Philippines for trade
with the Chinese, who needed it for coinage to
expand their own trade empire. In exchange, the
Spanish received huge quantities of silk, cotton, oriental rugs, jade, ivory, porcelain and precious gems,
as well as pepper, cloves and cinnamon. The Chinese
were so eager for Mexican silver that they even ex-
changed gold bullion for it. When these goods went back
through Mexico to Spain, they were sold throughout
Europe at many times the worth of the silver they were bought
with. Suddenly, Spain was the most prosperous nation in Europe.

The Manila galleons were the largest ships ever built until the 20th century.

Spain expanded its Manila fleet by hiring Chinese ship-
wrights in the Philippines to build new galleons in exchange for
the abundant Mexican silver. This international partnership re-
sulted in ships that combined elements of European sailing vessels and of Chinese junks. The new galleons were built bigger
and bigger; eventually they had more than three times the cargo
capacity of the ships that traveled between Spain and Mexico.

The need for a Spanish colony on the Baja coast was clear to
captains of the Manila galleons: They were often critically short
of food and water by the time they sighted California. A resupply point at the tip of the Baja peninsula would have done much
to alleviate the hardships of the trip. But the Mexican viceroy, re-
membering Cortés' failures, could not be interested in another attempt to colonize Baja. It was the British, not the Spanish, whose
ships next made landfall there.

Francis Drake was a privateer—a freelance warship captain
chartered by the British government to commit piracy against
Spanish ships in the Caribbean. As word got out about the incredible riches of the Manila galleons, Drake decided to rob one.
He sailed around Cape Horn and north to the tip of Baja, where
he lurked in wait for the Spanish ships. His attack came as a
complete surprise, since no British ship had ever entered the Pacific Ocean before. Drake returned to England with all the treasure he could carry.

A few years later, another British privateer, Thomas Cavendish, anchored at Cabo San Lucas and robbed the Manila galleons again. He, too, made it safely back to England with his loot. By 1598, British privateer ships were pouring into the Pacific and gathering around Los Cabos to wait for their prey. By 1615, Dutch pirate ships had joined the pack, setting up their own stronghold in the Bahía de la Paz. The viceroy belatedly realized that a colonial presence on the Baja Peninsula was essential to the security of the Manila galleons. But colonizing the Baja was easier said than done. Expeditions in 1596, 1644 and 1663 ended in failure. The token colony of San Bruno, near present-day Loreto, lasted for 19 months but was abandoned when the colonists' supplies ran out. A resupply station on Baja finally became a reality in 1730, thanks to Jesuit priests.

The Manila galleons crossed the Pacific every year for two and a half centuries, until just a few years before Mexican independence. During most of this time, pirates ruled the seas off the coast of Baja. Fighting them became a predictable part of the arduous return trip from the Philippines.

THE MISSIONS The first successful settlements in Baja were established at the end of the 17th century by the Jesuits, a Catholic order that had been founding missions across mainland Mexico for a century. Inspired by an encounter with Father Keno, the legendary mission builder of northern Mexico, Jesuit priest Juan María de Salvatierra applied for permission to start a mission in Baja. Considering the many failed attempts to colonize that barren, waterless peninsula, neither the viceroy nor the Mexican Jesuit leadership was willing to finance another attempt. But Father Salvatierra's enthusiasm impressed Jesuit officials in Europe; in 1697, with 21 other priests and some soldiers, he began construction of a mission church at Loreto to convert the local Guaycuros to Catholicism.

Father Salvatierra presided over the Loreto mission until his death 20 years later. During that time, he built four other missions, at San Javier, Ligui, Mulegé and Comomdu. Each mission was comprised of a church, clerical residences and an adjoining pueblo where Indian converts lived. The people worked on church land and shared in the crops. Under Spanish law, a mission was to last for only ten years, and then the land was to be turned over to the villagers, partly as private farms and partly as *ejido* land. In Baja, the Jesuits never quite got around to signing their land over to the Indians, but then again, they never succeeded in growing much on it. All through the missionary era, the priests and their Indian followers survived on food donated by wealthy patrons on the Mexican mainland.

Father Salvatierra's successors built 15 more missions in southern Baja during the 18th century, spanning most of Baja California Sur. The most important of these was San José del Cabo. Built in 1730 on a natural harbor, it was ideally situated to resupply the Manila galleons with fresh water from nearby springs. From then on, the ships put in at San José each year.

In 1733, outraged by a church prohibition against polygamy, the Pericús revolted against the four southern missions—San José, Todos Santos, Santiago and La Paz—killing several priests and all six guards assigned to the missions. When the Manila galleons sailed into San Jose, only to find the port in the hands of angry Indians, they hastened to report the uprising to the viceroy, who sent in the army. San José del Cabo became as much a military garrison as a mission, with soldiers outnumbering priests.

During the Jesuits' 70 years of mission work in southern Baja, the peninsula's total population fell to 7000. More than 85 percent of Baja's native people had died from epidemics of European diseases such as smallpox and measles, to which they had no natural immunity.

The arrival of soldiers and sailors at San José brought with it the beginning of a horror that would destroy the missions of southern Baja. Measles, syphilis and smallpox quickly spread from San José through the land of the Pericú. By 1748 the entire tribe was dead, and the missionaries had refocused their attention among the Cochimí, who were just beginning to experience the epidemics.

In 1767, suspecting that the missionaries might be amassing personal fortunes through fundraising and failing to turn mission land over to the villagers, the king ordered the Jesuit order expelled from the Spanish Empire.

With the expulsion of the Jesuits, Franciscan missionaries under the leadership of Father Junipero Serra took over the mission headquarters at Loreto for a few years. Soon, however, the king of Spain decreed that California would be divided between two religious orders—the Franciscans to do missionary work in Alta California, and the Dominicans in Baja. It was this decree that originally defined the boundary between the two Californias.

The Dominicans established half a dozen new missions in Baja California, from Santo Tomás with its vineyards and olive orchards to San Pedro Mártir, deep in the rugged mountains of the interior. They relocated Indians from the north to revive the southern missions. But wherever the missionaries went, fatal diseases accompanied them.

Mexico attained independence from Spain in 1821. Soon thereafter, the new government secularized missions throughout the country and confiscated their agricultural land. The only exceptions were the Dominican missions of northern Baja. These were allowed to continue as usual because, as the only settlements in the region, they provided way stations for travelers between the towns of Alta California and those of southern Baja. The missions' original purpose became little more than a memory, as there were hardly any Indians left to convert.

THE INVADERS   At first, the few people who cared one way or the other in Baja, like their counterparts in the other remote territories of Texas and Yucatán, generally favored the idea of being an autonomous republic. They changed their minds after British privateer Lord Thomas Cochrane, who had sailed around the tip of South America plundering isolated towns all along the Mexican coast, seized San José del Cabo and then attacked Loreto. Cochrane's landing party was repulsed by the city's military guard, which consisted of 15 soldiers. He returned to raiding the Mexican mainland and never bothered with Baja again. The people of both cities pledged their loyalty to Mexico in 1824. To reduce the power of the church, the capital was moved from Loreto, the headquarters of the Dominican missions, to La Paz.

With scarcely any population, mineral wealth or arable farmland, the national government took little interest in the peninsula. Instead, the few Mexican pioneers who crossed over from the mainland found that gringos coveted Baja far more than Mexico did. In the 1830s, Texas won its independence from Mexico. About the same time, U.S. diplomats initiated fruitless attempts to buy California from Mexico. As the pressure of western migration increased, the United States agreed to annex the Republic of Texas as a state. Mexico and the United States had radically different ideas about the location of Texas' southern border; the annexation touched off a military confrontation between the two nations. Texas was the excuse for the Mexican War, but California was the prize.

WHY THERE ARE TWO CALIFORNIAS

History records differing versions of why Baja, which was still occupied by U.S. troops and was initially part of U.S. negotiators' demands after the Mexican War (1846–48), was not included in the final settlement. Mexican students learn that their country balked at turning Baja over to the United States for reasons of national pride and security—it would have relinquished control of sea lanes to the mainland ports of Guaymas and Mazatlán. *Norteamericano* schoolbooks say that after U.S. military command in Baja reported the peninsula to be worthless and uninhabitable, negotiators decided to take New Mexico instead. There is probably some truth in both versions. In any case, in 1848 the partition of Baja and Alta California became permanent.

In May of 1846, when news arrived that fighting had started along the Rio Grande, a small fleet of American warships that had been stationed at the Mexican port of Mazatlán to protect the U.S. consulate there headed up the Pacific coast to seize San Diego, Monterey and San Francisco. There was no fighting. As U.S. Marines took control of the Alta California ports, the fleet returned southward to take control of Baja California.

U.S. Navy gunships blockaded the mouth of the Sea of Cortez. They then sailed to La Paz, where the American commodore informed the Mexican governor that he was placing Baja under U.S. control. There was no demand for surrender; instead, the authorities in La Paz were merely asked to pledge "neutrality" in the war—meaning that they would remain in charge of local affairs but would not resist U.S. military occupation. Six months later, U.S. ships took control of San José del Cabo under the same kind of neutrality agreement. Officials were happy to avoid a military confrontation: After all, there was no telling which nation would own Baja after the war. Baja's loyalty to Mexico had never been particularly strong, and it had eroded as the Mexican government had changed leadership no less than 50 times in 26 years, usually by assassination or military coup. Echoes of this "neutral" attitude toward both Mexico and the United States have helped shaped Baja's unique character ever since.

In September of 1847, the Mexican government ordered a small group of officers under the command of Capitán Manuel Pinada to cross the Sea of Cortez from Guaymas and land in Mulegé, north of the area held by the U.S. forces, now supplemented by two companies of infantry. Pinada did not bring many soldiers; every available man was needed for the last-ditch defense of Mexico City, which fell to an expeditionary force of U.S. Marines the same week that Pinada landed in Baja. Instead, the captain brought crateloads of rifles and conscripted the able-bodied men of Mulegé, Comondú and San Ignacio—about 300 in all—into a citizens' army to fight the gringos. After a skirmish at Mulegé, Pinada and his troops besieged La Paz, but after 12 days of fierce fighting the Mexicans ran out of ammunition and had to withdraw.

The Mexicans turned their attention upon San José del Cabo, which was occupied by a far smaller U.S. force, and fighting raged there for more than a month before American reinforcements arrived to save the day for the U.S. The final battle, near Todos Santos, ended in the surrender of Capitán Pinada and his troops. In all, the war in Baja involved fewer than 1000 soldiers on both sides. Sadly, the battles of San José del Cabo and Todos Santos took place after Mexico's surrender on February 2, 1848; news that the war was over had not yet reached the commanders of either side in the Baja conflict.

The treaty that ended the war ceded almost half of Mexico, including the modern-day states of California, Arizona and New Mexico as well as portions of six other western states, to the United States. In return, the U.S. agreed to pay Mexico a sum that was slightly less than negotiators had offered for California alone before the war.

Soon after Alta California became U.S. territory, the discovery of gold there brought a wave of more than 80,000 squatters and prospectors west from the United States to northern California. Alta California became simply California, the 31st U.S. state, in 1850. Suddenly an oppressed minority, many Hispanic Californians moved south to Baja, but few stayed; most eventually went to mainland Mexico.

By the end of the 19th century, Alta California's population would be only 2 percent Spanish-speaking, and Baja's population would be even smaller than it had been before the Mexican War.

Civil violence between liberal and conservative elements continued in mainland Mexico but rarely affected the Baja Peninsula; the biggest threat continued to be invaders from *el norte*. In 1853, backed by a group called the Knights of the Golden Circle, whose purpose was "to promote the benefits of slavery," American soldier of fortune William Walker and an army of mercenaries sailed into La Paz and seized the capital. Walker planned to establish Baja as the independent Republic of Sonora and Baja California, with himself as President, and then petition to be annexed by the United States. Mexican troops soon arrived to recapture La Paz, and Walker's army retreated first to Cabo San Lucas, then grudgingly northward along the Pacific coast, fighting battles at El Rosario, San Quintín and Ensenada. Walker finally returned to the United States, where he was arrested for violating the federal Neutrality Act of 1818.

Walker was later acquitted, and national press coverage of the trial earned him widespread support, including backing from newly elected U.S. President James Buchanan. He would invade Costa Rica and Nicaragua before he was executed in Honduras in 1860. An estimated 20,000 people died during Walker's forays, nearly matching the death toll of the entire Mexican War. Walker's tombstone reads, "Glory to the patriots who freed Central America of such a bloody pirate! Curses to those who brought him and to those who helped him."

Speaking of pirates: the wildest part of the Baja coast was invaded in 1857 by another kind of unscrupulous profiteer. American sea captain Charles Melville Scammon followed migrating gray whales to their calving waters in Laguna Ojo de Liebre. Using explosive harpoons, his men slaughtered more than a thousand of the whales and filled his ship to the brim with whale oil. But when Scammon returned to San Francisco with his huge haul, it could not be kept secret. The following year, Scammon's Lagoon became a scene of slaughter on an unprecedented scale as more than 50 whaling ships "harvested" thousands of whales. By the end of the 1859 season, no more gray whales could be found around Scammon's Lagoon. Nor would they be seen along the California coast until 1900, and Baja's gray whale population would not reach pre-whaling levels until 1996.

THE LAST WILDERNESS After centuries of failed attempts to conquer Baja, investment began to accomplish what military might could not. As the population of southern Baja's few small settlements dwindled, businessmen from north of the border eyed the possibilities for exploiting the peninsula. Unscrupulous real estate operators dealt in dubious mining claims and acreages. The biggest of these frauds got its start in 1863, when Mexican president Benito Juárez leased the northern two-thirds of Baja to an American promoter, who turned around and sold his claim to an investment cartel, which gave "free California farmland" to new arrivals from the East. The company made its profits on ship passage to the new land and on selling supplies—construction materials, for instance. And fresh water. Settlers soon found that their 160-acre "farms" were located along the salt-encrusted shoreline of Bahía Magdalena. Within a few years, the most tenacious settlers had abandoned their holdings, and the Mexican government revoked the lease.

The idea of leasing the Baja wilderness to foreigners for hard currency was reinvented in 1883, when the Mexican government under President Porfírio Díaz passed the *ley de colonización*. The law allowed the government to replenish its treasury by opening up vast Baja land concessions for sale to American and European corporations. They would then theoretically help tame the frontier and develop a viable economy on the peninsula.

Foremost among these would-be developers was the International Company of Mexico, a Connecticut-based investment group, that envisioned a wheat-farming empire on northern Baja's Pacific coastal plain, from Ensenada to San Quintín. American farmers bought land and began to develop the plain, but when their first year's crop died from lack of rain, most decided that they had been duped and went back to the United States. The shareholders sold the International Company of Mexico to a British corporation with still more grandiose plans. Bringing shiploads of English farmers—who would not find it so easy to quit and go back home—they not only established a large flour mill and a shipping pier at San Quintín but even started construction on a railroad that, if completed, would have linked San Quintín with San Diego. But as it became obvious that the drought that had destroyed the American colony was not just a bad season but a permanent condition, the English farmers, too, abandoned Baja.

More successful were several mining concessions, especially the copper mine at Santa Rosalía started by a German company in 1885. The world's largest copper mine, it was later sold to the French, but a German shipping company retained a monopoly on transporting the copper back to Europe. The foreign companies shaped the economy and architecture of the area, and many local residents today claim German or French ancestry.

Most of the concession holders in Baja did little to promote economic development. By the last years of the 19th century, Baja theoretically belonged to two dozen or so *ranchos* owned by wealthy Californians who rarely, if ever, set foot there. In fact, so many hundreds of acres of the parched and largely unexplored landscape were required to support a single steer that the Mexican cowboys who ranged this desert landscape were less herdsmen than bring-'em-back-alive hunters.

The discovery of gold in the northern mountains of Baja fueled the development of Ensenada, a port that was readily accessible from California but not from mainland Mexico; but the ore played out within a few years. Four centuries after its discovery, Baja remained Mexico's Alaska, irresistible to adventurers and almost impossible to live in.

THE HIGHWAY   The peninsula languished in the desert sun. The Mexican Revolution brought a brief flurry of action in 1911, when an independent rebel group known as the Magonistas joined forces with labor activists from the United States in a grandiose plan to seize Baja and form a leftist border republic. The rebels captured Mexicali and Tijuana with ease, but were soon forced to retreat into the mountains as Mexican Army reinforcements arrived.

During the early 20th century, the border between the United States and Mexico was "open," without immigration restrictions. In 1920, the United States adopted the 18th Amendment, prohibiting the possession, sale and use of alcoholic beverages. Californians responded by hastening across the border to the saloons and dance halls of Old Mexico. The first luxury resorts were built in Rosarito and Ensenada, along with a plush gambling casino, and Hollywood celebrities flocked there. Tijuana, meanwhile, started earning a reputation for easy-to-find vice that has persisted to the present day. The tourist boom lasted only 12 years before Ensenada's high life was dealt a double blow: Prohibition was repealed in the United States, and gambling was declared illegal in Mexico.

Tijuana's sleazy side continued to thrive, especially after 1941, when World War II brought hundreds of thousands of

Where the Commons Survive

The biggest factor that shaped Baja in the first half of the 20th century was land reform. As you drive the Baja Highway today, you'll see many signs for place whose names are preceded by "EJ." This cryptic abbreviation stands for *ejido,* the Spanish word for "common." In rural Spain at the time Mexico was colonized, villagers used community land ("commons") owned by the church for grazing livestock and gathering firewood. The system was carried over to the New World by missionaries, and these *ejidos* fostered the growth of Indian villages near the missions until 1840, when church land was confiscated by the government. (The commons had largely been privatized out of existence in Europe by this time.) The *ejido* concept was revived in another land reform movement in 1930, when the government distributed millions of acres to landless *campesinos* for communal use.

The system has served to encourage settlement of Baja California, as irrigation wells have created more arable land. In recent years, such settlements have provided at least a small safety valve for Mexico's explosive population pressures, as thousands of Indians from the poor southern state of Oaxaca have taken the government up on offers to relocate to Baja.

New *ejidos* are created when rural people form a group and petition the government to grant them land that is currently not in use. The government finances the purchase of equipment and seeds, as well as the cost of drilling irrigation wells, through a chain of special banks called Banco Rural; the villagers pay the loans back with a share of the crops. The government's share is sold throughout Mexico in federally operated CONASUPO stores. In some areas today, *ejido* land is used for other purposes. Many tourist campgrounds along both coasts of Baja are owned and operated by *ejidos*.

All *ejido* land was owned by the government, and the people who lived and worked there were merely its custodians, until 1993, when the law was changed to give legal title to the *ejido* members; they could decide by majority vote whether to keep the land as community property or divide it among themselves as private property. The idea was to make it easier for *ejido* farmers to borrow money to modernize. Opponents have claimed that the privatization is a plot to expose *ejido* lands to the threat of bank foreclosure. So far, many *ejidos* in Baja are prospering in enterprises that range from cotton plantations to tourist campgrounds; others have not been so fortunate.

With the population growth brought by the *ejido* system and irrigation, Baja California achieved statehood in 1952.

young men to the naval base in San Diego, just a short bus ride from the border. But fears started to grow that Mexicans would take American fighting mens' jobs and women while they were overseas. In Los Angeles' 1943 Zoot Suit Riots, Anglo soldiers and sailors assaulted hundreds of Latinos in the streets while the police stood by and arrested the victims. The U.S. government closed the Mexican border, passed a series of stringent immigration laws, and deported from the border states large numbers of Mexican Americans who could not prove that they had been born in the U.S.A. The deportations more than doubled the size of Tijuana. Ever since, it has been easy for United States citizens to enter Mexico but very difficult for Mexicans to come to the U.S. legally.

In 1952, the United States installed a radar station at San Felipe and built a highway (now Route 5) there from Mexicali. It was the first paved road into the Baja desert, opening Sea of Cortez beaches to travel-trailer campers, the RVers of that era.

The rugged, rocky road that linked Ensenada and the San Quintín Valley to the southern towns of Loreto, La Paz, San José los Cabos and Cabo San Lucas remained the kind of journey that legends are made of—a 2000-mile round trip with few food and water stops, no reliable gasoline supply and no tow trucks. Today, the rusted shells of abandoned cars and trucks from the 1950s are a common site along the highway, relics of the days when many vehicles that started off across the Baja wasteland never came back. The custom of caravanning in groups started in the early days of the Baja Highway to provide a way out of the desert in case of a breakdown. The Baja 1000, originally a motorcycle race from Tijuana to La Paz (since rerouted and expanded to include cars, trucks and all-terrain vehicles) and first held in 1967, brought the Baja Highway into the U.S. public consciousness.

Paving of the Baja Highway was completed in 1972, about the same time that motor homes were enjoying their greatest vogue in the United States. The flow of RV adventurers and "snowbirds" was immediate and enthusiastic. It has never slowed down. At the same time, the highway made farming on southern Baja's coastal plain feasible—since there was now a way to get crops to market—and spurred the development of new population centers at Ciudad Constitución and Ciudad Insurgentes. Farming and tourism have made Baja one of the most prosperous areas of Mexico in recent years.

Baja California Sur, the southern half of the peninsula, was granted statehood in 1973; it was the last territory in Mexico to become a state.

Today, some areas of Baja are experiencing unprecedented population growth—up to 15 to 20 percent per year—thanks to retiring baby boomers, who have discovered that oceanfront condominiums or home lots cost about one-third what they do in California, taxes can be one-tenth as much, and the overall cost of living, including medical treatment, is less than half as much. One real estate developer who has caught the wave of retirement in Baja is Donald Trump, whose Trump Ocean Resort condominium megacomplex is his first project outside the United States. Trump's resort is located south of Rosarito, a short drive from San Diego (if you don't count the long wait to cross the border), where The Donald's high-rise towers fit right in with the skyscraper hotels. Other areas to which retirees are swarming include Ensenada, La Paz (now ranked as one of the world's ten fastest-growing retirement areas), Loreto (a fishing village with a major, underutilized airport which the Mexican government has been trying unsuccessfully for years to transform into a Cancún-style megaresort) and Los Cabos, where most condos come with golf course privileges and at least one has its own fleet of communal yachts for condo owners' use. Condominium developments are also being built, though not at such a furious pace, in San Felipe, and real estate promoters in the area predict that condos will soon proliferate in the border town of Tecate and the wine country of Valle de Guadalupe.

> More than 95 percent of Baja's two million residents are mestizo, a blend of Spanish and Indian cultures.

Culture

PEOPLE

Inhospitable terrain and lack of water severely limited the population of Baja until recent years. If all the various peoples—American Indian, Spanish, Anglo American, British, German, French and Japanese among them—who settled on the peninsula at one time or another had stayed, Baja would be a cultural melting pot on the same order as Alta California, its neighbor to the north. But instead, the population of Baja is made up of three ethnicities: mestizo, Indian and Anglo.

Mestizo (commonly called *mexicano*), the dominant race of Mexico, is a synthesis of Spanish and indigenous Indian cultures mingled over nearly five centuries. Seventy-five percent of the peninsula's people live along the border with the United States, and fewer than half of them were born in Baja. Newcomers are drawn by job opportunities in *maquiladoras* (duty-free factories) along the border, and by prospects of seasonal farm work on both sides of the border. People also move from mainland Mexico to Baja to be close to relatives living in California and to enjoy the peninsula's *tranquilo* way of life.

Few of the peninsula's native Indian people survived the epidemics that wiped out entire tribes in colonial times. Their only descendants are a few hundred Paipái Indians living in the Sierra de Juárez southeast of Ensenada. The Indian population of Baja today comes from the southern state of Oaxaca, where people have been encouraged by the government to relocate to Baja *ejidos* to alleviate tribal poverty and overpopulation. While most work on farms, growing numbers of Indians sell trinkets or beg in resort areas, and others travel from beach to beach selling souvenirs and provisions from the backs of trucks. Indians account for about 2 percent of Baja's permanent population. The polite word for American Indians in Mexico is *indígen* (pronounced almost like "Indian" in English), not the pejorative *indio*.

Although Anglos from the United States, Canada and England have sometimes accounted for a large part of the peninsula's population in the past, those not born in Baja were expelled following the Mexican Revolution of 1910–12. Today, official census figures show that only 2 percent of Baja's population is Anglo. But this is misleading, since most retirees and other expatriates who make their homes in Mexico legally reside in the United States; they are officially tourists, even though they may live in Baja year-round and return to the U.S. for a few days once or twice a year.

CUISINE   The regional cooking of Baja begins and ends with seafood. Shrimp *(camarones)*, lobster *(langosta)*, crab *(cangrejo)*, clams *(almejas)*, scallops *(callos)*, octopus *(pulpo)*, squid *(calamar)*, along with many varieties of fish *(pescado)* are ubiquitous ingredients all over Baja.

Baja tacos are wrapped in corn tortillas, but that is the extent of their resemblance to the familiar taco found in the United States. The Baja version will contain strips of stir-fried fish, crab or other seafood, salsa, guacamole and a cabbage marinade similar to cole slaw. Tacos are served at beachfront stands, open-air

NOT QUITE FARM-FRESH

Baja lacks the abundance of tropical fruits and vegetables available in other parts of Mexico. Though much of northern Baja California is farmland, most of its produce is exported to the United States. If a restaurant serves vegetables other than the standard side dishes of beans and rice, they usually come out of a can. During harvest times, which vary depending on the crop, vendors sell local produce at roadside stands. Surplus crops are also sold from the backs of trucks that make the rounds of beaches in areas inhabited by campers. One week the crop may be tomatoes, the next week strawberries or onions. *Elotes*—steaming hot ears of corn served with chili powder, lime and cream—are a specialty at some roadside stands.

fast-food eateries called *comedores,* and inexpensive restaurants in all coastal areas of Baja.

Shrimp, crab and octopus are often served as cocktails *(cokteles)*—uncooked, marinated in lime juice, vinegar, oil, cilantro and spices and served in a tall glass. Similarly, fish is chopped or grated and marinated to make *ceviche.*

Shrimp is commonly served in garlic sauce *(al mojo de ajo)* or breaded *(empanizados)*. Prawns *(gambas)*, like shrimp but larger, may be sliced open and stuffed *(rellena)* with cheese, crab meat or other fillings. Crabs are typically steamed *(al vapor)* or deviled *(al diablo)*. Stone crab claws come cracked and sauteed in butter.

Pacific spiny lobsters, the kind commonly caught off the Baja coast, are sliced in half lengthwise with a big, sharp knife and grilled with butter, garlic and spices. This way of preparing lobster, called *estilo Puerto Nuevo* after the major lobster-fishing port south of Rosarito, is favored throughout Baja.

Clams of several varieties are among the most common foods along the Sea of Cortez coast. Chocolate clams (pronounced "cho-co-LAH-tay") are not to be missed. These fat clams in dark brown shells are almost the size of hamburgers; order a half-dozen and you may need a doggie bag. They are steamed and sliced in half inside the shell before serving.

Menus often say just "pescado" and serve whatever white-fleshed fish the sea provides that day—typically snapper *(huachinango)*, yellowtail *(jurel)*, mackerel *(sierra)*, tarpon *(sabalo)* or halibut *(lenguado)*. These are prepared in many ways—in garlic sauce *(al mojo de ajo)*, in a salsa of chopped tomatoes, onions, olives, cilantro and spices *(veracruzano)*, in a savory fish stew *(guisado)*, or cleaned, breaded and fried whole *(empanizado entero)*. Order one of these and you'll often get a red snapper big enough to feed a whole family. Better restaurants feature steaks from large fish such as tuna *(atún)*, swordfish *(pez espada)*, shark *(tiburón)* and the most delicious of all fish in Baja waters, mahi-mahi *(dorado)*.

The Mexican food served in restaurants is much the same as you would expect to find in a typical "Mexican" restaurant in the United States. Since many more gringo tourists than locals eat in restaurants, the menus focus on the dishes that are most familiar north of the border—tacos, enchiladas, tamales and burritos. *Chiles rellenos*, a popular dish in Baja restaurants, are different from their U.S. counterparts. Poblanos—large, mild, dark green chiles shaped like bell peppers—are filled with cheese or seafood, breaded and fried.

The Mexican food served in most restaurants is not as *picante* as elsewhere in Mexico. The *salsa fresca* that comes with tortilla chips is fresh, as the name implies, but usually not very hot. If you request *salsa picante*, you will invariably get Tabasco sauce bottled in Louisiana. Another concession to gringo tastes? No: imported Tabasco is the kind of hot sauce most often found in Baja grocery stores. Like most things, it's cheaper and easier to get hot sauce from southern California than from the Mexican mainland. Another popular hot sauce, Tapatio, is made in Guadalajara but exported to the United States, then reimported to Baja.

By far the most common meat in Baja is machaca, which is beef that has been marinated, cooked, shredded and then dried like beef jerky to preserve it. (Some grocery store meat departments sell machaca that has not been dried. Otherwise, the dried beef is steamed to reconstitute it before serving.) Machaca originated on the other side of the Sea of Cortés, in the state of Sonora, which has many cattle ranches. Since Mexican cattle are not fattened in feedlots, their meat is not marbled with fat like North American beef. As a result, beef steak (*bistec* in Spanish) is quite tough, and if you've ever tried to eat one, you'll appreciate why machaca is shredded. It is often served wrapped in flour tortillas to make burritos—the authentic northwestern Mexico kind, not the kind with beans and such that is sold at Taco Bell. It is also scrambled into eggs and omelettes for breakfast or simply heaped alongside beans and rice.

LANGUAGE The language barrier between English and Spanish should never be perceived as an obstacle to visiting Baja. Locals have a long history of contact with gringos and may even have one or two in their family trees. Surrounded by bilingual and tourist-oriented signs, and bombarded by American television, even locals of limited education understand a fair amount of English, though they may be self-conscious about trying to speak it. In fact, "Spanglish"—a crazy-quilt mix of Spanish and English words with elastic rules of grammar—approaches the status of an unofficial "official language" in Baja. So many people like to practice speaking English that the language barrier you're most likely to run into is when you find yourself in a lengthy conversation *in English*—and can't understand a word.

Today, more and more Baja residents come from the mainland, where English is not heard as much. Mexican students are required to attend school until the age of 14. Unless they drop out, they are required to take two years of English in high school. The dropout rate is high in some poor regions of Mexico, but not in Baja. Students in Mexican universities must be reasonably fluent in English to graduate. So in general, educated middle-class Mexicans speak English well; unskilled laborers do not. Indian children who grow up on tribal land are not required to attend

school, so adult Indians rarely understand English and sometimes cannot even speak much Spanish.

Speaking fluent Spanish enhances any trip to Mexico, of
course. But what if, like most people who live in the United States,
you don't? Many people who have never stud-
ied Spanish worry more than they ought to about
traveling south of the border. One of the funda-
mental lessons of foreign travel is that people can
communicate even though they don't know a word
of each other's languages. Words help, but your tone
of voice, the expression on your face, and gestures or
sign language often count for more.

> In the border region, it's
> not unusual for the
> newer *corridas* (folk
> songs) to tell how
> brave drug smugglers
> met their sad fates.

Even though English is widely understood, people
will relate to you better if you attempt to speak Spanish,
no matter how poorly. It pays in smiles if you study for your trip
by practicing a few useful phrases like *"¿Cuánto vale esto?"*
(How much is this worth?), *"La cuenta, por favor"* (The check,
please), *"¿Tiene usted una habitación para la noche?"* (Do you
have a room for the night?) and *"¿No habría modo de resolver
el problema de otra manera?"* (Isn't there another way to resolve
this problem?). If your comprehension of Spanish leaves something to be desired, try to ask questions that can be answered
with a yes or no, with one word, or with a number. It can be very
frustrating to ask for directions and receive a cheerful reply that's
so long, fast and complicated that you can't make sense of it.
Better to ask questions like "Is this the right way to _____?"
"How many blocks?" "On the right or left?".

Of the many books available for studying Spanish on your
own, the one I have found most helpful and friendly is *Spanish
Lingo for the Savvy Gringo* by Elizabeth Reid, who spent eight
years teaching English to Mexicans in Rosarito. Her Spanglish
approach to vocabulary building is ideal for Baja travelers. The
book is available in many southern California and Baja bookstores or from In One EAR Publications, 29481 Manzanita Drive,
Campo, CA 91906-1128; 800-356-9315.

Many people who have studied Spanish in school find themselves helpless when it comes to actually communicating in Mexico. Once you've learned it, the vocabulary stays stored in the
deep recesses of the mind, but it's often hard to bring it to the
surface after years of disuse. Before you leave for Baja, a few
weeks of using aids such as instructional CDs can help attune
your ear and tongue to the language. A painless way to tune into
Spanish is to spend your TV-viewing hours watching Spanish-
language cable channels or rented videos. The Mexican motion-
picture industry is undergoing a renaissance these days; internationally acclaimed films such as *Y Tu Mama Tambiem* and

Amores Perros are well worth watching in Spanish, with or without the English subtitles. Most U.S. video stores can order Mexican films and Spanish-version DVDs (subtitled or dubbed) of almost any popular Hollywood film.

MUSIC   In many restaurants, especially in Ensenada, La Paz and Los Cabos, you will be approached by groups of strolling musicians. They play at tables for a fixed rate per song, often cutting the restaurant in for a small amount. In Baja, the going rate is about five pesos per song for each band member. In dollars, a romantic trio gets about US$2 for a song, and a large *mariachi* or *conjunto norteño* may get up to about $6 a song.

The most familiar Mexican musical groups are mariachis, the ensembles of musicians dressed in big sombreros and tight clothes decorated with gold or silver piping. The bands, made up of five to eight or more guitar, *guitarrón* (bass guitar), violin and trumpet players, originated in Guadalajara in the 19th century, and their ornate outfits represent the suits worn by *charros*, or cowboys, of that era on formal occasions. Though Guadalajara is still the mariachi capital, all parts of Mexico have good mariachis. Their music follows traditional forms, especially *rancheras,* cowboy songs that usually have to do with love or drinking, and *corridas*, folk songs that tell stories, often with patriotic, topical or tragic themes. Most of the standard *rancheras* sung by mariachis today were composed from the 1920s to the 1950s. The most famous and prolific of *ranchera* composers, José Alfredo Jiménez, is memorialized by a larger-than-life statue in Mexico City's Plaza Garibaldi. Musicians continue to write *corridas*, though.

Conjuntos norteños are the traditional musical groups of the Mexican border states. Neither as large nor as formal as mariachis, a *norteño* group usually numbers from three to five members, dressed in cowboy hats, boots, jeans and Western shirts. Though they may look like *norteamericano* country-western bands and play many of the same standard *rancheras* and *corridas* as mariachis do, the *norteños* have a distinctive style that people in other parts of the country sometimes ridicule as provincial but which Mexicans from both sides of the border adore. Besides guitars and a *guitarrón*, common *norteño* instruments include the accordion and the snare drum, neither of which is ever used by mariachis, as well as the violin.

Tríos románticos usually wear modern business suits and consist of a guitar player, a *requinto* player (the instrument looks like a miniature guitar and sounds like a mandolin) and a percussionist who plays *maracas* and other small rhythm instruments. Their repertoire typically includes contemporary Mexican pop music, translations of American easy-listening tunes set to latin rhythms, and traditional Mexican songs.

Listen to any Mexican musical group playing requests in a tourist restaurant, and you may get the impression that the only songs they know are "Guantanamera," "Cielito Lindo" and "El Rancho Grande." In fact, hundreds of traditional Mexican songs are included in the repertoire of every strolling musician. Get familiar with a few others and impress your companions when the musicians come around to your table. For starters, try "Las Laureles" (The Laurels), a classic Mexican love song that few gringos know, or the haunting "Peregrina" (Traveler), written to honor a blonde American reporter with whom Mexican governor Felipe Carrillo Puerto had fallen in love.

FOUR

The Border

 Coils of razor wire top the 150-mile-long chain-link steel fence, nicknamed the Tortilla Curtain, that stretches from the Pacific Ocean to the Colorado River delta, separating the state of California from the state of Baja California. Most of Baja's population lives within seven kilometers of the border, enticed from all over Mexico by the promise of steady factory jobs in the *maquiladoras,* the dream of crossing the border for better pay in southern California or, in some cases, the fast-money gamble of smuggling drugs or guns. Rich with opportunity, wracked with poverty and desperation, the California–Baja border forms a sociological fault line between two lands that are utterly unlike one another.

Although it seems unlikely that many readers would opt to spend their vacations in the high-stress border zone when so many fantastic beaches and fascinating hideaways lie farther south, crossing the border—twice—is unavoidable. Fortunately, it's also easy. Crossing northward, however, takes considerably longer.

This chapter contains complete information on crossing the U.S./Mexican border in both directions at each port of entry between California and Baja California. It shows you how to appreciate Baja's largest city, Tijuana, as well as the smaller border towns of Tecate and Algodones. Along the way, dirt-road side trips can take you to two hidden destinations in little-known Parque Nacional Constitución de 1857, far removed from the border cities—Laguna Hanson, Baja's only natural lake, and the secluded hot springs of Cañon de Guadalupe.

▼▼▼▼▼▼▼▼▼▼▼▼▼

Crossing the Border

You can enter Baja California via any of five border crossings. The two in Tijuana are among the world's busiest, and the lack of freeways on the Mexican side of the border means dealing with many stoplights and sometimes traffic snarls. An easier crossing point that is convenient to southern California cities and on a direct route to Ensenada and that points south is the much smaller town of **Tecate.** You can also cross farther east at Baja

California Norte's capital city, **Mexicali**, though it's hard to imagine many circumstances in which this would be your most convenient option. Finally, the small-town border crossing at Algodones, just south of Yuma, Arizona, can be a convenient "back-door" crossing point for travelers coming from states other than California.

You don't need a tourist card or car permit if you're only visiting the *frontera*—the area within 25 miles south of the U.S.-Mexico border, though if you're driving you will need Mexican car insurance. Remember that as of January 2008, you must have a valid passport to return to the United States, even from a day trip to Tijuana.

TIJUANA Tijuana's main port of entry, San Ysidro, is said to be the world's busiest border crossing. More than 60 million people cross here each year—pedestrians and bus riders as well as motorists in 33 million private vehicles.

Crossing south into Tijuana is easy. Route 5 from San Diego takes you directly to the border, where Mexican officials normally wave cars with U.S. plates right through. Keep to the center lanes as the freeway takes you over the Río Tijuana, a deep concrete ditch that flows northward into the United States, on the rare occasions when it flows at all. Right on the other side of the river, you'll find yourself in a dizzying three-level freeway interchange. Follow the signs to "Downtown/Centro" to reach the downtown tourist zone, "Paseo de los Héroes" to reach the cultural center and public market, and "Mex 1-D Cuota" to get onto the toll highway south to Ensenada.

Reentering the United States is a different story. Not only is access to the border crossing bewilderingly difficult from the northbound freeway, but also border security has been tight in the wake of the 9-11 terrorist attacks. Every car must come to a complete stop, and all drivers and passengers must be prepared to present ID and citizenship documents; this obstructs the traffic flow enough so that you can expect to wait in line before reaching the gates. And wait, and wait . . . it often takes four to six hours to get across the border. Make sure you fill up your gas tank before getting in the traffic line. Sundays and U.S. holidays should be avoided, when you can sometimes wait all day. Lines are shortest on weekdays before 10 a.m. and after 10 p.m.

Here's a secret for those who simply must brave the border at rush hour: The U.S. inspection area has 24 gates, of which 16 are open at any given time. They are evenly divided between the east and west sides of a center median filled with street vendors' stalls. The west lanes come from Highway 1, downtown and Paseo de los Héroes—all the places gringo tourists go. The east lanes are fed by Via Oriente, Paseo de Tijuana and Avenida Padre

Kino, the main thoroughfares on the northeast side of the river. Rarely used by visitors from the U.S., these lanes typically take half as long as the west lanes. To reach them, cross the river on Avenida Independencia, which runs between the Centro Cultural and the Palacio Municipal, and turn left on any of the three main streets.

For many daytrippers, the easiest way to get to Tijuana's tourist zone is to take the **San Diego Trolley**, which shuttles passengers from downtown San Diego to and from the San Ysidro Border Crossing, within walking distance of downtown Tijuana, every 15 minutes from 5 a.m. to midnight. **Greyhound** also operates bus service across the border from San Diego to Tijuana and from Calexico to Mexicali. ~ www.greyhound.com.

On Avenida Cuahutémoc there is a statue of the 16th century Aztec leader for whom the avenue is named.

A second port of entry to the U.S., the **Otay Mesa** border crossing, is located 20 minutes east of downtown Tijuana's San Ysidro crossing, past the airport. Located in a major industrial zone, it is the border's truck route, used by most tractor-trailer rigs and many passenger buses. Until recently, it was a better place to cross into the United States because it had less private car traffic, but now the secret is out, so this route also has an endless line of cars, complicated by several cross-streets without traffic signals, as well as a parade of souvenir vendors, fire-eaters, acrobats and windshield-washing beggars. Hours are 6 a.m. to 10 p.m., and the trucks stack up for the morning opening; traffic eases a little after mid-morning. To get there, take the *libre* highway from Rosarito or Boulevard Agua Caliente from downtown Tijuana, continuing on Avenida Cuahutémoc (beware the dizzying *glorieta*, or traffic circle) and following the signs to "Airport" and "Otay Border Crossing." Sounds easy, but a co-pilot is almost essential for navigating the *glorietas*. You can also get there by taking the "Otay" exit from the Route 2 freeway and following the signs. You'll know you're on the right track when you find yourself in a miles-long line of almost motionless traffic.

TECATE You can avoid the hassle of driving in big-city traffic by crossing at Tecate, 49 kilometers east of Tijuana on Route 2 or 41 miles east of San Diego on Route 188. This is by far my favorite way to cross the border in either direction. Southbound, it bypasses Mexico City and takes you through the pastoral wine-growing Valle de Guadalupe before depositing you in the back streets of Ensenada. Northbound, this route has less traffic than any other border-crossing option. The border crossing there has only two U.S. Customs booths and a tiny Mexican *aduana*, or customs office, that apparently is never open. An average of 1500 cars and trucks a day cross the border here in each direction, or fewer than 100 an hour when the border crossing is open—daily from 6 a.m. to 10 p.m.

Crossing southward, you probably won't have to stop at all. The only trick is finding Tecate. There are no signs anywhere directing you to Mexico, let alone to Tecate. To get there, follow Interstate Route 8 east through suburban San Diego to the second El Cajon exit, marked Route 54. Proceed south through town on Second Street, which angles left onto Jamacha Road. This is Route 54, which heads straight south for several miles before curving right and intersecting Route 94, or Campo Road. Turn left on Campo and follow Route 94, a rural four-lane highway that winds among horse farms and country homes. This is not as simple as it sounds, because Route 94 has a couple of tricky road intersections as it makes its way through the Jamul Mountains on National Forest and Indian land. A navigating device in your car is a big help here. Eventually, you'll come to a fork in the road where Route 188 heads downhill to the right. Follow it, and you're practically at the border crossing. From the port of entry, stay on the same street, Calle Lázaro Cárdenas, for four blocks and you'll reach the quaint little Plaza, which would be worth visiting except that you will have a slim chance of finding a parking space anywhere nearby. Jog left one block to Calle Ortiz Rubio and you'll soon find yourself crossing the river and heading out of town on Mexican Route 3, the road to Ensenada.

Returning northward, you'll learn why so many experienced Baja buffs like the Tecate border crossing. It's easy to find from the Mexican side, and there is rarely a long line. Saturday is the busiest day. Sunday is quiet. After you cross the border, simply get on Route 94 and follow it all the way back to suburban San Diego.

MEXICALI   You can see the smoggy orange glow of city lights at night from U.S. Interstate 8, a mere 11 miles north of the border crossing, but you won't find much civilization in Calimex, north of the line between San Diego and Yuma. It was built to accommodate wheat and vegetable shipments to U.S. supermarkets from the farms of the Valle Mexicali. Today the city of Mexicali has grown large and heavily industrialized, and trying to find your way around as a novice is more hassle than it's worth. I've stopped suggesting that visitors take time to explore the meager sights of this city. Crossing the border here only makes sense for tourists if they are bound for San Felipe.

Baja California's sprawling capital city is so far from anything on the U.S. side that the crossing is rarely busy. It's open 24 hours a day, so there is no early-morning truck stack-up, and it's easy to follow fast, four-lane Calzada López Mateos from the border diagonally across the city to the junction of Route 2, west to Mexicali or east to San Luis Colorado and the Mexican mainland, and Route 5 south to San Felipe.

Heading north, it's easy to stray from Calzada López Mateos onto Boulevard Benito Juárez, a main drag that marks the east edge of the city. Stay on it and you'll eventually come to the low concrete walls and high chain-link-fence that mark the border. Avenida Cristóbal Colón parallels the border for miles and eventually brings you to the port of entry.

ALGODONES The small town of Los Algodones (usually just called Algodones, also known by its older name, Vicente Guerrero) is located off U.S. Interstate 8 on Route 186 where the California–Arizona state line and the by-now-dry Colorado River meet the Mexican border. It is the obvious port of entry for travelers from points east who are bound for the San Felipe area. Theoretically it is possible to cross the border here and continue west on Mexican Route 2 through Mexicali and Tecate to Tijuana, though the slowness and complexity of the road network in the Colorado River Delta makes Algodones a poor alternative to other border crossings farther west.

The border crossing is open from 6 a.m. to 10 p.m. Algodones is in the Pacific time zone (barely). Mexican auto insurance, a must for those driving their own vehicles into Baja, is available at offices within a block on each side of the border crossing.

Tijuana

Tijuana is a city of paradoxes: one of the wealthiest cities in Mexico, brimming with free-trade economic opportunities—yet sobered by the suffering of hundreds of thousands of people living in desperate poverty. All Spanish-speaking illegal immigrants found in California, Nevada, Oregon and Washington are deported to Tijuana, regardless of their state or country of origin. According to unofficial estimates, as many as half a million Tijuana residents either are on their way to the United States or have recently been expelled from there. If you wander too far from the main drag, you may find where they live—in makeshift huts of cardboard and salvaged plywood without electricity or plumbing, jammed haphazardly onto vacant lots around the industrial zone. It's an aspect of "hidden" Tijuana that most visitors are content to leave undiscovered.

Tijuana got its start in 1889 as a customs house on the edge of a large cattle ranch called Rancho Tía Juana, meaning "Aunt Jane." The "Aunt Jane" after whom the Tía Juana River and Tijuana were named established the first travelers' inn in the area in 1769. The outpost was of little importance until the 1920s, when Prohibition sent hordes of Californians across the border for liquor, as well as horse races, casino gambling and sleazy nightclubs featuring stage shows whose depravity has passed

into legend. In the early thirties, Prohibition was repealed in the United States, and casino gambling was banned in Mexico. Tijuana's fortunes floundered.

President Lázaro Cárdenas sought to rescue the city's economy by declaring Baja a free-trade zone, a move designed to stimulate retail sales of imported goods to southern California shoppers at tax-exempt discount prices. The plan initially met with only limited success, as the Great Depression strangled the flow of free-spending shoppers across the border. When economic salvation finally arrived, it came in the form of World War II, bringing a huge U.S. naval force to San Diego, just 18 miles north of Tijuana. A hectic red-light district flowered overnight as hookers and street hustlers from all over Mexico were drawn to Tijuana like pelicans to a fishing fleet.

Tijuana earned its reputation as the quintessential badass border town, and it has yet to live down that reputation. Half a century later, many Americans' mental picture of Tijuana is a city brimming with dark-alley easy, slightly slimy, sticky-fingered guilty pleasures. The fact is, today you can find more lowlife and scary cops in Los Angeles than in Tijuana.

For motorists headed down the Baja Peninsula, this city of more than two million is an obstacle to be gotten through as soon as possible. If you're driving a large motor home, it can be your ultimate traffic nightmare. If you want to spend some time in Tijuana, the best plan is to leave your vehicle on the U.S. side of the border, cross the pedestrian bridge, and explore on foot or in taxis, which are plentiful. Go back and retrieve your vehicle when you're ready to head farther south. To avoid driving in Tijuana at all, you might even consider retracing your route all the way back to Interstate 8 and heading for the Tecate border crossing. I would.

SIGHTS

Visitors who cross the border into Tijuana on foot or on the Tijuana Trolley from San Diego can proceed directly from the Customs and Immigration area through **Viva Tijuana**, a mall full of curio shops and restaurants, then over a pedestrian bridge that spans the Tijuana River, and be in the downtown tourist zone in a matter of minutes. It's so easy that you might consider leaving your car at one of the huge parking lots on the U.S. side while you check out downtown Tijuana, then reclaiming it when you're ready to hit the highway south.

Avenida Revolución, the heart of the tourist zone, runs south from the border for 11 blocks. Visitors crossing the pedestrian bridge get there by walking two blocks along Calle 1, encountering many street vendors along the way. Motorists cross the river a few blocks to the east and immediately find themselves in an amazing multilevel traffic whirl. The Calle 2 and Calle 3 exits lead to Avenida Revolución, where parking lots are plentiful if not cheap. Curio shops, boutiques and galleries share the avenue with nightclubs, sports betting parlors, hotels and restaurants, all packed with Americans. Along Avenida Revolución, the sleazy character of old-time Tijuana has been transformed for better or worse by international chains; within a couple of blocks are a Jack in the Box, a KFC, a Burger King and a Hard Rock Café. Older buildings converted to mini-malls house hundreds of small shops side-by-side with chic international designer outlets, all vying to assist tourists with their duty-free shopping needs. Strangely enough, you'll also encounter quaint relics of old-time Tijuana such as donkeys painted like zebras, waiting to be photographed for money, and an abundance of restaurants that turn

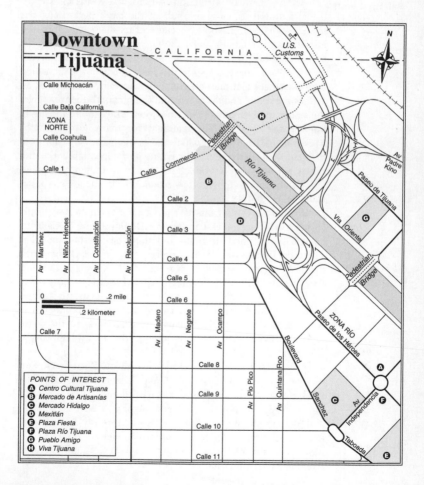

Downtown Tijuana

CALIFORNIA

U.S. Customs

N

Calle Michoacán

Calle Baja California

ZONA NORTE

Calle Coahuila

Pedestrian Bridge

Río Tijuana

Av Padre Kino

Paseo de Tijuana

Calle Commercio

Calle 1

B

Calle 2

D

G

Via Oriental

Calle 3

Av Martinez

Av Niños Héroes

Av Constitución

Av Revolución

Calle 4

Calle 5

Pedestrian Bridge

0   .2 mile

0   .2 kilometer

Calle 6

Calle 7

Av Madero

Av Negrete

Av Ocampo

ZONA RÍO

Paseo de los Héroes

A

Calle 8

Boulevard

Sanchez

Av Independencia

F

POINTS OF INTEREST
- **A** Centro Cultural Tijuana
- **B** Mercado de Artisanías
- **C** Mercado Hidalgo
- **D** Mexitlán
- **E** Plaza Fiesta
- **F** Plaza Río Tijuana
- **G** Pueblo Amigo
- **H** Viva Tijuana

Calle 9

Av Pío Pico

Av Quintana Roo

C

Calle 10

Taboada

Calle 11

E

into raunchy nightclubs after dark, ready to live up to tourists' stereotypical expectations.

Running diagonally away from the border crossing along the west bank of the Tijuana River, the **Zona Río** represents contemporary Tijuana in sharp contrast to the traditional tourist zone. Interspersed among financial institutions, upscale hotels and stylish retail stores line the broad Paseo de los Héroes. Even though a 30-foot-tall bronze statue of U.S. President Abraham Lincoln presides over the paseo from a traffic circle, local government has been largely unsuccessful in its strategy of enticing American tourists to this flashy urban redevelopment area.

You can't take fresh fruits or vegetables from Baja California Norte to Baja California Sur because of Mexican agricultural regulations designed to control fruit flies and other pests.

The main attraction of the Zona Río is the **Centro Cultural Tijuana**, the hub of the city's performing-arts scene, nicknamed "La Bola" because of its shape, which resembles the world's largest golf ball. The symphony orchestra, the ballet folklórico, repertory companies and lecturers use the center's 1000-seat theater. Also in the cultural center are an art exhibition gallery that presents changing shows by local artists, an astronomy room, and the big, round Omnimax theater that gives the center its distinctive shape; it shows wraparound movies in English and Spanish. The highlight for many visitors is the **Museo de las Californias**, which traces the history of Baja from prehistoric times to the present with wax figures, miniature dioramas, artifacts and reproductions of ancient Indian cave paintings. Admission to museums. ~ Avenida Paseo de los Héroes at Calle Mina; 664-487-9600.

If you drive south from the tourist zone, Avenida Revolución curves around to the east to become **Boulevard Agua Caliente**, lined with big, modern hotels and shiny new restaurants. The **Toreo de Tijuana** (see "Seda, Sangre y Sol" in this chapter), the older of the city's two bullrings, marks the beginning of the hotel strip. Route 1 *libre*, the free highway to Ensenada, turns off to the south at the bullring. For a slightly more scenic alternative, head west on Avenida Internacionál, exit the Libramiento at Avenida Paseo Playas de Tijuana and drive west to the coast, where the road veers south, joining the main highway at Rosarito.

At the east end of the hotel zone is **Caliente Race Track**. Formerly called the Hipódromo de Agua Caliente, the famous race track for which the boulevard was named ended live horse racing in 1993. Greyhounds race there nightly as well as Saturday and Sunday afternoons. There is also betting on closed-circuit horse race broadcasts from California, viewed on television monitors in the track's sports club. ~ Boulevard Agua Caliente at Avenida Salinas; 664-686-3958.

Hotels in Tijuana tend to cluster in three areas. Tourist-oriented (and usually rundown) hotels are found downtown along Avenida Revolución. Brand-name hotels stand in a row near the golf course and racetrack on Boulevard Agua Caliente and cater to visiting businesspeople and politicians. Sterile, mostly utilitarian hotels are found around the airport on the southeast side of the city. Below is a selection of the best-known Tijuana hotels, most of them located in the tourist zone.

Pink and art deco-ish, the **Hotel Nelson** has 92 clean, plain, somewhat threadbare rooms with carpeting and private baths, some with TVs and windows overlooking the heart of Tijuana's tourist zone. ~ Avenida Revolución 501; 664-685-4304, fax 664-685-4302. BUDGET.

Hotel Caesar's, an atmospheric old-timer from Prohibition days, offers 42 clean, comfortable, air-conditioned rooms with "character." Walls are decorated with framed photos and posters of bullfights. ~ Avenida Revolución 827; 664-688-1666. BUDGET.

The six-story **Hotel Lucerna** is a centerpiece of the Zona Río district. Its 167 guest rooms and suites have a lived-in look and a resort feel, as well as views of the swimming pool and surrounding gardens. ~ Paseo de los Héroes 10902; 664-633-3900, fax 664-634-2400, or 800-582-3762 in the U.S.; www.hotel-lucerna.com.mx, e-mail lucerna@telnor.net. DELUXE.

At the **Holiday Inn Express—Tijuana Agua Caliente**, rooms are spacious and modern, but the real draws are the swimming pool, sauna and large whirlpool tub fed by natural hot springs. ~ Paseo de los Héroes 18818; 664-634-6901, fax 664-634-6912. DELUXE.

The **Grand Hotel Tijuana**, the largest and finest hotel in the city, has 422 light, spacious rooms splashed with fiesta-color accents in twin 25-story towers that are Tijuana's tallest buildings. The higher the room, the better the view and the steeper the rate. ~ Boulevard Agua Caliente 4500; 664-681-7000, fax 664-681-7016, or 866-472-6385 in the U.S.; www.grandhotelj.com.mx, e-mail reservaciones@grandhotelj.com.mx. DELUXE.

For semisecluded accommodations on a side street just off Avenida Revolución and the Zona Río, try **La Villa de Zaragoza**. The 66-room hotel is designed to suggest a Spanish colonial hacienda (though the Colonial era was over long before the first buildings in Tijuana were erected). Guest rooms are spacious, carpeted, air-conditioned and clean—uncommon in Revolución-area hotels. Avoid the rooms with windows facing the street, ask for one facing the inner courtyard to get a peaceful respite from the din of all-night partying along the main drag. ~ Avenida Madero 1120; 664-685-1832, fax 664-685-1837; www.hotellavilla.biz, e-mail reservation@hotellavilla.biz. BUDGET TO MODERATE.

◄ *HIDDEN*

Some of the most pleasant and affordable lodgings in town are found along the outskirts of the trendy Playas de Tijuana area, though the taxi fare to get there from downtown Tijuana can offset any savings made on room rates. A longtime favorite HIDDEN ► of young gringo visitors is **Hostal Barnes**, a guesthouse within sight of the ocean. The plain, utilitarian single and twin rooms rent for little more than the price of a dormitory stay at most youth hostels (of which, at this writing, Tijuana has none). No smoking. ~ Calle Relampago 1230; 664 630-1126. BUDGET.

Secluded in a canyon between the highway and the ocean, with picturesque views of the Coronado Islands offshore, the HIDDEN ► **Real del Mar Marriott Residence Inn** offers golf enthusiasts an international playground just 11 miles south of the border. In low Mediterranean-style buildings scattered around the resort grounds, the 76 brightly appointed guest suites range from spacious to palatial. Besides 18 holes of golf, the resort has tennis courts, spa facilities and horseback riding. ~ Route 1-D Km. 18; 664-631-3671, 664-631-3677, or 800-662-6180 in the U.S.; www.marriott.com. ULTRA-DELUXE.

DINING

Along Avenida Revolución are dozens of budget-priced places for lunch—many of them hauntingly familiar. For something completely different from the international burger franchises, try **La Especial**, a busy taco-and-enchilada eatery that still feels like a typical Mexican *comedor*. ~ Avenida Revolución 718; 664-685-6654. BUDGET.

One of the longest-established and best-known restaurants in the tourist zone, **TiaJuana Tillies** is packed with noisy gringos morning, noon and night. There's a good reason. Tillies serves big portions of some of the best Mexican food on the border—not only familiar dishes but also more exotic ones from distant parts of Mexico—*cochinita pibil* (pork barbecued in a Seville orange marinade), *pollo en mole* (chicken in chile-and-chocolate sauce) and enchiladas *suizas* (chicken enchiladas in a tangy sauce with ranch cheese melted over them). ~ Avenida Revolución at Calle 7; 664-685-9015. MODERATE.

A pleasant refuge from the shopping frenzy of Avenida Revolución is **Restaurante Circa Barcelona**, a Spanish-style *tapas* bar between the jai alai *frontón* and TiaJuana Tillies. Patio dining lets you watch the sea of passersby as you savor delicacies like dates and bacon in apricot sauce and eels in olive oil and garlic. There are also full dinner entrées such as paella, duck in peach brandy and curried lamb catalán. ~ Avenida Revolución at Calle 7; 664-685-60-24. BUDGET TO DELUXE.

The Caesar salad was invented at **Caesar's**. As atmospheric now as in Prohibition days, the restaurant still serves salads made according to the original recipe (though not by the same

chef). Dinner only. ~ Avenida Revolución 827; 664-688-2794.
MODERATE.

For some of the freshest, most unusual seafood dishes in the
city, go to **Los Arcos**, a bright, family-style restaurant near the bull
ring. You'll find a selection of dishes like marlin tacos and *caldo
pescado* (fish stew), as well as the house specialty, *zarandeado,* a
large whole fish scored and broiled with heaps of chiles and
onions. ~ Boulevard Salinas 1000; 664-686-4757. MODERATE.

The dozens of fast-food stalls at **Mercado Hidalgo**, the city's
main public market near the Zona Río, offer a varied choice of
inexpensive dishes from all over Mexico. For a dollar or two,
you can buy a fistful of fish tacos or pineapple tamales, a grilled
pork sandwich, a steaming bowl of *posole* stew or a plastic plate
of beans and rice with an egg on top, and eat it at a picnic table
at a little distance from the market fray. ~ Avenida Independencia at Boulevard Sanchez Taboada. BUDGET.

In the Zona Río, **Victor's** has been a local favorite for more
than four decades. The restaurant is divided into an elegant,
clublike dining room and a casual café under an atrium. While
the dining room menu features a larger choice of priccy entrées—
mostly thick slabs of beef—most items are available in both dining room and café, including the house specialty, *carne adovada*
(beef strips marinated in a red chile sauce and grilled). ~ Boulevard Sanchez Taboada at Calle Joaquín Clausell; 664-634-3355.
BUDGET TO MODERATE.

When it comes to beef, Argentinians are the experts. A glance
at the menu in **Restaurante Argentino de Tony** may lead you to   ◄ HIDDEN
believe that's all they eat in South America. A Colonial-style
ambience of dark wood, beamed ceilings, potted plants and spotless white linen sets the stage for huge servings of sizzling red
meat. Try the mixed grille, an artery-clogging meal big enough
for two that includes some surprise ingredients you wouldn't
likely find north of the border. This local favorite rarely sees
tourists. ~ Pueblo Amigo Shopping Center; 664-682-8111. MOD-
ERATE.

AUTHOR FAVORITE

I thought I'd tasted just about everything in Mexico—until I dined
at **Cien Años**, Tijuana's trendy pre-Columbian restaurant where the bill
of fare includes such delicacies as ant eggs in garlic sauce, washed down
with more kinds of tequila than one can sample without falling over.
See page 84 for more information.

The penetrating stare of a huge portrait of Salvador Dali sets the stage for the artsy atmosphere of **Gypsys.** (Check out the life-size nude figures in the restrooms.) This long, narrow restaurant specializes in Spanish-style *tapas* and also serves full meals, such as Spanish *tortillas*—an omeletlike egg-and-potato dish, no relation to the Mexican tortilla—and vegetarian paella. The restaurant is in a shopping center just half a mile from the San Ysidro border crossing. Closed Monday. ~ Pueblo Amigo Shopping Center; 664-683-6006. MODERATE.

Reputed to be the best restaurant in Baja, or at least the trendiest, is **Cien Años**, the Pacific coast's premier example of the new wave in Mexican restaurants—resurrecting Aztec and other pre-Columbian ingredients and recipes, prepared with careful attention to authenticity and served with gourmet flair. Yet to appear in the United States, this cuisine includes items bizarre enough to challenge the most adventurous palate—fried cactus worms, ant eggs in garlic sauce, crêpes *de huitlacoche* (corn fungus), manta ray burritos and *medula con sesos* (spine marrow soup) to mention a few. Though nothing on the menu is likely to be familiar, there are also plenty of choices for the gastronomically timid, such as squash blossom soup, filet mignon *en salsa borracha de pulque* (marinated in Mexican Indian corn liquor) and *mixote* (an Aztec dish made with shrimp and thin-sliced nopal cactus leaves). There's also a separate menu listing 38 brands of tequila. Reservations are essential. ~ Calle José María Velazco 1407; 664-634-3039. MODERATE TO DELUXE.

Two blocks south of the intersection of Cuauhtémoc and Agua Caliente, **La Fonda de Roberto** is part of the new gourmet trend in Mexican restaurants. The friendly, contemporary upstairs dining room is best known for its specialty, *chiles en nogada*, poblano chiles stuffed with meat and fruit and smothered in walnut sauce topped with pomegranate and cilantro, a favorite Mexican dish that is traditionally eaten on Día de la Independencia because its colors—red, white and green—are the same as those of the national flag. The "menu," which features a choice of five entrées and changes daily, isn't really a menu at all; instead, the waiter brings out actual plates of food as examples, and you can order simply by pointing. Closed Monday. ~ Boulevard Cuauhtémoc 2800; 664-686-4687. DELUXE.

In the Agua Caliente area with a view of the Tijuana Country Club golf course, **La Leña** is a clean, modern steak house serving thick mesquite-broiled slabs of beef and northern Mexico ranch specialties such as *carne asada*—beef strips barbecued in a spicy red-chile marinade—and *gaonera,* a steak sliced down the center and stuffed with guacamole and cheese. ~ Boulevard Agua Caliente 4560; 664-686-4687. MODERATE.

Seda, Sangre y Sol

The poetic turn of speech "silk, blood and sun" is often used to refer to bullfighting, a spectacle that is popular throughout Mexico, and nowhere more so than along the Baja California border. Latinos who live across the border in California and Arizona, where bullfights are illegal, flock to the *corridas de toros* in Tijuana and Mexicali on Sundays. Mexicans and Mexican Americans believe that gringos misunderstand the nature of bullfights, unable to see beyond the horror and cruelty of hacking livestock to death with barbed darts, spears and swords.

Though the rules and trappings of the spectacle originated in 18th-century Spain and came to Mexico in the last years of colonial rule, bullfighting also mirrors the ritual public sacrifices of the Aztecs and Toltecs in earlier times. Mexicans see each bullfight as display of courage—not a sport like boxing or riding in *charreadas* (rodeos), but a ritual that links them to heritage and primal instinct. Several mounted *picadores* and *banderilleros* on foot participate in the first half-hour of a fight, but the *matador* (literally, "killer") is the star of the show, so icy of nerve that he—or she—can not only stand within inches of a charging thousand-pound behemoth with horns that can rip a horse apart or toss a man in the air, but at the same time execute customary cape passes with the precision and grace of a ballet dancer. The bull too is judged on its courage. Though it is hand-selected at an early age for belligerence and trained in the art of fighting on a special ranch for four years, there is no predicting how a bull, bloodied and tormented, will face the certainty of death.

Any gringo who wishes to understand the Mexican people on their own terms must attend at least one *corrida de toros*. A word of caution, though: Take care not to give voice to feelings of horror or disgust unless a human is gored. Mexican spectators take offense at negative reactions by gringos at bullfights, and they may bring various nasty substances to throw at disgraced *matadores*—or rude tourists.

Six bulls are fought in an afternoon's *corrida*, which lasts about six hours. Tijuana has two bullrings—the older **Toreo de Tijuana** (Boulevard Agua Caliente 100; 664-686-1510) and the larger **Plaza Monumental** (Route 1-D; 664-680-1808). Bullfights are held every Sunday from May through September at one ring or the other—in August at both. Mexicali's bullfights are held every other week from October through May at the **Plaza Calafia** (Calle Calafia; 664-657-0681). Admission at all three bullrings is around $15 for seats in the sun and $25 in the shade.

Long considered one of Tijuana's finest restaurants, **Pedríns** has moved from downtown to the Real del Mar Resort, where it overlooks the golf course. Upscale and not at all Mexican, it features dishes such as lobster bisque and chateaubriand, served in an atmosphere that's clean, shiny and sterile. ~ Route 1-D Km. 18; 664-631-3671. DELUXE TO ULTRA-DELUXE.

GROCERIES Travelers camping out and RV sojourners stocking up on food for the trip south will find an abundance of fresh produce, along with meat stalls that may convert the squeamish to vegetarianism, at the big, busy **Mercado Hidalgo**, the city's main public market, located a block from the Centro Cultural Tijuana. Especially tempting to travelers are the stands selling exotic tropical fruits such as mamay, zapote, cherimoya, tunas (candied cactus fruit) and giant papayas. This is also a good place to shop for "real" souvenirs such as fresh spices, uniquely Mexican kitchen utensils and curiosities like mango-flavored bubble gum. Don't miss photographing the vendors' shrine to the Virgin of Guadalupe, conveniently situated on the roof of the cleanest restrooms in Tijuana. Parking can be a problem, especially for RVs, so it's best to leave your vehicle parked elsewhere and take a taxi to the market and back. ~ Avenida Inde pendencia at Boulevard Sanchez Taboada.

The major supermarket chain in Tijuana and all of Baja California is **Calimax**. There are branches on Avenida Constitución between Calles 1 and 2; on Avenida Revolución between Calles 9 and 10 on Paseo de los Héroes at Avenida Cuauhtémoc and on Boulevard Agua Caliente across from the Caliente race track. All are open 24 hours a day. ~ 664-688-0894.

Look for Mexican and imported gourmet foodstuffs at **Ley**, located in the Pueblo Amigo. ~ Via Oriente 9211; 664-684-2771.

SHOPPING It doesn't get much more touristy than Tijuana's **Mercado de Artisanías**, located where visitors step off the pedestrian bridge from the border over the Tijuana River. Here, vendors display Mexican "arts and crafts"—mostly factory-made curios and gift items—along with a fair selection of Guatemalan clothing. The main purpose in establishing this open market was to keep street vendors from clogging the sidewalks of Avenida Revolución. ~ Calle 2 between Avenidas Ocampo and Negrete.

Apple, S.A. also offers a large selection of *artesanía* and leather goods, as well as duty-free imports ranging from Swiss watches to Asian electronics. ~ Avenida Revolución 812; 664-685-1609.

Avenida Revolución is so shopper-friendly that you'll find an array of possibilities for every taste and budget here. You may have to fend off youths whose job is to steer you into their families' stores, and you may have to dig through endless clutters of onyx elephants and huge, brocaded mariachi sombreros, but in the end you'll most likely find something that tugs at your purse-strings. Leather goods, from boots and belts to suitcases, are the best bargain in Tijuana, and there are plenty of others. A wooden dance mask from Michoacán? A delicately embroidered Oaxacan wedding dress? Guess jeans or Ralph Lauren sportswear? Avenida Revolución is the place to look.

Start your shopping spree at **Tolán**, reputedly Tijuana's finest Mexican folk art gallery. Prices here may be high, but the quality and selection of both museum-quality indigenous work and contemporary ethnic paintings, jewelry, sculpture, weaving and ceramics set the standard for comparison in Baja gift shopping. ~ Avenida Revolución between Calles 7 and 8; 664-688-3637.

Tijuana's free-trade status enables vendors to sell quality imports, from Japanese consumer electronics to French perfume, at prices somewhat lower than you'd expect to find in San Diego or L.A.

A good one-stop shopping center for Mexican *artesanía* is the **Bazar de Mexico**, where 40 permanent vendors sell quality gift items from all parts of the country—Talvera pottery, rustic wood furniture, fountains large and small, Huichol Indian art, pre-Columbian reproductions, handmade leather goods, Oaxacan *albrijes* (wood carvings of animal dreams) and much more. ~ Avenida Revolución at Calle 7; 664-638-4737, fax 664-688-3526; www.bazardemexico.com, e-mail info@bazardemexico.com.

Nearby is **Sanborn's**, part of the nationwide department store chain that is the Mexican counterpart of Macy's. Sanborn's has responded to the invasion of international discount stores like Wal-Mart and Sam's Club by stocking higher-quality merchandise to attract a more upscale clientele. The restaurant and book-and-magazine department of Sanborn's are reputed to be among the most popular gay meeting places in the city. ~ Avenida Revolución at Calle 8; 664-688-1462.

Though you'd never know it if all you saw was ultra-touristy Avenida Revolución, Mexicans too come from far and wide to indulge in Tijuana shopping sprees. **Pueblo Amigo**—within easy walking distance of the border crossing—and **Plaza Río Tijuana** and **Plaza Fiesta**, farther along Paseo de los Héroes, are landmarks in the Zona Río. All three indoor shopping malls contain an improbably large number of stores selling silver jewelry from Taxco, the famous silversmithing center in the southern Mexico state of Guerrero. Across the street from the Plaza Río, vendors at **Plaza Zapato** sell shoes, bags, leather clothing, saddles and tack at a fraction of U. S. prices. There are also many stores featuring quality European and Asian imports—as well as imports from the United States, aimed at Tijuana's growing young urban professional market.

◄ HIDDEN

NIGHTLIFE   From the sleazy to the ultrachic, nightlife is one of the main attractions that lures visitors over the border to Tijuana. Many never get farther than Avenida Revolución, which becomes a bright, loud, touristy dance club scene after dark. Street barkers will try persistently to lure into their clubs any gringo male who looks like he has money to spend. You know you're not drunk enough yet if you find yourself trying to figure out why you went to another country just to hang out in a **Hard Rock Café**. ~ Avenida Revolución 520; 664-685-0206. For something a little more un-American, check out **Red Square**, with its vaguely Kremlinesque facade and its rooftop bar overlooking the main street. ~ Avenida Revolución at Calle 6; 664-688-2782. The last of the old-timers, **Bar San Marcos** dates back to World War II and entertains its patrons with lavish mariachi productions. ~ Avenida Revolución at Calle 5; 664-688-2794. **Disco Salsa** blares high-energy Latino dance music until dawn. ~ Avenida Revolución between Calles 1 and 2; 664-634-8615. Bars and discos along Revolución typically stay open until 3 a.m. on weekdays, 5 a.m. on weekends.

Just off Avenida Reforma are a number of "hidden" places that you don't have to be a tourist to go to. You'll find Latino dance rhythms, cheap tequila and plenty of usually amiable Mexican rowdiness at **La Estrella**. Cover for men. ~ Calle 6 east of Avenida Revolución; 664-688-1349.

Another side of Tijuana nightlife can be found in the **Zona Río**, the recently redeveloped commercial district around Paseo de los Héroes and Calle Diego Rivera, east of the traditional downtown tourist zone. Discos here tend to be sleek and trendy, catering to upper-class Mexicans as much as to gringos. Many have dress codes and are selective about who they allow in. **Baby Rock**, part of a chain of chic Mexican rock-and-roll clubs found mostly in beach resort towns, is frequented by the city's young, moneyed and fashionable. Cover. ~ Boulevard Paseo de los Héroes at Avenida Río Tijuana; 664-634-2404. **Jala la Jarra**, next to the Guadalajara Grill, is another popular disco, always packed on weekends. Cover. ~ Calle Diego Rivera at Paseo de los Héroes; 664-634-3065.

The three-level **Rodeo Santa Fe** in the Pueblo Amigo Shopping Center has live *norteño* dance music downstairs and a contemporary disco upstairs, as well as a *quebradita* (mechanical bull) and, nightly at midnight, a live indoor rodeo. Cover. ~ Avenida Paseo Tijuana; 664-682-4967.

The hot dance club in downtown Tijuana is **El Lugar de Nopal**, where live salsa or rock music is featured most nights. Cover. ~ Cinco de Mayo 1328; 664-685-2413.

Tijuana has the liveliest gay scene between the border and Puerto Vallarta. Things get started late. **Mike's Disco**, a prominent club in the heart of the tourist zone, draws mostly male crowds with its nightly Mexican female impersonator stage shows. They start at midnight and continue until nearly dawn. ~ Avenida Revolución 1220; 664-685-3534. For more information on the city's constantly changing GLBT world, call or visit the **Tijuana Gay and Lesbian Center.** ~ Calle 1 no. 7648; 664-685-9163.

Tijuana's red-light district is the **Zona Norte**, between Calle Comercio (Calle 1) and the Tijuana River, within walking distance of the pedestrian bridge from the border crossing. The district centers on Calle Coahuila between Avenida Martinez and Avenida Niños Héroes, which run one-way in opposite directions for convenient cruising. No-nonsense gay bars, strip joints and sordid little establishments of every description pack this self-consciously seedy district where for a price you can get anything you want and (if you're not careful) more. Assume that everyone you meet here, regardless of gender or putative sexual preference, is a trained professional.

If gambling is your preferred vice, there are ten branches of **Caliente Race & Sports Books** around the city, including the big Centro Caliente on Revolución, where you can bet on televised sporting events daily until midnight. ~ Avenida Revolución at Calle 4; 664-686-3958. Or you can phone your wagers in to **Caliente Phone Bet** (664-682-8448) and watch the game on a big-screen TV at **Yuppie's Sports Café** in the Zona Río. ~ Paseo de los Héroes at Calle Diego Rivera; 664-634-2227. Another option is jai alai, a fast-as-a-horserace game played by teams hurling a hard rubber ball at speeds up to 160 miles an hour according to rules guaranteed to bewilder the ignorant. You can watch it, and place parimutuel bets, at the **Palacio Frontón**, an entertainment complex that also houses three restaurants and a disco. Closed Wednesday. Cover. ~ Avenida Revolución at Calle 8; 664-686-3958. There's video horse racing and live greyhound racing nightly and on weekend afternoons at the **Caliente Race**

AUTHOR FAVORITE

I have no qualms about venturing into the desert or the depths of the ocean, but I have to admit that the back streets of Tijuana make me nervous after dark. To get away from the laser discos of Avenida Revolución without leaving the relative safety of the tourist zone, I head down the pedestrian alleyway that starts by the tourist information office at Revolución and Calle 1 and runs diagonally to Avenida Constitución. It's lined with no-name, hole-in-the-wall bars showcasing mariachis and marimba groups in a ceaseless battle of the bands.

Track, an 11-kilometer drive or bus trip south of downtown. You can't miss its grandiose Moorish-style entrance, which dates back to 1916. ~ Boulevard Agua Caliente; 664-686-3958.

BEACHES & PARKS

PLAYAS DE TIJUANA 🏃 This string of narrow beaches, where Route 1-D, the toll highway south to Ensenada, reaches the Pacific coast and turns south, is fronted by Tijuana's nicest residential area. The concrete and chain-link border fence runs across the north end of the beach. Although the beaches are open to the public, neighborhood security and border patrols make sunbathing uncomfortable and camping unthinkable. Most visitors pass by Playas de Tijuana in favor of the developed resort area of Rosarito, ten minutes' drive farther on (see Chapter Five). Still, you can often spot dolphins frolicking just offshore here. ~ Paseo Playas de Tijuana, off Route 1-D less than a kilometer north of the tool booths.

ISLAS LOS CORONADOS 🌊 🚤 ⛵ Seven miles off the coast of Playas de Tijuana lies a chain of four tiny desert islands, occupied by the ruins of a Prohibition-era resort hotel and a small Mexican Navy detachment that enforces the law prohibiting humans from setting foot on the islands. Boaters can circle around and between them, though, for fishing, diving and wildlife watching. Los Coronados host one of the largest pelican rookeries on the Baja coast, along with a large sea lion colony and smaller groups of elephant and harbor seals. ~ Accessible by fishing *panga* from San Antonio, south of Playas de Tijuana on the toll highway.

▼▼▼▼▼▼▼▼▼

Tecate

Tecate is set at an elevation of 1690 feet in a bowl-shaped valley surrounded by jagged, rocky hills. Picacho Tecate (Tecate Peak, 5884 feet), part of the coastal mountain range, towers above the town. Tecate's permanent population is 45,000. The major industry is brewing beer.

Tecate got its start in 1831 as the private ranch of a wealthy Peruvian who went on to become governor of San Diego while it was still part of Mexico. When farmers flooded into the rich Valle de Guadalupe in the 1880s to grow wine grapes, olives and wheat, the ranch headquarters became first a supply station and then a full-fledged town. In 1915, the completion of a railroad between Tijuana, Tecate, Mexicali and Tucson, Arizona, made Tecate an important shipping center as it opened United States markets to local growers.

A few years later, when the United States imposed Prohibition, Tecate businessman Alberto Aldrete built a whisky distillery that employed most of the townspeople. It was as hard for U.S. agents to stop bootleggers from smuggling liquor through the mountains and canyons along this part of the border as it is to catch unauthorized immigrants here today. The whisky distillery went out of business when Prohibition ended in the United States, but its huge malt factory was converted to manufacturing beer, the town's most famous product today.

Several U.S.-based companies have built *maquiladora* manufacturing plants on the border outside of Tecate's city limits. Factory workers, who live in *colonias* of tiny, identical cinderblock houses near the plants, account for about half the valley's population but are not included in the official census figures for Tecate because most *maquiladora* laborers are categorized as temporary residents whose families and permanent homes are in rural areas of central and southern Mexico.

Considering its location at San Diego's mountainous back door, you might expect Tecate to be a smugglers' haven. Although you'd probably be right, so far Tecate has not experienced the disastrous rise in gun violence that has accompanied increased drug and firearm smuggling in other border cities. Built around a peaceful town plaza, Tecate is the most typically Mexican town on the Baja border. It is also, in all likelihood, the town with the most dentists per capita in North America. Many San Diego residents visit Tecate routinely for dental work at a fraction of southern California prices.

Tecate

SIGHTS   The **Cervecería Cuauhtémoc-Moctezuma,** the biggest building in town, fills up to 1600 bottles a minute with two of Mexico's best-known export beers, Carta Blanca and Tecate. (Only bottled Cerveza Tecate is actually made in Tecate; the canned beer is made at the original Carta Blanca brewery in the mainland city of Monterrey.) The beer is made differently depending on whether it is headed for Mexico or the United States.

Tecate beer sold in Mexico has a slightly higher alcohol content, more hops and a stronger taste than the export version. Group tours of the factory, which individuals can join, are given on most Saturday mornings, and parties of five or more can usually arrange a tour on weekdays. Either way, advance reservations are essential. Located one block south and four blocks west of the plaza. ~ Avenida Hidalgo and Calle Carranza; 665-654-2011.

HIDDEN ►   High in the Sierra de Juárez east of Tecate, the open-air **Museo El Vallecito** offers a chance to explore an archaeological site adorned with pictographs by nomadic Yumano Indians as much as three thousand years ago. The rock paintings, done on protected cliff surfaces in hues of red, black and white made from pulverizing colored stones, consist mainly of human figures and geometric patterns. Both the designs and their locations probably had shamanic significance, and some have been found to possess astronomical implications. Crude artifacts—grinding stones, arrowheads and tool fragments—have also been found in the area, which served as a temporary campsite for hunters and gatherers for thousands of years. Admission. ~ Located three kilometers off Route 2 on an unpaved road that turns off near the Restaurant El Chipo in La Rumerosa and passes the Rancho Santa María del Oro before reaching the site; no phone.

LODGING   The main downtown hotel is the modest **Hotel Tecate,** located on the southwest corner of the plaza. Its 24 guest rooms are clean, though slightly frayed around the edges, with double or twin beds, ceiling fans and private baths; some have TVs. There's no heat, so this hotel is a dubious option in winter. ~ Calle Libertad at Avenida Presidente Cárdenas; 665-654-1116. BUDGET.

The more comfortable **Motel El Dorado** has 41 spacious guest rooms with one queen-size or two double beds, wall heaters, air conditioning, in-room phones and cable color TV. ~ Avenida Benito Juárez 1100; 665-654-1101, fax 665-654-1333. MODERATE.

Although a stay at **Rancho La Puerta,** five kilometers west of Tecate, may be beyond the means of most casual vacationers, the curious traveler can get a peek at the grounds by visiting the all-vegetarian café near the entrance for lunch or just a latte and biscotti. Simultaneously elegant and rustic, the resort has no TVs or phones in the guest casitas. It *does* have some of the best fitness

Backcountry Adventure:
Cañon de Guadalupe

One of Baja's most delightful secret spots is hidden at the end of a long dirt road less than 40 miles south of the border. Cañon de Guadalupe, the most accessible of five spectacular palm-filled canyons in the Sierra de Juárez escarpment within Parque Nacional Constitución de 1857, is a nature-lovers' alternative to exclusive spa resorts like Rancho La Puerta (see page 92), the canyon has three campgrounds at its mouth, run by different members of the same family. Primitive campsites near a common hot-springs pool cost $15 a night, while luxury sites cost $50 and up per weekend during the winter season and as low as $15 a day off-season. ("Luxury" is not meant to suggest that there are such niceties as water or electric hookups. There aren't. But each site has its own geothermal hot tub and room for several vehicles and tents.

As if the spectacular sunrises, magnificent rock massifs like Trono Blanco and 4500-foot-high Picacho Rasco and hot springs rich in the natural tranquilizer lithium were not enough, hiking trails shaded by tall date palms lead deep into the lush canyon of white granite, where a year-round stream supports stands of cottonwoods, willows, mosses and ferns and feeds waterfalls and swimming holes. Paipais and Cucapas Indians made this canyon oasis their home for an estimated 9000 years, and guides can lead campground guests to little-known archaeological sites for a look at petroglyphs, pictographs and cave dwellings where ancient pottery shards and other artifacts still litter the dusty ground.

Although the canyon and its campgrounds lie within an easy morning's drive from San Diego, curiously few gringos come to visit. Instead, the camp-grounds cater primarily to Mexican guests from Mexicali and Tijuana who come to get away from the stresses of city life. For this reason, they are full to capacity on most weekends and much quieter during the week.

To reach the canyon and hot springs, take the unpaved, wide but wash-board road that turns off Route 2 to the south near kilometer 28 east of Mexicali; it's a 57-kilometer trip to the hot springs. (Watch for the turnoff between two large irrigated fields.) An alternate route, more suitable for large vehicles but treacherous if there has been recent rain, turns off at kilometer 25; the sign says "Laguna Salada." Snow may make areas of the park inaccessible in winter. ~ Reservations are essential and can be made through Guadalupe Canyon Hot Springs and Campground, P.O. Box 4003, Balboa, CA 92661; 949-673-2670; www.guadalupe-canyon.com, e-mail rob@earthlink.com.

facilities anywhere, including a complete spa, tennis courts and swimming pools, enough exercise equipment to train an army, and more than 20 miles of jogging trails through spectacular foothills. Celebrities such as Oprah Winfrey and Barbara Streisand come here to relax and restore their minds and bodies. The minimum stay is a week, from Saturday to Saturday, at a cost of about $200 per person per night, double-occupancy. Guests can arrange complimentary transportation across the border to the resort from Lindberg Field in San Diego. Reservations should be made up to a year in advance. ~ Route 2; reservations c/o The Golden Door, P.O. Box 463057, Escondido, CA 92046; 760-744-4222, 800-443-7565, fax 760-744-5007. ULTRA-DELUXE.

Look for first-rate resort accommodations at surprisingly affordable prices at the **Hacienda Santa Veronica**, a half-hour's drive east of Tecate on the highway to Mexicali. The resort's condominium-style mini-suites have contemporary furnishings, private patios and fireplaces. There are six tennis courts, an outdoor swimming pool, mountain trails for hiking, jogging and horseback riding, race tracks for motorcycles and all-terrain vehicles, as well as bullfighting lessons. ~ Route 2; reservations c/o Hacienda Santa Veronica, 74818 Vellie Drive, Suite 4, Palm Desert, CA 92260; 665-655-2195 or 664-681-1428 in Tijuana, or 619-341-9811 in the U.S. MODERATE.

DINING

The often noisy, no-frills **Jardín Tecate** on the south side of the main plaza serves tasty, low-priced soups, salads and fish dishes, as well as *comidas corridas*—fast-service daily specials. Locals outnumber tourists, and there's sidewalk dining in hot weather. ~ Andador Libertad 274; 665-654-4353. BUDGET.

El Passetto, in an alleyway on the westside of the plaza, specializes in traditional Italian food and also has a few Mexican and seafood selections. The owner serves his own homemade red table wine. ~ Callejón Libertad 200; 665-654-1361. MODERATE.

La Carreta is a cool, dim sit-down restaurant featuring *norteño* Mexican cooking—the familiar burritos-and-enchiladas fare, typical of Mexico's northern cattle ranching region and

AUTHOR FAVORITE

That special place in my psyche that sometimes wishes I were Ernest Hemingway finds a special kind of thrill at **Hacienda Santa Veronica**, a former fighting bull ranch turned luxury resort where you can take bullfighting lessons and pit your nerves and skill against a sharp-horned training cart or, if you dare, a small yearling bull—thrilling without killing. See above for more information.

often called Tex-Mex in the United States. ~ Avenida Juárez 270; 665-654-0462. BUDGET.

Panadería El Mejor Pan has, as the name claims, some of the best **GROCERIES** bread in Baja. The little bakery is located two blocks east of the plaza. Open 24 hours. ~ Avenida Juárez 331.

PARQUE NACIONAL CONSTITUCIÓN DE 1857 🏃 This 12,400-   **PARKS** acre park surrounds **Laguna Hanson**, which is an important refuge for migratory water birds (though it does not always contain water). The lake is in the heart of the Sierra de Juárez, a pine-covered mountain highland that separates the Mexicali Valley and Colorado River delta from the Pacific coast. ~ Laguna Hanson is located midway along an unpaved 100-kilometer road that runs between Route 2 and Route 3. From Route 2 between Tecate and Mexicali, high-clearance vehicles can take the park road that turns off to the south four kilometers west of the tiny roadside village of La Rumorosa at the highest point along the highway—this is challenging for passenger cars because of a rocky stretch just inside the park entrance. Most vehicles, including cautiously driven motor homes, can get to the lake by driving north from Route 3 at kilometer 55 east of Ensenada.

On the other side of the park, Cañon de Guadalupe offers natural 105°F hot springs shaded by palms at the base of the sierra's steep eastern escarpment. (See "Backcountry Adventure: Cañon de Guadalupe" in this chapter.)

▲ Camping around Laguna Hanson is informal and free. There is no water, so bring your own drinking water. At Cañon de Guadalupe, there is a commercial campground by the hot springs. Sites range from $15 to $50 per night; no hookups.

▼▼▼▼▼▼▼▼▼▼

Formerly so arid that humans could not survive there, the Valle Mexicali came to life in 1902 with the completion of the Imperial Canal, which diverted water from the Colorado River on the U.S. side of the border to irrigate California's Imperial Valley as well as the desert around Mexicali, which was controlled by the Colorado River Land Company, a consortium of U.S. businessmen who had leased vast holdings from the Mexican government. The company brought thousands of Chinese laborers who had helped build the canal to farm the Mexicali Valley as sharecroppers. The population of early-day Mexicali was 93 percent Chinese.

Mexicans came gradually to the Mexicali area—first for the fast money to be made from Prohibition-weary Americans, then for the vast areas of *ejido* farm acreage made available when land reform swept through 1930s Mexico, cancelling the leases of foreign landholders like the Colorado River Land Company. Land

Mexicali

reform also disenfranchised many Chinese farmers, forcing them to look for work in the thriving capital. Today, Mexicali's La Chinesca district is the largest Chinese-Mexican community in the entire country. A unique dialect of border Spanish mixed with Chinese is often heard in shops and restaurants.

Mexicali's economy turns on agriculture, not tourism. An elaborate irrigation system connected to Morelos Dam, on the Colorado River just south of the border, has transformed more and more arid desert into fields green with crops for export to U.S. and Canadian supermarkets. *Maquiladora* factories lure thousands of workers from areas of mainland Mexico where jobs are hard to find. "Temporary" *maquiladora* workers swell Mexicali's official population from 775,000 "permanent residents" to more than a million. Though surrounded by the squalid housing projects that go along with *maquiladora* plants, the long-established parts of the city are more befitting the capital of Baja California—palm-lined boulevards, monumental statues, flower-filled parks, fountains and quiet residential neighborhoods with manicured lawns.

SIGHTS   **Parque Niños Héroes de Chapultepec**, Mexicali's formal downtown plaza, is located three blocks east of the border crossing and less than one block south of the border. From here, the downtown area continues eastward for almost two miles, though it is only four blocks wide. ~ Between Avenidas Cristóbal Colón and Francisco Madero and Calles Ayuntamiento and Altamirano.

The graceful **Catedral de la Virgen de Guadalupe**, the city's primary house of worship, is located a block east and a block south of the plaza. Most of the old, historic churches of Baja had crumbled into memory long before this 20th-century Spanish Mission Revival–style edifice was built. ~ Avenida Reforma at Calle Morelos.

La Chinesca, the largest Chinatown in Mexico, is "on the other side of the tracks," along Avenida Altamirano a few blocks south of the plaza across the diagonal Calzada López Mateos and the train tracks that run alongside it. The mainly residential district has a smattering of the exotic little shops and mysterious signs you'd expect in a Chinatown, along with dozens of inexpensive Chinese restaurants.

The **Universidad Autónomo de Baja California** has several facilities around the city. The administration buildings, on the main campus two miles east of the center of downtown, occupy the most historic building in town—the original Palacio de Gobierno or state capitol. ~ Avenida Reforma at Avenida Sebastian Lerdo de Tejada; 686-554-0400; www.uabc.mx. The Colorado River Land Company's corporate headquarters once occupied another impressive office building just north of the former capitol. ~ Avenida Reforma at Calle F.

The University's top attraction, the **Museo Regional** (**Museo Hombre, Naturaleza y Cultura**), is eight blocks east of the main campus. The biggest and best museum on the peninsula—almost by default—its eight galleries contain exhibits on geology, fossils and the mission churches of Baja. The main focus is on anthropology, especially the Yumano and other nomadic peoples who inhabited the Sierra de Juárez and Sierra San Pedro Mártir in pre-Columbian times. All interpretive signs are in Spanish. ~ Avenida Reforma at Calle L; 686-552-5717.

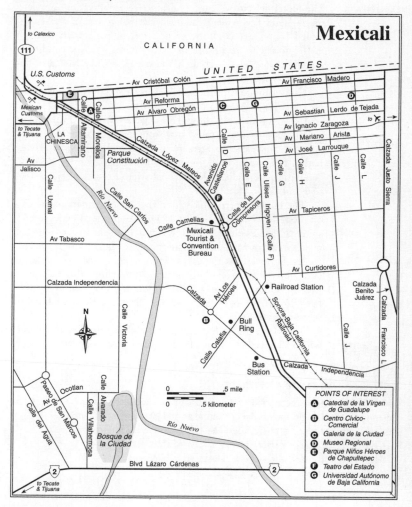

Mexicali

CALIFORNIA

to Calexico

111

U.S. Customs

UNITED   STATES

Av Cristóbal Colón

Av Francisco Madero

Mexican Customs

Av Reforma

Av Alvaro Obregón

Av Sebastian Lerdo de Tejada

to Tecate & Tijuana

LA CHINESCA

Av Ignacio Zaragoza

to

Av Mariano Arista

Av José Larrouque

Calzada López Mateos

Parque Constitución

Av Jalisco

Río Nuevo

Calle San Carlos

Av Tapiceros

Calle Camelias

Av Tabasco

Mexicali Tourist & Convention Bureau

Av Curtidores

Calzada Independencia

Railroad Station

Calzada Benito Juárez

N

Bull Ring

Bus Station

Calzada   Independencia

0   .5 mile

0   .5 kilometer

Río Nuevo

Ocotlan

Bosque de la Ciudad

Blvd Lázaro Cárdenas

2

2

to Tecate & Tijuana

POINTS OF INTEREST

Ⓐ Catedral de la Virgen de Guadalupe
Ⓑ Centro Civico-Comercial
Ⓒ Galeria de la Ciudad
Ⓓ Museo Regional
Ⓔ Parque Niños Héroes de Chapultepec
Ⓕ Teatro del Estado
Ⓖ Universidad Autónomo de Baja California

The **Teatro del Estado**, Baja's largest performing-arts theater, presents Mexican plays, dance concerts and musical events. Schedule information is available across the street at the Comité de Turismo y Convenciones (COTUCO) office. ~ Calzada López Mateos at Avenida Castellanos; 686-564-0757.

Baja California's governor, state legislature and judiciary are housed in separate buildings of the **Centro Civico-Comercial**, an ambitious urban renewal project on the south edge of the city near the Plaza de Toros Calafia bullring. There's not much to see. ~ Avenida Los Héroes.

LODGING   The **Hotel del Norte**, with its distinctive architecture—art deco meets Santa Fe—is near the border crossing. Its 52 well-maintained rooms are comfortable and full of personality, though traffic noise can be a problem. Some rooms have air conditioning and color TV. ~ Avenida Madero 203 at Calle Melgar; 686-552-8101. BUDGET TO MODERATE.

One of the most affordable places to stay in the downtown area, the **Hotel Mexico** caters mainly to Mexican families. The rooms are spotless but show signs of severe wear and tear. Guest accommodations (and rates) vary from spartan rooms with a bed and not much else to attractively furnished ones with private baths, TVs and air conditioning. All rooms have one thing in common: pink walls. ~ Avenida Sebastian Lerdo de Tejada 476; 686-554-0669. BUDGET.

The **Hotel Lucerna**, located in the southeast part of the city on the road to San Felipe, has 175 air-conditioned guest rooms, suites and individual bungalows in a lush garden setting that makes it one of Mexicali's prettiest hotels. Many rooms have balconies that overlook the two swimming pools and the fountains and palm trees surrounding them. Guest facilities also include an exercise room. ~ Boulevard Benito Juárez 2151; 686-564-7000, fax 686-566-4706, or 800-582-3762 in the U.S.; www.hotel-lucerna.com. DELUXE.

Top of the line in Mexicali is the **Holiday Inn Crowne Plaza**, with 158 spacious, colorfully decorated guest rooms that are up

AUTHOR FAVORITE

One of the attributes that fascinates me about Baja is its amazing blend of Anglo, Latino, American Indian and Japanese inhabitants. For yet another aspect of this cultural kaleidoscope, plus an abundance of Chinese restaurants that serve Mexican-style Cantonese food, visit Mexicali's **La Chinesca**, the largest Chinatown in Mexico. See page 96 for more information.

to the standards of better motor inns in the United States. The air-conditioned rooms have phones, cable color TV and even computer modem ports. ~ Avenida de los Héroes 201 at Calzada López Mateos; 686-557-3600, fax 686-557-0555. DELUXE.

Mexicali's youth hostel, the **Instituto de la Juventud y el Deporte,** has dormitory accommodations designed more for the use of visiting sports teams than gringo travelers. Its location, a long way from the border, the bus depot or anyplace you might want to visit, makes it a doubtful choice. There is no food service. ~ Calle Coahuila 2050; 686-557-6182. BUDGET.

DINING

Mexicali boasts more Chinese restaurants than any other Mexican city—over 100. In fact, about half of the restaurants in town are Chinese. In the Chinese district south of Calzada López Mateos, check out **Alley 19,** the granddaddy of all Chinese restaurants, operated by the same family in the same location since 1928. The menu presents a choice of stir-fries, mostly beef and vegetarian dishes, served over heaps of fried rice. Try the *chau men*, which contains different vegetables from the familiar American-style chow mein. ~ Avenida Benito Juárez 8. BUDGET.

◄ HIDDEN

Restaurant Buendía, a hole-in-the-wall eatery also in La Chinesca, offers an authentic taste of Mexicali's unique Chinese-Mexican cuisine—items like stir-fried beefsteak with vegetables, and spicy egg rolls that bear a striking resemblance to burritos. The prices are worth walking a few extra blocks for. ~ Avenida Altamirano 263; 686-552-6925. BUDGET.

◄ HIDDEN

More upscale is **El Dragón,** atmospherically Asian in a pagoda-shaped building on the east side of town. The elegant restaurant serves shrimp and lobster dishes as well as exceptional presentations of local standards such as beef broccoli and *chau men*. ~ Calzada Benito Juárez 1830; 686-566-2020. MODERATE. The same management also operates **La Misión Dragón,** where the food meets the same high standard and the ambience strikes a strange synthesis of classic Chinese and Spanish Colonial mission styles that expresses Mexicali's unique Chinese-Mexican character perfectly. ~ Boulevard Lázaro Cárdenas 555; 686-566-4400. MODERATE.

Several blocks south of the main Universidad de Baja California campus, the **Cenaduría Selecta** is a little off the beaten path, but that does not stop a mostly Mexican clientele from packing the place most evenings. In business since 1945, the restaurant serves an assortment of Mexican combination plates and thin, Mexican-style beefsteaks. ~ Avenida Arista 1510; 686-562-4047. MODERATE.

◄ HIDDEN

The place to go for great seafood is **Los Arcos,** in the Centro Cívico-Comercial. The menu includes the Baja California favorite, Puerto Nuevo style lobster, along with sea bass, shrimp sauteed in garlic, and a wealth of other culinary delights. The light, somewhat sterile atmosphere seems to have been created with business lunches in mind. ~ Avenida Calafia 454; 686-556-0886. MODERATE.

SHOPPING One of the few shopping spots that rises above downtown Mexicali's usual run of curio shops is the **Galería de la Ciudad**, a large, privately owned art gallery that displays works by contemporary Baja artists. ~ Avenida Obregón 1209; 686-553-5044.

Desarrollo Artesanal de Mexicali, a government-sponsored store, sells arts and crafts handmade in Baja California. Prices are good. It's too far to walk there from the border, though. ~ Boulevard Lázaro Cárdenas 1190; 686-561-6444.

NIGHTLIFE Although a few sleazy bars and strip joints survive as reminders of bygone days when Mexicali hoped to lure rich gringos across the border with various vices, most of the city's scant nightlife these days is in the plush, flashy discos at the better hotels. Check out **La Capilla**, a dance club in the Hotel Lucerna that's a favorite hangout for the young and prosperous. Cover. ~ Boulevard Benito Juárez 2151; 686-566-1000.

PARKS **BOSQUE DE LA CIUDAD** This large city park contains a lake surrounded by forest, a zoo, carnival rides and a miniature train that takes visitors on a quick tour of the park. Admission is three pesos. Closed Monday. ~ Calle Alvarado, north of Boulevard Lázaro Cárdenas on the southwest side of the city; 686-555-2833.

▼▼▼▼▼▼▼▼▼▼

Algodones

The small town of **Los Algodones** (usually just called Algodones), located off U.S. Interstate 8 where the California–Arizona state line meets the Mexican border, is the obvious port of entry for travelers from points east who are bound for the San Felipe area.

Named for the cotton fields that surround it, Algodones is the commercial center for residents of the agricultural area near the mouth of the Colorado. The town, with its narrow, nameless dirt streets, covers an area of just one square mile and has a population of 15,000. Yet during the winter months, almost that many visitors from the United States come through each day. Many are motorists bound for San Felipe, but more are senior citizens from the retirement meccas of southern Arizona who pay to park on the U.S. side and walk across the border to avail themselves of Mexico's much less expensive dental work. In fact, Algodones has 35 dentists and 15 optometrists, whose prices are often less than half as much as those charged in Arizona. Until recently, many seniors living in southern Arizona retirement communities flocked to Algodones to fill prescriptions at a fraction of U.S. prices, and some of the *farmacias* that used to line the streets of town are still in business. But since U.S. Customs started cracking down on imported pharmaceuticals a few years ago, you risk getting apprehended as a "drug smuggler" merely for your personal stash of Lipitor, Rogaine, Prozac or Viagra.

As you drive east from Algodones, following the signs that mark Route 3 on its circuitous path to join Route 5 to San Felipe, you pass through the eastern part of the **Valle de Mexicali**, Baja's largest agricultural area. Irrigated by water diverted from the Colorado River at Morelos Dam, about two miles south of Algodones, the area has seen explosive population growth in recent years.

SIGHTS

During the hot months, when visitors from the U.S. are rare, almost all activity in Algodones shuts down, though the border remains open.

Roads linking Algodones and the many small farming communities of the valley with Mexicali were unpaved until the early 1990s. Poverty is more obvious here than in most other parts of Baja. Most people who live here are essentially sharecroppers who struggle along on subsistence farms and work seasonally, harvesting crops at large farms on both sides of the border. Watch to the north and you'll glimpse the **Algodones Dune Field** beyond green fields of alfálfa. More than a hundred feet high in places, the 50,000-acre expanse of sand sprawls across the border and is inaccessible from the Mexican side.

There is little reason to consider spending the night in Algodones, since you'll find motels and motor inns galore just off U.S. Interstate 8 in Yuma, Arizona, just a few miles east of the Algodones border crossing.

LODGING

Numerous vendors sell tacos, *elotes* (corn on the cob) and fruit salads on the streets of Algodones during the winter.

DINING

For a sit-down meal, **El Rancherito**, a tourist-oriented place two blocks south of the border crossing, serves typical border cuisine: burritos, enchiladas and several varieties of tamales. ~ Plaza Gisela 12; 657-512-7008. MODERATE.

Or try **El Gourmet**, where you can order calamari steak, clam chowder or filet mignon and dine in the sports bar with 32 TVs and a betting concession operated by Caliente, the company that holds a monopoly on gambling throughout Mexico. ~ Avenida B between Calles 1 and 2; 657-517-7009.

Carlota's Bakery, in the Real Plaza del Sol mini-mall two blocks south and a block east of the border crossing, tempts travelers with breads and sweet rolls. A small open-air café serves continental breakfasts and snacks.

GROCERIES

Almost any time is harvest time for one vegetable or another in the Valle de Mexicali, and many small farmers make extra cash by carrying veggies in to Algodones to sell to gringo tourists. Don't be surprised if every third person you meet offers to sell you a bundle of asparagus. Another week, it could be onions. Most vegetables can be taken across the border into the U.S., though without a special permit you can't bring in avocados, potatoes (including sweet potatoes and yams) or sugar cane.

Outdoor Adventures

FISHING

Near Tijuana, **Islas los Coronados** is a favorite area for yellowtail, sea bass, halibut and barracuda. Charters can be arranged informally at San Antonio del Mar. Most fishing charters that operate in this area are based in San Diego. Contact **H&M Landing**. ~ 2803 Emerson Street, San Diego; 619-222-1144; www.hmlanding. com. You can also book a charter at **Fisherman's Landing**. ~ 2838 Emerson Street, San Diego; 619-221-8500; www.fishermans landing.com.

DIVING

Islas los Coronados is an enormously popular area for scuba diving. Although the islands may not look like much from the surface, they are the summits of a cluster of steep underwater mountains whose rock faces, like coral reefs, teem with sea life. The best dive areas lie 60 to 90 feet below the surface and can be hazardous for inexperienced divers. A popular spot for easy diving is the kelp forest off the southern tip of the southernmost island. There are no regularly scheduled commercial dive trips, and most scuba enthusiasts come in their own boats.

TENNIS

Tennis courts are hard to find in Tijuana; most visitors who are inclined toward gringo sports head for the resorts at nearby Rosarito. The best bet for Tijuana tennis is the **Gran Hotel Tijuana**, which has two hard-surfaced courts for guest use. ~ Boulevard Agua Caliente 4500; 664-681-7000.

Mexicali has a number of municipal and semiprivate *clubs deportivos* that have tennis courts as well as swimming pools and other facilities. The lowest fees are at the **Ciudad Deportiva**, where you'll find four hard-surfaced courts available on a first-come,

AUTHOR FAVORITE

As an aficionado of dramatic contrasts, I like to stop on my return trips from the deep desert of central Baja to hike through the pine forests that line the shores of **Laguna Hanson**, the peninsula's only freshwater lake. It's also the only natural lake in Baja California. See page 103 for more information.

first-served basis, along with a public swimming pool, baseball diamond, running track and jai alai *frontón*. ~ Boulevard Cuauhtémoc; 686-555-3025. Visitors can rent courts at the private **Club Raqueta Britania**, which also has a workout room and spa. ~ Boulevard Anahuac at Calle Mar Baltico; 686-557-1307.

GOLF

The semiprivate **Tijuana Country Club** (also called the Club Social y Deportivo Campestre) has a long 18-hole course that sometimes hosts the Mexican Open Golf Tournament. ~ Boulevard Agua Caliente; 664-681-7851.

South of Tijuana on the way to Rosarito, the 18-hole course at the **Real del Mar Golf Resort** is open to the public and has club and cart rentals and a complete pro shop. ~ Route 1-D Km. 18; 664-613-3401; www.realdemar.com.

The **Club Deportivo Campestre de Mexicali** is another 18-hole semiprivate country club course, so similar to Tijuana's that the two courses must have shared the same designer and possibly the same blueprints. ~ Route 5 south; 686-563-6171.

BIKING

It's hard to imagine vacationers visiting Tijuana by bike. The risk of theft is tremendous, and most places of interest to tourists are within walking distance of the border crossing. But if you choose to bike to Tijuana, you'll be pleased to learn that a newly opened bike lane, designed to accommodate the thousands of Mexican workers who commute daily to San Diego, makes cycling the fastest way to get through U.S. Customs.

HIKING

The cool pine woods that surround Laguna Hanson in the **Parque Nacional Constitución de 1857** are one of the best hiking areas in Baja. A well-defined trail makes its way around the lake (which does not always contain water). A complete circuit of the lake involves more than 20 miles of walking, all fairly level. Other trails wander off into the forest. Those who venture out of sight of the lakebed should be sure to take a compass, since the secondary trails are unmapped and can be confusing.

Transportation

AIR

Delta and Aeroméxico have has frequent flights to **Tijuana International Airport** from Los Angeles. Aero California also has flights from Los Angeles to Tijuana, Loreto, La Paz and Los Cabos. Mexicana has flights between Tijuana and Los Cabos, and Aeroméxico links Tijuana with Guadalajara and other major cities of western Mexico. The airport is located east of Tijuana near the Otay Border Crossing.

Mexicali International Airport has daily Mexicana and Aviasca flights from Los Angeles, Mexicana offers daily service to Mexicali from Mexico City and Guadalajara.

Tecate and Algodones do not have commercial airports.

CAR   Tijuana's San Ysidro Border Crossing is at the end of U.S. Interstate 5 south from San Diego. The Otay Border Crossing is
reached via the last exit from U.S. Interstate 805 before it merges
into I-5 at the border.

Tecate is 32 miles southeast of San Diego. To get there, follow the directions in "Crossing the Border" at the beginning of
this chapter.

Mexicali is on Route 111, 11 miles south of Interstate 8 near
El Centro, California.

Algodones is also just off Interstate 8. Take the Andrade exit,
three miles west of Yuma, Arizona; it is about three miles south
to the border crossing.

**CAR
RENTALS**

Car rentals are easy to come by in Tijuana. At Tijuana International Airport, try **Alamo** (664-686-4040), **Avis** (664-683-0603),
Budget (664-634-3303), **Hertz** (664-683-2080), **National** (664-
683-8115) or **Thrifty** (664-683-8130). Most of these chains also
have locations in the Zona Rio and Agua Caliente hotel zones.

In Mexicali, rental agencies are found along the Boulevard
Juárez strip near the border crossing. They include **Budget** (Boulevard Juárez 2220; 686-566-4840), **Dollar** (Boulevard Juárez
1000; 686-565-6262), **Hertz** (Boulevard Juárez 1223; 686-568-
1973) and **National** (Boulevard Juárez 1004; 686-568-3963).

BUS   The **San Diego Trolley—Blue Line** shuttles passengers from
downtown San Diego's Old Town Transit Center and intermedi-
ate stops to and from the San Ysidro Border Crossing, within
walking distance of downtown Tijuana, every 15 minutes from
5 a.m. to midnight. The cost is about $3 each way.

Greyhound operates bus service across the border from San
Diego to Tijuana and from Calexico to Mexicali. ~ www.grey
hound.com. **Autotransportes de Baja California** has frequent bus
service along Mexican Route 2 between Tijuana, Tecate, Mexicali and Algodones.

**PUBLIC
TRANSIT**

Tijuana's colorful, modern buses run to all parts of the city and
make it easy to reach Zona Río and Agua Caliente district attractions from Avenida Revolución.

Mexicali's old-fashioned public buses run from a central
downtown loading zone on Calzado Justo Sierra, two blocks
from the border crossing, and go to every part of the city.

Besides private taxis, both Tijuana and Mexicali have *com-
bis* (also called *taxis de ruta*), shuttle vans that travel specific
routes and cost more than a bus ride but less than a taxi cab.

TAXIS   In Tijuana, taxi service from the airport is provided by **Transportes Tijuana** (664-682-3903) and **Transportistas Terrestres**

(664-683-8054). For transportation from the border and other parts of the city, call **Radio Taxis of Tijuana** (664-683-1801) or **Yellow Cabs** (664-682-4617). In Mexicali, call **Ecotaxi** (686-562-6565) or **Taxi Flash** (686-567-2424). Both Tijuana and Mexicali have many independent taxis. Look for them around the border crossings and the major hotels. Cab rates are regulated, and authorized fare cards are supposed to be posted. Price gouging is common on border pickups, though, so it is a good idea to ask first what the fare will be. Some taxi drivers like to drive tourists across the border to U.S. Customs—where Mexican price controls do not apply—and then ask for an outrageous amount.

> Mexican entrepreneurs have started renting bicycles at the border in five-minute increments. When you get across you drop the bike off and a youngster pedals it back to Mexico for the next customer.

TOURS

The **Comité de Turismo y Convenciones de Mexicali** offers all-day tours of the city from the tourist office near the Monumento Vicente Guerrero in Mexicali or from the tourist office in Algodones. ~ Calzada López Mateos at Calle Camelias, Mexicali; 686-557-2376, 686-557-2561.

Addresses & Phone Numbers

Hospital ~ Tijuana, 664-684-0922; Mexicali, 686-557-3700

Police ~ Emergencies (all cities), 134

United States Consulate ~ Avenida Tapachula 96, Colonia Tipódromo, Tijuana; 664-681-7400, fax 664-622-7400

Secretaría de Turismo del Estado de Baja California Norte ~ Tijuana; 664-681-9492

Comité de Turismo y Convenciones de Tijuana ~ 664-684-0537, or 800-252-5363 in the U.S.

Comité de Turismo y Convenciones de Mexicali (Mexicali Tourism and Convention Bureau) ~ López Mateos at Calle Camelias, Mexicali; 686-557-2376, 686-557-2561

Green Angels (Federal roadside repair and assistance units) ~ Tijuana, 664-623-3877; Mexicali, 686-654-0443

Internet access ~ Cafe-Online, Boulevard Sánchez Taboada 4002 local no. 11, Zona Río, Tijuana, 664-634-2872; Café Internet, Reforma 1991, Colonia Nueva, Mexicali

FIVE

Northern Baja

A cool morning fog drifts in off the ocean to shroud the hills behind the port city of Ensenada. On the other side of the peninsula, dust devils spin crazily across the sunbaked Desierto de San Felipe, one of the driest places on the continent. Northern Baja is a land of striking contrasts, where the fertile farmland of the Pacific coastal plain, the evergreen forests and granite peaks of the Sierra de San Pedro Mártir, and the stark desert shoreline of the Sea of Cortez exist within 90 miles of one another.

The two most popular tourist areas in the state of Baja California—Ensenada and San Felipe—have one feature in common. Both are close enough to the border for a weekend getaway from San Diego, Los Angeles or Phoenix. Beyond that, they couldn't be more different. Ensenada, the third-largest city in Baja, accommodates cruise ships with the biggest, busiest tourist-oriented shopping district between Tijuana and Los Cabos. The lazy little sportfishing village of San Felipe, by contrast, rarely sees any vessel larger than a shrimp boat, and every store in town seems to sell the same T-shirts. The Pacific coast around Rosarito and Ensenada is the setting for numerous luxury beach resorts; San Felipe provides beachfront campsites for astonishing numbers of motor homes and other recreational vehicles.

The hidden aspect of northern Baja awaits discovery in the high sierra between the two coasts, a magnificent wilderness of oak and piñon hill country and the highest mountains on the peninsula. The drive in is beautiful, and hiking or biking the trails of Parque Nacional Sierra de San Pedro Mártir is even more so. But not all the hidden spots in northern Baja involve long backroad expeditions. Some of the nicest Pacific beaches in Baja California are just a few miles off the Baja Highway, near the farm town of San Quintín. The elbow-to-elbow party atmosphere that characterizes the weekend beach scene around Rosarito and Ensenada rarely reaches as far south as San Quintín, and you're likely to find that you have the whole beach to yourself.

Steep hills on the landward side and a ten-mile-long
peninsula on the ocean side protect the Bahía de
Todos Santos from storms, making it the best location for a shipping port on the entire Pacific coast of Baja. The
exclusive gringo neighborhoods that blanket the hillsides swell
the port's population to an estimated 370,000 full-time residents;
it is Baja's largest city that is not on the border.

Ensenada Area

Spanish ships first dropped anchor in the bay in 1542, and over
the centuries it sheltered both the Spanish Empire's treasure galleons from Manila and the pirate ships that preyed on them. In the
1700s, Todos Santos became a favorite hunting area for whalers.
The one obstacle to settlement was the absence of fresh water.

Relying on rain catchments and intermittent streams from the
eastern mountains, ranches sprang up during the early 1800s, but
it was not until 1872, when gold was discovered in the Sierra de
Juárez, that a port settlement began to flourish. Ten years later, Ensenada was declared the capital of the Territory of Baja California.
But in time, the mines played out and Ensenada faded into obliv-
ion. In 1915, the territorial capital was relocated to Mexicali, leaving Ensenada as nothing more than an obscure fishing village.

Prosperity returned in the 1920s, as Prohibition in the United
States drove Hollywood's party set south of the border. The Playa
Ensenada Hotel and Casino opened as the most lavish resort in
Baja, but this playground of the rich and famous lasted less than
a decade before the Mexican government outlawed casino gambling and closed it down. Ensenada's dependence on tourism and
foreign money, however, has continued to the present day.

Today, the city's shipping port hosts several cruise ships from
Los Angeles each week, spilling stampedes of daytrippers into
the curio shops that line Avenida López Mateos. Thousands of
gringo retirees and expatriates have swelled the city's permanent
population to a quarter of a million. This is not a place where
people retire to live cheaply; the property prices and overall character of the *norte americano* Chapultepec Hills district are not
much different from comparable neighborhoods in San Diego or
Orange County, though property taxes are much lower. A major
reason gringos move here, rather than someplace farther down
the peninsula, is that Ensenada has the best medical facilities in
Baja, including the only hospital that accepts U.S. medical insurance instead of requiring patients to pay cash and file for insurance reimbursement on their own. Mexicans from all parts of the
peninsula also travel to Ensenada for health care.

The **Carretera Escénica**, or scenic route, from Tijuana to Ensenada covers 190 kilometers, hugging the coastline the whole

SIGHTS

way. Two roads follow the same route—the *cuota*, or toll high-way, which speeds you from the border to Ensenada in about an hour and costs around $6, and the traffic-clogged libre, or free highway, which serves the coastal resorts and takes three times as long.

Between **San Antonio del Mar**, on the southern outskirts of Tijuana, and **San Miguel**, just over the hill from Ensenada, once-upon-a-time fishing villages now merge in an unbroken strip of high-rise beachfront hotels, restaurants and condominium complexes. The epicenter of all this beach fun is the string of towering ocean-view condos at the south end of **Rosarito**. The Hotel California is located directly across the highway from Rock'n'Roll Taco in this whitewashed, red-tile-roofed strip town of 50,000 sandwiched between the beach and the Route 1 *cuota*. Rosarito has signs not only in English but also in Spanish. This is because resorts in the area enjoy a modest summer season of visitors from mainland Mexico. In the winter, Rosarito is overrun by hordes of rich gringos every weekend, laid-back and mainly Mexican during the week.

Twentieth Century Fox built **Fox Studios Baja** on the southern outskirts of Rosarito in 1996 for the filming of *Titanic*. Since then, Fox has used the "Baja Tank" to represent both the Atlantic and the Pacific for the 2003 film *Master and Commander: The Far Side of the World*. It has also rented the facility out to several other Hollywood studios for such films as *Pearl Harbor* and the James Bond thriller *Tomorrow Never Dies*. One-hour tours of this starkly industrial site, offered on Sundays only, include a look at the 20-million-gallon water tank sound stage where Leonardo DiCaprio's character sunk into the icy depths, as well as an opportunity to explore remnants of the giant *Titanic* cruise ship set. A "Making of Titanic" video and footage from the original film let visitors compare illusion with reality. Another exhibit focuses on the Mexican film industry. A "Foxploration" tour takes visitors behind the scenes to view production work and see the sound stages. Admission. ~ Route 1 Km. 32.8; 646-614-9000, fax 646-614-0184; www.foxbaja.com, e-mail info@foxbaja.com.

El Mirador, high on a rocky promontory north of Bahía de Todos Santos, is the most scenic rest area between Rosarito and Ensenada. Whale watchers throng to this place during migrations, and at any time of year the sunset view is as magnificent as any on the Pacific coast.

Entering the city on Route 1, motorists find the **Comité de Turismo y Convenciones** tourist information office at the crowded intersection near the port entrance gate. ~ Boulevard Costero 540; 646-178-2411. Road access to the **Port of Ensenada**, on a spit of land that juts into the bay parallel to the waterfront, is restricted.

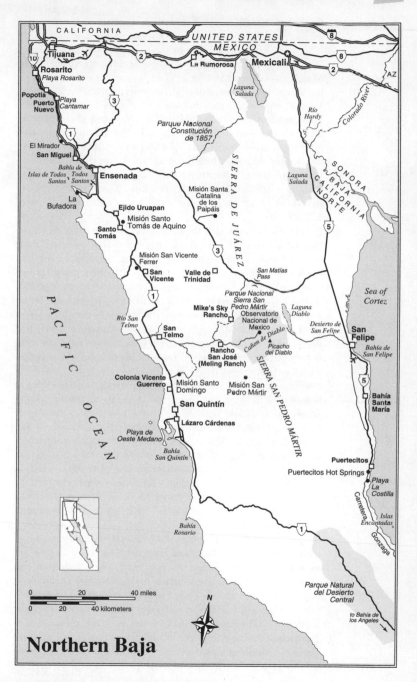

Northern Baja

Passengers from the cruise ships that dock at the port's wharf take a shuttle to the downtown shopping district.

Located two blocks west of the tourist information office, a 19th-century Mexican customs house has been resurrected as the **Museo Ex-Aduana Maratima**. The museum does not have much in the way of permanent displays of artifacts from the local area. Instead, it provides space for touring exhibits from the Instituto Nacional de Antropología y Historia, which has jurisdiction over all of Mexico's historical districts and ancient ruins. If you stop here on your way south, you may find an exhibit on the colonial missions of Baja California, for instance, and then discover on your northbound return trip that it has been replaced by Mayan sculptures or Empress Carlotta's furniture. Exhibits are captioned in Spanish only. Closed weekends. ~ Avenida Reyerson 99; 646-178-2531.

Three blocks south of the tourist information office on Boulevard Costero is the **Plaza Cívica**, nicknamed Tres Cabezas ("three heads") because the broad paved square contains 12-foot-tall busts of three revered Mexican historical figures: priest-turned-rebel-leader Miguel Hidalgo, organizer of the 1810 rebellion that would lead to Mexico's independence from Spain; President Benito Juárez, who led the fight to drive the French imperialist government of Emperor Maximillian out of the country in 1867; and President Venustiano Carranza, who reigned over the constitutional convention that created modern Mexico in 1917. ~ Boulevard Costero at Avenida Alvarado.

HIDDEN ▶

From downtown, museum buffs can follow Avenida Obregón north (away from the waterfront) for 14 blocks to visit the **Caracol Museo de Ciencias**. Situated in a two-story house, the science museum emphasizes astronomy, paleontology, oceanography and marine biology. Its educational displays on environmental protection and endangered species are aimed more at school classes than tourists. This museum is one of the best places to learn about the California gray whale and its migrations—if you can read the Spanish-only explanations. Closed Monday. Admission. ~ Avenida Obregón 1463; 646-178-7192; www.astrosen.unam.mx/~museo-en/mus-0.html.

The big edifice that houses the **Museo de História** was originally built in 1930 as the Playa Ensenada Hotel and Casino, the most elegant hotel in Baja for a few years, and it's worth a visit as much to see the building itself as for the museum's exhibits on Baja's indigenous people, early European explorers and missionaries. Managed by retired prizefighter Jack Dempsey, reputedly with financial backing from Al Capone, the resort played host to Hollywood's beautiful people until 1938, when the government outlawed casino gaming. Visitors can stroll through the Moorish-style lobby with its striking murals, the ballroom with its dazzling wrought-iron chandelier, the chapel where eloping movie stars used to tie the knot, and the old casino, which has repeatedly inspired Ensenada residents to petition the Mexican federal government to legalize gambling again in the Baja free trade zone as an economic stimulus. Although, until recently, the government showed no inclination to consider the idea, some politicians have begun voicing support for legalized casino gambling in Mexican tourist areas. Admission. ~ North end of Riviera del Pacifico at Boulevard Costero; 646-177-0594.

Baja history buffs may also want to visit the **Museo Histórico Regional**, featuring a permanent exhibit on the people and cultures of Mesoamerica, which occupies a 19th-century military headquarters that served as the city jail until 1996. Closed Monday. ~ Avenida Gastelum at Paseo Calle 1; 646-178-2351; www.inah.gob/mx/muse2/htme/mure0201a.html.

Ensenada's best-known sight is **La Bufadora**, a sea geyser at a rocky point across the bay from the city. Its name comes from *bufa*, Spanish for "snort" and colloquial Mexican for bison; La Bufadora is commonly translated as "the buffalo snort." This

Ensenada

N

POINTS OF INTEREST
- **A** Bodegas de Santo Tomás
- **B** Caracol Museo de Ciencias
- **C** Comité de Turismo y Convenciones
- **D** Museo Ex-Aduana Maratima
- **E** Plaza Cívica
- **F** Port of Ensenada
- **G** Tourist Information

Calle Ambar

Calle 15

Calle 12

Calle 11

Av Azteca

Av Neizahalcoyotl

Av Ryerson

Clark Flores

Av General

Av Alemán

Colinas Chapultepec

Av Moctezuma

Av Obregón

Av Ruiz

Av Gastelum

Av Ruiz

Av Gastelum

Av Miramar

Av Riveroll

Ensenada

Av Moctezuma

Av Miramar

Av Alvarado

Av Blancarte

Av Castillo

Arroyo

Calle

Av Espinoza

Calle 9

Calle 7

Av Guadalupe

Av Iturbide

Av Reforma

11

Av Reforma

Av Juarez

Calle 4

Calle 2

Av López

Boulevard Azueta

Boulevard

Boulevard

Av Riveroll

Mateos

Lázaro

Cárdenas

Calle Diamante

Calle Agustin

Av Cipres (Loyala)

Sangines

3

1

0   .4 mile
0   .4 kilometer

Bahía de Todos Santos

Av Mateos

Boulevard Costero

waterspout is created by the entrance to a long, narrow cavern just above sea level, between steep cliffs that narrow to a "V." When a wave rolls in, water crashes over the cavern's mouth, compressing the air inside. As the surf subsides, the air trapped in the cave blasts the water back out with amazing force, beginning with a low rumble and climaxing with a plume of sea spray that can reach almost 100 feet. The phenomenon is at its most spectacular with a high tide and big waves. La Bufadora becomes quite crowded on weekends. Parking fee. ~ Carretera Punta Banda.

La Bufadora is at the end of the long, narrow **Peninsula Punta Banda**, which shelters the Bahía de Todos Santos from the open ocean. It's a 40-kilometer trip from Ensenada. The well-marked road to La Bufadora turns off Route 1 south of the city and runs along a ridge high above the bay. Several parking areas along the road provide fantastic views—especially during the southward whale migration, December to mid-February. Peninsula Punta Banda is one of the best whale-watching spots in Baja California Norte. Gray whales are bottom feeders, so they travel close to shore. Many of them veer into the bay and must swim the length of the Peninsula Punta Banda to find their way back to the open ocean.

HIDDEN ►   Just outside the mouth of the bay are the **Islas de Todos Santos**. The smaller northern island contains a Mexican Navy base and is off-limits to civilians, but you can visit the larger southern island by tour boat or sea kayak. Pelicans, ospreys and many other bird species nest there, and sea caves and grottos dot the island's south end. Surfers say the Todos Santos waves reach 30 feet in height. Local legend holds that the islands inspired the setting for *Treasure Island*, which Robert Lewis Stevenson is said to have written while living at the north end of the bay. Most historians agree that in fact Stevenson never set foot in Baja, though his widow lived farther south on Isla Cedro for a while after his death.

From Ensenada, paved two-lane Route 3 runs 250 kilometers across the Baja's mountainous spine to San Felipe, climbing gradually along a series of high, cool agricultural valleys sepa-

AUTHOR FAVORITE

The best view of the city is from the **Colinas Chapultepec**, which enclose the downtown area on the west. The Spanish name sounds more poetic than its English translation—"Grass hopper Hills." Irregardless, the panorama is a sight to behold and I enjoy doing so while cruising slowly through this exclusively gringo hillside suburb. To get there, follow Calle 2 west from downtown; it immediately starts climbing into the hills. There is an overlook where the street joins Avenida Alemán, which loops all the way around the hills before returning you to the same overlook.

rating the Sierra de Juárez from the Sierra San Pedro Mártir. Pygmy forests of juniper and piñon shelter vast fields of hay and pastures where dairy cows graze.

Ninety kilometers into the trip, an unpaved road turns off to the north and goes about ten kilometers to the adobe ruins of **Misión Santa Catalina de los Paipáis.** Only adobe wall fragments remain of this mission church. Built in 1797 to minister to the Paipai Indians, the mission lasted for more than 40 years but did not prosper. The high altitude made conditions less than ideal for growing crops, and the priests were often forced to turn to the Indians for food to survive harsh winters. In the end, the Indians' resentment erupted into violence, and the missionaries were driven from the valley in an 1840 uprising. Several hundred Paipai Indians live around the old mission and in tiny villages scattered through the wilderness to the north; they are the last surviving indigenous people of Baja. Farther on, past the fast-growing farming town of Valle de Trinidad, the highway crosses 5000-foot San Matias Pass and begins its descent into the San Felipe Desert.

LODGING

Beachfront hotels from Rosarito to Ensenada fill up on Friday and Saturday nights, so reservations are advised. Except during the mid-July to mid-September peak season, there is no problem finding vacancies on weeknights, when room rates drop as much as 30 percent. *Note:* Kilometer markers on Route 1 north of town indicate the distance from Tijuana, while south of town they show the distance from Ensenada.

The **Rosarito Beach Hotel** is one of the few remnants from the days when Rosarito was a tiny, hard-to-reach fishing village on a great beach where silent-movie stars went to hide from the outside world. Built in 1926, this elegant hotel originally had only 12 rooms; it was the only hotel in town with running water. Expanding with each road improvement and corresponding tourist influx, the hotel has grown to 275 rooms. The exterior of today's big, white Mediterranean-style hotel is typical of the beach resort complexes toward the south end of Rosarito; inside, the restored lobby, dining rooms and ballroom ooze Roaring Twenties ostentation. The mix of old and new buildings offers a full range of room choices, from older, very affordable and relatively plain rooms (some without air conditioning) facing away from the ocean to spacious luxury suites with private balconies overlooking the beach at triple the cheap rooms' price. All guests have the use of facilities that include two heated swimming pools, tennis and racquetball courts, jacuzzis and a steam room. The hotel offers a special "half-your-age" discount. If you're 30 years old, for instance, you get 15 percent off the regular room rate; if you're 50, you get 25 percent off. Availability of these discounted rooms is limited, and reservations must be made in advance to qualify for the discount. ~ Boulevard Benito Juárez 31, Rosarito; 661-612-0144, 661-612-1111, fax 661-612-1125, or 800-343-8582 in the U.S.; www.rosaritohtl.com. MODERATE TO ULTRA-DELUXE.

A peculiar blend of surprisingly affordable resort ambience and theme park–style contrivance, the **Hotel Calafia** proclaims itself a "historic and cultural center" because it is built around a cluster of white facades replicating the various colonial missions of Baja California. There's also an ecological park with tidepools and a conference center where talks on Baja history are sometimes presented. The 72 guest rooms and suites have ocean views, and the open-air dining terrace is perched above surf crashing on the rocks. ~ Route 1 Km. 35.5, Rosarito; 661-612-1581, fax 661-612-0296; www.hotel-calafia.com, e-mail info@hotel-calafia.com. MODERATE.

Quintas Papagayo Resort is 11.5 miles north of Ensenada. The natural seashore is mostly boulders, but a retaining wall holds a sandy beach. This old-timey cluster of 50 units, built in 1947 by the owners of Hussong's Cantina, is rapidly being eclipsed by the highrise hotels springing up around it. Still, rates here are less than half of those charged at other resorts on the same beach. Guest rooms and beach bungalows have decks overlooking the bay, Mexican tile floors and handcarved furniture; the bungalows have kitchenettes and fireplaces. Amenities include a swimming pool and tennis courts. None of the guest rooms have TVs, and many rooms have no air-conditioning. ~ Route 1, Km. 110; 646-174-4575, fax 646-174-1455, or 619-491-0682 in the U.S.; www.hussongs.com.mx. MODERATE.

HIDDEN ▶ You'll find the best youth hostel in Baja California Norte six miles north of Ensenada. The **Hostel Sauzal** offers male, female and co-ed dormitory accommodations in four-bed rooms, each with a writing desk, and a wide porch with a hammock and an ocean view. There are hot showers, laundry facilities, a kitchen and barbecue, picnic facilities and a library of Baja books and maps—all for $15 per person per night. ~ 344 Avenida L, Sauzal; 646-174-6381; hostelsauzal.tripod.com. BUDGET.

Queen of Ensenada's casually elegant small resort hotels is **Las Rosas**, magnificently located on a bluff overlooking the beach at the north end of Bahía de Todos Santos. Downtown is a two-mile drive away. All of the two-story hotel's 31 spacious, pastel-hued rooms and suites have balconies with ocean and pool views, and many have jacuzzis and fireplaces. There is a two-night minimum stay. ~ Route 1, Km. 105; 646-174-4310, fax 646-175-9031; www.lasrosas.com, e-mail reservation@lasrosas.com. DELUXE.

Centrally located between the main shopping and restaurant street and the Centro Artesanal next to Tres Cabezas Plaza, the 12-story **Hotel Villa Marina** is within easy walking distance of everything downtown, and there's no problem finding your way back—it's the tallest highrise in town. The upper floors on the ocean side offer great views of the port and bay, though on weekend nights the din from the nightclub on the top floor can make guests wish they'd settled for a lower angle of view. Other rooms overlook Avenida López Mateos and the heart of the downtown tourist zone. The 130 cozy, cool and contemporary guest rooms are decorated in shades of blue, and most have narrow private balconies. ~ Avenida López Mateos at Avenida Blancarte; 646-178-3351. MODERATE.

A little farther south on López Mateos and a little more affordably priced, the Mediterranean-style **Hotel El Cid** is a Best Western with standard motor inn accommodations in 52 guest rooms (many with queen-sized beds) that are individually decorated to represent the state capital cities of Mexico. There's a heated swimming pool, plus cable TV, phones and air conditioning in every room. Room rates plunge almost into the budget range during the winter/spring off-season. ~ Avenida López Mateos 993; 646-178-2401, fax 646-178-3671. MODERATE.

The **Estero Beach Resort** fronts on a secluded stretch of sand toward the south end of Bahía de Todos Santos, far from the pandemonium of downtown Ensenada. This beautifully landscaped complex has 106 light, modern guest rooms, ranging from small, bungalow-style units and spacious one- and two-bedroom units with balconies overlooking the ocean to large suites, equipped with kitchens, that can sleep four adults. There are no phones in the rooms. Outdoor sports are the best reason to pick this resort (the resort is the site of the world's biggest international beach volley ball tournament). There are tennis courts and a boat ramp, and you'll find saddle horses, fishing equipment, Wave Runners, kayaks, canoes and bicycles for rent. The two-story resort sits at the edge of an estuary that attracts abundant pelicans, cormorants, egrets and hawks. Most of Ensenada's population growth has been southward, so the main route from here to the tourist zone is lined with supermarkets and discount

AUTHOR FAVORITE

Topping my list of Ensenada-area hideaways is **Estero Beach Resort**, thanks to its peaceful out-of-town setting with abundant bird life and an occasional whale cruising past just offshore, plus affordable lodging and all kinds of sports-gear rentals. Sure, it's far enough away so you have to drive into town; but then again, if you stayed in town, you'd have to drive to get here. Estero Beach is better. See above for more information.

department stores and so packed with traffic that it can take almost an hour to get downtown, but the resort has a restaurant and nightclub. ~ Route 1, Km. 10.5; 646-176-6225, fax 646-176-6925, or 800-762-2494 in the U.S.; www.hotelesterobeach.com. MODERATE TO DELUXE.

The **Joker Hotel and RV Park**, south of Ensenada near the turnoff to La Bufadora, adds a touch of whimsical fun to what would otherwise be a routine hotel stay. The 40 guest rooms are contemporary and plain, with balconies overlooking the pool and pink walls and minimal furnishings, but the exterior is a riot of eccentric architecture. Tudor gables and latticework and Gothic towers fill the facade of this essentially ordinary two-story motel to overflowing, and the crenelated turret of a medieval castle stands by the swimming pool and jacuzzi, rising ten feet above the roofline and affording an ocean view. ~ Route 1, Km. 12.5; 646-178-2601, fax 646-177-4460; www.hoteljoker.com. BUDGET TO MODERATE.

There are no lodging accommodations along Route 3 between Ensenada and San Felipe. Well . . . actually there's one, but **HIDDEN ►** **Mike's Sky Ranch** (some signs say Rancho Mike) is a little off the beaten track, at 4000 feet elevation on the northern boundary of Parque Nacional San Pedro Mártir, surrounded by mountains, waterfalls and pine forests, with a trout stream running right through the camp. Established by the late Mike Leon, a pioneer Baja 1000 racer, the Sky Rancho has traditionally been the private domain of dirt bikers and other off-roaders for one good reason: getting there requires a 35-kilometer drive on an unpaved road. These days, the resort is getting more family vacation trade, though the families often bring off-road vehicles with them. The road to Mike's, which turns off to the south from the main highway at the summit of San Matías Pass (near kilometer marker 138), is graded and well maintained during the summer months, though it can deteriorate badly over the winter. A passenger car capable of climbing steep hills can usually make the cautious journey from the highway in about two hours. Accommodations are in about 27 rustic motel-like rooms, electricity is furnished by a gasoline-powered generator, and there are no phones. Moderately priced meals are served family-style in a central dining room. There's a swimming pool. ~ Reservations: P.O. Box 1948, Imperial Beach, CA 92032; 619-428-5290 in the U.S. BUDGET.

DINING

The place to go for elegant dining in Rosarito is **Chabert's Restaurant**. Located at the Rosarito Beach Hotel and Spa, in the mansion of the hotel's founder, the restaurant evinces nostalgia for the opulence of the 1920s. The French and Continental cuisine may be the best in the Baja. ~ Boulevard Benito Juárez, Rosarito; 661-612-0144. DELUXE.

For more casual fare, **Ortega's Place** in Rosarito offers $1.99 breakfasts and an all-you-can-eat soup-and-salad bar. The specialty in this upstairs restaurant is *langosto estilo Puerto Nuevo*— lobster sliced in half lengthwise, fried in a pot of boiling oil and served with butter, lime and salsa. The Ortega family also operates several lobster restaurants under the same name in Puerto Nuevo. ~ Boulevard Benito Juárez 200, Rosarito; 661-612-0022. BUDGET TO MODERATE.

El Patio, one of eight restaurants in Rosarito's Festival Plaza Hotel serves gourmet "Aztec-style" Mexican food—the kind you won't find north of the border. The shopping-mall atmosphere of this place does little to distract from the savor of such delicacies as *crepas xochimilco* (crêpes stuffed with shrimp and smothered in mole *pepián*, a spicy sauce made from poblano chiles and crushed pumpkin seeds). Other intriguing entrées include *huachinango estilo guayabitos* (red snapper in a sweet coconut-mango sauce) and Chihuahua-style quail in tangy *rielera* sauce. ~ Boulevard Benito Juárez, Rosarito; 661-612-2950. MODERATE TO DELUXE.

Puerto Nuevo, often called "New Port," just down the road from Rosarito, is a fishing village turned food court. Prime lobster waters lie just offshore, and roadside vendors started selling fried lobster here soon after the road to Ensenada was built. Today, the lobster stands have evolved into a complex of about three dozen side-by-side, permanent, full-service restaurants. Ranging in appearance from slightly funky to nearly fancy, all serve the same thing—fried lobster—at about the same prices, ranging from about US$16 to $24 depending on size. Most of the families who operate these restaurants catch their own lobsters during the October-to-March season; the rest of the year, the restaurants serve lobsters imported from Baja Sur and from as far away as Cancún. Reservations are not taken.

> Bigger isn't always better. In Rosarito, the smaller lobsters are more tender and tasty; those that weigh in at more than a pound are likely to be tough.

La Casa de Langosta has a sizable menu of dishes ranging from lobster omelettes to lobster burritos and lobster thermidor as well as the standard lobster Puerto Nuevo. ~ Route 1, Km. 49, Puerto Nuevo; 661-614-1072. MODERATE.

The upstairs area of **Ortega's Patio** offers one of the best ocean views in town and charming tropical decor. ~ Route 1, Km. 49, Puerto Nuevo; 661-614-1320. MODERATE. Both of these restaurants are large, seating 200 people or more. For a small, family-run place where your dinner was probably caught by your waiter's uncle, try **Josefina y El Negro**. ~ Route 1, Km. 49, Puerto Nuevo; 661-612-1083. MODERATE.

Text continued on page 120.

Tour
Valle de Guadalupe

Though not well known outside the region, Baja California Norte produces excellent wines and has been doing so for centuries. Most vineyards are located in the beautiful Valle de Guadalupe, along Route 3 between Tecate and Ensenada. Recently, the state tourism department and the wineries of the valley have started promoting the **Ruta de Vino**, a self-guided auto tour that takes you to the valley's wineries.

Whether you're coming from Tecate or Ensenada, the place to start is **L.A. Cetto Winery**, 73 kilometers south of Tecate and 33 kilometers north of Ensenada. Follow the unpaved road for 5 kilometers through the vineyards to Latin America's largest winery, though it has only recently begun distributing its award-winning wines to the United States in limited quantities at ten times the price you'll pay at their tasting room. Founded in 1974 by Don Luis A. Cetto, heir to an Italian immigrant family that owned a beverage bottling company, and world-renowned winemaker Camillo Magoni, they are known for their nebbiolo wine, of which they are the largest producer outside Italy. They have also received more than 20 international gold awards for their petite syrah, cabernet sauvignon and zinfandel. Their white zinfandel, a trash wine blend at most California wineries, is a revelation here—flavorful, subtly scented and so good you'll wish you could buy it back home. Winery tours are available, and the tasting room offers free samples as well as wine by the glass, which you can sip while relaxing on the patio surrounded by peacocks and palm trees. ~ 646-155-2264.

A little farther along the road past L.A. Cetto, the small **Doña Lupe Organic Winery** specializes in selling its estate wines, as well as jams, jellies, salsa and natural herbs, to tour bus groups. The beautiful setting makes for one of the best rest stops on the *Ruta de Vino*.

Across the highway from the turnoff to L.A. Cetto, the **Domecq Winery** is headquartered in a charming old-style hacienda with grandiose entrance gates. The first commercial winery in the valley, it was founded in 1972 by the company that makes El Presidente brandy. Wines range from the expensive reserva magna, a blend of cabernet sauvignon, merlot and nebbiolo aged 18 months in French oak barrels, to the very affordable blanc de blanc, an unaged blend of chenin blanc, riesling and chardonnay. There is a small fee for winery tours and wine tasting. ~ 646-155-2249.

About three kilometers down the road toward Ensenada, a road turns off the main highway toward the village of Francisco Zarco, where the **Museo Comunitario del Valle de Guadalupe** exhibits historical photos of the valley and artifacts of the Kumiai Indians, who once lived here. Of particular interest is the story of the Molokans, Russian religious refugees who arrived in 1906 to settle the valley in the name of the Cooperative Society of the Russian Empress Colonizers of Baja California. Many of their descendents still live here, including the owners of the remote Bibayoff Wines. Just past Francisco are two other prestigious wineries, the **Monte Xanic Winery** (646-174-6155; tasting by appointment only) and **Chateau Camou** (646-171-9300; tastings Monday through Saturday until 2:00 p.m.). Also near Francisco Zarco is the small boutique **Vinos Sueños Winery**, where award-winning vintner José Ochoa Calderón makes less than 1000 cases of premium wine a year.

Between this northern cluster of wineries and the outskirts of Ensenada are half a dozen other wineries, all situated well off the main highway, as well as vineyards belonging to the Santo Tomás wineries in Ensenada and the town of Santo Tomás. If you're looking for adventure, search out **Three Women Winery**, an artisan winery and gallery hidden in the hills. Turn east off the highway at Km. 87 and drive between two rock pillars, straight to the end of the road, then turn left up the hill. ~ 646-171-5674.

Adventuresome souls who prefer to seek out the catch of the day in an authentically ramshackle fishing village with nary a T-shirt shop or curio hawker in sight will find it in **Popotla**. This little town just south of Rosarito seems determined to avoid the notoriety that has brought tourists to neighboring Puerto Nuevo in overwhelming numbers. In fact, the fishermen's wives who run the 30 or so nameless seafood stands along the waterfront often outnumber the gringo visitors. Stroll among them and take your pick of huge chocolate clams, conch, oysters, octopus cocktails, sea urchins, deep-fried barracuda, crabs, lobsters and whatever else the morning's fishing brought in—all lovingly prepared before your eyes. To get there, follow Rosarito's main street for four miles south of town, watch for a concrete archway near kilometer marker 33, turn right and drive under the arch. Continue down the rough, unpaved road for half a kilometer to the parking lot at the edge of the village. Visit early; having no electricity, Popotla is an early-to-bed, early-to-rise kind of town. ~ Route 1, Km. 33. BUDGET TO MODERATE.

As you approach Ensenada from the north, watch for **Enrique's Restaurant** on the ocean side of the highway. Long a local institution, this hole-in-the-wall place got its start as a roadside fried-shrimp stand. Over the decades, it has expanded into a romantic restaurant with a great view of the port. The menu has expanded, too, highlighting exotic Continental dishes like frog legs and glazed quail, but it's still the shrimp that justify the restaurant's reputation. ~ Route 1, Km. 101; 646-178-2461. MODERATE.

Ensenada's **Mercado de Mariscos**, at the north end of the waterfront near the tourist information office and sport-fishing docks, is surrounded by open-air stands selling fish tacos—sticks of fresh fish battered, deep-fried and wrapped in a corn tortilla. Condiments range from guacamole to sliced radishes. ~ North end of Boulevard Costero. BUDGET.

The downtown tourist zone is packed with overpriced Mexican restaurants with menus so unimaginative that you might as well be back home at a Taco Bell. Locals who work downtown

AUTHOR FAVORITE

There's nothing like seafood right off the boat. That's why I make a point of stopping at **Popotla**, a small fishing village south of Rosarito, where fishermen's wives grill fresh fish, lobsters and other *mariscos* at open-air stands along the beach. It's the "hidden" counterpart to the more famous lobster village of Puerto Nuevo nearby. See above for more information.

join the tourist throngs in **El Charro**, which offers some of the best prices around on enchiladas, burritos and *chiles rellenos*. The specialty is *pollo asado*—whole chickens roasted on spits in the restaurant's front window. ~ Avenida López Mateos 475; 646-178-3881. BUDGET.

One of the longest-established restaurants in Ensenada, **El Cid** (located in the hotel of the same name) serves a full range of less familiar Mexican specialties, such as *pescado veracruzano* (fish in a tangy salsa) and *chiles Gertrudis* (a special kind of stuffed chile), as well as international gourmet dishes like quail in rosé sauce and the restaurant's award-winning "Oscaritos"—baby squid stuffed with clams. The atmosphere is shadowy, candlelit and Spanish. ~ Avenida López Mateos 993; 646-178-2401. MODERATE.

El Rey Sol has been serving authentic French cuisine in Ensenada since 1947, when the restaurant was opened by a French man and his Mexican wife; they met while working as chefs in Paris. Under their family's management ever since, El Rey Sol maintains the highest standards in food and service. Stained glass and heavy, dark furniture set the mood. The bill of fare includes beef, lamb, poultry and seafood; this is probably the only place in Baja where *pollo en mole* shares the menu with duck au beaux arts. Besides using freshly caught fish, the chef uses produce from the owners' farm in Santo Tomás. Bread and pastries are baked on the premises. ~ Avenida López Mateos 1000; 646-178-1733. DELUXE.

The exterior of **Bronco's Steak House** proclaims "¡LA NUEVA COSTUMBRE MEXICANA—DE COMER STEAKS!" ("The new Mexican custom—of eating steaks!") In fact, many local Mexican families who would never set foot in a downtown tourist restaurant come to Bronco's to celebrate birthdays and other holidays. The interior is wood-paneled and decorated with ranch memorabilia, and the food contains a good selection of traditional Mexican dishes such as *carne asada* (beef strips marinated in red chile sauce and barbecued) as well as steaks cut thick and grilled over mesquite coals and south-of-the-border specialties like *boca del rio*, a strip steak that is split and stuffed with chiles and spices. The all-you-can-eat luncheon buffet and Sunday brunch mix Mexican and gringo food. ~ Avenido Lopez Mateos 1525; 646-176-4900; e-mail broncos@telnar.net. MODERATE.

One of the most popular restaurants in Ensenada is **La Embotelladora Vieja**, serving seafood and Continental fare in a big converted warehouse that was once a wine-aging room for the Bodegas de Santo Tomás winery next door. The food is first-rate and the atmosphere makes up in country French romanticism for whatever it may lack in the way of quiet intimacy. But the real attraction is the spectacle of all that wine. The walls are literally covered with 30-foot wine casks and racks of wine bottles from every vintner in Baja and many Californian and European wineries as well, and the wine list is formidable. It has become a fashionable place to sample Mexican wines and savor Cuban cigars, so diners may wish to steer toward the far end of the nonsmoking section. ~ Avenida Miramar 666; 646-174-0807. MODERATE.

While Ensenada boasts more than its share of fine dining, most Mexican food in downtown restaurants is Americanized for the gringo palate. To try authentic local food, stop at one of the roadside **tamal stands** that line Route 1 south of town on the way to the La Bufadora turnoff. Tamales—cakes of corn meal mush that are stuffed, wrapped in corn husks and steamed—come not only in the meat-stuffed variety familiar in the United States but also with an assortment of other fillings ranging from diced shrimp to pineapple. Some vendors may stare dumbfounded when you order, because of the widely held belief that gringos can't eat real Mexican food without getting sick. My experience with roadside stands in Ensenada and most other parts of Baja suggests that this fear is unfounded. ~ Route 1 south. BUDGET.

You can enjoy a spectacular view along with your dinner of fresh seafood, pasta or gourmet Mexican food at **Restaurante Costa Azul**, a four-story open-air restaurant overlooking the bay at La Bufadora. Local fishermen deliver their catch fresh daily, and the international team of cooks prepares it in styles that range from Puerto Nuevo to Cajun and Pacific Northwestern. ~ La Bufadora; 646-154-2540. MODERATE.

GROCERIES **Supermercado Gigante** carries most of the same food items you'd expect to find in a supermarket in the United States. ~ Avenida Gastelum 672; 646-178-2644. Additional locations of Gigante and Calimex supermarkets are opening along Route 1 on the south side of town. The waterfront **Mercado de Mariscos**—a genuine public fish market, not just another tourist trap—is the place to go for fresh-caught fish, shrimp, squid, octopus, clams and lobsters if you have a refrigerator or a good, big ice chest. ~ North end of Boulevard Costero. For natural foods, organic produce and herbal remedies, try **La Milpa**. ~ Calle 4 1329; 646-176-1005.

SHOPPING Ensenada is the best gift-shopping town north of Los Cabos, thanks to the large numbers of free-spending cruise ship passengers who stroll the sidewalks of Avenida López Mateos. There's a wide selection of merchandise in all price ranges, and although you won't find Third World prices in Ensenada—or anywhere in Baja—there are bargains to be found in items such as leather goods, silver jewelry, Mexican designer fashions and ceramics. The

The Lost Treasure of Rosarito

You don't have to travel far south of the border to discover the kind of remote, rugged wilderness that adventurous travelers expect of Baja. Look inland (left) from Route 1-D as you drive south from Tijuana to Rosarito and you'll see a jagged volcanic peak rise in the distance from the flat coastal plain. Its name is El Coronel, after a mysterious hermit who lived more than a century ago in the caves you can see with binoculars high on the almost sheer mountain slopes.

In the 1870s a U.S. Army colonel absconded with an undisclosed amount of army gold and paper currency and fled south down the old Camino Real, which ran near the base of the mountain. He made his home on the mountain, an ideal defensive position commanding a view of the entire coastal plain, and moved from cave to cave over the years. Artifacts of his occupation remain to this day. That much is documented by the Rosarito Historical Society.

The rest of the story is a mystery. What became of the colonel, whose remains have never been found? Although several locals have found small caches of gold and old U.S. dollars on the mountain, none of them approximate the fortune that legend says the colonel stole. Does the rest of the treasure still lie hidden somewhere on El Coronel? Or did it ever exist at all? What of the gringo ghost who, many say, roams the mountains guarding the gold? And what would the colonel have thought if he could look out over modern Rosarito—an array of condos, beach resorts and even an oceanic movie studio, all served by a fast four-lane superhighway—and realize that his hideout more than a century ago is as hidden as ever.

Although the mountain and its caves are easy to spot, getting there is another matter. There's no established trail; the approach is hot, dry and covered in dense brush, leading to a climb that traverses slippery rock slopes and edges along treacherous cliffs. Visitors can reach the caves and the hidden lake that kept the colonel supplied with fresh water and wild game on a long day's horseback ride with a guide from the stables south of town on old Route 1. To attempt the trip on foot, head south from Rosarito on old Route 1 and turn left between kilometer markers 39 and 40 at the sign for "Ciudad de Misericordia," which leads to an old mine in the foothills. This road will take you within day-hike distance of El Coronel. From there, you're on your own as you scramble your way up the slope without a trail.

Ensenada Arts And Crafts Center, actually a mall of small, open-front shops selling typical Mexican village handicrafts at only slightly inflated prices. ~ Boulevard Lázaro Cárdenas 1094. (Be aware that many low-priced arts and crafts today are actually knock-offs imported from China, a practice that has reduced the incomes of many artisans in small villages who depend for their living on selling their work to curio vendors.) Bartering is inappropriate in stores here, although street vendors are willing to negotiate prices, as are merchants at La Bufadora's flea market and Mercado Los Globos.

There are two distinct downtown shopping areas. The recently facelifted, tourist-oriented dining-and-shopping promenade along Avenida Lopez Mateos between Avenida Castillo and Avenida Ryerson has gift items in all price ranges, with an emphasis on jewelry and high-end arts and crafts. Four blocks inland, Avenida Juárez is where people who live in Ensenada go for their everyday necessities, though this area has been losing much of its trade to American discount department stores on the south side of the city.

Silver prices in retail shops are highly competitive and significantly lower than in U.S. jewelry stores. One reliable shop is **Los Castillo,** a family-owned jewelry chain that started in Ensenada in 1969 and has expanded to resort areas throughout Mexico. The Castillos represent many of the finest designers in Taxco, Mexico's premier silversmithing center, with jewelry in both .925 (sterling silver) and .950 purities. They also carry pewter and ceramic items and handcarved furniture. ~ Avenida López Mateos 815, 646-176-1187; second location at Avenida López Mateos 656.

The best feature of the **Santa Paula Bazar,** a crowded curio mini-mall in the heart of the tourist zone, is the stained glass and handblown glass of Armando Ozuna, who practices his craft daily in the front display window to the fascination of onlookers. ~ Avenida López Mateos 537.

There are bargains to be found in Mexican leather goods, including leather jackets, hats, huaraches, handbags, daypacks,

THE SIGN OF SILVER

Many street vendors in the tourist zone offer jewelry that they insist is made of sterling silver. Mexican law requires manufacturers to stamp a number—".925" (the percentage of silver in sterling), ".950" or ".999" (pure silver)—into each piece of jewelry, along with a mark showing who made it. If the number and the mark aren't there or are illegible, chances are it's alpaca. Sometimes called German silver, *alpaca* is an alloy of copper, nickel and zinc and actually contains no silver.

belts, boots and even saddles. Many small shops in the cruise-ship shopping zone along Avenida López Mateos carry similar selections at similar prices. You'll find a wider choice of leather clothing and accessories at **Nuevo México Lindo Talabarteria**, a shop known for its handmade saddles. ~ Calle 1 688; 646-178-1381.

Look for authentic Paipai and Kumai Indian arts and crafts at **Taller de Artesanos Indigenes** in the Bodega de Santo Tomas shopping complex. ~ Avenida Miramar at Calle 6; 646-178-8780. Another good source for Indian arts from both Baja and the northern Mexico mainland is **Galería de Perez Meillon** in the Centro Artesanal. ~ Boulevard Costero 1094-39; 646-174-0394.

Though the main tourist zone has turned upscale to capitalize on the steady flow of cruise ship passengers, you can still find hidden-away shops that specialize in contraband—especially Cuban cigars, firecrackers and switchblade knives. All are illegal in the U.S.; that's the only reason they're sold here. As a practical matter, the risk of being caught at the border with any of these items is low enough to put this kind of casual smuggling in the cheap-thrills category. Mexican vendors mock U.S. laws that let Americans buy all the firearms they want but outlaw cherry bombs.

Although quite a few stores in the Ensenada tourist zone offer "Cuban" cigars for sale to Americans who can't get them north of the border, the reality is that many of these cigars come from the Dominican Republic and are disguised to look like Cuban counterparts. The Dominican Republic is the world's largest cigar exporter, and connoisseurs from Canada and elsewhere often consider their cigars superior to the ones from Havana. Many counterfeit Cuban cigars have labels just slightly different from the real thing. For instance, fake Cohibas may have one or three rows of white dots above the brand name, instead of two. Some counterfeits sold today are so good that only an expert can tell them from the real thing. Unfortunately, U.S. Customs agents can't tell either.

Ensenada does have a swap meet–style flea market, **Mercado**   ◄ HIDDEN
Los Globos. On the east side of town in an area rarely frequented by tourists, the vast eight-block market operates every day but has the most vendors, as well as the biggest crowds, on Saturdays and Sundays. Browsers can spot occasional Mexican collectibles and curiosities scattered among the produce stalls and piles of cheap plastic housewares. ~ Calle 9 east of Avenida Reforma.

You'll find original paintings, sculptures and handcrafts by Baja artists at the **Galería Los Arcos**, located on the road to La Bufadora. ~ Ejido Esteban Cantú; 646-614-2066.

At La Bufadora, the street that leads to the geyser overlook is lined with curio shops for blocks. The merchandise is similar to that found in many stores downtown, with an emphasis on leather goods; asking prices start higher than downtown but are negotiable. This tourist shopping area has been dubbed the **flea market** by tour guides, and if you ask a taxi driver to take you to the flea market, this is where you'll wind up. ~ Carretera Punta Banda.

South of Ensenada, olive orchards cover thousands of acres. Not so long ago, farmers' daughters used to sell olive oil and several varieties of olives in glass jars at **roadside stands** along Route 1. As the highway has become more congested, these stands have become fewer, though you can still find some. You'll also find a good selection of local olives and olive oils in tourist shops and at winery tasting rooms.

Travelers crossing the peninsula from Ensenada to San Felipe on Route 3 may want to check out two modest shops in **Ejido Héroes de la Independencia** that sell crude coil pottery made by the Paipai Indians. The last remnant of Baja's original inhabitants, the Paipai live in small groups around the site of Misión Santa Catarina, eight kilometers east of the *ejido*, though the mission itself has been abandoned for more than 150 years. ~ Route 3, Km. 92.

NIGHTLIFE Rosarito's **Papas and Beer** (*papas* means "potatoes," or in this case, french fries) is not so much a nightclub as a huge nonstop beach party. With a big dancefloor, live music, food, drink and volleyball courts and a rock-climbing wall, all that's missing is Frankie Avalon and Annette Funicello . . . or maybe they're just lost in the crowd that packs this place on weekends. Papas and Beer claims the dubious distinction of being the largest bar in Baja. ~ Playa Rosarito, one block north of the Rosarito Beach Hotel; 661-612-2140.

Equally popular is **Iggy's Son of the Beach Bar**, a huge, hip-hoppy club where the fun includes foam parties, mechanical bull riding and bungee jumping. ~ Avenido Coronado 11337; 661-612-0537.

If you plan to make the bar scene in Ensenada, the one place you must not miss is **Hussong's Cantina**, Baja's oldest saloon. It hasn't changed much inside or out, they say, since it opened in 1892, when it catered to Ensenada's then mostly-non-Mexican population of gold miners, gamblers and adventurers. Especially on weekends, loud and rowdy doesn't begin to describe this place—sort of like a historic landmark on perpetual spring break. ~ Avenida Ruiz 113; 646-178-3210.

There are a half a dozen or so other big discos downtown. Designed for crowd management during spring break, these places can seem cavernous on many nights.

Mexico's
Wine Legacy

The most enduring legacy of the Spanish missionaries who first colonized Baja is vineyards. Just as Alta California is regarded as having the United States' best wineries, so northern Baja has a well-deserved reputation for producing Mexico's finest wines.

Situated in the grapevine-filled Valle de Santo Tomás, **Bodegas de Santo Tomás** makes wine from some of the oldest vines in California. The vineyards themselves are down in the Valle de Santo Tomás, 51 kilometers south of the city on Route 1, where Dominican brothers founded a mission in 1791. There they planted cuttings from grape vines that had originally been brought to the Baja peninsula by Jesuits more than a century earlier. Underground springs and coastal fog helped create an exceptionally good environment, and the vineyards flourished until 1840, when the Mexican government seized all agricultural land owned by the church, and the grapevines were abandoned. Spanish immigrants bought the the old vineyards and revived them in 1888, and Russian immigrants later brought new strains of grapes.

The winery was moved to Ensenada in 1937 to make shipping easier. In 1995, they opened a new state-of-the-art gravity-flow winemaking facility in the midst of their vineyards in the Santo Tomás Valley, where all their red wines are now made; white and sparkling wines are still made in Ensenada. Today, Bodegas de Santo Tomás produces fine pinot noir, cabernet sauvignon and chardonnay varietal wines, which are exported to Europe as well as to the Mexican mainland but are not sold in the United States. The winery's pride is the relatively pricey duetto, a dual-component wine blended with about 80 percent cabernet sauvignon from Santo Tomás and 20 percent merlot from the northern California–based Wente Winery. Guided tours of the Ensenada winery, including tastings, are offered several times daily. Admission. ~ Avenida Miramar at Calle 7; 646-178-2905, 646-178-3333; www.santotomas.com. mx, e-mail info@sdro.com.

Wine, whether red (*tinta*) or white (*blanco*), is properly called *vino de uva* (grape wine). The more generic *vino* is used to refer to all types of alcoholic beverages, and low-quality tequila is sometimes called *vino blanco*.

For a less rowdy crowd and a panoramic view, visit **El Navigante**, the nightclub on the top floor of the Hotel Villa Marina, the tallest building in the city. There's live music Thursday through Saturday nights and disco during the week. Cover. ~ Avenida López Mateos at Avenida Ruiz; 646-178-3351.

Ensenada's original gay bar is the low-profile **Coyote Club**. Cover. ~ Avenida Costero 1000. Newer clubs on the scene include **Club Ibis**. ~ Boulevard Costero at Avenida Sangines. There's also **La Ola Verde**. ~ Calle 2 #459.

BEACHES & PARKS

The Pacific Ocean beaches of Baja California Norte are most attractive in the summer and early fall, when they present a less crowded alternative to San Diego and L.A. beaches. The water is too cold for comfort in winter and spring, and it is often windy.

PLAYA ROSARITO This is the closest great Mexican beach to the U.S. border, so it is full of funseekers on most weekends. People live in luxury condos along Playa Rosarito and commute to work in San Diego. If peace and quiet is what you want, Rosarito isn't the place to look for it. Surfers say the waves here are awesome. ~ Located 24 kilometers south of Tijuana on Route 1.

▲ **Chuy's Trailer Park** has 26 RV campsites on the beach with full hookups, hot showers and a restaurant; $25 per night. ~ Costa Azul 75; no phone.

PLAYA CANTAMAR Calmer than Rosarito, this pretty three-mile beach is separated from the highway by a broad field of sand dunes—a favorite weekend playground for noisy ATVers. There are resort hotels but no camping. ~ Located 47 kilometers south of Tijuana on Route 1.

PLAYA MAL PASO This wide, soft beach runs for almost three miles and is largely undeveloped. It is known for its grunion runs, which draw a small crowd of fish-watchers and curiosity seekers every full-moon and new moon night in spring and summer. Silvery, seven-inch adult fish lay their eggs in the beach sand, somehow timing it so that ten days later they will hatch during a peak high tide. When they do hatch, the surf boils with thousands of baby fish, as locals scurry around catching them in buckets. ~ You can reach this beach through the Mal Paso RV Park, 71 kilometers south of Tijuana on Route 1, or Outdoor Resorts of Baja, one kilometer farther south.

One out of every four U.S. residents who travel to Baja is a Californian on a brief getaway to Ensenada.

▲ Despite its name, the **Mal Paso RV Park** is rustic enough to suit tent campers better than RVers. Sites are undefined; beach camping is permitted. No hookups, though there are restrooms and cold showers. Sites cost just $4 per night. ~ Route 1 Km. 71, La Misión. In contrast, **Baja Seasons Villas & RVs**, a kilometer down the highway on the same beach, has it all: hot showers, a laundry room, a sauna, a swimming pool, a hot tub, a game room, lighted tennis courts and even a miniature golf course. The 137 sites are on concrete pads and have full hookups, including cable TV. Sites cost $24 to $35 per night, with an extra charge for pets. Reservations are accepted. ~ Route 1 Km. 72; reservations: 4492 Camino de la Plaza, San Diego, CA 92173; 800-754-4190, fax 619-422-5953.

BAHÍA DE TODOS SANTOS 🚶 🐎 ⛵ 🛶 🚤 🛥️ 🚣 ⛵ All the way around the rim of the bay, beaches arc north and south from the Port of Ensenada. The northern reaches, around Las Rosas Resort, are the most attractive segment of the beach, and the southern part around Estero Beach Resort is also good. Closer to the port, the beach is less appealing, its waters clouded and discolored by oil films and muck stirred up from the bay's shallow bottom by ship propellers. Even in its urban sections, though, the beach makes for an interesting walk. ~ Route 1 from Punta San Miguel north of Ensenada to Ejido Chapultepec south of the city.

▲ Ensenada's most centrally located beach campground is **Campo Playa RV Park**, just over the bridge south of downtown on the east side of Boulevard Lázaro Cárdenas; you must walk across this bridge to reach the beach. There are 90 sites, all with concrete pads and hookups, and hot showers. Fees are $16 per night. ~ Boulevard Las Dunas at Calle Diamante; 646-176-2918. For a few dollars more you could camp at the **Estero Beach Resort**, toward the south end of the bay, and enjoy the resort's facilities, including snorkeling, horse, bicycle, sailboard and jet ski rentals and tennis courts. There are 60 sites, all with concrete pads and hookups, and hot showers. Fees are $20 per night. ~ Route 1, Km. 10.5; 646-176-6225, fax 646-176-6925; www.hotelesterobeach.com, e-mail reservations@hotelesterobeach.com.

PLAYA PUNTA BANDA 🚶 🚴 ⛵ 🎣 🏊 🚤 🚣 A long, straight, sandy beach runs along the north side of Punta Banda, the narrow peninsula that encloses the Bahía de Todos Santos. Like the peninsula itself, the beach is largely undeveloped. Surf fishing here is said to be the best in the area. ~ Turn west off Route 1, 18 kilometers south of Ensenada.

▲ **La Jolla Beach Camp** is a modest resort for RVers and tenters, with hot showers, a restaurant, a boat ramp and horse rentals. Campsites are on the beach and undefined; $6 per night. No hookups. ~ Carretera Punta Banda Km. 12.5. Several **ejido camping areas** are located on the Punta Banda road between Km. 2 and Km. 8, offering primitive camping without such niceties as

◄ *HIDDEN*

hookups, flush toilets or water. The steep dirt-road descent from the main road to the beach in this area makes these campgrounds all but inaccessible to motor homes but pleasantly secluded for tent and pickup campers. The fee is minimal.

San Felipe Area

One of the most popular destinations in Baja, San Felipe has managed to preserve a "hidden"—if not an undiscovered—feel. Catering primarily to the motorhome and camper crowd, it lacks the big-resort ambience that characterizes other Baja hot spots like Ensenada and Los Cabos. On a remote bay near the northern end of the Sea of Cortez, San Felipe is separated from the heavily populated Pacific Coast by the highest mountains on the peninsula. To get there, you must cross the Baja's most arid desert; once you arrive, you'll find a friendly little town where English is spoken everywhere and U.S. dollars are the preferred currency. Since the bottom fell out of the local fishing industry, tourism and vacation real estate development account for virtually all commercial activity in San Felipe. And it has proven to be a solid economic base in recent years, as the town's full-time population has doubled since the turn of the 21st century, and the population increases by 5000 during the cold months.

Jesuit priests landed on San Felipe's beach in the 18th century and established a small port for the purpose of delivering supplies to the Misión San Pedro Mártir in the forbidding mountains to the west. In 1806, when the mission closed, San Felipe was abandoned.

Drawn by the astonishing abundance of marine life in the northern Sea of Cortez, fishermen gradually migrated to San Felipe's bay and beach to establish a ramshackle village where people had no problem feeding their families but could not export their seafood for cash income because there was no way to carry fresh fish across the vast desert to market.

Prosperity came a step closer in 1952, when Mexico granted the United States the right to put a radar station at the south end of Bahía de San Felipe in exchange for funds to pave the road south from Mexicali. San Felipe was soon exporting huge quantities of shrimp to California and Arizona in refrigerated trucks. Sport fishermen from the United States started coming to San Felipe to catch *totuava*, a challenging 250-pound game fish known to anglos as sea trout. For 15 years, the fishing capital of San Felipe reigned as the most thriving community in the Baja.

Disaster struck in 1967, when a tropical storm totally destroyed San Felipe. While residents were struggling to rebuild, the Mexican government leased fishing rights in the Sea of Cortez to the Japanese fleet. In an operation that was unprecedented in scale, huge factory ships moved in and used long-line drift nets and giant underwater vacuum cleaners to extract most of the marine life from the northern gulf. The Mexican government finally terminated Japan's fishing rights by declaring the area off-limits to all commercial fishing for export. Today, San Felipe's small fishing and shrimping fleet only supplies local restaurants. The *totuava* has been declared an endangered species, and it is against the law to catch one.

San Felipe's economy was rescued from total collapse by RVs. With low prices and miles of undeveloped beaches just a few hours' drive from Phoenix or San Diego, San Felipe has become Mexico's top-ranking destination for trailer, camper and motorhome travelers, as well as dune buggy and all-terrain-vehicle enthusiasts. Though the winter months can be chilly, gringo "snowbirds" outnumber local residents between Christmas and Easter. The gringo presence reaches a frenzied peak during March, when college students from all over the western United States descend on San Felipe for spring break. Since the typical San Felipe visitor is fairly self-sufficient, the restaurant and resort hotel industry

San Felipe

has not kept pace with the rise in tourism. Curio shops and liquor stores are plentiful, though.

SIGHTS

Getting to San Felipe is half the fun. The distance from Mexicali is 198 kilometers; from Algodones, it's about the same, though unlike the Mexicali highway, the first part of the trip before you join Route 5 is quite slow. As it leaves the Valle de Mexicali agricultural zone, Route 5 crosses a broad green wetland along the west bank of the **Río Hardy**, a short tributary of the Colorado River. It forms an estuary, lush with reeds and tall grass and alive with herons, egrets and other wading birds, as it flows alongside the highway for about 12 kilometers before merging with the Colorado River. Most years, the Colorado itself is completely dry, since the water is diverted to irrigate farms on both sides of the border.

As it veers away from the river, the road plunges across the heat-shimmering **Laguna Salada**, the largest dry lake bed in Baja. This usually empty "Salt Lake" was part of the Sea of Cortez until 400 years ago, when the buildup of silt on the river delta separated the lake from the gulf. It has taken from then until now for the lake bed to dry out completely. Some areas toward the north end still fill with water in times of heavy rain. In fact, Route 5 is elevated as much as nine feet above the barren, parched desert because even this part of the lake bed can still occasionally flood. Do not stop on the levee or walk or drive on the lake bed: the apparently hard, dry surface can conceal patches of soft mud or quicksand.

> The Laguna Salada is so salty that plants cannot grow there.

Beyond the Laguna Salada, the north end of the Sea of Cortez begins to come into hazy view across the vast, shimmering mud flats of the **Colorado River Delta**. Fifteen miles wide and up to 60 miles long, the flats are so nearly level that normal tides shift the coastline in and out by many miles twice a day. Before the Colorado's flow was completely diverted, the area was a green wetland teeming with life. As the freshwater supply dropped, the marshes' rising salt content killed the plants, leaving only sterile mud flats where seagulls glide in search of clams and crabs.

The highway gradually nears the sea as it runs south across the **Desierto de San Felipe**. In the rain shadow of the high peaks of the Sierra San Pedro Mártir, this is the driest desert in Baja. Most of this area receives between one and two inches of rain per year—though near the mountains there are places where, locals say, rain has never fallen in human memory. The desert is a pale, gravelly, alkaline expanse without the smallest tuft of grass. Not even cactus grows. The only plant life consists of creosote bushes, ocatillos and diminutive, green-barked palo verde trees. With only the tiniest of leaves, these plants do little to relieve the stark, dry look of the landscape—except during late April of some years, when the ocatillos erupt in a spray of flamingo-pink blossoms and the branches of the palo verdes fill to overflowing with yellow flowers.

Expect a military checkpoint with drug-sniffing dogs where Route 3 from Ensenada joins Route 5 to the town of San Felipe. They are on the lookout for southbound guns and northbound drugs, and "tourist immunity" will get you through without problems. However, thorough searches of suspicious Mexican vehicles can cause delays of an hour or more at busy times.

It is 72 kilometers from the Route 3/Route 5 highway junction to the town of San Felipe. From there, the road angles closer and closer to the sea. The last 15 kilometers before reaching San Felipe run less than a kilometer from the beach. Packed-sand roads provide access to beachfront campgrounds, fish camps and vacation lot developments. Because of explosive growth, the 11-kilometer stretch of highway between El Dorado and San Felipe has become one of the most dangerous stretches of highway in Baja. The government plans to widen it into a four-lane roadway soon.

An improbable four-lane divided boulevard, Calzada Chetumal, whisks you out of the desert and straight into the middle of San Felipe, passing a towering modernist monument and circling a landmark traffic roundabout, known in these parts as a *glorieta*. Despite this grand entrance, the town has only 13,000 residents, and the "downtown" commercial area is only two streets wide and four blocks long. The two main streets are one-way in opposite directions: the beachfront street, called simply Malecón, runs north; one block inland, Avenida Mar de Cortez runs south.

The center of activity is the **malecón**, the sidewalk promenade along the wide, white beach that borders the business district. Young lovers linger on the steps and low walls at the foot of a crude statue that depicts a fisherman dragging a huge *totuava*. Nearby, (normally) gentle waves lick the sand and beachgoers relax in the shade of a few thatched-roof shelters or pitch their own tents on the sand for relief from the sun's glare. North of the statue, fishermen beach their motorized *pangas*. Beyond the north end of the *malecón*, in a large, bowl-shaped sand lot, lies a jumble of fishing boats wrecked by storms.

San Felipe's best sight is the view from the **Virgin of Guadalupe Shrine,** located on the conical hill above the cliffs at the north end of town. A 120-step climb up the concrete stairway to the squarish, white concrete block shrine is amply rewarded with a spectacular view of San Felipe's mountains, desert, beaches and bay.

To experience the Desierto de San Felipe up close, head north of town on Route 5 for 11 kilometers to a wide road that runs toward the mountains. A sign says "El Dorado Ranch Estates," and there is sometimes an army security checkpoint at the intersection. **El Dorado Ranch Estates** was a scheme hatched in the mid-1980s to attract vacationers to San Felipe. Thousands of lots were given away to gringos in a mail-order contest. The giveaway lots were worthless, waterless, arroyo-slashed, rattlesnake-infested land, but for an extra payment owners could trade them in on better lots close to the highway. Over the years, the "upgrade" subdivision evolved into a sizeable community of snowbirds in RVs and prefab cottages. With the present influx of retiring baby boomers from the U.S., the area has grown into a full-fledged suburb called El Dorado.

A wide dirt road that turns off the main highway at El Dorado heads east across pale, sandy ground studded with ocatillo and palo verde. Beyond the last signs of civilization, the road forks. Turn around here if your vehicle is not suitable for driving in sand. The left fork meanders south along the base of the mountains, passing through several small ranching villages before it dead-ends. Drivers of fat-tire trucks, Baja bugs, all-terrain vehicles and dirt bikes who take the right fork will soon find themselves crossing the **Laguna Diablo**, a long, narrow lakebed of dry sand. The lakebed is normally hardpacked, and a standard passenger car can cross it with no problem. But in relatively wet years, it can become the kind of place that even off-roaders must speed across for fear that if they slow down, they'll sink up to their axles in the drifting sand. Before taking this route, be sure you have a full day's supply of water. Before crossing sandy areas, get out and walk the road to see where the soft and hard parts are. And if you do get stuck, dig the sand away from the wheels, let half the air pressure out of each tire and don't slow down until you get back to the highway. You can pump your tires back to the correct pressure at the Pemex station in San Felipe.

After the road crosses the first segment of the Laguna Diablo, a two-track ranch road exits to the left and heads for the base of 10,154-foot **Picacho del Diablo**, the highest mountain on the Baja peninsula. I'm told it is possible to climb to the summit from a trailhead parking area, but gazing up at the sheer cliffs and steep, rocky canyons, it doesn't look possible. (Climbing the forested, less steep west side of the mountain from Parque Nacional San Pedro Martir is by far the easier way to reach the summit.) Most hikers content themselves with exploring the lush

HIDDEN ► hidden landscape of **Cañon del Diablo**, where year-round springs feed pools, waterfalls and streams, creating a long, hidden oasis whose flora ranges from *cardón* and barrel cactuses to cedars, oaks and willows. Past the turnoff to Cañon del Diablo, the road continues across the broader part of the Laguna Diablo and eventually meets Route 3 about 100 kilo meters north of San Felipe on the way to Ensenada.

A less risky side trip from San Felipe is down the narrow, paved coastal **road to Puertecitos**, 76 kilometers to the south. Though interrupted by *vados*—eight-foot-deep dips designed to control the course of flash floods after occasional mountain rainstorms—the road is recently paved and generally good until the final approach to Puertecitos, where its surface is the wreckage of past pavement. The route is easily passable by motor homes, passenger cars and trucks with boats in tow. Rarely out of sight of the sea, the route takes motorists through a landscape that is stark, pale, flat and arid. Besides the ocatillos and palo verdes of the San Felipe area, the vegetation includes occasional giant *cardón* cactuses. An unusual dwarf tree found along this route is the incense tree or *torote colorado*, whose twigs give off a distinctive perfume scent when burned like incense. The squat, pinkish tree's trunk is shaped like an elephant's foot, so some people call it a kind of elephant tree; however, it belongs to a completely separate genus from the white-barked elephant trees found in the Desierto Central and farther south.

> Laguna Diablo's lake bed is usually so hardpacked that smugglers have been known to use it as an airstrip.

The strange little village of **Puertecitos** is segregated into a Mexican barrio, where local fishermen and their families live in small, crude shacks, and a gringo enclave where snowbirds and expatriates hide out, as far beyond the reach of telephones, TV ads and the IRS as you can get towing a boat. You'll know this is no ordinary retirement community as soon as you enter the village, passing the Public Library and U.S. Post Office, twin edifices that appear to be remodeled outhouses, and the sign that reads "Sobriety Checkpoint Ahead." There is also a small store, a nameless restaurant and a Pemex station that is sometimes open. Don't count on there being gas, though; fill up before leaving San Felipe.

◄ HIDDEN

On a rocky beach near the point south of the village are **Puertecitos Hot Springs**, a cluster of sulfurous pools, each a different temperature. Bathers here quickly become so relaxed that they don't mind the mineral odor. Admission.

For most sightseers, including anybody in a rental car, Puertecitos is the end of the trip; return to San Felipe by the same route. If your vehicle has high clearance and four-wheel drive, the rough road that continues south from Puertecitos, known as the **Carretera Gonzaga**, offers an adventurous short cut to points south on the Baja Transpeninsular Highway. The Mexican government has been promising for years to pave this road. It's a notion that looks great on paper—an alternate route to Baja California Sur that would stimulate tourism on the gulf coast and relieve overcrowding at the Tijuana border crossings. But anyone who has driven the road from Puertecitos to Gonzaga knows that it is not likely to become a highway any time soon. Walk each questionable segment before attempting to drive it. In dry weather, most of the route is manageable in a passenger car whose driver has nerves of steel; but a series of steep, rocky grades beginning 27 kilometers south of Puertecitos and continuing for about 20 kilometers makes for a hair-raising trip. The roadbuilding effort so far has consisted of pouring bags of wet cement down the daunting slopes.

HIDDEN ▶

The Carretera skirts volcanic coastal mountains on its way to **Bahía San Luís Gonzaga**, as isolated a piece of paradise as you're likely to find in Baja. Long, soft sand beaches along the north part of the bay offer good swimming; fishing is best toward the south end of the bay with its mountainous coastline. Scattered vacation homes have sprung up along the water even in this remote place; their owners get there by boat, not by car.

From Alfonsina's, a beachfront restaurant and sometime gas station with basic rooms to rent near the north end of Bahía San Luís Gonzaga, the road veers inland, goes 60 kilometers across a plateau and joins The Baja Transpeninsular Highway in the middle of the Desierto Central, halfway between Cataviña and the turnoff to Bahía de los Angeles.

LODGING

The **Motel El Cortez,** on the beach about five blocks south of the statue at the center of the *malecón,* is ideally located for taking in all the local action. You know, the ATVs and monster trucks that cruise the waterfront from breakfast time to mid-evening. Its 81 clean, modern rooms and suites and 28 luxury beach bungalows have TV, air conditioning and a pleasantly all-American ambience. Facilities include an outdoor pool and a boat ramp. ~ Avenida Mar de Cortez; 686-577-1055, or 888-313-7409 in the U.S.; reservations: P.O. Box 1227, Calexico, CA 92232. MODERATE.

Rock-bottom lodging can be found at the **Motel El Pescador,** which caters mainly to Mexican workers. The 24 spartan guest rooms are clean and air-conditioned, with tired double beds, private toilets and not much else. Staying here costs about twice as much as camping. Though not on the beach, it's close to everything in town. ~ Avenida Mar de Cortez 101; 686-577-2648. BUDGET.

The 140 rooms in the centrally located two-story **Hotel Costa Azul** are clean and modern, with minimalist decor and such American motor inn–style conveniences as satellite TV, in-room phones and air conditioning. The location at the south end of the *malecón* is excellent, and the carefully tended landscaping creates an oasis against San Felipe's stark desert backdrop. There is a heated outdoor pool. ~ Avenida Mar de Cortez at Calle Ensenada; 686-577-1548, fax 686-568-3991. MODERATE.

The newest lodging in town, the Mediterranean-style **George's Motel** is blindingly pink inside and out. The 12 sparkling clean guest rooms have two double beds each, terracotta tile floors, arched doorways and nice new bathrooms with an abundance of toiletries. ~ Avenida Mar de Cortez 336; 686-577-1970. MODERATE.

New among the comparatively high-end beach hotels springing up around San Felipe is the **Capricho D'Marmol Baja Retreat**, a small, European-style resort shrouded in banana and palm trees that vividly contrast the stark desert shoreline. The guest accommodations are unusually spacious studio suites, decorated in cool blue and green hues in one of four themes that range from Polynesian tropical to ancient Inka. All have kitchenettes and ocean-view patios or balconies, and many have special features such as oversized baths or private waterfalls. ~ 2700 Misión San Fernando, Playa San Felipe; 686-577-1585; e-mail capricho@mind spring.com. MODERATE TO DELUXE.

The fanciest address in town is the **San Felipe Marina Resort**. The 60 luxury beachfront suites have sea-view balconies or patios and kitchenettes with microwaves. There are also a master suite and villas that can sleep up to eight; these rent in the ultra-deluxe range. Mexican handicrafts decorate the walls. Facilities include tennis courts, an exercise room, saunas and outdoor and indoor heated swimming pools. Despite the resort's name, the planned 100-slip yacht marina is still just a dream, though there are 140 "land yacht" slips with full hookups in the resort's deluxe RV park. ~ Carretera Aeropuerto Km. 4.5; 686-577-1455, fax 686-577-1566, or 800-291-5397 in the U.S.; e-mail snmarina@telnet.net. DELUXE.

> Puertecitos residents have elevated stealing U.S. road signs to an art form, and houses all over town are festooned with notices of nonexistent School X-ings, Mansion Districts, Bus Stops, Unauthorized Areas and Freeway Entrances.

Two blocks from the beach but—as the name suggests—with an ocean view from the rooftop party patio, the **Vista del Mar B&B** is a short walk to downtown. The two-story lodging has just five guest rooms, plus common facilities that include a swimming pool and spa, a barbecue pit and a shared living room and TV room. ~ Avenida Baltico 354; 686-577-1954. BUDGET.

DINING

Located at the end of the *malecón*, **Rosita Restaurant** specializes in fish, lobster and clams—like every other restaurant on the San Felipe waterfront. But it also serves steaks. There is a fine beachfront sea view. Open for breakfast, lunch and dinner. ~ North end of Malecón; 686-540-6218. MODERATE.

Just down the street, **Rice and Beans** is owned and operated by the brother of Rosita Restaurant's owner. Both men are engaged in an ongoing friendly competition over who's the best chef on the beach. The last time I visited, Ricardo at Rice and Beans seemed to have the title in the bag with his fantastic shrimp soup (or maybe it was the margaritas). Diners have a choice of shady indoor seating or an outdoor table with a front-row view of the action on the waterfront. ~ Malecón 262; 686-577-1770. MODERATE.

Larger indoor restaurants are found away from the ocean along the town's main street. **Cachanillas** serves assorted shrimp and fish dishes, *chiles rellenos* and other Mexican standards in a simple, air-conditioned atmosphere. (The same family also runs Cachanillas Taco Stand on the *malecón*.) ~ Avenida Mar de Cortez 146; 686-577-1039. MODERATE.

Practically next door, **Los Gemelos** is a cool, clean little restaurant with a varied menu of seafood and Mexican fare including *pollo en mole*—chicken in a delicious chile-and-chocolate sauce. Starting at 7 a.m., the breakfast menu offers a full range of American (bacon and eggs) and Mexican (*chilaquiles* and fruit plates) selections. ~ Avenida Mar de Cortez 136; 686-577-1063. MODERATE.

The **Restaurant China Ocean** serves exceptional Chinese stir-fries in a dimly lit Asian atmosphere. Not surprisingly, the best choices on the menu involve shrimp, scallops, squid and other local fruits of the sea. ~ Avenida Mar de Cortez 148; 686-577-1866. MODERATE.

George's Restaurant, adjacent to the motel of the same name, prides itself on great steaks, including filet mignon smothered in mushrooms. It also offers a standard selection of Mexican fare and seafood, as well as a "surf-'n-turf" steak and shrimp combo, and a long menu of American and Mexican breakfasts including huevos rancheros, *machaca* (shredded beef) with eggs and vegetables, and shrimp omelets. ~ Avenida Mar de Cortez 336; 686-577-1057. MODERATE.

The **Lighthouse**, a picturesque, atmospheric restaurant set alongside the actual lighthouse on the hill south of the Malecón,

SEAFOOD AND SEA VIEWS

San Felipe is a great place to enjoy seafood on the cheap. The *malecón*, the three-block beachfront promenade in the center of town, is lined with small open-air restaurants called *comedores*—**Mariscos Norma's, Tacos y Cockteles Blanca**, and a dozen or so others—that serve fish tacos, shrimp cocktails, steamed clams, seven-seafood chowder and whole fried fish. The decor at these simple eateries is limited to picnic tables or plastic chairs and tables with checkered tablecloths; whatever they may lack in ambience, they recoup with sea views. ~ Malecón. BUDGET.

serves chile cheese omelettes for breakfast with a view. Dinner entrées range from cheeseburgers and enchiladas to beef steaks and local seafood. ~ Calle El Faro; 686-577-2540. MODERATE.

The dining room at **San Felipe Marina Resort**, the undisputed best in town, features local seafood dishes such as shrimp in cilantro sauce and corvina in garlic sauce. The dining room with its three-story lofted cedar ceiling commands a panoramic view of the Sea of Cortez. ~ Carretera Aeropuerto Km. 4.5; 686-577-1455. MODERATE.

Like many Baja towns, San Felipe has no public produce market. **GROCERIES** Though the rich farming valley of Mexicali is just two hours away, the fresh fruits and vegetables to be found in San Felipe are usually disappointing. Look for them, along with assorted packaged foods and canned goods, at the main supermarket, **Abarrotes La Vaquita Dos**, at the north end of the Malecón. ~ Puerto Peñasco 292; 686-577-1710. You can get catch-of-the-day fish and other fresh seafood for a cookout at **Mariscos La Chona**, a fish market located in a residential neighborhood just north of Calzada Chetumal. ~ Avenido Puerto de Guaymas 200; 686-577-1019. **Panedería Especial** is one of several family-run bakeries in town that sell delicious fresh-baked bread and pastries at very low prices. ~ Avenida Mar Caribe; 686-577-2948.

Avenida Mar de Cortez, San Felipe's main commercial street, is **SHOPPING** lined with souvenir shops. The main stock in trade is T-shirts, bathing suits, sun hats, dark glasses and other assorted beach paraphernalia. Determined shoppers will find better-than-average selections of Mexican arts and crafts at **Curios Mitla** (Avenida Mar de Cortez 100; 686-577-1132) and **Curios Roberta** (Avenida Mar de Cortez 222; 686-577-1066). For local arts and crafts, many of them for sale on consignment, there's **The People's Gallery** (Avenida Mar de Cortez Sur 148; 686-577-2898). You can find Cuban cigars at **Smoke Signals**, just north of Rockodile on the *malecón*.

San Felipe is not a place to go for glamorous nightlife. The after- **NIGHTLIFE** dark scene is dominated by **Rockodile**—a big, youth-oriented club, built around a volleyball court, that strives for a spring break atmosphere all year. The sound system blares rock and disco and the beer flows freely until the wee hours. ~ Malecón 199; 686-577-1453. The next-best bet is the mellower **San Felipe Beachcomber**, under the same management as Rockodile and located just down the street, it's a huge two-story club with three separate bar and dance areas, featuring laser lightshows and Thursday night karaoke. ~ Calzada Chetumal at Malecón; 686-577-1044.

Centrally located under a big blue Cerveza Corona sign, the **Bar Miramar** has been a fixture on the Malecón for more than 15 years. Much smaller than the other party places in town, the bar and beer garden are packed on weekends. ~ Avenida Mar de Cortez; 686-577-1192.

The best-hidden bar in town, **Al's Backstreet Cantina** is a Margaritaville kind of joint decorated in tropical clutter with pool tables, dart boards, sports TV and music and dancing nightly. It's located behind the *malecón*'s Bancomer on an alley that's one-way going the wrong way; park on Avenida Mar de Cortez and walk. ~ No phone.

BEACHES & PARKS

PLAYA LAS ALMEJAS 🏊 🚣 ⛵ 🛶 ⛵ "Las almejas," Spanish for "the clams," refers to the good clamdigging on Playa Las Alemeja's vast, wet sand flats that form at low tide as the surf recedes by half a mile or more. This eight-mile-long beach north of San Felipe is lined with campgrounds and private-lot developments, which are separated from the beach by steep sand banks in many places. More people seem to choose this beach than anyplace else in the San Felipe area to blast around on ATVs. ~ The beach runs from Playa Blanca, eight kilometers north of San Felipe, to Campo Los Amigos, 22 kilometers north of town. Any road that does not have a guarded gate or a "members only" sign can provide beach access, though campgrounds may charge you a small day use fee.

▲ A number of large private campgrounds may be found along this beach. Though their main trade is RV travelers, tent campers are welcome at all of them, and after paying the site fee you can leave your car at the campground and pitch your tent right on the beach. Centrally located on the beach, **Pete's El Paraiso Camp** is the largest and has the most amenities, including a restaurant, bar, laundry room and exercise room; $10 per night. ~ Route 5, 13 kilometers north of San Felipe; reservations: 909-676-4224, fax 909-699-6673; www.petescamp.com, e-mail rafael@petescamp.com. Facilities are more limited at **Campo Los Compadres** at the north end of the beach, but they do include hot showers for a small extra charge; $10 per night. ~ Off Route 5, 12 kilometers north of San Felipe.

PLAYA SAN FELIPE 🏊 🚣 ⛵ 🛶 ⛵ ⛵ This beach starts at the hill where the Virgin of Guadalupe Shrine stands at the north end of town and curves around the Bahía de San Felipe, in an arc broken only by the marina, to Punta Estrella at the south end of the bay. The "downtown" part of the beach, along the *malecón*, is young and lively on winter weekends and frenetic during spring break. Toward the south end of town, the same beach is enjoyed by resort hotel guests. Still farther south, lot developments line the quieter part of the beach; free access is easy through any of several

HIDDEN ▶

defunct developments that have vanished over the years, leaving landscaped but unpaved boulevards in the sand beyond the ruins of ostentatious entrance gates. ~ Access is from the *malecón* in San Felipe and points south along the road to Puertecitos.

▲ San Felipe has more than a dozen private campgrounds, almost all of them on the beach. Most welcome tenters, though several have only sites with concrete pads—best for motor homes but bad for backpackers' backs. One of the most luxurious is **San Felipe Marina Resort and RV Park**, a 143-site campground with full hookups (including cable TV), a restaurant, a swimming pool and a laundry room; sites are $25 to $35 per night, depending on the season. ~ Carretera Aeropuerto Km. 4.5; 686-577-1455, fax 686-577-1566, or 800-291-5397 in the U.S. San Felipe's most se-cluded in-town campground is **Campo Numero Uno**. On a small cove just north of town, it is separated from the main beach by the cliffs below the Virgin of Guadalupe Shrine. There are rest-rooms, palapa shelters and not much else at this campground, which is popular with Mexican families. There is a small beach and a gravelly tidal flat where locals gather mussels. Tent and RV sites are $10 to $12 per night. ~ Avenida Mar de Cortes.

NORTH OF PUERTECITOS 🏃 🏊 🎣 A nameless, almost unbro-ken 24-mile strand of beach extends from the village of Bahía Santa Maria south almost to Puertecitos. Intermittent beachfront campgrounds and lot developments dot the northern part of the beach. It becomes wilder and harder to reach by road the farther south you go. ~ The north end of the beach is 40 kilometers south of San Felipe on the road to Puertecitos.

▲ There are at least 15 beach campgrounds along the road from San Felipe to Puertecitos. Most are primitive, lacking the niceties of some of the motor-home camps around San Felipe but ideal for tenters and tailgaters who want to be far away from tourist crowds. **Campo Jacaranda** is among the most basic and affordable—in fact, camping here is free. There are no hookups or other amenities, except outhouses. ~ Located 85 kilometers south of San Felipe; no phone. **Octavio's Campo Playa Escondido**

AUTHOR FAVORITE

Although I'd never tried clamdigging before, I found that the per-fect place to practice is **Playa Las Almejas**, north of San Felipe, where the water recedes half a mile when the tide goes out, and locals and visi-tors armed with shovels and buckets head out across the wet sand. (Just don't get caught out there when the tide comes back in; it's a long way to dashwade—back to shore.) See page 140 for more information.

may have the nicest location along this stark stretch of coastline, sharing a pretty, sandy cove with a local fish camp where the fishermen will often take campers out in their *pangas* for a small fee. Sites cost $5 per night, and there are outhouses and cold showers. ~ Located 88 kilometers south of San Felipe.

SOUTH OF PUERTECITOS 🏃 🏊 🎣 There are several beautiful beaches along the rugged four-wheel-drive road that continues south from Puertecitos. Playa La Costilla, 10 kilometers south of the village, is calm and ideal for swimming, with an offshore reef that makes for good snorkeling. Playa Bufeo, 63 kilometers south of Puertecitos, is a wide, sugar-white beach renowned for great surf fishing. Seven miles farther down the road, Playa El Faro also offers excellent swimming and fishing; it is one of the most remote beaches in Baja, and you'll probably have it all to yourself.

▲ There are no established campgrounds south of Puertecitos, but primitive camping is permitted on all beaches.

San Quintín Area

The San Quintín Valley doesn't look much like the land of big cactuses and stark, jagged mountains that the word *Baja* conjures in many travelers' minds. For most of the 196-kilometer trip south from Ensenada, the highway runs through orchards and crop fields on a broad, flat plain inland from the coast. As you drive among vineyards, olive orchards and tomato fields, pause to consider the miracle.

Land reform and irrigation have transformed this region from a landscape so arid that all pre-20th-century attempts to settle it met with failure. Faint outlines of old adobe walls are all that remain of the early missions that first introduced agricultural crops to the area. A cemetery filled with English names and a ruined pier are the only evidence of grandiose gringo land development schemes in the 19th century.

Today, resorts are few and most of the Pacific coast remains wild and windswept. To see the ocean, take your chances on any of the numerous farm roads that turn off to the west from the main highway.

SIGHTS   Kilometer markers on the highway to San Quintín tell how far south of Ensenada you are. The town of Santo Tomás, 51 kilometers south of Ensenada, is the site of the **Misión Santo Tomás de Aquino**, founded by Dominican priests in 1791. Some of the grapes grown in the valley today, and used in making Ensenada's Bodegas de Santo Tomás varietal wines, are descendants of the Dominican vineyards. Only fragments of melted adobe walls remain of the former mission church, located on the east side of the highway. Santo Tomás wines are for sale in the store adjoining the town's only restaurant, as well as in tasting rooms in Ensenada, Rosarito and Tijuana.

The ruins of **Misión San Vicente Ferrer**, located 88 kilometers south of Ensenada near the present-day town of San Vicente, date back to 1781, when the Dominicans built it as the headquarters for their northern missions. The sad remains of old adobe walls are all that remain of the fortresslike church. The ruins are half a mile west of Route 1 on an ungraded dirt road.

At kilometer 169 you'll come to an unpaved road to the left (east) that leads eight miles to the village of Santo Domingo, site of the ruins of **Misión Santo Domingo**. One of the first missions in northern Baja, it was established by Dominican priests in 1775 and operated for 64 years. Though deteriorated beyond recognition, the church's three-foot-thick adobe walls are still visible after two centuries. The ruins are located in a pasture just west of the village school.

San Quintín and its adjacent southern "suburb," Lázaro Cárdenas, form a community of more than 30,000 at the southern end of Baja's Pacific agricultural plain. San Quintín dates back to 1884, when Mexican President Porfirio Díaz granted vast land concessions covering most of Baja California Norte to a New York–based corporation with plans to sell the land to expatriate U.S. wheat farmers and make flour for export. The company built a flour mill and port facility along the shore of San Quintín's sheltered estuary, but the few pioneers who bought farms in the area retreated northward as drought destroyed their crops year after year. The next time a wet year came along, the New York company seized the opportunity to sell San Quintín—land, town, port and mill—to a British investment group, which brought settlers from England and built a larger mill, shipping docks and a customs house. They even started construction of a railroad line to San Diego. But the wheat farmers fared no better than their predecessors. Drought returned, and the last of the colonists left San Quintín by 1900.

Remnants of the failed enterprise can still be seen. A wide gravel road to the right (west) one kilometer south of Lázaro Cárdenas leads to **Puerto San Quintín** on the grassy shores of the sheltered estuary. The old grist mill has been extensively restored

PACIFIC PRESENCE

Ejido Uruapan, an ordinary-looking farm community near kilometer 41, exemplifies the growing presence in Baja of other Pacific Rim powers. The village of 1000 people has a factory that processes sea urchins for export to Japan, where they are used to make sushi. A Japanese company built the plant and runs it under a cooperative agreement with the *ejido*. The strawberry greenhouses are also a Japanese joint venture.

Sierra San Pedro Mártir

Got time for an all-day side trip? Here's an easy expedition to one of the most unexpected places in hidden Baja—the Sierra San Pedro Mártir.

PICACHO DEL DIABLO   The sierra are the highest on the Baja Peninsula thanks to a single massive, white granite crag: 10,498-foot Picacho del Diablo, the "Devil's Peak," looms at the extreme eastern edge of the sierra. Although it seems to drop straight down on the east side for 9000 feet to the floor of the Desierto de San Felipe, the road up the west side is a beautifully scenic drive up long, gentle grades. As you go south on Route 1, watch for the side road on the left (east) just after kilometer 140 and just before crossing the bridge over the little Río San Telmo. A sign says "San Telmo/Observatorio." This is one of the widest, smoothest unpaved roads in Baja. It's a 200-kilometer roundtrip from the highway, so it might be wise to gas up at the Pemex in Colonet first.

RANCHO SAN JOSÉ   The road takes you through a progression of contrasting landscapes as it makes its way into the high country. Soon after you pass through **San Telmo**, a tiny hillside village comprising half a dozen farmers' houses and a white concrete chapel with a lawn where cows graze, fields of hay and wheat give way to juniper, piñon and oak. An hour's drive will take you past a turnoff on the left for a very rough four-wheel-drive road that goes 26 kilometers north to **Mike's Sky Rancho** (page 116), a legendary bed and breakfast for bikers. Immediately after this, another road turns off on the right and plunges down a long hill to Rancho San José, also called Meling Ranch, a 10,000-acre working cattle spread that doubles as a guest ranch. Visitors are welcome, though no gas or food is for sale there.

PARQUE NACIONAL SIERRA SAN PEDRO MÁRTIR   At higher elevations, where the ground is covered with snow (and the road is often closed) in winter, tall pine and fir trees grow, with scattered groves of

and is now the site of the Old Mill Restaurant. The British shipping pier is about a mile down the coast, behind the Muelle Viejo Motel, and still farther along is a graveyard known as the Old English Cemetery, although today few English names are to be found on the headstones and wooden crosses there. Irrigation has transformed the arid fields that defeated American and British farmers into some of the richest vegetable farmland in Baja. Once again, the Valle de San Quintín is occupied by newcomers from a distant land—this time Mixtec Indians from the poor aspen and a few San Pedro Mártir cypress, a rare species that grows only in these mountains. More than 170,000 acres of tall, cool forests and wildflower meadows have been set aside as Parque Nacional Sierra San Pedro Mártir, a vast wilderness that is virtually roadless except for this route. One of Mexico's least-known national parks, it receives only an estimated 300 carloads of visitors per year!

OBSERVATORIO NACIONAL DE MEXICO   After crossing the cattle guard that marks the park entrance, the road winds its way up to the Observatorio Nacional de Mexico, set on a ridgeline at 9300 feet above sea level. The observatory is only open on Saturdays from 11 a.m. to 1 p.m., at which time guided tours in Spanish are offered to any sightseers who may show up. Not many do. The rest of the week, the gate two kilometers below the observatory is locked, but hikers can park and walk up to two nearby overlooks for spectacular views of Picacho del Diablo and Cañon del Diablo.

VALLECITOS   From Vallecitos, a parklike meadow six kilometers before the locked gate, the three-story, domed white observatory due north on the ridgeline makes a reliable landmark while you're exploring the forest of sugar pine, lodgepole pine and white fir that surrounds the meadow. Were it not for the profusion of jays and songbirds, Vallecitos would be absolutely silent—on weekdays, at least.

MISIÓN SAN PEDRO MÁRTIR   The mountain range and the park were named for the Misión San Pedro Mártir, established in 1794 about 18 miles—as the crow flies; more like 30 miles by hiking trail—south of the present-day observatory, in a part of the mountains that remains all but inaccessible to this day. The mission proved to be a hopeless folly for the Dominican priests who came to Christianize the indigenous people of Baja. Even though more Indians lived in these cool, wet, forested mountains teeming with wildlife than in any other part of the peninsula, it was so hard to bring in supplies from either coast that the mission was shut down after only 12 years. Today, you have to be an amateur archaeologist to spot the melted adobe ruins, which have fared worse than most others because of the higher rainfall.

state of Oaxaca in southeastern Mexico. They struggle as stoop laborers to support families on Mexican minimum wage in the agri-industrial farmlands that fill the valley today.

The **Old Mill Motel** offers 34 units, including simply furnished sleeping rooms, studios with kitchenettes and two-bedroom suites with fireplaces. The bayside location is exceptional for birdwatching and fishing. The restaurant here serves the best food between Ensenada and San Quintín; it also has the most popular gringo

LODGING

fishermen's bar on this part of the coast. Rowdiness can last late into the night, and fishermen get up early in the morning, so ask for a unit as far away from the restaurant and bar as possible. No phones. ~ Puerto San Quintín Road, about 8 kilometers south of San Quintín. Reservations: 619-428-2779. BUDGET TO MODERATE.

Right next to the Old Mill, the new **Don Eddie's Landing** has 20 clean, simple rooms and a clientele that seems to consist almost entirely of sportfishermen. Room-and-fishing packages are available. ~ Puerto San Quintín Road, 8 kilometers south of San Quintín; 646-162-2722; www.doneddies.com. MODERATE.

Rancho Sereno Bed & Breakfast has just three guest units on the shady, wooded grounds adjacent to the headquarters of a working ranch. Each unit is individually decorated, and the largest has a king-sized bed and a fireplace. There is electricity for limited hours, no air conditioning, TV or phones. Reservations are essential. ~ Located 2.5 kilometers west of Route 1 south of San Quintín; 909-982-7087 in the U.S. MODERATE.

Adobe bricks, if not regularly coated with fresh layers of mud stucco, dissolve from rain over time.

The **Hotel La Pinta**, at the north end of Playa Santa María, would be a fairly conventional budget motel in many parts of America except for its location. Most of the sprawling one-story complex's 60 rooms look out on Bahía San Quintín, and it's the only hotel in sight on the gentle, grassy shoreline. Most guests come here for the fishing, which is said to be exceptional. No phones or air conditioning. ~ Route 1, Km. 16 south of San Quintín; Reservations: 800-800-9632 in the U.S. MODERATE.

Meling Ranch (Rancho San José) is a guest facility and working cattle ranch high in the Sierra San Pedro Mártir, near the park boundary. The ranch has a spectacular hill country setting and a remarkable history. It was founded in 1899 by Harry and Ella Johnson, who bought a franchise from the Mexican government giving them dominion over a vast expanse of the sierra. It succeeded where other Baja ventures of that era because Johnson discovered a deposit of gold on his land and made a quarter of a million dollars from his mine before 1911, when the ranch was destroyed and Johnson's family was slaughtered while he was on a business trip to the United States. His only surviving daughter, Alberta, married Norwegian expatriate Salve Meling, who rebuilt the ranch in the 1920s. The Melings acquired a reputation for hosting travelers in the Sierra San Pedro Mártir, and their ranch became a popular celebrity retreat in the 1950s. The late Alberta Meling was the first woman to drive the newly paved Baja Highway in 1973, arriving in Cabo San Lucas on her 90th birthday. Recently reopened after being closed a year for refurbishing, the guest ranch is now operated by the fourth-generation of the Meling family to live here. The ranch's ten guest rooms are rustic. Deer hunters in autumn are the primary clientele; spring and summer adventurers wishing to explore the 10,000-acre ranch and the wilderness of the Sierra San Pedro Mártir are more than welcome. The ranch has no phones but does have an airstrip for fly-in guests and a swimming pool. ~ Reservations: 858-454-7166 in the U.S.; e-mail info@melingguestranch.com. MODERATE.

The ranch's ten guest rooms are rustic. Deer hunters in autumn are the primary clientele; spring and summer adventurers wishing to explore the 10,000-acre ranch and the wilderness of the Sierra San Pedro Mártir are more than welcome. The ranch has no phones but does have an airstrip for fly-in guests and a swimming pool. ~ U.S. reservations: Rancho Meling, P.O. Box 189003, Coronado, CA 92178-9003; 646-177-5897; e-mail meling-ranch@ensenada.net.mx. MODERATE.

DINING

◀ HIDDEN

The **Old Mill Restaurant** is one of the Baja Highway's pleasurable surprises. Set on the grassy shore of Bahía San Quintín, it stands on the site of an old flour mill built by an anglo land development company as part of an overly optimistic plan to transform the sunbaked coastal plain into the breadbasket of the Californias. The original mill has been expanded by disassembling a former fish cannery, shipping it from northern California and rebuilding it plank by plank. The house specialty is lobster. In season (October to March), dozens of them crawl, huddle and clack their claws in a large aquarium tank in the front room, unwittingly waiting to be boiled at your pleasure. The restaurant doesn't import lobsters off-season, though. You can always also order fish, though. A guitarist sings ballads from the dinner hour on, the sunset view is exquisite, and gringo fishermen swap yarns up and down the restaurant's central bar late into the evening. ~ Puerto San Quintín Road, south of San Quintín. MODERATE.

The restaurant at **Don Eddie's Landing** features steamed lobster, steamed clams, steamed oysters and steamed crabs; but the real specialty of the house is cooking up the fish you catch yourself on fishing expeditions guided by Don Eddie and his crew. ~ Puerto San Quintín Road, next to the Old Mill; 646-162-2722. MODERATE.

The commercial strip of San Quintín and Ejido Lázaro Cárdenas runs along both sides of the highway for ten kilometers. The restaurants and *comedores* along this busy stretch of road cater more to truck drivers than to gringo tourists. They serve spicy Mexican food and seafood at low prices. A cut above average, **El Alteño** serves plentiful food in a simply furnished concrete block building, with live music while you eat. It is located near the town movie theater. Closed in summer. ~ Route 1, Km. 189. BUDGET.

Another hole-in-the-wall eatery worth looking into, **La Bota** serves American-style steaks and baked potatoes to a mainly Mexican clientele. It is located near the Pemex station at the south end of town. ~ Route 1, Km. 189. BUDGET.

Jardines Restaurant and Bar, a new place off the highway south of San Quintín, features a Mexican-style steak and seafood menu and a pleasant indoor-outdoor garden setting. Closed Monday. ~ One block past the Old Mill turnoff; no phone. MODERATE.

GROCERIES Very basic provisions are available at dozens of tiny, family-run grocery stores along the highway in San Quintín and Lázaro Cárdenas. You can get cornmeal, wheat flour, canned goods, Coca-Cola and candy; don't expect much else. Vegetable sellers wander up and down the long commercial strip with boxes of tomatoes and whatever other fruits or vegetables are currently being harvested in the valley.

BEACHES & PARKS

PLAYA MALIBU SUR 🏃 🛶 Travelers looking for a secluded hideaway near the route south from Ensenada may want to consider this remote stretch of shoreline where stone shelves pocked with tidepools flank fragments of sandy beach. The 25-kilometer unpaved road from the main highway to the shoreline can be washboarded and sandswept enough to keep the tourist traffic away. The road runs through tomato rows and vast fields of *nopales*, a cactus that is dethorned, peeled, sliced in strips and marinated to make a vegetable dish called nopalitos. Other than the campground restrooms, there are no facilities on this road.

▲ Despite the enticing name, the ejido-run Malibu Sur campground is pretty basic. The 14 spaces have full hookups (but don't drink the water or fill your RV's water tank with it; the electrical generator only runs during the evening hours). The plumbing in the restrooms and laundry room sometimes works. The managers live in a trailer on the premises. Sites are $10 per night. ~ Turn west off the main highway 28 kilometers south of the small town of Santo Tomás and follow the main dirt road. The beach and campground are at the end of the road; no phone.

PARQUE NACIONAL SIERRA SAN PEDRO MÁRTIR 🏃 🚲 🐎 Picacho del Diablo, the highest mountain peak in Baja, presides over the vast, pine-clad sierra. The climate is alpine and cool. The wildlife is abundant. The only access for passenger cars is the unpaved road that runs from Route 1 to the park entrance, a distance of 79 kilometers, and continues through the national park to the Mexican National Observatory. ~ Carretera San Telmo-Observatorio.

▲ There is a small, primitive campground within the national park. Facilities are minimal and the setting is beautiful, but nights are cold. Camping is free.

PLAYA SAN RAMÓN 🏃 🏄 ⚓ This popular surfers' beach spans 12 miles of the Pacific coast west of San Quintín. It is wide and fringed with sand dunes, and the flats at low tide are a good place to dig for Pismo clams. People fish from the shore near the rocky point at the southern end of the beach. ~ Turn west off Route 1 two kilometers south of Colonia Vicente Guerrero and continue on the unpaved road for four miles to the dunes; walk to the beach from there.

> Some homes in San Quintín are constructed of volcanic rock quarried from the 12 dormant volcanoes that encircle Bahía San Quintín.

▲ There are no camping areas right on the beach—the soft sand makes vehicle travel treacherous. On the road to the beach, **Don Pepe RV Park** has 50 campsites with concrete pads and full hookups, as well as a tent area. The restrooms have hot showers. Fees are $4 for tents, $8 for motor homes. ~ Colonia Vicente Guerrero; 646-176-2216. Nearby on the same road, the larger **Posada Don Diego RV Park** has similar facilities plus a volleyball court. The 100-site campground caters to caravans and seems deserted when they leave. Sites cost $11 per night. ~ Colonia Vicente Guerrero; 646-166-2181, fax 646-166-2248.

PUERTO SAN QUINTÍN 🏃 ⚓ There's no beach on the inner bay, which was once the port for American and British wheat-farming colonies, but the grassy banks are fine for strolling and fishing. ~ Turn west off the main highway four kilometers south of the Army base at Lázaro Cárdenas and follow the unpaved road for six kilometers to the shore.

▲ You can camp near the shore of Bahía San Quintín at the **Old Mill RV Park**, an attractively landscaped park that has 30 tent and RV campsites and a clean, central bathhouse. Fees are $10 per night for tents (no hookups) and $16.50 for RVs (full hookups). There are restrooms with showers. ~ Puerto San Quintín Road; no phone.

PLAYA DE OESTE MEDANO 🏃 🏃 ⚓ This long, lonely strand runs along the Pacific side of the narrow spit of land protecting Bahía Falsa and Bahía Quintín. There are two popular surfing areas: the north end offers a long, rolling break, while the southern tip, known as Cabo San Quintín, has a wicked point break. Surfers usually have the place to themselves; wind and heavy surf discourage sunbathers and casual swimmers. ~ Follow the unpaved road west from Lázaro Cárdenas to the shore, a distance of about 12 kilometers, and then continue south along the beach. Beware of sand traps.

▲ There are no facilities for campers. Nobody is likely to stop you if you want to pitch a tent, but if you spend the night out here, alone with the banshee wind and smashing waves, you'll know why the early settlers chose a more sheltered location on the other side of the bay.

PLAYA SANTA MARÍA 🏃 ⛵ 🏄 🛶 🛶 Another surfers' secret, this wide white beach stretches for miles along the coastline of the Bahía Santa María. While the northern part of the beach is best for surfing, the whole bayshore is a good place to fish the surf for corbina or dig for large Pismo clams. Toward the south, Playa Santa María blends seamlessly into Playa Pabellón—the distinction between the two beaches seems to depend on which road you take to get there—forming a continuous ten-mile strand that ranks as one of the most beautiful Pacific beaches in Baja. ~ Thirteen kilometers south of the bridge that separates San Quintín and Lázaro Cárdenas, turn off Route 1 at the sign for La Pinta Hotel. Go past the hotel and the end of the pavement, six kilometers to the beach.

▲ There is a decrepit excuse for a campground at the **Cielito Lindo Motel and RV Park**, located where the road stops at the north end of the beach. There are no hookups or designated campsites, and the restrooms leave much to be desired; this discourages the RV crowd and suits surfers just fine. Sites cost $5 per night for tents and $8 for RVs. ~ Turn west off the highway 12 miles kilometers of San Quintin at the La Pinta Hotel sign and drive seven kilometers to the end of the dirt road. No phone.

PLAYA PABELLÓN 🏃 ⛵ 🛶 Backed by low sand dunes, this lonely beach continues south along the shore of Bahía Santa María. Fishermen beach their *pangas* here between dawn and dusk forays out onto the bay. The water is good for swimming in the summer and fall, and there's interesting beachcombing all year. Huge clamshells lie strewn in the sand, along with occasional pieces of driftwood, packaging debris printed in Japanese, and other mysterious objects that have floated across the Pacific on ocean currents.

▲ A large sign at the entrance to **El Pabellón RV Park** warns, "No Racing Motor Cycle or etc. in Camp Ground"— that's how flat and open this sandy park at the dunes' edge is. The local *ejido* that owns it has planted rows of casuarina trees to protect campers from the constant winds of winter and spring. The entrance road is landscaped with bright flowering bushes, and there is a central restroom with hot showers and flush toilets. Other than that, you're on your own; there are no hookups or clearly defined campsites. Fees are just $5 per night. ~ Watch for the sign and turn right off Route 1, 28 kilometers south of San Quintín. The campground is about two kilometers off the main road.

ENSENADA The waters around Ensenada are famed for California yellowtail. Other game fish include white sea bass, albacore, bonito and barracuda. Fishing charter offices are located near the fish market, and you can save money by joining a group charter with any of several outfitters, such as **Gordo's Sport Fishing** (Paseo Costero at Avenida Gastelum; 646-178-3515) and **Sergio's Sportfishing Center** (Paseo Costero at Avenida Gastelum; 646-178-2185 or 800-336-5454).

FISHING

SAN FELIPE Barracuda, rockfish and yellowtail are among the fish commonly found in San Felipe waters. Bonefish also run here in the summer months. For charters, contact **Alex Sport Fishing**. ~ Malecón 241; 686-577-1442. The sand flats at low tide offer excellent clamming.

SAN QUINTÍN Tuna is the catch of choice along this part of the coast. When you arrive, arrange a charter for the next day. Boat charters can be arranged at the fishing supply store at the **Old Mill Motel and RV Park**. ~ Puerto San Quintín, no phone. **Don Eddie's Landing** also operates sportfishing charters. ~ Puerto San Quintín Road, 8 kilometers south of San Quintín; 646-162-2722; www.doneddies.com.

ENSENADA Scuba diving adventures off the rocky coast of Bahía Bufadora can be arranged at **Dale's La Bufadora Dive Shop**. ~ La Bufadora turnoff from the Transpeninsular Highway; 646-154-2092.

DIVING

ENSENADA The beaches around **Rosarito** have been attracting hordes of surfers since the Beach Boys were kids. But the pros say the greatest surfing in the Ensenada area is to be found at **Islas de Todos Santos**, a pair of islands six and a half miles offshore at the mouth of Bahía de Todos Santos. Waves here can reach a height of 30 feet. The beach on the ocean side of the south island catches the waves in a long, rolling break that is a surfer's dream, and the accelerated swells that speed through the narrow passage between the south and north islands are a super-

SURFING & WINDSURFING

◆◆◆◆ ◆◆◆◆◆◆◆◆◆◆◆◆◆◆◆◆◆◆◆◆◆◆◆◆◆◆◆◆◆◆◆◆◆◆◆◆◆◆

AUTHOR FAVORITE

I often have to vie with the bevy of surfers at **Playa Santa María** in San Quintín for the best waves, but there are certainly worse things in life. Great surfing, warm white sand and cool Pacific breezes highlight why this beachfront strip is one of Baja's most beautiful stretches of shoreline.

thrill. You'll find current surf information and boards for sale (but not for rent) at **Tony's Surf Shop**. ~ Boulevard Juárez 312; 646-172-1192.

SAN QUINTÍN Those who have discovered the well-hidden beach at the north end of **Playa de Oeste Medano** in San Quintín call it one of the best surfing spots on the Pacific coast. If you don't have a dune buggy, you'll have to carry your board for about a mile, skirting a dormant volcano cone, to get there.

SAILING & PARA-SAILING

SAN FELIPE Parasailing can be arranged through **Rainbow Aquatic Sports**, which also rents Yamaha Wave Runners—sort of like motorcycles that run on water—and offers discounts to senior citizens. ~ Malecón Sur 142; 686-577-1940.

KAYAKING

ENSENADA The **Islas de Todos Santos**, at the mouth of the Bahía de Todos Santos, are a six-and-a-half-mile paddle from Punta Bandas. Visitors to the islands will find soaring cliffs and sun-soaked beaches, harbor seals sea lions and abundant bird life. Kayak trips to the area, including transportation and kayaks, can be arranged through **Southwest Sea Kayak** in San Diego. ~ 619-222-3616 in the U.S.

SAN FELIPE Kayakers head for the remote **Bahía de San Luís Gonzaga**, about 70 kilometers south of Puertecitos on a rugged four-wheel-drive road. The bay makes a good jumping-off point for exploration of the **Islas Encantadas**, six small islands with seabird rookeries at the mouth of the bay. One of Baja's more ambitious kayak challenges is the 75-mile trip along the rugged, deserted coast from Bahía de San Luís Gonzaga south to Bahía de los Angeles. Rental kayaks are hard to find in the San Felipe/Puertecitos area; most adventurers bring their own.

WHALE WATCHING

ENSENADA During winter, whale-watching excursions to the Islas de Todos Santos can be arranged through the **Caracol Museo de Ciencias**. ~ Avenida Obregón 1463; 646-178-7192.

TENNIS

ENSENADA A number of resorts in the Rosarito and Ensenada area have tennis courts for guest use, but only the **Baja Beach and Tennis Club** is open to the general public. Court fees are expensive. ~ Isla San Benito 123, south of Ensenada; 646-176-2113.

GOLF

ENSENADA The only game in town—or anywhere in the region—is the 18-hole course at the **Hacienda Don Juan Resort**. Club and cart rentals are available. ~ Playa Faro; 646-177-4094.

OFF-ROADING

SAN FELIPE Riding all-terrain vehicles (ATVs)—those big-tired little vehicles like four-wheeled motorcycles—on beaches, desert roads and the main street of town is a favorite San Felipe sport.

Even though it's called "off-roading," you'll want to stay *on* the roads in the Baja backcountry, which can be as hazardous as it is fragile. You can rent an all-terrain vehicle at **Tito's ATV Rentals**. ~ Next to the tourist office on Avenida Mar de Cortez.

San Diego–based **Trail Boss Tours** organizes three-day group motorcycle trips to Mike's Sky Ranch, the legendary bikers' getaway high in the Sierra San Pedro Mártir. ~ 760-598-2930 or 888-228-6878 in the U.S.; www.trailbosstours.com, e-mail trailbos@ trailbosstours.com.

ENSENADA   Riding horses on the beach is a popular activity in Rosarito. Every day, cowboys bring strings of rental horses to the beach to wait for customers, especially in the area of the Rosarito Beach Hotel.

RIDING STABLES

SAN FELIPE   The ultimate hike in the area is an ascent of the east face of 10,154-foot **Picacho del Diablo**, Baja's highest peak. The 11-mile trail goes along the floor of **Cañon del Diablo** most of the way, through vegetation that changes gradually from desert to the lushness of a tropical oasis as it passes waterfalls and bathing pools. The last part, beyond the backpackers' campground at the upper end of the canyon, is a steep, challenging Class 2-5 climb, gaining 4000 feet in less than two miles. The roundtrip takes four days. Shorter treks into Cañon del Diablo are also rewarding.

HIKING

SAN QUINTÍN   The **Parque Nacional Sierra San Pedro Mártir** offers some of the finest hiking on the Baja peninsula. A trail up the gentler western slope of Picacho del Diablo to the summit starts from the end of a two-track road that branches off the main park road at Vallecitos and continues southeast for about eight miles. The ten-mile roundtrip can be completed in a (long) day. Another trail that starts near the astronomers' residences below the Mexican National Observatory gate leads to a stand of shimmering aspen trees and a viewpoint overlooking Cañon del Diablo. It's a four-mile round trip to the overlook. For a longer trek, a right fork in the trail at the aspen grove continues to the rim of Cañon del Diablo.

ENSENADA   Ensenada has no regularly scheduled passenger flights at this writing. The only airport in the city serves the military.

Transportation

SAN FELIPE   Private planes and charters land at **San Felipe International Airport**. There is no regularly scheduled passenger service.

AIR

ENSENADA   Autotransportes de Baja California ("ABC"; 664-683-5681) and **Tres Estrellas de Oro** (664-626-1701) operate

BUS

frequent first-class bus service up and down the Baja peninsula from the main Tijuana bus terminal (Calzado Lázaro Cárdenas at Rio Alamar, La Mesa), stopping in Ensenada at the bus terminal at Calle 1 and Avenida Riveroll; 646-178-6680. ABC also runs buses between Ensenada and San Felipe. **Transportes Norte de Sonora** runs daily buses between Ensenada and both Tecate and Mexicali.

SAN FELIPE **Autotransportes de Baja California** operates daily bus service to and from both Ensenada and Mexicali. San Felipe's bus terminal is at Avenida Manzanillo and Avenida Mar de Caribe; 686-577-1516.

CAR

Route 1, the Carretera Transpeninsular or Baja Highway, runs from Tijuana to Ensenada, a distance of 190 kilometers. On this segment of the route, you have two choices—the *carretera libre* (free highway), which makes its slow way through the busiest part of Rosarito, or the fast, four-lane *carretera cuota* (toll highway), which covers the distance in no time. From Ensenada, if you continue south on Route 1, you will reach San Quintín in another 196 kilometers.

Route 3 crosses the peninsula from Tecate to Ensenada, a distance of 106 kilometers. From Ensenada, Route 3 continues across the peninsula toward San Felipe, joining **Route 5** from Mexicali, San Felipe is 263 kilometers from Ensenada, 314 kilometers from Tecate or 184 kilometers from Mexicali. There are no gas stations between Tecate and Ensenada, Ensenada and San Felipe or Mexicali and San Felipe, so be sure to start with a full tank. All these routes are well-maintained, paved two-lane highways.

CAR RENTALS

ENSENADA **Ensenada Rent-Car** is located at 582 Avenida López Mateos; 646-178-1896. There's also **Fiesta Rent A Car** at Boulevard Lázaro Cárdenas; 646-176-3344. Rental rates run considerably higher in Ensenada than in Tijuana. Vendors around the Plaza Cívica have motor scooters for rent.

SAN FELIPE **El Dorado Travel Center** rents cars. ~ Mar Caribe 395; 686-577-1278. All-terrain vehicles are available from **ATV's San Felipe** ~ Calzada Chetumal and Mar de Cortez; and from **C.J. ATV Rentals** ~ Avenida Mar de Cortez.

PUBLIC TRANSIT

ENSENADA Ensenada has many independent taxis. It is not customary to hail taxis when they are moving; instead, you board them at any of the many taxi stands, called *sitios*, all along Avenida López Mateos and Avenida Benito Juárez, as well as elsewhere around the downtown area and in front of the larger hotels.

Several private companies provide inexpensive bus service along main avenues in Ensenada. Minibuses serve nearby villages and rural areas from a station on Calle 4 between Avenidas Macheros and Riveroll.

SAN FELIPE Taxis are not plentiful in San Felipe, perhaps because almost all visitors arrive in their own vehicles. The central taxi stand is on Avenida Mar de Cortez, or you can call for a cab at 686-577-1293. There are no public buses here.

▼ ▼

Addresses & Phone Numbers

Ambulance ~ Ensenada, 646-178-1400; San Quintín, Paramedicos Vicente Guerrero, 646-166-2034

Hospital ~ Hospital General, Avenida Reforma at Fraccionmiento Bahía, Ensenada, 646-172-4500; San Felipe; 686-577-0117

Cruz Roja (Red Cross) ~ Ensenada, 646-174-5335; San Felipe, 686-576-5132

Police ~ Rosarito, dial 060; Ensenada, 646-176-2421 or dial 134; San Felipe, 686-577-1134

Green Angels (roadside help) ~ 646-176-4675

Secretaría de Turismo del Estado de Baja California Norte ~ Rosarito, 661-612-0200; Calles Las Dunas and Las Rocas, Ensenada, 646-172-3022; Avenida Mar de Cortez at Calle Manzanillo, San Felipe, 686-577-1155; San Quintín, 646-166-2728

Comité de Turismo y Convenciones de Rosarito ~ 661-612-0396, or 800-962-2252 in the U.S.

Comité de Turismo y Convenciones de Ensenada ~ 646-178-2411

Internet access ~ Internet Café, Avenida Juárez 1449-8, Ensenada, 646-176-1331; or Lost Civilizations, Avenida Ruíz 168-2, Ensenada, 646-178-1226; Network Café, center of town, San Quintín.

SIX

Central Baja

A vulture perches motionless atop a thirty-foot cactus spire, tiny eyes peering through the sun's glare at the motor homes, Baja bugs and eighteen-wheelers that speed along the narrow strand of two-lane blacktop. A wild burro loiters in the shade of a stone grotto where painted symbols mark the spot of an ancient shamanic ritual; the thousand-year-old magic lingers. A whirlwind sweeps across a sand flat, exposing the million-year-old fossil of a sea snail as large as a dog. Baja's vast, surprisingly green central desert reveals the wonders of life spanning the centuries in such abundance that it is doubly remarkable that almost no human beings live there today.

The population of Baja lives along the border and the coasts. In the central section of the peninsula, however, both the Pacific and Sea of Cortez shores are mostly uninhabitable, and nearly unreachable, because of steep cliffs that plunge from jagged mountain ridges into the watery depths. The Baja Highway heads straight down the peninsula's centerline in a two-stage crossing of North America's wildest desert. For the adventurous, this 200-mile stretch of empty highway is the heart and soul of the Baja. It's like Alaska with 100-degree heat, or like the loneliest road in Nevada but with fewer people. It's one of the last great North American wildernesses.

Before the 1974 completion of the Baja Highway, the vast desert formed an all but impassable barrier between the relatively modern north, with its factories, agribusiness and weekend beach-party towns, and the southeast coast with its easygoing tropical ambience and centuries of colonial history. Today, motorists can cross this vast desert in an easy 50-mile-an-hour day—or take their time and experience the natural wonders of environments that are unique on earth.

Between the fanciful landscapes of the Desierto Central and the stark vastness of the Desierto Vizcaíno, travelers can detour to the coast and visit two remote oases that couldn't be more different—Bahía de los Angeles, a mecca for sport fishermen and kayakers on the shore of an idyllic, island-studded bay, and Guerrero Negro, a wind-blasted salt company town with cheap motels, good and not-so-good restaurants, and, in the winter, more whales than anyplace else on the continent. It is also the only place covered in this chapter that has TVs or phone service. Travelers with tough vehicles can bounce farther off the highway on unpaved back roads to explore vanished desert settlements—old mine camps and 18th-century Spanish colonial mission churches; two of the most remote are still used today. Still longer backcountry trips lead to Baja's most remote beaches. Finally, there are the islands, large and small, that lie off both coasts. As uninhabitable as the desert, some harbor huge seabird colonies and elephant seal rookeries, while others boast world-class surfing beaches and scuba-diving sites.

▼▼▼▼▼▼▼▼▼▼▼▼

Desierto Central

The journey south on the Baja Highway changes character suddenly and dramatically as you leave the coastal plain and plunge into the Desierto Central, a bone-dry, spiny wonderland whose diversity of drought-resistant vegetation makes it the most magical desert landscape in North America. Here you can wander among spirelike cardones, surreal cirios, squat and twisted elephant trees, giant century plants, treelike yuccas and a myriad of other exotic subtropical flora. Even if you never leave your vehicle, the half-day drive through this uninhabitable wonderland is an experience you'll never forget. Bring plenty of water.

SIGHTS

The Baja Highway turns away from the Pacific coast, winding through volcanic hills and down the side of a canyon to reach **El Rosario**, a tiny town that boasts a famous café, the last Pemex station before the desert, and not much else. The pavement ended at El Rosario for many years before 1974, when the Mexican government, flush with oil revenues, undertook the monumental project of paving the road all the way to the tip of Baja. Today, El Rosario marks the point where the coastal plain gives way to deep desert.

The highway takes a sharp left turn in the center of town. To see the hidden sights of El Rosario, at the left turn in the highway turn right instead. Take the next left and ford the Río del Rosario (an arroyo that normally contains little or no water); crude road signs mark the 16-kilometer route to **Punta Baja**, a long, rocky spit of land reaching out into the Pacific. The rugged beaches there are used by the fishermen of the tiny village of **Agua Blanca** but rarely seen by travelers.

◄ HIDDEN

Along the way, about two and a half kilometers from the highway on a bluff above the arroyo, sections of adobe wall still stand from **Misión Nuestra Señora del Rosario de Abajo**, built in 1802 to replace an earlier mission whose spring had run dry. Only the sketchy outlines of walls remain of the older mission—**Misión Nuestra Señora del Rosario Viñadaco**, the first Dominican mission in California, built in 1774—just off the main highway near the

Motel Sinai. The mission at El Rosario closed in 1832; diseases imported by the Spanish had so devastated the local Cochimí population that there were too few converts to work the fields.

HIDDEN ► Fishermen at Agua Blanca can often be hired to take visitors to **Isla San Jerónimo**, ten miles offshore to the south. The barren island has a small fishing camp and an old lighthouse, as well as the wreck of a large tuna-fishing boat. Other wrecks lie just offshore; they're hard to dive because of choking seaweed. A sizable sea lion colony inhabits the south end of the island. Other wildlife includes a strange legless lizard found only on Isla San Jerónimo.

Leaving El Rosario, the highway soon narrows as it begins a gradual, winding ascent through volcanic hills and mesas. This is mining country. The area no longer produces copper, but semiprecious stones such as turquoise, onyx, hematite, azurite and malachite are mined here. The adobe monoliths visible a short distance west of the highway on a side road from the tiny village of El Progreso, 63 kilometers south of El Rosario, were part of the
HIDDEN ► two-foot-thick walls of **Misión San Fernando Velicatá**. The mission was built in 1769 by Padre Junípero Serra to minister to the Guiricata Indians. It operated for 49 years but, like most Spanish colonial missions in Baja, was abandoned after epidemics wiped out the indigenous population.

Just beyond El Progreso, an unpaved road turns south to the small village of **Santa Catarina**. The road is well used but has steep grades and should be traveled only in a high-clearance vehicle beyond Santa Catarina village. Fifty-six kilometers from the highway is an area where fossilized ammonites—giant snail-shaped sea creatures—are found. Another 11 kilometers on the same road
HIDDEN ► brings you to **Puerto Catarina**. Scattered ruins mark the site of an old shipping port built for exporting onyx from the quarries at El Mármol during the early years of this century. The makeshift shacks of a fish camp are all that lies at the end of the road today.

HIDDEN ► **El Mármol** is an abandoned onyx quarry 16 kilometers from the highway on an unpaved road that exits to the east near tiny San Agustín, 85 kilometers south of El Rosario. This is an interesting and easy side trip that mineral buffs should not bypass. From 1900 to 1958, the quarry produced some of North America's finest, most delicately hued onyx, a type of translucent silicate that is layered in different colors. Created by mineral deposits
HIDDEN ► from a fuming spring called **El Volcán**, a hot two-mile hike beyond the quarry, the onyx at El Mármol is translucent and striated in green, ochre and umber. Easier to work than marble, yet able to take a high polish and resist staining, onyx was only found in Algeria before the discovery of the deposits at El Mármol, and it was very expensive. The stone was quarried in huge blocks at El Mármol, then freighted by wagon more than 50 miles across the desert to Puerto Catarina, where as much as 100 tons of it

per day was shipped to the United States and Europe, where it was used for statuary, doorknobs, tabletops, and floor and wall facings. At its peak, El Mármol was a thriving company town inhabited by hundreds of Mexican workers and their families as well as two generations of gringo owners. With the development of modern plastics, demand for onyx declined until the stuff was not worth hauling to the coast. The quarry was abandoned and the town gradually died. Visitors can see what's left of a one-room schoolhouse and a jail, both built of massive blocks of onyx. The

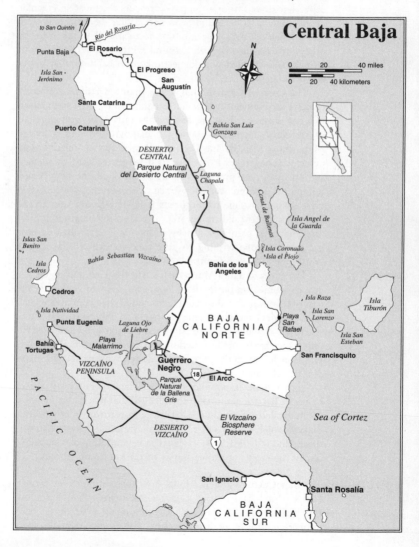

Central Baja

to San Quintín
Punta Baja
El Rosario
Rio del Rosario
Isla San Jerónimo
El Progreso
San Augustín
Santa Catarina
Puerto Catarina
Cataviña
DESIERTO CENTRAL
Parque Natural del Desierto Central
Bahía San Luis Gonzaga
Laguna Chapala
Canal de Ballenas
Isla Angel de la Guarda
Islas San Benito
Isla Cedros
Bahía Sebastian Vizcaíno
Isla Coronado
Isla el Piojo
Bahía de los Angeles
Cedros
Isla Natividad
Punta Eugenia
Laguna Ojo de Liebre
Isla Raza
Isla San Lorenzo
Isla Tiburón
Playa Malarrimo
BAJA CALIFORNIA NORTE
Playa San Rafael
Isla San Esteban
Bahía Tortugas
VIZCAÍNO PENINSULA
Guerrero Negro
San Francisquito
Parque Natural de la Ballena Gris
El Arco
Sea of Cortez
PACIFIC OCEAN
DESIERTO VIZCAÍNO
El Vizcaíno Biosphere Reserve
San Ignacio
Santa Rosalía
BAJA CALIFORNIA SUR

0   20   40 miles
0   20   40 kilometers

quarry is intermittently mined on a small scale by men from a nearby *ejido*, who sell the onyx to factories in Tijuana that make it into curio items such as chess sets and elephant statuettes.

The **Cataviña Boulder Field** marks the northern extent of Parque Natural del Desierto Central, a 100-mile-long scenic area protected from development by Mexican law. The park flanks the highway for about six miles on each side, with frequent parking areas and a number of unpaved roads that provide back-country access to mines and ranches beyond the park boundaries. The drive through the park presents the most spectacular desert scenery to be found anywhere along the Baja Highway, and the boulder field is even more spectacular than the rest. The area is strewn for miles with round white boulders the size of houses, and studded with majestic *cardón* cactuses that tower above the giant rocks.

The town of **Cataviña** has fewer than ten buildings, mostly garages for highway maintenance equipment, and a population of a few dozen hardy souls, but it is the only oasis with any kind of travelers' amenities—namely a campground and a motel. Maps show it as having the only Pemex station on this long desert crossing but when I passed through recently, the Pemex station was in the process of being demolished, the new Pemex pumps at the motel were not yet in operation and two old men were selling gasoline to motorists from five-gallon cans in the back of a rickety old trailer. Yet with a scenic location and interesting cave paintings nearby, Cataviña is the obvious base camp for anyone wishing to take time to explore the Parque Natural del Desierto Central.

The ruins of **Santa María de los Angeles Cabujacaamag**, the last Jesuit mission on the Baja Peninsula, located 29 kilometers east of town on a road so sandy and rutted that even four-wheel-drive vehicles have a hard time getting there. Dirt bikers sometimes rise to the challenge. The mission was built in 1767 and used for only two years before jurisdiction over the northern Baja missions was transferred to the Dominican Order, which chose to abandon this remote site.

Sixty kilometers south of Cataviña, the Baja Highway crosses **Laguna Chapala**, a normally dry lake bed that marks the midpoint of the Desierto Central crossing. Rare rainstorms briefly fill this "lake," which has no outlet, and then evaporate, leaving deposits of salt and minerals. A short distance beyond Laguna Chapala is one of the most impressive stands of *cardón* cactus in Baja.

LODGING   The **Baja Cactus Motel** is a long, slow renovation of the former, funky Motel El Rosario, next to the town's Pemex station. Originally built as a travelers' way station in 1902, it has been in operation for more than a century. Today, six of the old, spartan guest rooms are still in use, along with 16 new ones with king-sized beds, in-room phones and 29-inch TVs. ~ Route 1, Km. 55, El Rosario; 616-165-8850, fax 616-165-8700. BUDGET TO MODERATE.

The **Motel Sinai** on the east edge of El Rosario offers a dozen remarkably plain cinder block motel units with double beds and satellite TV, designed more for truck drivers than gringo tourists. The motel also operates a walled 12-unit RV park—$12 per night with restrooms, showers and a laundry room but no hookups. ~ Route 1, Km. 56, El Rosario; 616-165-8818. BUDGET.

In Cataviña, the 28-room **Hotel Desert Inn Cataviña**—the largest building in town—is typical of the Desert Inn (formerly La Pinta) chain of motels found up and down the peninsula. It has pleasant though plain air-conditioned rooms, an outdoor swimming pool and tennis courts. A noisy electrical generator runs from 6 p.m. to midnight. ~ Route 1, Km. 174, Cataviña; 800-262-4500; www.lapintahotels.com. MODERATE.

There's also the **Mini-Hotel Cabañas de Linda** across the highway from the La Pinta, with 14 basic, almost-bare rooms. ~ Route 1, Km. 174, Cataviña. BUDGET.

Rancho Santa Ynez, three-fourths of a mile off the highway, offers very simple hostel-style dormitory accommodations. This is a favorite dirt bikers' haunt, though it's hard to see the advantage over camping out. Electricity goes off at 9:30. ~ Route 1, Km. 176, Cataviña. BUDGET.

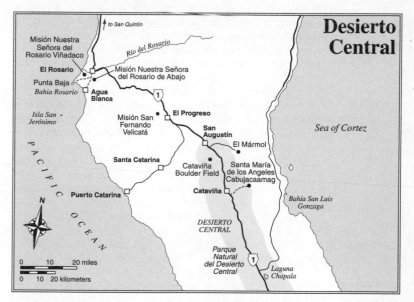

DINING

Mama Espinosa's in El Rosario has been a Baja Highway landmark since 1946. Until 1974, the pavement ended right in front of this plain little restaurant, making it the natural rendezvous and departure point for innumerable expeditions into the desert wilderness. Still prepared under the sharp eye of Mama Espinosa herself, a matriarch who was born in 1908, breakfast here is good, and the lobster burritos—a surprise reminder that the little desert village of El Rosario is only seven miles from the Pacific coast—are among central Baja's best roadside attractions, though a tad pricey. T-shirts and cartoon place mats perpetuate the restaurant's mystique, though there's little competition in sight. The centerpiece of the simple decor is a collection of fossilized ammonites—giant snails that lived during the dinosaur era and reached almost two feet in diameter. They were found by fishermen on a remote part of the coast about 40 miles south of El Rosario. ~ Route 1, Km. 55, El Rosario. BUDGET.

Also good in El Rosario is the **Mount Sinai Restaurant**, located at the motel and campground of the same name. Standard Mexican fare is served here, along with lobster enchiladas and other seafood specialties. The decor, featuring works by local painters and craftspeople, is strangely reminiscent of Mexican restaurants in the United States. ~ Route 1, Km. 56, El Rosario; 616-165-8818. MODERATE.

Las Cazuelas, the restaurant at the Hotel Desert Inn Cataviña, offers a predictable menu of Mexican and American dishes, including a taco-and-enchilada combination plate just like you'd expect to find in a typical Mexican restaurant in the U.S. The restaurant is cool, clean, cheerful and open from around noon to well after dark. (Though they may bear little resemblance to one another, restaurants at all the hotels in Baja's La Pinta chain are called Las Cazuelas, which means "the cookware.") ~ Route 1, Km. 174, Cataviña. MODERATE.

Near Cataviña, **Rancho Santa Ynez** serves breakfasts of *huevos rancheros con chorizo* (fried eggs smothered with chile sauce, with spicy, crumbly Mexican sausage on the side) and, in the afternoon, taco-and-enchilada dinners. (Mexicans are accustomed to eating the main meal of the day during afternoon siesta; don't count on finding this place open during the gringo dinner hour.) The ambience is simple, with wooden picnic tables and hard benches under a shade roof with open sides. The menu is limited and the prices very reasonable. ~ Route 1, Km. 176, Cataviña. BUDGET.

GROCERIES

In El Rosario, near Mama Espinosa's and the Pemex station, there is a fairly complete food store, called **Supermercado**.

**BEACHES
& PARKS**

PLAYA DEL ROSARIO 🏃 🏊 Sunbathers may be disappointed by this remote, stony beach, but beachcombers are likely to love it.

Mystery of the Ancient Artists

The Cataviña area is where the greatest concentration of **Indian cave paintings** are found. The geometric patterns measure from about 12 to 18 inches in size, made with mineral hues—mainly black, white, various shades of red and sometimes ochre. Several "schools" of rock art are found in central Baja, apparently painted by different groups of the same ancient race. Farther south, in the vicinities of San Ignacio and Mulegé, the sites are less numerous but far more elaborate, depicting human and animal figures in huge murals. The largest known site, hard-to-reach Gardner Cave in the rugged Sierra San Francisco, contains a mural more than 500 feet wide and 30 feet high. These mysterious paintings date back as much as 1500 years. At many sites, several layers of newer motifs have been painted over older ones, suggesting that the paintings were made over a span of centuries.

The meaning of the images is not known; they may have had shamanic or other ritual significance. More puzzling is the question of who painted them. The Cochimí people, who lived in the area when the first Spanish explorers and missionaries arrived, had no evident artistic tradition and disavowed any knowledge of the paintings' origins. Anthropologists attribute them to an ancient race known only as "the Painters," about which nothing at all is known.

The most extensive painted-cave sites can only be reached by a long four-wheel-drive trip. Some paintings, however, are close to the highway. Look for good examples in a small grotto among the largest boulders on the skyline about half a mile north of the highway near kilometer marker 171. Another site is 400 meters up the trail from the rest area located one and a half kilometers north of the Hotel La Pinta Cataviña. Small roadside signs that say "Pinturas Rupestres" mark other painting sites.

The beach lies at the edge of a fossil-rich expanse of petrified forest, and the surf continually exposes fragments of fossilized dinosaur bone and petrified wood. The road from the highway to the beach passes through the heart of the petrified forest, where broken stone trunks of prehistoric palms and tropical evergreens litter the sunbaked terrain. Fossil remains of duckbilled dinosaurs known as hadrosaurs have been found in this area, along with prehistoric crocodiles, some of the oldest evidence of mammal life and a unique "missing link" between dinosaurs and modern birds. ~ Turn right where the main highway turns left in El Rosario. Take another right at the first fork, then keep right at each subsequent fork in the road. It's seven and a half kilometers to the beach.

PARQUE NATURAL DEL DESIERTO CENTRAL 🚶 🚲 On a series of mesas stretching for a hundred miles down the middle of the peninsula, some of the world's most fantastic desert forests grow. Towering *cardón* cactuses, blue palms, squat elephant trees and tapered, slender cirios cover the slopes of the mesas, and everywhere is a profusion of prickly pear, barrel cactus, candelaria, ocotillo, cholla, velvet cactus, galloping cactus and agave. Ravens, hawks and vultures perch atop the cactuses, and woodpecker holes in the trunks of the big *cardones* make nests for many kinds of desert songbirds. Ancient Indian rock art is found several places in the park. The area is protected by stringent environmental laws intended to make it eligible for UNESCO Biosphere Reserve status, but don't expect park rangers or entrance gates, much less a visitor center. The area has been preserved in its natural state, and the only amenities are roadside pull-outs where you can park and stroll among the cactuses. ~ Route 1 runs through the center of the park from the Cataviña Boulder Field, 75 kilometers south of El Rosario, to the turnoff for Bahía de Los Angeles.

▲ The village of Cataviña, the only human settlement within the natural park, has two campgrounds. The *ejido*-run **Cataviña Trailer Park** has 67 tent and RV sites, some with electricity, and restrooms with hot showers. Sites cost $9 per night. There is also an informal camping area—little more than a big graded parking lot—at Rancho Santa Ynez south of Cataviña. There are no amenities except restrooms; bring your own drinking water. Sites cost $3 per night. Side roads provide boundless camping opportunities for tent and small-truck campers.

Bahía de los Angeles

Near the southern edge of the Parque Natural del Desierto Central, where a Pemex station (sometimes open but don't count on it) stands alone in the desert, a paved 66-kilometer road branches off the Baja Highway and runs through forests of boojums and elephant trees to the Sea of Cortez coast, an hour's drive away, to dead-

end at Bahía de los Angeles—the Bay of Angels. Named after the
bay, the town, with its seasonal population of about 1500, is one
of the most remote coastal settlements of any size on Baja.

On first impression, the gringo fishing village of Bahía de los
Angeles is an unappealing little place. Since there is no simple way
to dispose of such items as defunct washing machines and broken
sofas, over the last 50 years the main street
has become lined with discarded furniture
and appliances, creating the ambience of a
Goodwill store in paradise. Most residents
live in rows of mobile homes and bungalows
radiating inland from the beach. The rumble of
the gasoline-powered generator that supplies the
only electricity carries from one end of town to
the other. (After ten at night the power plant runs a
smaller generator.) The water supply comes from an
artesian well in the mountains 30 miles away and
flows through the small blue pipe that runs beside the
road into town. The water fills a community tank, where town residents wait in line to replenish their household water supplies. You
could count the number of telephones in town on your fingers.

> Isolated on both sides by inacces-
> sible coastlines where volcanic
> cliffs plunge straight down into
> the sea depths, Bahía de los
> Angeles is certainly the most
> out-of-the-way place in
> Baja that you can reach
> by paved road.

It's not the town's character that lures so many snowbirds from
the United States to Bahía de los Angeles each winter. It's the bay,
one of the most magnificent spots on the Sea of Cortez. Sport fishermen from California started colonizing Bahía de los Angeles in
the 1940s, when the only way to get there was by private plane.
Today, while the area continues to attract anglers, a new breed of
sea kayakers and whale and dolphin watchers is infiltrating this
Hemingwayesque community with eco-consciousness notions.

All the Spanish colonial mission ruins north of the Baja California
Sur state line have been abandoned for so long that little is left
to see—except Misión San Francisco de Borja Adac, commonly
known as **Misión de San Borja**. Natural springs—one hot, one
cold—created an oasis in the mountains that made it an Indian
population center and an obvious place for missionary work. The
solid stone church, built by Dominicans in 1801, replaced a Jesuit
mission established on the site in 1762. Although the church was
abandoned by the missionaries in 1818, ranchers who came to
graze cattle in the high mountain meadows preserved it and their
families continue to worship there to this day. The hot and cold
springs still flow a short walk from the church. A cowbell clangs
in place of the original church bells, and a cemetery bears witness to the generations who have inhabited this isolated place. A
few still do, though the condition of the road that takes you there
shows infrequent use. To reach the mission from the paved road
in to Bahía de Los Angeles, you need a high-clearance vehicle.
Follow the narrow, unpaved road that turns off to the south 22

SIGHTS

◀ *HIDDEN*

kilometers from town (or 45 from the Baja Highway). Then it's 26 kilometers of slow, careful driving to the old mission.

Bahía de los Angeles—the town—is not a sightly place. A few minutes' drive in either direction, though, the pavement ends and you have your choice of great beach hideaways. An adventuresome driver in a rugged vehicle can continue around the bay to spots where no human has left a footprint in years.

The **Museo de Naturaleza y Cultura**, a block west of the main road near the center of town, packs an extraordinary hodgepodge of area artifacts into its cramped quarters. There are whale skeletons, Seri Indian tools carved from turtle shells, fossils of prehistoric horses, and exhibits on 19th-century gold mining around Bahía de los Angeles. Open for about two hours most afternoons. ~ Bahía de los Angeles.

Bahía de los Angeles—the bay—conceals a mostly submerged mountain range whose peaks form a protective chain of islands along the mouth of the bay. These islands provide safe haven for more than 500 species of fish by making the bay too treacherous for the big industrial fishing ships that have devastated the fish population in other parts of the Sea of Cortez. Further protected from storms and surf by Isla Angel de la Guarda, the largest of all the islands off the Baja coast, the bay first offered a safe harbor to sailing ships in 1746.

Some of the islands across the mouth of the bay show massive, rocky ridgelines; others are round, barren rocks so caked with guano that they look like snowcapped mountaintops rising pure white out of the turquoise bay a few miles offshore. **Isla Coronado**, the northernmost island, is four-and-a-half miles long and has more land area than the other 14 islands combined. Because the longest distance between any two islands is two miles, Bahía de los Angeles is an ideal spot for sea kayaking. Ospreys inhabit Isla Coronado and other islands, and there is a large pelican colony on Isla el Piojo.

On the eastern skyline, an entire mountain range looms above the water, giving Bahía de los Angeles more the feel of a large lake than a sea harbor. The mountains are on **Isla Angel de la Guarda**—Guardian Angel Island—and rise more than 1300 feet above sea level. Between Bahía de los Angeles and Isla Angel de la Guarda lies the **Canal de Ballenas**. The deep, calm channel with its abundant marine life is a favorite rest stop in the winter months for no less than five species of whales—including blue whales, the largest animal species that has ever lived on earth. Dolphins, too, are often spotted cruising the channel in pods of as many as a hundred.

LODGING   RV sites outnumber motel rooms by at least fifty to one in Bahía de los Angeles. The best accommodations are at the **Villa Vitta**

Hotel, a modern 40-room place with air conditioning, a swimming pool and a jacuzzi. No phone or TV, but there is electricity most of the day, thanks to the noisy generator nearby. On the main road in the center of town, the Villa Vita has access to the beach and boat ramp a block away. The motel also has a large RV park with hookups ($12 per night). ~ Bahía de los Angeles; 686-650-3208, or 760-741-9583, fax 760-489-6687 in the U.S.; e-mail villavitta@aol.com. BUDGET TO MODERATE.

The original tourist facility in Bahía de los Angeles, **Casa Díaz** has 15 spacious though spartan stone cabanas with simple furnishings, private baths, solar-heated showers and a beachfront location. There is also a handful of run-down RV campsites on the premises. ~ Bahía de los Angeles. Reservations: Apdo. Postal 579, Ensenada, BC. BUDGET.

Somewhere between a campground and a cabana complex, **Gecko Camp** has ten stone-walled palapas. Unfurnished except for crude tables, they are nonetheless cozy and private, and each one has the beach and bay right out the front door. Bring your own lantern, hammocks, bedding and kitchen gear, and you can easily go native for the season here at $10 per night. The central restrooms have solar-heated showers. ~ Six kilometers south of Bahía de los Angeles (keep left at the fork). BUDGET.

Farther south along the bay shore, the **Las Animas Wilderness Resort** consists of a series of luxuriously appointed yurts scattered along a picture-perfect beach far removed from any other signs of civilization. It is only accessible by boat, and lodging priority is given to guests on the four- to six-day getaways offered by Baja Air Adventures, which include transportation by private plane

◄ HIDDEN

Las Flores and San Francisquito

In the last decades of the 19th century, long before the present-day town of Bahía de los Angeles was born, the mountains that surround the bay saw a brief flurry of gold, silver and copper mining. Remnants from this era offer the best excuses for landlubber adventuring in the area.

LAS FLORES   The ghostly old mining camp of Las Flores dates back to the 1890s, when nearby Mina San Juan produced more than $2 million worth of silver. To get there, follow the only road south from Bahía de los Angeles for 16 kilometers, bearing right at the fork where the south shore road turns off to the left. A three-foot-thick stone vault where silver ingots were stored marks the site of the old refinery. Ore was brought down from the mine in two miniature trains linked by a pulley cable, then lowered in buckets over impassable cliffs from one train to the next. (One of the little locomotives that pulled the ore trains to and

from San Diego. Sea kayaking, whale watching and pretending you're stranded on a desert island are among the main activities. ~ 800-221-9283; www.bajaairadventures.com. DELUXE.

DINING   The best restaurant in Bahía de los Angeles is **Guillermo's**, located near the center of town in the white building at the big RV park of the same name. Fresh seafood fills the menu, with several shrimp choices, lobster *estilo Puerto Nuevo*, and catch-of-the-day fish dishes. Sea bass, when available, is a specialty. Diners on the outdoor terrace overlook the bay from the cool comfort of palapa sunshades. (This restaurant and the RV park were closed during my most recent visit, but it has since reopened after a much-needed repaving and rewiring.) ~ Bahía de los Angeles. MODERATE.

The clean, modern, friendly restaurant at the **Villa Vitta Hotel** in the center of town serves Mexican seafood specialties such as lobster, scallops and oysters and big, chilled fruit smoothies. Seating is in the air-conditioned dining room, shady and decorated with Mexican tilework, or outdoors at tables beside the swimming pool. ~ Bahía de los Angeles; 686-650-3208. BUDGET TO MODERATE.

Two blocks north of Guillermo's on the town's main street, **Las Hamacas** serves seafood at slightly lower prices, along with from the mines can be seen outside the Museo de Naturaleza y Cultura in Bahía de los Angeles.) Ruined buildings, machinery and heaps of reddish mine waste are scattered across the abandoned town.

SAN FRANCISQUITO   The road continues past Las Flores, paralleling the coastline from afar for 130 kilometers, winding among volcanic peaks of over 3000 feet before descending to a hidden beach, **Playa San Rafael**, and following the coast to the still more remote fish camp of San Francisquito—a secluded beach on the Sea of Cortez with a few very basic palapas that can be rented if anybody is around to rent them from. It is on a small cove with good fishing for sea bass and barracuda. Travelers on this adventurous back-road route can take a different route upon leaving San Francisquito and drive 72 kilometers to rejoin the Baja Highway south of Guerrero Negro. The rough trip requires a sturdy high-clearance vehicle, and extra cans of gasoline may be a fine idea. Gasoline is sometimes sold from drums at San Francisquito, but you can't count on it.

standard Mexican dishes. Especially popular for breakfast, the restaurant features both gringo fare (eggs, bacon, pancakes) and Mexican favorites such as *chilaquiles*—tortilla pieces and chicken scrambled in a creamy red chile sauce—and tropical fruit salad. This place, too, has a great bay view. ~ Bahía de los Angeles. BUDGET TO MODERATE.

GROCERIES Fish and other fruits of the sea are abundant. You can get such staples as macaroni and cheese, canned peas and Pan Bimbo (Mexico's answer to Wonder Bread) at several small stores in Bahía de los Angeles. The best of the lot, and the only place that offers much in the way of fresh fruits and vegetables, is the relatively large **Mercado Xitlali**, located at the south end of town, a block or so past where the paved road curves around to the right (and about a block before the pavement ends.) It's across the street from the local internet café.

NIGHTLIFE Get enough sportsmen together, add booze, and there's bound to be after-hours action even in the most out-of-the-way places. The boys swap fishing stories late into the evening around the bar at **Guillermo's,** and the restaurant's atmospherically lighted patio is as romantic a waterfront setting as you could want (if it's open). There's another gringo bar up the street at **Villa Vitta Hotel.**

BEACHES & PARKS

BAHÍA DE LOS ANGELES BEACHES 🏄 🏊 🚤 🛥 ⏤ Ten miles of unbroken beach line the western shore of Bahía de los Angeles from the rocky outcropping of Punta La Gringa in the north to the Estero de la Mona wetlands at the south end of the bay. Windsurfers and kayakers head for the north beaches, best for launching. Sun worshippers find blissful seclusion at both ends, as far as possible from the center of town, where the beach feels practically urban; with several boat ramps, it's the hub for sport fishing on the bay. ~ Unpaved roads, wide and well-graded though steep in places, run north and south from town for the length of the beach.

▲ There are numerous campgrounds along the north beach from town to **Punta la Gringa**, all casual affairs designed with fishermen and kayakers in mind, including **Daggett's Beach Camping** (664-650-3206, fax 664-650-3206; $8 per night). Daggett's is clean and well-run, with beautiful sunrise views from the beach, although since it caters mainly to fishermen you should not be surprised to find fish skeletons and entrails baking in the sun here and there; the restrooms are only open for limited hours. Another possibility is **Camp Archelon**, owned by marine biologists who conduct a sea turtle rescue project there. The campground is set up mainly for student volunteers but is open to the public when not full. (Second right turn after Daggett's; no phone; $8 per night.) Ten kilometers past the end of the pavement are the ruins of a former campground at **Playa la Gringa**. There are no facilities, but camping is free, and the views from Punta la Gringa are magnificent. Six kilometers south of town, Gecko Camp has tent and RV sites without hookups for as little as $5 per night.

> Since there is no fresh water on Isla Angel de la Guarda, it has never been inhabited by humans.

PARQUE NACIONAL ISLA ANGEL DE LA GUARDA 🚶 🏊 🚤 ⏤ The largest island off the Baja coast, Isla Angel de la Guarda was once part of the peninsula but broke away a million years ago. Pristine but not very inviting, its steep slopes grow the same vegetation as the mountains west of Bahía de los Angeles—*cardones*, agave, elephant trees and boojum trees. There are sea caves on the exposed eastern coast and a sea lion colony on a small cay off the northern tip, and the mountains host an abundance of bird life along with some rare lizard species. ~ Located seven to ten miles off the coast, east of Bahía de los Angeles. By asking at Guillermo's or any fishing shop, you can often locate a fishing guide to take you to the island. It is also possible—though strenuous and potentially hazardous—to get there by sea kayak.

▲ Camping is allowed. The best campsites are at the northern and southern tips of the island.

MID-RIFT ISLANDS WILDLIFE SANCTUARY 🏃 ⛵ 🚤 ⛵ Isla
Raza is off-limits to humans in March and April, when elegant terns,
royal terns and rare Heermann's gulls numbering in the hundreds
of thousands make their nests there. Guides operate tours from
Bahía de los Angeles to view the bird colonies at Mid-rift Islands
from a distance during nesting season. At other times of year, you
can visit the island and ponder the mysterious mounds of rock
that cover its surface. There are more than a thousand of these
"monumentos" on the island, neatly piled to heights of five feet.
Perhaps built by Seri Indians, egg gatherers or convicts at hard
labor, their origin and purpose has been forgotten. To the south, Isla
San Lorenzo and smaller neighboring islands host the world's largest
brown pelican colony. ~ Southeast of Bahía de los Angeles, a chain
of 45 large and small islands parallels the coast at a distance of
about ten miles. Getting there by sea kayak is possible, though risky.
▲ Camping is allowed on Islas San Lorenzo and San Esteban.

Following the Baja Highway south for 133
kilometers past the Bahía de los Angeles turnoff, motorists cross the state line between

Guerrero Negro Area

Baja California and Baja California Sur, where a monument with
an eagle statue commemorates the opening of the highway in
1974. A few miles down the road, near the turnoff to Guerrero
Negro, there is often an Army check point—the only one you're
likely to encounter in laid-back Baja California Sur.

With a population of more than 7000, Guerrero Negro is the
first large town south of San Quintín. The people of the town
work for Exportada de Sal, S.A. de C.V., the world's largest salt
producer. The operation gathers salt from evaporating ponds
that cover more than 300 square miles near the shore of the extremely saline lagoon south of town, and takes it by truck and
ferry to its port on Isla Cedros for shipment to the United States,
Canada and Japan. The company ships out 6.5 million tons of
salt each year—more than 35,000,000 pounds of the stuff each
day! Until recently, the company was under American ownership
and could not sell salt within Mexico because of trade restrictions; when the Japanese-based multinational Mitsubishi
Corporation bought the salt works, it immediately gave 51 percent ownership to the Mexican government and received in return the right to sell salt to Mexicans—a profitable deal because
it meant a dramatic reduction in shipping costs.

Despite its size, this company town has fewer lodging and restaurant options than little Bahía de los Angeles, but it has more
stores selling groceries and basic necessities. Guerrero Negro is
more than just a pit stop between the Desierto Central and Desi-

erto Vizcaíno, however. From December through March, salt-encrusted Laguna Ojo de Liebre south of town is one of the best whale-watching spots in North America—the calving ground for thousands of gray whales. The weather is windy and often chilly in winter; if you're looking for sunny tropical beaches, this is not the place. Wildlife watchers, however, will rate it as a high point of their Baja expedition. Even when the whales are gone, the abundance of bird life on this lagoon is beyond belief.

SIGHTS

Eagles, not whales, are the official symbol of Guerrero Negro. The **Monumento Aguila**, a dramatic bronze sculpture of a Mexican eagle greets travelers at the state line as they approach the town; sea eagles, or ospreys, are so abundant in the area that they nest atop many of the power poles along Guerrero Negro's streets. Crossing the state line takes you from the Pacific time zone to the Mountain time zone. Set your clock forward an hour when heading south, and back on the return trip.

There is nothing approximating a tourist sight in Guerrero Negro itself. Drive the length of the main street to the salt company and Pemex station, then turn right and continue past the traffic *glorieta* to take the road to the **old salt port**. The smooth, wide unpaved road runs north for ten kilometers along the top of a levee, through coastal wetlands teeming with herons, egrets, and other wading birds. The site of the old salt-shipping facility overlooks Laguna Guerrero Negro. The lagoon and later the town were named for the S.S. *Black Warrior*, an American ship that was overloaded with whale oil in 1858. Its sails could not move the overweight ship, which foundered on the sand bar at the mouth of the bay. The wreck was visible for many years. In the 20th century, the salt company found that the same sand bar limited the size of the ships that could use their salt port and moved the port offshore to Isla Cedros after a few years. Ruined walls of huge warehouses and loading docks remain, providing pelican perches and osprey nesting places. Whales often congregate around the mouth of the lagoon; they're sometimes visible through binoculars from the parking area above the salt port. Whale-watching boats sometimes depart from here, too.

South of town, Laguna Ojo de Liebre—also called Scammon's Lagoon—is a more popular whale-watchers' destination. Whales often come to Scammon's Lagoon to birth because the shallow lagoon has a high salt content, making for more buoyancy and easier births. The road to **Parque Natural de la Ballena Gris** turns off the main highway 10 kilometers south of town and runs for 24 kilometers west to the shoreline. It is unpaved but wide and smooth. Other roads in the area are marked off-limits to unauthorized vehicles. Heed the signs: monster salt trucks that seem the size of cruise ships, twice the width of a semi truck and rolling on tires ten feet in diameter, careen down these roads at high speed, and woe be unto the mere passenger car or motor home that gets in the way. The park is situated along a windy, soggy coastline green with creeping plants, close to the mouth of the narrow, salt-crusted estuary where the whales go to give birth to their calves. Whale-watching boats leave frequently from the park dock in season. An observation tower lets you survey the distant water with binoculars searching for whale spouts. When the whales are gone, the park is closed.

The **Hotel Desert Inn**, seven kilometers out of town near the state line, offers the nicest lodging in the Guerrero Negro area. The 28 rooms are modern and spacious, with hot water, satellite TV, air conditioning and a swimming pool. ~ Paralelo 28; 615-157-1305, fax 615-157-1306, or 800-542-3283 in the U.S. MODERATE.

LODGING

On the road that leads into town from the highway, the **Hotel El Morro** has 35 clean, spare and spacious rooms with ceiling fans, private baths and hot showers. ~ Boulevard Emiliano Zapata (Apdo. Postal 144 Guerrero Negro, BCS 23940); 615-157-0414 BUDGET.

Room rates are even more affordable at nearby **Motel Dunas**. At under $20 a night, you wouldn't expect anything special here, and you'd be right. Each of the 25 clean, modest rooms has a private bath with shower, a double bed and not much else. There is also an RV park on the premises. ~ Boulevard Emiliano Zapata, Guerrero Negro; 615-157-0057. BUDGET.

Cabañas Don Miguelito, attached to the Malarrimo Restaurant and RV Park, has 16 guest units. The walls seem to be made of plywood, but comfortable beds, hot showers, TVs, coffee makers and cheerful decor make for a welcoming stopover between two vast expanses of desert. Behind the motel and restaurant is an RV campground with hookups for 55 rigs ($10 to $14 per night). The sites are paved or graveled, making for uncomfortable tent camping. The only alternative for tent campers is

KEEPING TRACK OF THE TIME

Baja California Sur is one time zone later than Baja California Norte, so when you cross the state line north of Guerrero Negro, set your watch forward an hour. Just to make things confusing, Baja California Norte observes daylight-saving time from early April to late October, while Baja California Sur is only on daylight-saving time from early May to late September. Since there's not much out here to be on time for anyway, the best strategy may be to pack your wristwatch away in your suitcase until you reach civilization again.

the windblown coastal campground at Parque Natural de Ballena Gris. ~ Boulevard Emiliano Zapata, Guerrero Negro; 615-157-0250, fax 615-157-0100. BUDGET.

Three blocks west on the other side of the street, by the radio tower, the **Motel Don Gus** has 18 plain rooms with TVs and private baths that boast hot water 24 hours a day. There's a guarded parking area. ~ Calle Rosaura Zapata, Guerrero Negro; 615-157-1611. BUDGET.

Across from the Catholic church near the park, the **Casa Laguna Bed & Breakfast Guest House** is owned by a company that operates whale-watching tours from the U.S. When it's not being used to lodge their tour groups, the fully furnished and equipped house is rented out to travelers. It can sleep eight to ten people. ~ Boulevard Emiliano Zapata, Guerrero Negro; 615-157-0500; e-mail lagtours@nextgeninter.net.mx. MODERATE.

Motels get smaller and cheaper the farther west you go on Boulevard Emiliano Zapata, closer to the salt company headquarters. Places such as the **Motel Gámez** near city hall cater to transient workers, not tourists, and offer the bare minimum in comfort—mattresses on concrete pedestals in cramped, colorless quarters, with shared showers—but if you're looking for a roof over your head and a little privacy all for the same price as a campsite, this 12-room hotel will fill the bill. ~ Boulevard Emiliano Zapata, Guerrero Negro; 615-157-0370. BUDGET.

DINING

Several good restaurants are found seven kilometers north of town at the state line. **Las Cazuelas**, the dining room at the Hotel Desert Inn, features a substantial menu of seafood, Mexican fare and American-style breakfasts. It poses no serious competition for Guerrero Negro's legendary Restaurant-Bar Malarrimo, but

AUTHOR FAVORITE

A culinary highlight of driving the Baja Highway is the **Restaurant-Bar Malarrimo**, the finest dining between Ensenada and La Paz. It is the principal attraction at the little tourist center of the same name at the east end of Guerrero Negro's main street. Seafood is prepared with a flair that is part Continental, part California nouveau. Besides the lobster, shrimp and catch of the day typical of Baja seafood restaurants, the menu features big Pismo clams, abalone and a rich *marisco* soup. The wine cellar is the best in the Baja backcountry. Soft lighting, heavy, rustic chairs and tables, and real cloth tablecloths help make for a little splurge of luxury to celebrate achieving the Baja Highway's halfway point. ~ Boulevard Emiliano Zapata, Guerrero Negro; 615-157-0100. MODERATE TO DELUXE.

if you're spending the night out here, it's certainly convenient. ~ Paralelo 28; 615-157-1305. MODERATE.

Near La Pinta, **Mario's Palapa** specializes in American-style omelets and serves a full range of seafood and Mexican dishes. The food is equal to that at Las Cazuelas, the prices are lower, and the lavishly tropical palm-frond decor is unique. ~ Paralelo 28. BUDGET.

Don Gus, at the motel of the same name, gets my vote as the best restaurant in town. The atmosphere is rather plain (but that's true of just about every place in town), but the service is attentive. Lobster, clams and seafood stew are among the menu offerings, which also include a hodgepodge of American and European dishes. ~ Calle Rosauro Zapata, Guerrero Negro; 615-157-1611. BUDGET TO MODERATE.

During the afternoon, dozens of open-air *comedores* open up along the main street to serve salt company workers on their mid day siesta breaks. The food—fish tacos, *birria* (goat), tamales, *carne asada* and other Mexican favorites—is as good as you'll find in Guerrero Negro's budget-priced restaurants, and prices are so low that you can fill a picnic basket to the brim for a few dollars.

Restaurants in Guerrero Negro provide soy sauce on the table instead of salt: until recently, the town's huge Japanese-owned salt-mining operation was forbidden to sell its product in Mexico. All the salt was exported, while Japanese soy sauce was imported for local consumption. The practice has persisted; most likely, by the time they get off work, local people don't want to look at any more salt.

GROCERIES

The **Supermercado la Ballena** has as good a selection of nonperishable foodstuffs as you'll find in central Baja. It carries such convenient on-the-road fare as pop-top fruit juices, packaged cookies, dried fish and that ubiquitous backcountry staple, canned peas. ~ Boulevard Zapata, Guerrero Negro; 615-157-0666.

NIGHTLIFE

Gringo travelers congregate after dark in the **Restaurant-Bar Malarrimo.** ~ Boulevard Zapata, Guerrero Negro. Look for the local version of disco action late into the night at **Mario's Restaurant-Bar,** at the Motel El Morro on the road into town.

BEACHES & PARKS

PARQUE NATURAL DE LA BALLENA GRIS 🐋 This coastal park provides access to Laguna Ojo de Liebre near the narrow, salty estuary where the whales calve. In the winter, when 18,000 to 20,000 whales gather in the lagoon, the park's dock is busy with low, open, motorized boats that take sightseers out among the whales. There is also an observation tower where visitors can often view the whales from shore through binoculars. Open December through March only. ~ Turn west off the main highway at the big hand-lettered sign 10 kilometers south of town; follow the wide, unpaved road for 24 kilometers to the park. Admission costs about US$3, and you are required to register your vehicle upon entering the park.

▲ A vaguely defined row of tent and RV sites without hook-ups lines the lagoon shore north of the boat dock. Camping costs $12 per night. Tenters may find camping uncomfortable on this chilly, windy stretch of coastline.

Desierto Vizcaíno

South of the salty oasis of Guerrero Negro lies the widest and wildest part of Baja—the Vizcaíno Desert. From the Pacific coast to the Sea of Cortez, a distance of 140 miles as the crow flies, stretches the Vizcaíno Biosphere Reserve. No road signs mark the reserve's boundaries, but it is the largest protected habitat area in Mexico. Reserves like this are created around the world under the UNESCO "Man and the Biosphere" program. A "core area" is protected by regulations more stringent than those that apply to federally designated wilderness areas in the United States; commercial and industrial exploitation is banned in adjacent populated areas but local people are permitted to use the natural resources. In the case of the Vizcaíno Biosphere Reserve, the human population is found almost entirely in fishing camps along the Pacific coast, as a jagged range of extinct volcanoes makes the Sea of Cortez coast inaccessible by both land and sea.

Motorists on the Baja Highway cross the center of the Vizcaíno Desert on the 140-kilometer journey from Guerrero Negro to San Ignacio. Compared to the cactus wonderland of the Desierto Central, this stretch of desert is bleak. Giant *cardón* cactuses, many of them thickened, crippled or scarred by brutal sandstorms, stand sentinel over the landscape, alongside the woody gray skeletons of *cardones* from centuries past. The climate is too dry for decay, and there is no one around to break them up for firewood. Many of the smaller cactuses are colorless and nasty—galloping cactus, which creeps along the ground as it grows to form impassable thickets, and jumping cholla, whose stiff, sharp spines grip anyone who brushes against it so tight that removing them may require pliers. Dust devils scour the glaring desert and send writhing white plumes of sand a hundred feet or more in the air.

Adventurous travelers who are not deterred by this howling wilderness can explore westward from the main highway and discover some of the most remote coastline in Baja.

SIGHTS   From Route 1, motorists with rugged vehicles or dirt bikes will find an intriguing side trip 29 kilometers south of Guerrero Negro (near kilometer marker 154), where another major road turns off

to the east and goes to a cluster of old mining towns—**El Arco,** ◄ *HIDDEN*
Pozo Alemán and **Calmallí.** The three old towns were booming
gold camps in the 1920s, with a population numbering in the
thousands. Officially designated Route 18, the road was once
paved but has deteriorated so badly that high clearance and tough
tires are advisable, and a four-wheel-drive vehicle is a big help in
certain patches. It is 42 kilometers to El Arco; the former boom
town has a tiny population and a well-kept church that serves
the area's scattered ranches. Beyond El Arco, the "pavement" ends
and four-wheel drive is advisable. Four kilometers farther on, at
Pozo Alemán, little is visible but stone foundations and the old
well for which the town was named. There, a left fork goes nine
kilometers north to Calmallí, where tumbledown buildings and
the strewn wreckage of mining equipment are mute reminders
that it was once the site of the richest mine in the district.

A sharp right turn where the pavement ends at El Arco puts you
on the road to **Misión Santa Gertrudis,** one of the best-preserved   ◄ *HIDDEN*
and least-visited Spanish colonial missions in central Baja. The
road is wide and well maintained, but may require high clearance. Founded in 1752, the mission thrived despite its remote location because a freshwater spring irrigated its fields, orchards
and vineyards. It produced the finest wine on the peninsula for
many years, exporting it in stone vessels for lack of wood. In its
heyday, the mission supported a community of 1500 Cochimí
Indians. Although the missionaries abandoned it in 1822, a handful of Indians remained to keep the fields productive, and local
fruit and vegetable farmers have maintained the church ever since.

Desierto Vizcaíno

One unique feature of the old adobe church is its bell tower, built not on top of the church but 50 yards away. A small museum in the church displays Cochimí Indian artifacts. Pilgrims from all over Baja trek to this church to observe the Fiesta de Santa Gertrudis on November 16.

Back on the Baja Highway, another long side trip leads to Bahía Tortugas, on the tip of the Vizcaíno Peninsula. This road turns off Route 1 to the west, 71 kilometers south of Guerrero Negro. The first 26 kilometers are paved; the remaining 122 kilometers to the Pacific are not. They're sometimes badly washboarded but good enough to accommodate all passenger vehicles, including motor homes.

Staying on the main road, you cross a barren coastal plain and salt flats en route to **Bahía Tortugas**, the largest town on the Vizcaíno Peninsula, with a population of about 3000. Fishing for lobster and abalone is the main business here. Tourism has become a factor in the local economy, with a small but steady stream of gringo visitors arriving by boat and RV in roughly equal numbers. There are exceptionally fine beaches along the bay south of town—a good spot to dig for Pismo clams—and a few miles north, near the small village of Punta Eugenia.

Isla Cedros, the largest island off Baja's Pacific coast, lies 12 miles north of Punta Eugenia, the tip of the Vizcaíno Peninsula. The 12.5-mile-long, almost beachless island comprises two mountain peaks rising 3950 and 3488 feet above sea level; a broad saddle between them is sliced by the sheer cliffs of a deep, narrow canyon called the Gran Cañon. The north slopes of both mountains are covered by a "cloud forest" of evergreens that stand as much as 40 to 50 feet tall. Clumps of ball moss cling to the trees and obtain their moisture from the thick sea fog that often shrouds the island. Isla Cedros ("Cedar Island") refers to the juniper trees that grow here. The forest also contains two unique tree species, the Cedros Island pine and the Cedros Island oak, and provides habitat for a rare subspecies of mule deer and several unique rodent and lizard species. Pueblo de Cedros, on

AUTHOR FAVORITE

If I were to be stranded on a desert island, my top choice would be **Isla Cedros**. Not only does it offer spectacular vistas, a hidden canyon and cool, lush cloud forest, but the daily air service makes it easy to rescue yourself at the end of the adventure. Author Robert Louis Stevenson's widow, Fanny, discovered her own "Treasure Island" here when she came here to spend a season in solitude after her husband's death in 1904. See above for more information.

the east side of the island, has been a fishing village for centuries, ever since Cochimí Indians lived on the island. They were the only native people to hunt gray whale, killing the great beasts with spears.

Exportación de Sal moved its shipping port to Isla Cedros in 1967, and today the prosperous Pueblo de Cedros has a population of more than 3000—about half that of Guerrero Negro. As in Guerrero Negro, almost everybody on the island works for the salt company. Aside from the town, the island is undeveloped, and the northern half is practically inaccessible by land.

LODGING

Several very basic concrete-block motels have popped up along the main drag in Bahía Tortugas lately. The best bet remains the longest-established lodging in town, the clean, well-run **Vera Cruz Motel**. Somewhat upgraded in the face of competition, it has twin beds, baths with solar-heated showers, and little in the way of decor. When chilly winds blow off the ocean, which is often, the rooms can be drafty. ~ Bahía Tortugas. BUDGET.

Several Isla Cedros residents offer simple rooms for rent in their homes or adjacent guest cottages. Availability depends on the presence or absence of transient dock workers. Watch for "se renta" signs. ~ Isla Cedros. BUDGET.

DINING

Several *comedores* along the main road in Bahía Tortugas offer fish tacos. For a full Mexican dinner, try the no-frills restaurant at the **Vera Cruz Motel**. ~ Bahía Tortugas. BUDGET.

GROCERIES

If you're heading for the Vizcaíno Peninsula, stock up on food before leaving Guerrero Negro. Groceries are scarce in these parts.

BEACHES & PARKS

PLAYA MALARRIMO 🚶 Along the way to Bahía Tortugas, a turnoff goes north to one of the most interesting out-of-the-way beaches on the Pacific coast—if you're equipped to get there. The side trip to Playa Malarrimo requires four-wheel drive to cross rocky areas and deep sand drifts. This hard-to-reach beach near the mouth of Scammon's Lagoon has a reputation for some of the best beachcombing in the world. Ocean currents from the North Pacific swirl into the north coast of the Vizcaíno Peninsula, depositing Japanese floats, huge logs from British Columbia and plastic containers from many lands along the powdery beach. There are no travelers' facilities of any kind, and you can spend days at Playa Malarrimo without seeing another human being. ~ The road, marked with a small sign that says "Malarrimo," turns off from the route to Bahía Tortugas about 80 kilometers from the Baja Highway. It's another 42 kilometers to the beach.

▲ There are no restrictions on camping at Playa Malarrimo. Fierce winds can make the experience less than idyllic, though.

Outdoor Adventures

FISHING

BAHÍA DE LOS ANGELES Although old-timers will tell you that fishing in the Bahía de los Angeles is not what it used to be, it's still the top sportfishing center on the Sea of Cortez. Especially during the summer months, the catch includes sea bass, dorado (mahi mahi), tuna, halibut and grouper, as well as many exotic species of tropical fish (including triggerfish, considered a delicacy in these parts). Yellowtails run during the winter months. Fishing guides and limited fishing supplies are available at **Guillermo's** (686-650-3209) and **Casa Díaz** (686-650-3206). Fishing is said to be better farther south at the remote outpost of Bahía San Francisquito.

DIVING

EL ROSARIO AREA There's good diving on the reef of the south end of **Isla San Geronimo**, off Punta Baja near El Rosario, though sea lions can be possessive about the area. They are unaccustomed to human visitors, whose presence may set off a din of barking. **Arecife Sacramento**, a reef a few miles south of the island, lies so close to the surface that it can only be dived on a calm day when swells are less than two feet. Its top is a forest of surf grass—a slender, waving seaweed that grows up to 12 feet tall here and harbors an amazing array of underwater life, including huge lobsters, giant sea bass and benign horn sharks. Several ships have wrecked here, including the reef's namesake, the paddlewheel steamer *Sacramento*, which went down in 1872 with a fortune in silver and gold. Another good shipwreck dive on the reef is the *Goodwill*, a luxury yacht that sank in 1969.

BAHÍA DE LOS ANGELES Isla Coronado is the most popular diving area (scuba divers prefer the east coast, snorkelers the west coast around little Isla Mitlan), though the whole rock reef where the bay plunges into the Canal de Ballenas is scuba-suitable. Bring your own air—there is no dive shop in town.

VIZCAÍNO PENINSULA The **Islas San Benito**, a cluster of three tiny islands 16 miles northwest of Isla Cedros, has been the ruin of tuna boats, industrial fishing ships and even an oil tanker. Several of the wrecks make great dives. The waters around these islands

AUTHOR FAVORITE

I thought I'd been whale watching before, but nothing compares with gliding among thousands—yes, thousands!—of gray whales at **Parque Natural de la Ballena Gris**, in an open fishing boat so close to water level that you can dangle your fingers in the water, and maybe even touch a whale. The most amazing part of the experience is the realization that the whales are as curious about us humans as we are about them. See page 172 for more information.

also boast a junglelike kelp forest and rock reefs teeming with fish, supporting some divers' claim that the San Benitos offer the best scuba diving in Baja. Guides on Isla Cedros take divers and nature lovers out to these remote islands, which also have a large elephant seal colony. The main limitation is air, since the passenger planes that fly from Guerrero Negro to Isla Cedros won't carry many scuba tanks, and once there, there's no place to refill them.

EL ROSARIO AREA   **Punta Baja**, along the coast a few miles west of El Rosario, is a surfers' secret with a long right-point break.

BAHÍA DE LOS ANGELES   Windsurfing is becoming popular here because the protected waters develop little chop in the wind. The prevailing wind is out of the north, enabling windsurfers to sail seven miles from **Punta La Gringa**, north of town, through the cluster of islands in the middle of the bay before landing on the far shore.

VIZCAÍNO PENINSULA   Five miles offshore from Bahía Tortugas, **Isla Natividad** offers great surfing summer and winter. Known by surfers as the most powerful beach break in North America, the break on the east side of the island is known for big, long tubes and lots of them. Locals in Bahía Tortugas and Punta Eugenia take surfers across to the island, a 45-minute trip each way. **Baja Airventures** organizes four- to six-day surfing trips from San Diego to Isla Natividad by private plane from May through October. ~ 800-221-9283.

SURFING & WINDSURFING

BAHÍA DE LOS ANGELES   Seri Indians routinely crossed the Sea of Cortez by canoe just south of here. By following the coast of giant Isla Tiburón on the mainland side, then hopping through the Mid-Rift Islands, they could make the crossing without ever being more than seven miles from shore. Modern kayakers have made the crossing, too, but it's not an adventure to be taken lightly. Most kayakers restrict their island-hopping to stepping-stone expeditions across the mouth of the bay, where the longest distance between islands is two miles. **Guillermo's** has a few rental kayaks.

GUERRERO NEGRO AREA   Formerly a favorite kayaking spot, Scammon's Lagoon and nearby waters are now off-limits to kayaks and other private boats during whale season. Access to Scammon's Lagoon is difficult at other times of year, when the road to Parque Natural de Ballena Gris is closed, but kayaking on Laguna Guerrero Negro offers solitude and fine birdwatching. There are no kayak rentals in town.

KAYAKING

BAHÍA DE LOS ANGELES   While several species of whales are commonly spotted in the Canal de Ballenas between the bay and Isla Angel de la Guarda during the winter months, their appearance is unpredictable enough that local guides offer boat trips for

WHALE WATCHING & BOAT TOURS

Text continued on page 184.

Baja's Imaginary Stairway

If you follow the road that goes north from Bahía de los Angeles past a series of fishermen's campgrounds to Punta la Gringa, you will see signs pointing the way to the "Escalera Nautica" ("Nautical Staircase"). Similar signs mark the turnoff from Route 1 to Santa Rosalita (sometimes called "Santa Rosalillito"), a fishing village on the Pacific coast north of Rosarito (this is not the same Rosarito as the resort between Tijuana and Ensenada). But if you actually follow these signs, you'll soon discover that the Escalera Nautica doesn't exist.

The concept of the Escalera Nautica has been promoted on and off since 1976, and it was the top priority tourism development of President Fox's administration (2000–2006). The idea is that the Mexican government would establish a series of 22 recreational boating ports up and down both shores of the Baja Peninsula. These would include five ports that already exist, six that would be expanded and eleven that would be newly built. The marina ports would be located at intervals of 120 nautical miles, or one day's boat travel.

Patterned on the model of Cancún, the Escalera Nautica project would involve $2 billion in development funds from the government and would solicit private companies to build luxury resort hotels and golf courses. It would, in fact, be the most ambitious tourism project FONART, Mexico's tourism development agency, has undertaken since Cancún in the 1960s.

There's one problem with this scheme, though. Most of the northern marinas are on the Pacific side of the peninsula, while most of the southern ones are on the Sea of Cortés side. No problem, say project promoters. Simply dig a canal across the narrowest part of the peninsula, between Santa Rosalita and Bahía de los Angeles—a map distance of 82 miles. This notion looks good on paper, but anyone who actually flies over the rugged terrain of the Sierra San Borja, with its mazes of canyons, volcanic cones and lava flows, will soon conclude that an 82-mile canal through this terrain is unlikely to ever be built.

An alternative plan, put forth by the Fox administration, is to pave a special highway, exclusively for boats, from one side of the peninsula to the other. Boats up to 55 feet long would be loaded onto tractor trailers and pulled by truck between the Pacific and the Sea of Cortés. Yet this "dry canal" or "land bridge" seems unlikely, too. If a peninsula crossing were feasible here, it seems that the Baja Highway would have used the same route instead of the more southerly route through the Cataviña Boulder Field.

Still, the idea remains on the table as panel after panel of experts are commissioned to study it, while environmental groups pour their energy into protesting the project. Meanwhile, a dredging project was begun to widen and deepen the channel approaching Santa Rosalito, though it has already begun to fill with silt. And a mile or so of the proposed land bridge from Bahía de los Angeles has been completed (though not paved), enabling the state of Baja California to run tourism ads that seem to show a sailboat traveling by canal through the desert—artfully concealing that it is being towed by a truck.

Optimistic estimates by the Mexican government claim that by 2014 the marinas will attract 50,000 boats annually, while the resorts associated with them will bring 1 million visitors from the western United States alone. To judge for yourself the likelihood of this, simply follow the "Escalera Nautica" signs out past where the pavement ends and ask yourself how likely it is that there will ever be a Sheraton or a Fiesta Americana resort there. (But then again, people probably thought the same thing about Cancún back in the 1960s.)

birdwatching instead of whale watching. Whether you take one of these jaunts or paddle your own kayak among the islands, you stand a fair chance of encountering a Minke, gray or blue whale in the bay.

GUERRERO NEGRO AREA Scammon's Lagoon is the largest of three gray-whale calving grounds along the Pacific coast of Baja. The whales were all but exterminated in the 1850s, and only in the 1990s has their population returned to pre-whaling levels— 18,000 to 20,000 according to recent counts. From December through March, guides take whale watchers out in large motorized *pangas* from the dock at **Parque Natural de la Ballena Gris** south of Guerrero Negro. Reservations are not necessary; departures are intermittent through midafternoon. The boats are prohibited by international treaty from approaching within 100 yards of a whale, but it's okay if the whale approaches the boat. Since gray whales often seem as curious about humans as we are about them, close encounters with the great beasts are more likely than not. Whale-watching expeditions to the mouth of Laguna Guerrero Negro, offered by guides who advertise their services at restaurants in Guerrero Negro, depart from the **Old Salt Port** north of town. To book a trip in advance, call **Laguna Whale Watching Tours.** ~ 615-157-0050; e-mail lagtours@nextgeninter. net.mx. Another good outfitter is **Malarrimo Ecotours.** ~ Restaurant-Bar Malarrimo, Boulevard Zapata, Guerrero Negro; ~ 615-157-0100; e-mail malarrimo@telnor.net. From the United States, San Diego–based **Baja Jones Adventure Travel** organizes five-day whale-watching trips to Scammon's Lagoon by van, accompanied by an expert in cetacean zoology. ~ 310-831-1317; www.greywhale.com, e-mail keith@greywhale.com.

VIZCAÍNO PENINSULA Guides from Bahía Tortugas and Punta Eugenia are often available to take nature lovers by boat to the **Islas San Benito** to see the elephant seals and large colonies of sea birds.

HIKING **DESIERTO CENTRAL** The area around Cataviña invites short hikes in the marvelous cactus forest and boulder fields. There are few visible trails, and the baking midday heat makes it advisable to limit hiking to the early morning and dusk. Follow arroyos to avoid getting lost. Most examples of rock art seem to be found near arroyos, too.

BAHÍA DE LOS ANGELES The **Mina Santa Marta,** an abandoned mine from the 1880s, makes for the most spectacular hiking or backpacking trip in the area. From the public dump two miles south of town, the bed of a former railway runs six steep miles up the canyon to the mine site. Hikers can also follow the old narrow-gauge railroad bed partway up to **Mina San Juan** from the ghost town of Las Flores.

VIZCAÍNO PENINSULA Hikers will find challenging trails on **Isla Cedros**. A five-mile ascent from Pueblo de Cedros to the 3950-foot summit of Pico Cedros earns you a spectacular view of the nearby Islas de San Benito, Isla Natividad, the Vizcaíno Peninsula and the distant shore of Scammon's Lagoon. From the summit, the trail descends the north side of the mountain and splits. The right fork goes down into the Gran Cañon and eventually to a secluded beach at the canyon mouth, seven miles from the mountain summit. The left fork follows the canyon rim for several miles before veering into the heart of the forest. The total distance from the summit is eight miles.

Transportation

AIR

There is no commercial air service to El Rosario, Cataviña or Bahía de Los Angeles, though the latter has a good airstrip to accommodate the numerous private pilots who fly in.

At this writing, the daily flights that used to carry salt workers back and forth to Isla Cedros are suspended indefinitely because the company's old DC-3 crashed. The only air service to Isla Cedros is the twice-weekly flight offered by **Aero Cedros**, with tickets available from an open-air stand near the Guerrero Negro bus station on Boulevard Emiliano Zapata.

BUS

Autotransportes de Baja California operates four first-class buses daily from Tijuana and one from Mexicali, stopping in Guerrero Negro on their way south to La Paz and Los Cabos.

A first-class bus runs from the Tijuana terminal to Bahía de los Angeles once a week, leaving at 6 a.m. on Saturday and returning on Sunday.

CAR

El Rosario, Cataviña and the Parque Natural del Desierto Central are along **Route 1**, and Guerrero Negro is just a short distance off the main highway. Bahía de los Angeles is 67 kilometers off the Baja Highway on a paved road that, confusingly, is also designated as Route 1. The unpaved road from the main highway east to remote Bahía San Francisquito is designated as **Route 18**, while the road west to the tip of the Vizcaíno Peninsula has no route number but is referred to as the **Carretera Bahía Tortugas**.

Addresses & Phone Numbers

Policia Municipal ~ Guerrero Negro; 615-157-0222
Policia Federal (Highway Patrol) ~ 615-157-0848
Policia ~ Guerrero Negro; 615-157-0222
IMSS Hospital y Clínica ~ 615-157-0433
Secretaría de Turismo de Bahía de los Angeles ~ Avenida López
   Mateos 1250, Ensenada; 646-150-3206

SEVEN

Southern Baja

Imagine impossibly brilliant turquoise water—so still that each dip of your paddle leaves concentric ripples as your kayak glides along the surface of Bahía Concepción, so clear that you can see triggerfish darting below. Feel the thrill as curious dolphins surround you. On the distant shore, white sand beaches lined with palm trees and giant cactus provide the kind of camping spots that daydreams are made of.

If any one part of the peninsula represents the spirit of "hidden" Baja, this is it. In this chapter, you'll discover many of the best places on the peninsula for kayaking, sport fishing and whale watching, as well as the best-preserved old Spanish colonial mission churches, ancient Indian rock art and unexpectedly verdant canyons hidden deep in the mountains.

It's not that the towns of Southern Baja are off the beaten path—all of them lie along the Baja Highway. But they seem seem lost in time: the colonial outposts of past centuries live on as havens for gringos and Mexicans alike who choose to be refugees from civilization. At San Ignacio, Mulegé and Loreto you'll find 18th-century missions that did not return to dust, like the forlorn ruins of the north, but lived on thanks to the farm families who have cultivated the fields and orchards for many generations. These towns share a tropical, easygoing hammock-between-palm-trees feel that Los Cabos must once have had. Then there's Santa Rosalía, a unique old French colonial mining town that has survived both the departure of the French and the closing of the mine.

When it comes to great beaches, this area is hard to beat. Bahía Concepción, between Mulegé and Loreto, is so idyllic that many people camp along its beaches for months at a time, creating a do-it-yourself resort atmosphere with separate beaches for different camping styles, from full-hookup motor homes with boats in tow to four-wheel-drive tailgaters in search of utter solitude.

Two decades ago, the government agency that created Cancún and Los Cabos proclaimed its intention to create another mega-resort along the beaches south of Loreto, but dropped the project when hotel chains proved skeptical about investing there. Today, though the picture-perfect little resort area has fewer than

300 hotel rooms, it boasts the region's only international airport—with three planes a day—and the only golf course between Tijuana and Los Cabos.

This sandy stretch of low-rent paradise has avoided Los Cabos–style resort crowds and preserved its unique character because it is so hard to get to. You can get to Santa Rosalía by ferry from the Mexican mainland, or to Loreto by plane direct from Los Angeles, but there is no place to rent a car for hundreds of miles. This leaves the magnificent seascapes exclusively to the modest flow of tourists who come by motor home, van, camper truck, car or motorcycle. Many are in a hurry to reach La Paz or Los Cabos when they first discover this area and resolve to linger here on their trip back north. A growing number return year after year for longer stays.

San Ignacio Area

From its location on the map—in the middle of the Desierto Vizcaíno, separated from the Pacific coast by vast salt flats and from the Sea of Cortez by the Tres Vírgenes volcano field—travelers might expect San Ignacio to be another of those forlorn desert outposts that punctuate Central Baja's long, empty highway stretches. Those who take the winding, two-kilometer road that descends into town from the Baja Highway are in for a pleasant surprise. San Ignacio is a lush little desert oasis and the first town on the southward trip down the Baja Peninsula that feels like Old Mexico.

What maps do not reveal is that San Ignacio is set in a broad valley flanked on both sides by sheer volcanic cliffs and filled with date palm trees. Although the spring-fed Río de San Ignacio, which parallels the highway just north of town, doesn't go anywhere—its water normally evaporates in the desert sun long before reaching the Bahía de San Ignacio—it provides a reliable water source for the palm trees, as well as the oranges, pomegranates, grapes and corn grown on compact farms surrounding the town.

The palms were planted by Franciscan missionaries, who founded Misión San Ignacio Kadakaamán on the site in 1728. Thanks to the reliable water supply and rich soil, the mission grew to become the largest on the Baja Peninsula, ministering to more than 5000 Cochimí Indians. Since 1840, when the mission was abandoned, the palm trees have grown wild to dominate the town's skyline and colonize the river valley as far as the eye can see. Today, San Ignacio is a farming and ranching center with a population of 4000, including many fair-skinned descendants of German sailors who were stranded in nearby Santa Rosalía by a naval embargo during World War I.

In the summer of 1997, tinder-dry palm trees caught fire and set buildings ablaze throughout the north side of town. Townspeople and tourists rallied to fight the fire, stopping it just short of the church. Although the adjoining museum was damaged, the old mission survived the flames intact.

San Ignacio is the point of departure for two adventures into the Baja backcountry. Both are usually undertaken with guides from San Ignacio. Some of Baja's most magnificent Indian rock painting caves are found in the rugged canyonlands to the north; the most pristine of Baja's gray whale calving areas is Laguna San Ignacio, to the west. During the winter, some guides offer multi-day tours that include visits to both the caves and the lagoon.

SIGHTS

The tallest building in town, **Misión San Ignacio de Loyola** has the most ornate exterior of any Baja mission church; it recalls the great architecture of old Spain on a small scale. The timeworn, four-foot-thick volcanic stone walls were erected at the direction of Jesuit missionaries in 1728; Dominicans extensively renovated the church in 1786, adding false columns, biblical statuary, Moorish-style roof ornaments and elaborate stonework around the windows and doorways. The church is open to the public in the daytime and early evening. It contains an elaborate gold-leafed, viceregal-style altar framing a *nicho* that contains a statue of the town's patron saint, San Ignacio. There are also two side altars and several Colonial-era oil paintings. A sign at the entrance urges visitors to dress respectfully and refrain from chewing gum. A smaller structure beside the church houses a collection of Indian pictographs found on rocks nearby. ~ San Ignacio.

Across the street from the church is a **zócalo**, or town plaza, as shady and inviting as any in the tropics of mainland Mexico. Giant old Indian laurel trees form a sheltering canopy over the plaza. A handful of small stores and restaurants—pretty much all there is to the town—stands across the street from the south side of the plaza. ~ San Ignacio.

Laguna San Ignacio lies 67 kilometers west of the town of San Ignacio on a well-maintained—though unnervingly narrow—un-paved road that is usually suitable for passenger cars. It's the only one of Baja's three gray-whale calving areas (the others are Scammon's Lagoon and Bahía Magdalena) that remains untouched by development. The road leads past several tiny fish camps to Punta Yuca, a muddy, rocky point near the mouth of the 17-mile-long lagoon. This vantage lets whale watchers view the great beasts from shore much closer than at Scammon's Lagoon or Bahía Magdalena. Guides at the fish camps of La Laguna and La Fridera offer whale-watching boat trips during the winter months.

Continuing west from San Ignacio toward Santa Rosalía, the Baja Highway skirts the base of the 6300-foot **Volcanes Tres Vírgenes**. These barren peaks, their steep slopes splashed with color-ful red and black hues, are Baja's only active volcanoes. Major volcanic activity occurred here as recently as the 1850s, and con-temporary hikers sometimes report fumes in or near the south-ernmost of the three craters.

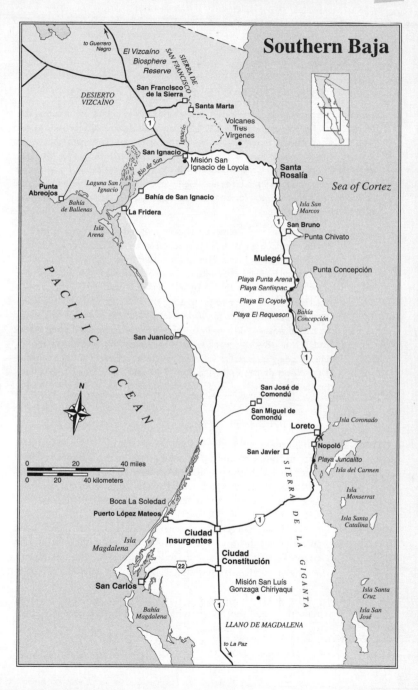

Southern Baja

to Guerrero Negro

El Vizcaíno Biosphere Reserve

SIERRA DE SAN FRANCISCO

DESIERTO VIZCAÍNO

San Francisco de la Sierra

☐ Santa Marta

Volcanes Tres Virgenes

San Ignacio ☐ Misión San Ignacio de Loyola

Río de San Ignacio

Santa Rosalía

Sea of Cortez

Punta Abreojos

Laguna San Ignacio

Bahía de Ballenas

☐ Bahía de San Ignacio

☐ La Fridera

Isla Arena

Isla San Marcos

1 San Bruno

Punta Chivato

Mulegé

Punta Concepción

Playa Punta Arena
Playa Santispac
Playa El Coyote
Playa El Requeson

Bahía Concepción

P A C I F I C

☐ San Juanico

O C E A N

N

0   20   40 miles
0   20   40 kilometers

San José de Comondú

San Miguel de Comondú

1

Loreto

Isla Coronado

San Javier ☐

Nopoló

Playa Juncalito

Isla del Carmen

SIERRA   DE   LA   GIGANTA

Isla Monserrat

Isla Santa Catalina

Boca La Soledad

Puerto López Mateos

Isla Magdalena

Ciudad Insurgentes

Ciudad Constitución

22

1

Misión San Luís Gonzaga Chiriyaqui ●

San Carlos

Bahía Magdalena

LLANO DE MAGDALENA

to La Paz

Isla Santa Cruz

Isla San José

San Ignacio's Painted Caves

Several of the most spectacular Indian cave-painting sites in Baja are found in the Sierra de San Francisco, due north of San Ignacio. Rising to 5200 feet above sea level, the steep, barren mountains conceal deep, palm-lined canyons that were home to a mysterious Indian race from about A.D. 500 to 1500. Unlike the rock art farther north around Cataviña, the murals in this region depict humans and animals—deer, mountain lions, birds and even whales. The sites are under the protection of Mexico's Instituto Nacional de Antropología e Historia and can only be visited with a licensed guide.

CUEVA PALMARITO   The most frequently visited rock art site in the San Ignacio area, Cueva Palmarito is reached by a five-mile hike or mule ride from Rancho Santa Marta. The spectacular mural covers a cliff face 150 feet long and 60 feet high, sheltered by a rock overhang. Guided tours can be arranged leaving from San Ignacio, or motorists with high-clearance vehicles can make the two-hour drive to the ranch and obtain a guide there. To reach the ranch, drive 14 kilometers east from San Ignacio on the Baja Highway and turn off to the north on the marked Santa Marta road. This narrow, rocky road winds higher and higher into the mountains, affording spectacular views of the Vizcaíno Desert and the canyons of the Sierra de San Francisco, for 29 kilometers to dead-end at Rancho Santa Marta.

LODGING   San Ignacio's best hotel is **Hotel Desert Inn,** similar in style, decor and amenities to the other properties in this ubiquitous Baja motel chain. On the way into town from the main highway, it has 28 bright, air-conditioned rooms around an interior patio, as well as a swimming pool and a game room. ~ San Ignacio; phone/fax 615-154-0300, 800-026-3605. MODERATE.

La Posada San Ignacio, a no-frills budget motel on a back street two blocks southeast of the *zócalo,* offers six plain, utilitarian rooms kept spotless by the friendly German-Mexican managers, who also guide cave-painting tours. ~ San Ignacio; 615-154-0313. BUDGET.

HIDDEN ▶   The **Casa Elvira,** an old adobe house in the center of town, rents one room short-term, with a three-day minimum stay. It has one full-size bed, an outside bath and kitchen privileges, and it opens onto a peaceful patio shaded by lush vegetation with a picnic table under a ramada. ~ San Ignacio. Reservations: Apar-

GARDNER CAVE   An even more challenging rock art expedition takes travelers up the west side of the sierra to the remote village of **San Francisco de la Sierra**, where guides are available for the three-day roundtrip by burro to Gardner Cave, also known as Cueva Pintada. Considered the finest known example of Baja rock art, this mural beneath the volcanic cliffs of Arroyo San Pablo measures 30 feet high and more than 500 feet long, with layer upon layer of images of men, women and wildlife. The cave was named for mystery novelist Erle Stanley Gardner, who devoted his later years to exploring the Baja backcountry and who wrote books and magazine articles about his discoveries—including Gardner Cave, which he found in 1962. To reach San Francisco de la Sierra, go 45 kilometers northwest from San Ignacio on the Baja Highway and turn east on the unpaved road near kilometer marker 118; a small sign reads "Pinturas Rupestres." The road serves several area ranches; it is wide and well graded, and passenger cars should have no problem, though motor homes may find some switchbacks difficult to negotiate. It is 37 kilometers from the highway turnoff to the village.

CUEVA DE RATÓN   Visitors who aren't up to the long burro trek to Gardner Cave can see a more modest mural just off the road, four kilometers below San Francisco de la Sierra. The site, Cueva de Ratón, is similar in character to that at Gardner Cave but only about 30 feet long. A guide is required, and local police patrol the area to stop trespassers.

tado Postal Urbana 2-62, La Paz 23070; 615-154-0158, fax 615-125-5750. BUDGET.

Set in a date palm grove beside the springs that feed the Río San Ignacio, the Canadian-owned **Ignacio Springs Bed & Breakfast** offers lodging in five Mongolian-style yurts with shared baths. Some have queen- or king-sized beds and some offer air-conditioning. There is also a luxury palapa at the water's edge. Kayaks are available for guests' use. Rates include a full breakfast and other meals are available by advance arrangement. ~ San Ignacio; phone/fax 615-154-033. BUDGET TO MODERATE.

The largest and best equipped of several campgrounds in San Ignacio is **El Padrino RV Park**, set among palm trees just south of Hotel Desert Inn. Seven of the 38 campsites have full hookups, and the restrooms have hot showers and flush toilets—luxuries that other campgrounds in the area lack! There's even a swimming pool. ~ San Ignacio; phone/fax 615-154-0089. BUDGET.

DINING **Restaurant Chalita**, a casual dining room with singing birds in an old home on the west side of the *zócalo*, has *comida corrida* dinner specials that change daily, as well as favorites like *chiles rellenos* (stuffed chile peppers) and *pescado al mojo de ajo* (fish in garlic sauce). ~ Calle Hidalgo 9, San Ignacio; 615-154-0082. BUDGET.

Farther up the same street, **Restaurant-Bar Rene**, a thatched-roof open-air eatery just off the *zócalo* by a small pond, serves American-style breakfasts and simple seafood dinners such as *calamar* (squid) and *camarones empanizados* (breaded shrimp). ~ Hildago 9, San Ignacio; 615-154-0256. BUDGET.

Located in the Hotel Desert Inn, **Las Cazuelas** is clean, classy and tourist-oriented. The traditional Mexican fare emphasizes regional specialties from the mainland, such as *pollo en mole* (chicken in a chocolate-and-chile sauce), as well as shrimp and lobster selections. ~ San Ignacio; 615-154-0300. MODERATE.

Restaurant-Bar Flojo, the plain-looking restaurant in El Padrino RV Park, specializes in surprisingly low-priced lobster tails and other seafood offerings, as well as heaping burrito plates. ~ San Ignacio; 615-154-0089. BUDGET.

On the main highway near the San Ignacio turnoff, **Restaurant Quichules** serves fresh seafood dishes as well as Mexican-style beefsteaks. The decor is minimal, the service is cheerful, and the cleanliness is striking. ~ Route 1, Km. 3. BUDGET.

GROCERIES There is a **Conasupo**—a government-run convenience store that sells milk, eggs, tortillas and other staples—at the intersection where the road to San Ignacio leaves the main highway.

SHOPPING San Ignacio is the home of a unique homebrewed liqueur called Damiana, known throughout Baja California Sur as a potent aphrodisiac. It is usually available in the little general store on the south side of the *zócalo*.

▼▼▼▼▼▼▼▼▼▼▼▼▼
Santa Rosalía Area

Baja Highway travelers (and travel writers) generally don't pay much attention to Santa Rosalía, a workingman's town with no beach to speak of and fewer recreational facilities than auto parts stores. The rare visitor who takes time to stroll around may find a rude charm there; the town's character is absolutely unique.

Santa Rosalía is the seaport for all the towns covered in this chapter. It lies directly across the 100-mile-wide Sea of Cortez from Guaymas, western Mexico's largest port city. Car ferries connect Santa Rosalía with the mainland and bring in cowboy clothing, hardware, kitchen utensils, magazines and all the other merchandise on display in the shops—much of it otherwise unavailable between Ensenada and La Paz. This connection with mainland Mexico sustains a population of 14,000, making Santa Rosalía the region's largest town, even though the copper mine that was the original reason for its existence shut down in 1985.

Santa Rosalía was founded in 1885 by the Rothschild family's Paris-based mining corporation, Compania de Boleo. A German shipping company, Casa Moeller, sold the House of Rothschild its rights to mine copper there but retained the exclusive right to transport ore from the mine. The French copper mine grew into a huge operation with nearly 400 miles of tunnels, a large smelter with fuming smokestacks, and a work force of thousands—mainly Yaqui Indians from mainland Sonora and Chinese immigrants managed by Colonialist French overseers. The cultural mix was further complicated during World War I, when the United States Navy impounded the German ships used to transfer the ore, stranding hundreds of German sailors in Santa Rosalía. Many married local women and settled down in Santa Rosalía and nearby San Ignacio, where their descendants still live.

Most of the French population left with the closing of the mine, but the names of the town's two residential districts—Mesa Francesa and Mesa Mexicana, situated on opposite sides of the canyon and downtown area—recall the segregation that divided the town in earlier times.

Motor homes have problems negotiating the narrow streets and tight corners in town. The best plan is to park in the vicin-

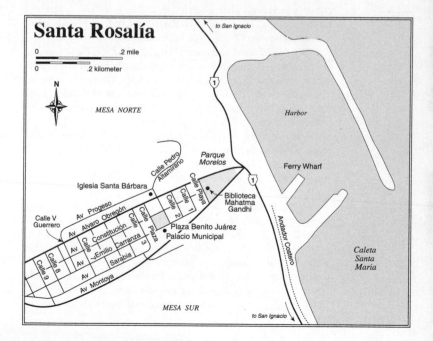

ity of Parque Morelos, at the east end of town just off the highway, and walk.

SIGHTS

Copper from the mine and smelter at Santa Rosalía was shipped up the Pacific coast to refineries in Oregon and British Columbia; the same ships brought back lumber. Santa Rosalía's French Colonial–style wood-frame houses and public buildings, now preserved under historic district regulations, are unique in Baja, giving the town its nickname—"the city of wood."

The best-known landmark in the city of wood is a unique latter-day "mission church" made of cast iron. The **Iglesia Santa Bárbara** is said to have been designed and built by architect Alexandre Gustave Eiffel for the 1889 Paris World Exposition, though no historical records have been found to confirm this. According to legend, Eiffel (who built the Eiffel Tower for the same fair) unveiled his prefab design as a prototype for churches to be erected by Catholic missionaries in tropical French colonies around the globe, since iron is termite-proof. The design won praise and awards, but enthusiasm for the concept waned after the exposition, and the disassembled pieces of the church ended up in a storage warehouse in Brussels, where officials of Santa Rosalía's mining company discovered it. They shipped the pieces around Cape Horn to Santa Rosalía, to be assembled in 1897 a block south of the town plaza. Painted battleship gray, the church's exterior is plain and simple. Inside, it is more ornate and traditional, and the stained-glass windows cast a heavenly glow. ~ Avenida Alvaro Obregón at Calle Altamirano.

The town's paved and rather plain *zócalo*, **Plaza Benito Juárez**, is located two blocks south of the Eiffel church, bounded by Calles Altamirano and Plaza and Avenidas Constitución and Carranza. Facing the *zócalo*, the block-long, many-windowed **Palacio Municipal** is one of the town's most elaborate examples of French colonial architecture. ~ Avenida Carranza.

Relics of Santa Rosalía's mining days are scattered around town. Historic photos are on display in the **Biblioteca Mahatma Gandhi**—the only public library between Ensenada and La Paz—near the east end of Santa Rosalía. ~ Avenida Constitución at Calle Playa.

An old **locomotive** that hauled ore from the copper mine to the smelter stands in front of the Hotel Frances, on the mesa north of town. ~ Calle Jean-Michel Cousteau.

Santa Rosalía's harbor lies to the east, beyond Route 1. The wide **Andador Costero** (coast walkway) runs south from the ferry dock at the harbor entrance. The most peaceful place in the bustling town, the walkway affords fine views of the harbor and Isla Tortugas, a dome-shaped, uninhabited island about 15 miles offshore.

Southeast of Santa Rosalía, and only four miles offshore, **Isla**   ◀ HIDDEN
San Marcos is an away-from-it-all possibility for fishing, hiking
and primitive camping. The mountainous island has a large seal
colony off the northern tip, and a mining camp and active gypsum
mine near the south end. It is within kayaking distance from San
Bruno, 29 kilometers south of Santa Rosalía. A free boat takes
mine workers to Santa Rosalía on Friday mornings at 6 a.m. and
returns to the island around 10:30 a.m.; visitors are welcome to
ride along, though a week is a long time to wait for the next boat
to leave the island.

A good bet for rock-bottom budget lodging, catering mainly to   **LODGING**
Mexican travelers coming and going on the ferry, is **Hotel Blanco**
y Negro, hidden away on a side street at the south end of Calle
3 (a one-way street running the wrong way; take Calle 4 to get
there). This 19th-century wooden building has nine rooms ranging from singles with shared bath to larger, two- and three-bed
rooms with private baths and local TV. ~ Avenida Sarabia at
Calle 3; 615-152-0080. BUDGET.

A mile south of Santa Rosalía on Route 1, **Hotel El Morro** has
24 modern, spacious rooms with air conditioning and TV. The
Spanish-style white stucco hotel overlooks the Sea of Cortez, and
some rooms have patios with sea views. The hotel has a swimming
pool. ~ Route 1 south Km. 15; phone/fax 615-152-0414. BUDGET.

Although there are no beachfront resort accommodations in
Santa Rosalía, there's a well-hidden one midway between Santa

AUTHOR FAVORITE

I'm partial to the **Hotel Frances** in Santa Rosalía because of its historic
ambience and the view from its second-floor balcony, not to mention it's the
only hotel I know of with a locomotive in the parking lot. Once the finest
lodging in town, it was built by the mining company on a hilltop above town
in 1886 to accommodate business visitors. It closed down along with the
copper mine in 1985 but continued to operate as a restaurant. A national
historic monument, the hotel reopened after a complete interior renovation in 2000. Its 17 guest rooms have air conditioning, private tiled
baths, balconies, local TV and touches of ersatz elegance. There's a pool
and a shaded patio. Not that Santa Rosalia is a prime tourist destination unless you're planning to take the ferry to the Mexican mainland
the next morning, but if you do find it convenient to spend the night
in the old mining town, this is the place to do it. ~ Calle Jean-Michel
Cousteau 15; phone/fax 615-152-2052. BUDGET.

Rosalía and Mulegé. **Hotel Posada de las Flores Punta Chivato** overlooks miles of deserted beaches on the Canal San Carlos from its solitary vantage on a rocky point. Its 28 rooms have fireplaces and two double beds apiece. There's a swimming pool and a sundeck suspended over the cliff, and mountain bikes, sea kayaks and a volleyball court are available for guests' use. Beachcombers will find seashells as well as tide pools teeming with life; snorkelers can explore the rock reef just offshore. To get there, turn east off Route 1 at kilometer 156 and follow the graded dirt road for 20 kilometers to the hotel. The hotel has its own airstrip for fly-in guests, and an RV campground. No children under age 13. ~ Punta Chivato, 613-135-1165, fax 613-135-1099. MODERATE.

DINING

Café Tokio is one of the better eateries in downtown Santa Rosalía. It is run by a Japanese-Mexican family whose ancestors came to work in the mine generations ago. Despite the name, and the Japanese sign painted on the front window, the fare is thoroughly Mexican, as are most of the patrons. Specialties include enchiladas and seafood cocktails. ~ Avenida Alvaro Obregón 15. BUDGET.

Near the park at the east end of town, **Terco's Pollito** serves rotisserie-roasted whole chickens, which you can eat there or take out. The small, no-frills restaurant also serves a tasty seafood soup. ~ Avenida Alvaro Obregón at Calle 1; 615-152-0075. BUDGET.

Restaurante Selene, south of the ferry dock, has sea views and nicely presented lobster dinners, as well as traditional Mexican food. Service can be on the slow side, but air conditioning makes it one of the more comfortable places in town to wait. ~ Route 1 south; 615-152-0685. MODERATE.

GROCERIES

Founded by the mining company nearly a century ago, the **Panadería El Boleo** still makes French pastries and baguettes as well as traditional Mexican *bolillo* rolls and sweet rolls. It has a reputation among Baja buffs as the best bakery on the peninsula. For the widest selection, stop by before 10 a.m. Later in the day, you may find only *bolillos*. ~ Avenida Alvaro Obregón at Calle 3.

BEACHES & PARKS

PUNTA CHIVATO 🏃 🚣 🎣 A series of white beaches parallels the rough dirt road to Hotel Punta Chivato for about 12 miles. The first, Playa La Palmita, is accessible by passenger car; others, farther from the main road, may require four-wheel drive because of sandy road conditions. Playa El Chivato, near the hotel, is among the prettiest spots on the Sea of Cortez. They're all good spots for collecting seashells. ~ The road to Punta Chivato turns off to the east at Kilometer 156, about 42 kilometers south of Santa Rosalía.

▲ The beachfront campground at Punta Chivato, operated by the hotel, has palapas, outhouses and unheated showers, but no hookups. Sites cost $10 per night.

During the winter, gringos make up the majority of the population in Mulegé. Stores in the little town of 4500 are geared to the needs of snowbirds. The Río Mulegé, also known as the Río Santa Rosalía, flows along the south edge of town from springs in the mountains to the west. It is lined with shady RV campgrounds and North American–style bungalows dripping with bougainvillea and greenery.

The river—one of the few freshwater streams in Baja that flows year-round—supports the effulgent vegetation that gives Mulegé its tropical feel. It's easy to believe you're in steamy southern Mexico. In reality, Mulegé lies almost 400 miles north of the Tropic of Cancer, at about the same latitude as Corpus Christi, Texas, or Palm Beach, Florida.

Mulegé was founded as a Jesuit mission in 1705. The original church was destroyed in 1770 by a tropical storm—one of several that have flattened this palm-thatched town over the centuries—but not before a new stone church had been built to replace it. Mulegé grew to become one of the largest settlements in Baja in the early 19th century. Its fortunes waned when a much larger shipping port was built to the north, at Santa Rosalía. The missionaries' date palm plantations and fruit orchards had fallen into neglect by the 1930s, when farmers banded together to work them as an *ejido*.

The opening of the Baja Highway transformed Mulegé's economy from agriculture to tourism practically overnight. Since then, land title complications have been a frequent source of friction between local *ejidatarios* and newcomers. In 1996, a group of peasant activists seized the Hotel Serenidad, the largest hotel in town. The group evicted the guests and held the hotel for a year while the *ejido* and the municipal government fought in court

AUTHOR FAVORITE

My favorite spot in all of Baja is **Bahía Concepción**, where I can park my camper right on the beach, snorkel among bright-colored tropical fish, let my dog chase pelicans and vultures, paddle a rental kayak alongside playful dolphins and count on local vendors to bring by fresh produce for dinner. In fact, you can choose from beachfront camping areas that range from RV parks to remote tent sites you can only reach with four-wheel drive. See page 198 for more information.

over who owned the land on which it stands. More than a thousand other pending land title disputes still hinder development in the Mulegé area.

SIGHTS **Santa Rosalía de Mulegé** was built between 1754 and 1766. The stone church was designed in an "L" shape, with the architectural simplicity and grace characteristic of southern Baja missions. The mission was abandoned in 1828, but the church has been restored several times and is still used for worship. Inside the dimly lit church are an 18th-century bell and a statue of Santa Rosalía. The church stands on a mound overlooking the town and the river. To get there from town, follow Calle Zaragoza as it goes under the main highway and crosses the river, then turn right and follow the river road for a quarter-mile.

The **Museo Mulegé** displays items from the original mission, as well as Indian artifacts, antique diving gear and a presentation on mining in the region. The museum is housed in an old territorial prison that was in use until 1975. It was known as the *cárcel sin cerraduras*—prison without locks—because inmates were free to leave during daylight hours to work on local farms: Mulegé's remote location was enough to preclude escape. Many local residents today are descendants of convicts from the mainland who were sent to Mulegé's prison. ~ Calle Cananea.

Mulegé's major attraction, **Bahía Concepción**, lies south of town. Thirty miles long and only three miles wide at the mouth, sheltered by a mountainous peninsula, the crystal-clear, turquoise bay with its multitude of beaches stands out as the most idyllic seashore in all of Baja and a world-class sea-kayaking mecca. All the beaches on the west side of the bay are easily accessible from the main highway, and all have campgrounds—some luxurious and others fairly primitive. At the bay's south end, a dirt road leaves Highway 1 and curves around the shore, where the beach is strewn with seashells and locals dig for the huge chocolate clams served in local restaurants. Continuing up the rugged, undeveloped eastern shore, the road gradually deteriorates into a four-wheel-drive track, passing many small beach areas on its way to the lighthouse at Punta Concepción.

Two of the best-known and most-studied Indian rock art sites in Baja are near Mulegé, and either one can be seen on a one-day HIDDEN ▶ guided tour. The murals at **Gruta San Borjitas** are unusual in that many of the large human figures depicted there are shown shot with arrows. These images, also found at other sites around Mulegé, are virtually the only evidence suggesting warfare among the Indian people of Baja. Some of the figures have male genitalia, not found in rock art elsewhere, and petroglyph drawings of female sex organs cover the side walls of the cave. Northwest of Mulegé, Gruta San Borjitas is reached by a 52-kilometer drive—

the last 30 kilometers on a ranch road requiring four-wheel drive—followed by a two-hour mule ride.

Cañon La Trinidad is closer to Mulegé. You can drive an ordinary passenger car to Rancho La Trinidad, where guides charge less than those in Mulegé—when they are around, which is not all the time. To get there, turn west from the Baja Highway on the road by the ice plant one kilometer north of the Mulegé turnoff. The network of back roads can be confusing; follow signs for San Estanislao until you spot the sign for Rancho La Trinidad. From there, it's a half-mile on foot to the canyon and the first murals—an adventurous hike that involves fording the river and scaling a 12-foot cliff. The murals, like those at Gruta San Borjitas, contain an image of a man shot with arrows and several drawings of genitalia, as well as the "Trinidad deer," cited in anthropology texts as the epitome of Baja rock art. Two other, lesser sites farther up the canyon can be reached by fording the river several times and swimming a quarter of a mile up a narrow slot canyon. The cool, clear spring water there is the beginning of the Río Mulegé, though it flows underground for several miles below the end of the canyon.

◄ HIDDEN ►

Mulegé

LODGING   The Mulegé area caters much more to campers than to the resort trade. The closest thing to a luxury hotel is the **Hotel Serenidad**, located on the beach four kilometers south of town. The 50 guest rooms, two-bedroom cottages and luxury villas are air-conditioned and have fireplaces. Facilities include a swimming pool, tennis court, boat ramp and runway for private planes. There's also an RV park with full hookups. ~ Route 1 south; 615-153-0530; www.serenidad.com, e-mail saralaurajohnson@hotmail.com. MODERATE TO DELUXE.

In town, the **Hotel Rosita** has eight huge, air-conditioned, haphazardly furnished two-bedroom suites, each with a separate living room and kitchenette. It's ideal for budget-minded families and groups. ~ Calle Madero 2; 615-153-0270. BUDGET.

The **Hacienda de Mulegé** offers a choice of 18 comfortably furnished rooms, some with air conditioning and the rest with ceiling fans, around a swimming pool and tropical courtyard landscaped with palms and banana trees. The central lounge area is a restored ballroom with a large fireplace for chilly winter evenings. The bar here is Mulegé's favorite party spot, so earplugs are a must for guests who retire early. ~ Calle Romero Rubio 3; 615-153-0021. BUDGET.

Despite their youth hostelish look, the several guesthouses along Calles Moctezuma and Madero tend to cost slightly more than the larger in-town hotels. **Casa de Huéspedes Manuelita** has eight small rooms with private baths, spartan furnishings, sagging beds and table fans. Campers can take a shower here for less than $2. ~ Calle Moctezuma; 615-153-0175. BUDGET TO MODERATE.

The **Nochita Casa de Huéspedes** has the lowest rates of the bunch. ~ Calle Moctezuma; 615-153-0140. BUDGET TO MODERATE.

HIDDEN ►   On a side road toward the sea off Route 1 and about a mile south of the main Mulegé turnoff (watch for the Orchard RV Park sign), **Clementine's Bed & Breakfast and Casitas** offers four modern, comfortable guest rooms as well as five individual casitas along the white-sand beach where the Río Mulege flows into the bay. Accommodations vary in size and decor. Most casitas are air-conditioned, while the B&B rooms have ceiling fans. Most units have refrigerators. The light breakfast included in the room rate is minimal, but guests have the use of the kitchen in the main house. Sea kayaks and bicycles are available for guests' use. Reservations are essential, and there is a minimum two-night stay. ~ Oasis Río Baja; 615-153-0319; www.clementinesbaja.com, e-mail clifftaylor1942@hotmail.com. MODERATE TO DELUXE.

DINING   The restaurant at the **Hotel Serenidad**—open to nonguests—is an outdoor buffet but it's the closest thing you'll find to fine dining in Mulegé. Weekly dining specials are featured, including the Thursday Italian Night with shrimp pasta primavera and chicken cacciatore. On Saturday evenings the hotel hosts an all-you-can-eat pig roast complete with mariachis and folkloric dancers. ~ Route 1 south; 615-153-0530. MODERATE.

There are no upscale restaurants in town, but you'll find an abundance of great Mexican food served in simple surroundings at very reasonable prices. Try **Restaurant El Candil**, a longtime favorite that has been run by the same family for nearly four decades, near the triangular town plaza. The specialty is a heaping combination plate of *chiles rellenos* and tacos served with beans, rice and tortillas. ~ Calle Zaragoza 8; 615-153-0185. BUDGET.

Los Equipales Restaurante, an upstairs eatery with cooling breezes and a view that takes in most of the town, has a wide selection of Mexican regional specialties, including big beef and chicken burritos and tangy *cocteles de almejas* (clam cocktails). ~ Calle Moctezuma; 615-153-0330. MODERATE.

Some of the tastiest food in town can be found at its numerous hole-in-the-wall *comedores*. Near the turnoff from the Baja Highway, **Taquería Doney's** serves good *carne asada* (barbecued beef) tacos and *mulitas* (open-face tacos), as well as some of the tastiest guacamole on the planet. ~ Calle Moctezuma. BUDGET.

On Playa El Sombrerito, the little beach at the end of Calle Morelos where the river meets the sea, you will find **Café La Almeja**, a large open-air palapa that serves a range of seafood dishes including fish tacos, chocolate clams and the house specialty, *sopa de siete mares* (seven seas soup)—a rich stew of just about every kind of seafood that can be found in the Sea of Cortez. ~ Calle Playa. BUDGET.

GROCERIES Campers can stock up at any of several grocery stores in Mulegé, including **La Tienda Y** on the way into town from the highway, **Casa Yee** (Calle Madero 46, 615-153-0018) and **Alba's Super Mercado** by the town plaza. The only bakery around—and it's a good one—is at **Villa María Isabel**, an RV park on the south side of the river about two kilometers from town. Oaxacan Indian vendors make the rounds of Bahía Concepción beaches most

AUTHOR FAVORITE

My favorite restaurant on Bahía Concepción is the nameless one at the RV campground on **Playa Buenaventura**, where you can feast on hamburger-sized "chocolate" clams while enjoying a view of the beach with its abundant bird life through the big picture windows. It also has the liveliest bar scene on the bay after dark (and sometimes in the middle of the day). ~ Located off Route 1 at Km. 94. BUDGET.

days, selling what ever fresh produce is currently being harvested in the Llano de Magdalena agricultural region.

NIGHTLIFE

What little evening entertainment Mulegé has to offer can be found at the poolside patio bar of the **Hotel Serenidad**. The hotel's weekly pig roast draws a crowd. ~ Route 1 south; 615-153-0111. People also get together at night to watch TV in the sports bar at **Los Equipales Restaurante**. ~ Calle Moctezuma; 615-153-0330.

**BEACHES
& PARKS**

PLAYA PUNTA ARENA This is the northernmost of several beaches separated by rocky points along the western shore of Bahía Concepción. Together they make up Baja's most beautiful seashore. Fishermen's shacks, some of them occupied by gringos, line part of the south-facing beach. ~ Turn east off the Baja Highway at Km. 119 south of Mulegé and follow the good unpaved road for three kilometers to the beach.

▲ There is informal camping along the beach. Facilities are limited to outhouses and a few palapas; no hookups. Primitive campsites cost $4 per night; sites with palapas cost $6.

PLAYA SANTISPAC A popular spot for self-contained motor-home, van and truck campers, this pretty, sheltered cove can be crowded during the winter season. Besides camping facilities, there are two small beachfront restaurants. ~ Just off Route 1 at Km. 114.

▲ Campsites with palapas cost $6 to $7 per night, with an additional $1 charge for using the outhouses and cold showers. There is a sewage dumping station, but no hookups.

PLAYA LOS COCOS A forest of palm trees and soft, sugary white sand give this beach a tropical-paradise feel. Fishermen's shacks—some inhabited by gringos, as evidenced by stolen road-sign decor and a Texas state flag or two—occupy the north end of the beach; the rest is camperland. ~ Located off Route 1 at Km. 111.

▲ Campsites cost $4 per night. There are no hookups or shade palapas, though there is a dump station. There are outhouses. No drinking water.

PLAYA EL BURRO This curved beach on a calm, sheltered cove is one of the most peaceful spots on the west side of the bay. Except when large RV caravans pull in, most campers here are long-term snowbirds who return year after year. It's an appealing spot for tent camping. There's a small beachfront restaurant. Across the highway from the beach is an arroyo where examples of Indian rock art can be found. ~ Located off Route 1 at Km. 109.

▲ Campsites cost $3 per night. There are shade palapas and outhouses, but no drinking water.

PLAYA EL COYOTE 🏃 ⛵ 🎣 🚤 🛥️ 🛶 Facilities at this beach have gradually been upgraded year after year as increasing numbers of snowbirds have made their winter homes here. El Coyote shares the same protected cove with Playa El Burro, just on the other side of a small, rocky point. Isla Bargo, a small L-shaped island less than a quarter-mile offshore, also has a secluded beach. ~ Located off Route 1 at Km. 108.

▲ Tent and RV sites cost $5. There are palapas, outhouses, showers and drinking water.

PLAYA BUENAVENTURA 🏃 ⛵ 🎣 🚤 🛥️ 🛶 The most-developed beach on Bahía Concepción, this beach has a big RV park complete with a restaurant and bar, a convenience store, a boat ramp and restrooms with showers and flush toilets. Although the exposed location makes it less appealing for swimming than most of the other beaches, there is a remarkable abundance of bird life along the beach, from sandpipers to great blue herons and pelicans. ~ Located off Route 1 at Km. 94.

> Mulegé was captured for a single day by U.S. forces during the Mexican War.

▲ Campsites with shade palapas cost $5 per night; no hookups. Thatched-roof camping cabins furnished with cots are $15.

PLAYA EL REQUESON 🏃 ⛵ 🎣 🚤 🛥️ 🛶 This popular beach is unique because of the long, sandy spit that projects out to a small offshore island at low tide, submerging as the tide rises. Locals come here to dig for dark brown, hamburger-sized chocolate clams in the shallow flats along the sand bar. ~ Located off Route 1 at Km. 92.

▲ Sites cost $2. There are outhouses but no other facilities.

PLAYA ARMENTA 🏃 ⛵ 🎣 🚤 🛥️ 🛶 The funkiest of the east-shore sites, this *ejido*-run camping beach is a graceful crescent of white sand around a turquoise cove flanked by steep, rocky hills where vultures perch on tall cactuses. It's generally the least crowded of the beaches accessible from the highway. The shallow cove is ideal for swimming, and a short hike takes you to hilltops with excellent views of the bay. ~ Located off Route 1 at Km. 91.

▲ Campsites cost $3. There are tattered shade palapas and fairly rank outhouses. You can rent the "honeymoon cottage"—an unfurnished palm-thatch cabin on a hilltop past the south end of the beach—for $10 per night.

Loreto Area

The oldest settlement on the Baja Peninsula, Loreto dates back to 1697, when Jesuit missionary Padre Juan María Salvatierra chose it as the site of the first mission in California. Misión Nuestra Señora de Loreto was the headquarters from which all other missionary expeditions in Baja and Alta California were sent forth. Loreto served as the capital of California through the entire Spanish colonial era. In 1829, a few years after Mexico gained its independence from Spain, the town was so devastated by a hurricane that the Mexican government ordered it abandoned and moved the capital to La Paz, bringing Loreto's rich history to an abrupt end.

In the years after the U.S. Civil War, the forgotten ghost town was resettled by a handful of immigrant gringos whose descendants, Mexican families with anglo surnames, make up a significant part of the population today. Fishing was the only occupation in town, and residents lived at the subsistence level for generations until, in the the 1950s, improved shipping methods made a small commercial fishing industry possible.

Loreto languished as little more than a fish camp amid the ruins of bygone grandeur until the 1970s, when the laid-back little town was selected by FONATUR, Mexico's tourism development agency, as the site of a planned mega-resort project similar to Los Cabos. Using proceeds from Mexico's booming national oil company, the government sponsored the construction of an 18-hole championship golf course, a professional tennis complex and a modern airport capable of landing jetliners. Resort hotel chains proved reluctant to make large-scale investments in the Loreto area, though, and eventually the government directed its tourism infrastructure funds elsewhere.

Today, Loreto seems undiscovered once again—a laid-back, palm-shrouded old town of 10,000 with cobbled streets, flanked by an estuary where herons wade in search of prey as cattle graze along the grassy banks. Fishing *pangas* line the stony seashore, and squadrons of pelicans patrol the waterfront in impressive numbers. There are renewed efforts to develop Loreto as an international destination, with an eye toward marketing condominiums to *norteamericano* baby-boomer retirees. So far these efforts have met with only limited success, although a 6000-unit residential development with two 18-hole golf courses, a tennis center and a marina is nearing completion on Bahía Nopolo south of town.

SIGHTS   Inscribed in stone above the entrance to **Misión Nuestra Señora de Loreto**, the words "CABEZA Y MADRE DE LAS MISIONES DE BAJA Y ALTA CALIFORNIA" ("head and mother of the missions of Lower and Upper California") and the date "25 OCT 1697" reveal the antiquity of Loreto's church and its importance in colonial times. Although the architecture is less impressive than that of the mission churches at San Ignacio and San Javier, Loreto's church is famous for the wooden figure known as the Virgen de Loreto, widely believed to possess miraculous healing powers. ~ Calle Salvatierra.

On the west side of the church stands the **Museo de las Misiones**. Operated by the Mexican Instituto Nacional de Antropología e Historia, the museum contains antique weaponry, artifacts from missions throughout Baja and exhibits about ranching and agriculture, all arranged chronologically to present a 300-year history of Baja. Oddly, no mention is made of the Indians who constituted most of the population of the mission settlements. Admission. ~ Calle Salvatierra.

Isla del Carmen, a long, mountainous island, lies about ten miles southeast of Loreto. *Pangas* can be rented to take groups to the island, which is a popular whale watching, fishing and diving area. Now uninhabited, Isla del Carmen was once the site of a mining operation that produced 80 million pounds of salt a year. This and the smaller islands of Coronado, Danzante, Montserrat and Santa Catalina are now protected as part of the new Loreto National Marine Park. ◄ *HIDDEN*

A popular day trip from Loreto is through the rugged Sierra de la Giganta to **San Javier**, site of Baja's most beautiful mission church. Though rough and steep in spots, the road is passable by passenger cars. It turns off the main highway at Km. 118, two kilometers south of Loreto, and goes 37 kilometers into the moun- ◄ *HIDDEN*

tains, climbing to 1700 feet above sea level. Though this remote mountain village has few year-round residents, its general store serves numerous ranches in the area. The mission, **San Francisco Javier de Viggé-Biaundó**, was first established in 1720, and the present stone church dates back to 1744. It is still in use and contains an ornate altar that was carried by burro from Mexico City, as well as several 18th-century religious paintings.

Beyond San Javier, the road gets even steeper as it continues for another 42 kilometers and descends into a canyon and the twin villages of **San José de Comondú** and **San Miguel de Comondú**. These villages were established in the early 1700s as farms growing food for the mission at San Javier, since the canyon has a reliable year-round water supply. A mission church was later built at Comondú; it no longer exists, but other buildings survive from the original mission complex. The orange groves, vineyards, date palms and fig trees planted by the missionaries still provide a livelihood for residents.

LODGING

Downtown at the plaza, the **Hotel Plaza Loreto** is a two-story white stucco building surrounding a traditional tiled Spanish courtyard with palm trees. The 24 guest rooms have stark white walls, Mexican tiles, two full-sized beds each and ceiling fans as well as air conditioning. The location, across the street from the old mission church, adds to the Colonial ambience. ~ Avenida Hidalgo 2; 613-135-0280, fax 613-135-0855. MODERATE.

HIDDEN ►

Also by the plaza, the **Hotel Posadas de las Flores** is in the pink stucco, beautifully restored colonial building just off the plaza on Avenida Salvatierra. Even if you choose not to stay here—it's Loreto's most expensive hotel—step in for a look at the lobby. There's a rooftop swimming pool with a translucent bottom that fills the hotel interior two stories below with rippling light. The rooms are spacious and individually decorated with handmade furniture and quality art pieces. ~ Calle Salvatierra at the plaza; 613-135-1162, or 877-441-2860 in the U.S; www.posadadelas flores.com. ULTRA-DELUXE.

Travelers in search of a cheap place to sleep may wish to head for the **Motel Salvatierra**, centrally located on Loreto's main street. The rooms, though frayed around the edges, are clean and air-conditioned, with modern private bathrooms. The motel is within easy walking distance of the bus station and eight blocks from the waterfront. ~ Calle Salvatierra 125; 613-135-0021. BUDGET.

The **Motel El Dorado** meets the standards you'd expect of a quality motor inn in the United States, with handcarved Mexican furnishings and artwork, TVs, air conditioning and ceiling fans in its 11 guest rooms. ~ Calle Pipilla, a half block off Avenida Hidalgo; 613-135-1500, or 888-314-9023 in the U.S. BUDGET TO MODERATE.

Small, affordable and secluded yet right in the middle of town, the **Iguana Inn** has four individual, bright pink casitas— ◄ HIDDEN three recently renovated and a fourth newly built—around a walled courtyard with a fountain. All guest units are air-conditioned and have either kitchenettes or small refrigerators and microwaves. The inn is just one block from the seashore and marina and two blocks from Loreto's mission church and central plaza. ~ Calle Benito Juárez between Avenidas Madero and Davis; 613-135-1627; www.igaunainn.com, e-mail iguanainn@yahoo. com. MODERATE.

Baja Outpost, the town's major scuba-diving outfitter, has an eight-room compound surrounding a shady yard across from the seashore. In adobe buildings with palm-thatched roofs and Mexican tile floors, the guest rooms are simply furnished with two large beds that can be pulled together as a king-sized bed. Continental breakfast on the veranda is included, and there is an honor bar. Lodging here is a real bargain, though guests are expected to take dive trips. ~ Calle de la Playa (Boulevard López Mateos); 613-135-1134, or 888-649-5951 in the U.S.; www.baja outpost.com. MODERATE.

Eight kilometers south of town lies the beachfront Zona Turística de Nopoló. The beautiful bay with its wide, white-sand beach is the site of a long-range plan to build the Villages at Loreto Bay, a 6000-unit, "eco-friendly" resort and retirement development with villas priced from US $200,000 to $1,000,000. The project has been slow to develop, but it does have an 18-hole golf course and a tennis club, open to nearby hotel guests, with a second golf course in the works. The main hotel at Nopoló, the **Inn at Loreto Bay**, has been swapped between major resort hotel corporations including Presidente and Camino Real since it was built in 2002. But none of them could

◆▸▴▸ ▪ ▸◆▸◆▸◆▸◆▸◆▸◆▸◆▸◆▸◆▸◆▸◆▸◆▸◆▸◆▸◆▸◆▸◆

AUTHOR FAVORITE

I get a kick staying at the most unique accommodations in Loreto: **Las Trojes Bed and Breakfast Hotel**, located on the beach just north of the Hotel Desert Inn. During the late 1980s, the owner, Augustin Salvat, located several ancient *trojes* (hutlike hand-hewn wooden granaries, built without nails in a style dating back to the 10th century) in the highlands of Michoacán. His crew of Tarascan Indians disassembled them, brought them by truck and ferry to Loreto and reassembled them along the waterfront. Now renovated as guest cabañas, the eight *trojes* have comfortable furnishings, private baths and air conditioning or ceiling fans. ~ Calle de la Playa (Boulevard López Mateos); 613-154-9770, fax 613-135-0277.

make a go of it and now it is independently operated. Its location, bordering the golf course on one side and the sea on the other, is ideal for beachcombing, sea kayaking, snorkeling and scuba diving, though the distance from town may make you feel trapped without alternatives to the bar and three restaurants. The hotel has sea views from the balconies of all 155 air-conditioned, brightly decorated guest rooms. Top-of-the-line suites have private jacuzzis, and all units have satellite TVs, in-room phones and high-speed internet access. ~ Boulevard Misión de Loreto, Nopoló; 613-133-0010 or 866-850-0333 in the U.S.; www.innatloretobay.com. DELUXE TO ULTRA-DELUXE.

HIDDEN ►

Set on a rugged hillside overlooking remote Bahía Ensenada Blanca, 42 kilometers south of Loreto, **Danzante Adventure Resort** has nine adobe luxury suites with king- and queen-size beds, a private bath, and twin terraces with spectacular mountain and sea views. All-inclusive rates cover meals, kayaking, horseback riding and snorkeling. The owners, authors of a book on diving in Baja waters, offer scuba trips in Loreto National Marine Park. ~ Route 1, Km. 158; reservations: P.O. Box 1166, Los Gatos, CA 95031; 408-354-0042, fax 408-354-3268; www.danzante.com, e-mail info@danzante.com. ULTRA-DELUXE.

DINING

The favorite gringo hangout for long, lazy breakfasts, **Café Olé** has good coffee and American-style bacon and eggs or *huevos rancheros*. Later in the day they serve burgers, fries, burritos and fresh fish filets. You order at the counter, then dine at one of the sidewalk tables. ~ Avenida Madero 14; 613-135-0495. BUDGET.

One of "downtown" Loreto's better restaurants is **La Terraza**. Upstairs from Café Olé, La Terraza's panoramic windows command the best view in town of Mission Nuestra Señora de Loreto, with the brooding mass of the Sierra La Giganta in the background. The menu presents a range of steak and seafood choices; you might start with the *sopa de mariscos* (lobster, crab, shrimp, fish and clam soup) and follow it with a filet mignon smothered in mushroom sauce or spicy Tampiqueña salsa. ~ Avenida Madero 16; 613-135-0496. MODERATE.

El Nido, a dimly lit, almost romantic steakhouse, has been owned and operated by the same local family for over 40 years. With ties to a large cattle ranch in mainland Sonora, the restaurant specializes in beef, from thick American-style porterhouse steaks and filet mignon to Mexican styles such as bistek *ranchero* and *carne asada*. Nonbeef entrées include quail and giant, burger-size chocolate clams topped with ranch cheese and *chipotle* sauce. ~ Calle Salvatierra 154; 613-135-0284. MODERATE.

The same owners have recently opened the **Lobster Trap**, a nautically decorated seafood restaurant located at the four-way stop sign in the center of town. ~ Quatros Altos. MODERATE.

El Canipole, an open-air restaurant behind the mission church, claims to be the oldest restaurant in Loreto. It is renowned for homemade *mole* sauce, which takes two days to make. Besides *pollo en mole*, the menu offers *conejo* (rabbit), *camarones al mojo de ajo* (garlic shrimp) and squash blossom quesadillas. Closed Sunday. ~ Piño Suárez; 613-133-0282. MODERATE TO DELUXE.

Plan on taking your time when you dine at **Mita Gourmet,** an elegant little restaurant across from the church. What may seem like unusually slow service is explained by the fact that everything is prepared fresh from scratch when you order it. While there is a large menu of traditional Mexican dishes, the house specialty—in season, at least—is big, juicy lobster tails. ~ Centro Historico 13; 613-135-2025. MODERATE TO DELUXE.

While commercial net fishing is banned within Loreto National Marine Park's boundaries, the waters offer outstanding catch-and-release sport fishing.

McLulu's ("Mucho Tacos Sold Aquí"), a ram-shackle four-table taco stand between the mission and the *malecón*, serves the kind of tacos that show you what you're missing at larger restaurants. Besides the fish and shrimp tacos typical of Baja, proprietress Lourdes "Lulu" Armendáriz serves Mexican favorites like chorizo (spicy sausage), *picadillo* (minced beef) and *machaca* (beef jerky cooked soft in a piquant sauce). ~ Paseo Hidalgo. BUDGET.

For some of the best pizza in Baja, stop in at **Tiffany's Pizza,** across the street from McLuLu's. The unpretentious little hang-out also sells gourmet coffee by the cup or by the bag and has a tempting selection of chocolates. Closed Thursday. ~ Paseo Hidalgo at Paseo Pino Suarez; 613-135-0577. BUDGET.

Located at the south end of the *malecón*, **Charlie's** offers glass-enclosed, air-conditioned comfort along with thatched-roof tropical ambience and a waterfront view. Owned by a northern Californian, the restaurant features gringo-style chicken and beef as well as seafood dishes and Mexican combination plates. ~ Boulevard Costero; 613-135-0577. MODERATE.

The largest of several grocery stores in town, **Mercado El Pescador** is where the locals shop. Located in the middle of town, it has a good stock of canned and boxed foods for campers, as well as fresh produce.

GROCERIES

Loreto is a very quiet place after dark. The place where you're most likely to find some semblance of nightlife is **Macaw's** (also known as JR's), which bills itself as a "sports bar," with two standard TV sets that the bartender will switch to American sporting events via satellite on request. But the real sportiness comes from the *norteamericano* expatriates and

NIGHTLIFE

snowbirds who gather here for happy hour and to hang around swapping fish stories late into the night. ~ On the *malecón* two blocks south of Salvatierra; no phone.

BEACHES & PARKS

LORETO NATIONAL MARINE PARK The waters offshore from Loreto were among the areas hit hardest by the Mexican government's ill-advised decision to permit large-scale industrial fishing by the Japanese in the Sea of Cortez during the 1980s. In order to allow the recovery of the depleted fishery and to realize the recreational potential of the area, the government established this national park, which protects the sea for up to 36 miles offshore and includes the deserted islands Isla Coronado, Isla del Carmen, Isla Danzante, Isla Montserrat and Isla Santa Catalina. The islands offer great scuba diving, and Isla del Carmen is ideal for extended sea-kayaking/camping expeditions. Whales are commonly spotted in the area in winter and early spring, and sea lions, sea turtles and dolphins abound all year, along with more than 200 species of tropical fish. ~ Accessible by boat from Loreto and Playa Nopoló.

> In summer, divers often encounter large schools of manta rays and sometimes 40-foot whale sharks at Loreto National Park.

PLAYA NOPOLÓ Loreto's resort area has the largest sandy beach on this part of the coast. The stretch fronting the empty resort property has been widened by previous owners and enhanced with loads of sand trucked in from elsewhere. Hikers who go any distance from the hotel find less impressive strands interrupted occasionally by patches of mangroves. A secluded beach area near the resort is designated clothing-optional. Camping is not permitted. ~ Eight kilometers south of Loreto, just off Route 1.

PLAYAS JUNCALITO, TRIPUI AND LIGUI Camping is permitted on three sandy patches along the mostly rocky coastline south of Loreto. The numerous small islands offshore present good fishing and snorkeling opportunities. There is a good boat ramp at the Puerto Escondido vacation home area adjoining Tripui Beach. ~ Located from 23 kilometers to 36 kilometers south of Loreto, the beaches are reached by three marked, unpaved roads that turn off the main highway and go about a mile before reaching the seashore.

▲ Camping is free at Juncalito Beach and Playa Ligui, both of which are favorites among tent campers and tailgaters and not easily accessible by motor homes; no hookups or other facilities are available. The only option for big rigs is the Tripui RV Park, which has restrooms with hot showers, a laundry room and a swimming pool. There are a restaurant and a general store at the RV park. The 50 campsites range from $15 to $18 per night, depending on location.

Ecotourism is coming slowly to Bahía Magdalena, the southernmost of Baja's whale
wintering areas. It is the hardest such area

Bahía Magdalena Area

to reach from the United States; although it is the closest whale-
watching spot to Los Cabos, this hasn't brought much tourism.
Instead, the limited development along the bay shore has focused
on shipping produce from the irrigated farmlands of the Llano
de Magdalena and phosphate mining for agricultural fertilizer.

Though its ragged, mangrove-choked shoreline has invited
little in the way of permanent settlement, Bahía Magdalena has
had a long history of transient visitors. Sea captain Sebastián Vizcaíno and missionary Clemente Guillén explored the bay shore
in colonial times, but each found that the lack of fresh water made
it unsuitable for a town or mission site. American whaling ships
out of San Francisco frequented the bay in the 19th century and,
between 1836 and 1846, wiped out the gray-whale population,
which has taken 140 years to recover from near-extinction. The
U.S. Navy seized Bahía Magdalena during the Mexican War and,
though forced to relinquish the bay at the war's end, later established a naval base there under a treaty with the Mexican government. During the same period, several American-owned companies
tried to establish agricultural colonies on the Llano de Magdalena,
but all failed. U.S. interests were driven from the area after the Mexican Revolution, but settlement by Mexican nationals did not
begin until the mid-1930s, when *ejidos* were established on the
Llano de Magdalena.

Today, there are two small seaports in the Bahía Magdalena
area—Puerto López Mateos and Puerto San Carlos. Both can be
reached from the Baja Highway on good paved roads. Guides in
both towns offer whale-watching trips during the winter months.
Puerto López Mateos offers better vantage points for whale
watching from shore but lacks even the minimal food and lodging available in Puerto San Carlos.

While Bahía Magdalena does not lure many motorists off the
main highway, it has long been a popular haunt for gringo yachts-
men. Sheltered from high seas by a hundred miles of barrier islands,
the bay is considered to be the finest natural harbor on the Pacific
coast between San Francisco and Acapulco.

Motorists traveling south from Loreto soon leave the coastal Sierra
de la Giganta and head out onto the **Llano de Magdalena**. *Llano*
means "plain," and this prairie is so flat and featureless that beyond
Ciudad Insurgentes, the Baja Highway runs due south without a
single hill or curve for almost 80 kilometers. A vast aquifer beneath the plain provides well water for irrigation on a grand scale.
The components for chemical fertilizer are found in the desert
nearby in seemingly limitless quantities. Cotton, oranges, grape-

SIGHTS

fruits, alfalfa and garbanzo beans are among the main crops. The agricultural *ejidos* of the Llano de Magdalena have proven so successful that it is now the fastest-growing area of Baja California Sur, boasting a larger population than Los Cabos.

Ciudad Insurgentes, the smaller of the two main commercial centers on the Llano de Magdalena, is home to about 15,000 people. Just over an hour's drive from Loreto, it is a clean, modern town with little of interest to travelers beyond the necessities—gas, groceries, telephones and auto repair shops. Here a good paved road turns off to the west and goes 37 kilometers to Puerto López Mateos.

HIDDEN ▶   A mere fishing village with a population of 2000 and no gas station, **Puerto López Mateos** is situated at the north end of Bahía Magdalena. The bay narrows into a channel less than a mile wide between the mainland shore and the sandy barrier island, Isla Magdalena. In the winter, the narrow channel brings large numbers of whales close enough to shore to offer great views through binoculars from the town dock.

HIDDEN ▶   An even better whale-watching vantage point is **Playa El Faro**, three kilometers to the north on the unpaved road from town. *Pangas* launch from Playa El Faro during whale season to take whale-watching groups to Boca la Soledad, where the greatest concentration of whales is found. This gap between barrier islands provides the only access from the bay to the open ocean for 50 miles.

Back on the Baja Highway, 26 kilometers south of Ciudad Insurgentes is **Ciudad Constitución**, the second-largest city in Baja California Sur. The commercial zone lies along the highway, which becomes the impressively wide, palm-lined Boulevard Olachea as it passes through the city, and along Avenida Juárez one block to the east. Banks, car dealerships and a large municipal performing-arts theater reflect the prosperity of this booming

ROSE-COLORED OASIS

The beautiful old **Misión San Luís Gonzaga Chiriyaqui**, built in 1751, makes for an adventurous side trip from the Baja Highway. Fifty kilometers off the main highway, the twin bell towers of the partially restored, rose-colored stone church stands on an isolated mesa near a small oasis of date palms around a pool. Turn east on the paved side road at Km. 195 south of Ciudad Constitución, marked with a sign that says "Presa Iguajil"—the name of a dam about 35 kilometers up the road. Past the dam, the pavement ends but the road continues for another 17 kilometers, passing scattered fruit farms at the base of the mountain before reaching the old mission.

agricultural center of 60,000. There is nothing to offer sightseers, though, unless you count as a point of interest the only stoplights between Ensenada and La Paz—a distance of more than 1100 kilometers.

At Ciudad Constitución, paved Route 22 turns off to the west and continues for 58 kilometers to **Puerto San Carlos**, the main shipping port for the Llano de Magdalena. Truckloads of cotton clatter through the dusty streets when a ship is in port. At other times, things couldn't be much quieter in this backwater town of 4000 people. A sandy beach runs north of town between the road and the bay. The whale watching from shore is less than awesome, but plenty of local boatmen stand by to take visitors on whale-watching excursions south to Punta Entrada or birding trips along the mangrove canals to the north.

◀ HIDDEN

Protecting Bahía Magdalena from the open sea, 70-mile-long **Isla Magdalena** consists mainly of sand dunes tufted with grass; a broad stretch of sandy beach runs along the ocean side for the island's entire length. More ships have wrecked along this shore than anyplace else in Baja, and the remains of several are still visible. The island, which is uninhabited, can be reached by kayak or *panga* from either Puerto López Mateos or Puerto San Carlos.

◀ HIDDEN

There are no real hotels in Puerto López Mateos, though a few residents put out signs offering simple bed-and-breakfast accommodations during whale-watching season.

LODGING

You'll find numerous lodging options in Ciudad Constitución, including the **Hotel Maribel**, with 20 modern, comfortable, air-conditioned guest rooms with telephones, shag carpeting and Spanish-only TV. ~ Calle Guadalupe Victoria 156, Ciudad Constitución; 613-132-0155. BUDGET.

The **Hotel El Conquistador** also offers all the comforts of a contemporary motor inn; its 24 rooms have dark wood Colonial-style furnishings, dim lighting, hot water, air conditioning and TV. ~ Calle Nicolas Bravo 161, Ciudad Constitución; 613-132-1731. BUDGET.

You'll find some of the lowest room rates on the peninsula— and worth every penny—at the spartan **Hotel Conchita** in the center of Ciudad Constitución. Parking is on the street, and you can't see your car from your room, but the rooms are clean. ~ Route 1 central, Ciudad Constitución; 613-132-0266. BUDGET.

Puerto San Carlos has three good, basic motels. The newest and most comfortable (despite its dubious name), the **Hotel Alcatraz** has 18 cheerful, spacious rooms with ceiling fans and TV. ~ Calle La Paz, Puerto San Carlos; 613-136-0017. BUDGET.

The **Hotel Palmar**, also clean and newish, has 12 plain, utilitarian guest rooms with ceiling fans. ~ Calle La Paz, Puerto San Carlos; 613-136-0035. BUDGET.

The oldest and least expensive lodging in town is the **Motel Las Brisas**, where eight spartan rooms with table fans surround a gardenless courtyard whose walls are muraled with paintings of gray whales. ~ Calle Madero, Puerto San Carlos; 613-136-0152. BUDGET.

DINING

In Puerto López Mateos, the **Restaurant Ballena Gris** serves tacos and other simple fare during whale-watching season. ~ Puerto López Mateos. BUDGET.

You'll find good seafood in Ciudad Constitución at the **Marlín Sonriente**, a pleasant, air-conditioned restaurant near the Hotel El Conquistador. ~ Avenida Juárez at Calle Hidalgo, Ciudad Constitución. BUDGET TO MODERATE.

Passing for high-class in a workingman's town, **Las Brasas Steak House** is more accustomed to tourist trade than most of the other spots along Ciudad Constitución's main drag. The menu features American-style steaks, hamburgers and salads. ~ Avenida Allende 217 (Km. 212), Ciudad Constitución; 613-132-0348. BUDGET TO MODERATE.

Low-priced Chinese food is served nearby at **Restaurant-Bar Calafia**, a dimly lit restaurant favored by locals. ~ Calle Nicolas Bravo at Boulevard Olachea, Ciudad Constitución; 613-132-0733. BUDGET.

Also in town, you can buy whole roasted chickens at **Super Pollo** to eat on the cramped, unpretentious premises or to take out. ~ Route 1 north, Ciudad Constitución. BUDGET.

For authentic Mexican *ceviche*, stop at the little roadside stand **Mariscos El Puerto**, located by the Pemex station at the intersection of Route 1 and the road to San Carlos. ~ Ciudad Constitución. BUDGET.

GROCERIES

You'll find one of the best selections of fresh produce on the Baja Highway at Ciudad Constitución's **Mercado Central**, a public market with nearly a hundred vendors. Prices are good, and bargaining is expected. ~ Avenida Juárez between Calles Nicolas Bravo and Hidalgo, Ciudad Constitución.

BEACHES & PARKS

PLAYA EL FARO The only beach with facilities on Bahía Magdalena, Playa El Faro has restrooms and a food stand. Besides being the departure point for whale-watching boats, it's a good spot for viewing whales from shore. The beach itself is not great—an intermittently sandy and sometimes soggy area flanked by low stands of mangroves. Other beaches, deserted and undeveloped, lie farther along the main dirt road north of Puerto López Mateos. ~ Three kilometers north of Puerto López Mateos.

▲ Free tent and RV camping is permitted on Playa El Faro.

The Sea of Cortez coast south of Santa Rosalía, and especially the Loreto area, is considered one of North America's top sportfishing areas. Although large-scale commercial fishing has depleted the area in the past, the government has enacted regulations placing the area off-limits to drift-netters and other big fishing boats, and the game fish populations are on the rebound.

Outdoor Adventures

FISHING

> The best beaches in the Bahía Magdalena area are on the ocean side of the barrier islands that shelter the bay. They can only be reached by boat, and local *pangueros* can be hired to take you there.

Yellowtail is the catch of choice during the winter and spring months. Marlin, sailfish and dorado (mahimahi) arrive in the summer; cabrillo and snapper are abundant year-round. Roosterfish, the challenging (though not especially edible) fighting fish prized by Los Cabos fishermen, are found in the spring as far north as Mulegé, and record-size specimens have been hooked in Loreto. Most charter operators, sensitive to the need to preserve and revive their fisheries, allow only catch-and-release big-game fishing.

SANTA ROSALÍA There is good deep-sea fishing in the waters east of Isla Santa Inez, and an abundance of smaller fish species in the channel between the Baja Peninsula and the island. Although the town has no fishing-charter reservation service, charter operators can often be found at **Marina Santa Rosalía.** ~ 615-152-0011. There's also **Los Frailes Sportfishing Adventures.** ~ 615-152-0373. Anglers can fish for yellowtail from shore at Punta Santa Inez and Punta Chivato.

MULEGÉ In fall and early winter you can fish from shore for snook, yellowtail and roosterfish at the mouth of the estuary where the Río Mulegé flows into the sea. Anglers with boats head for the open sea off the outer shore of the Concepción Peninsula in search of big game fish including tuna, marlin and dorado. Few fishing charters are available in Mulegé.

LORETO The water off the coast of Isla del Carmen is the top fishing area. Shore fishing is said to be incredible off the island's northern tip, though getting there may cost as much as chartering a boat for deep-sea fishing. Charters can be arranged through **Alfredo's Sportfishing** ~ Boulevard López Matéos at Calle Juárez; 613-135-0165 or **Ricardo's Sport Fishing** ~ Avenida Madero 118; 613-135-0126.

MULEGÉ The best diving is in the plankton-rich waters off Isla Santa Inez, swarming with colorful tropical fish. Snorkeling and scuba trips to the island can be arranged through **Mulegé Divers.** ~ Calle General Martínez; phone/fax 615-153-0059. Dive trips are also organized by **Cortez Explorers.** ~ Calle Moctezuma 75; phone/fax 615-153-0500.

DIVING

LORETO The waters off Nopoló and Puerto Escondido are ideal for snorkeling. Scuba enthusiasts head for the rock reefs of the islands in Loreto National Marine Park—Isla del Carmen, Isla Coronada and Isla Danzante—where big fish abound. Most dive sites are shallow and ideal for novice divers, though there are also some spectacular vertical wall dives. Snorkel and scuba gear can be rented at **Deportes Blazer**. ~ Avenida Hidalgo 24; 613-135-0911. Dive expeditions can also be arranged through **Baja Outpost**, Boulevard López Mateos; 613-135-1134, or 888-649-5951 in the U.S.; www.bajaoutpost.com.

KAYAKING

MULEGÉ Kayaking has become the most popular sport by far in the Mulegé area. Novices can practice paddling up and down the Río Mulegé before embarking on a fantastic journey across the (usually) smooth, crystalline waters of Bahía Concepción. **Baja Tropicales** rents lots of kayaks—reservations should be made well in advance—and organizes English-language guided all-day tours of the bay. ~ Hotel Las Casitas, Calle Madero 50; 615-153-0019.

LORETO The 84-mile trip from Mulegé to Loreto takes about a week and is one of the ultimate wilderness sea-kayaking adventures. The route follows a steep, rocky coastline that is unapproachable by land, with occasional, usually rocky landings suitable for camping. Tamer Loreto sea-kayaking possibilities include excursions to Isla Coronada and Isla del Carmen, ten miles offshore in the Loreto National Marine Park. Open-top kayaks are for rent in Loreto at **Deportes Blazer**. ~ Avenida Hidalgo 24; 613-135-0091. A permit is required for kayaking in the Loreto National Marine Park. You can get one at Deportes Blazer or any of the hotels and RV parks that have kayaks for rent.

BAHÍA MAGDALENA Sea kayaking is permitted in Bahía Magdalena outside of whale-watching season, though as of yet no kayak rentals are available in the area.

WHALE WATCHING

SAN IGNACIO The owners of **La Posada San Ignacio** guide tours to Laguna San Ignacio during the winter months to view the gray whales that congregate there. ~ 615-154-0313. Tours can also be arranged at the front desk of the **Hotel La Pinta San Ignacio**. ~ 615-154-0300.

LORETO Blue whales and minke whales are frequently sighted in the vicinity of Isla del Carmen during the winter months. Whale-watching trips can be arranged through **Alfredo's Sportfishing** ~ Boulevard Mateos at Calle Juárez; 613-135-0132 or **Arturo's Fishing Fleet** ~ Calle Juárez at Callejón 2; 613-135-0409.

BAHÍA MAGDALENA Whale-watching *pangas* depart from San Carlos and Playa El Faro near Puerto Lopez Mateos during the winter months.

Gray Whales' Hidden Lagoon

Remote, barren and pristine, Laguna San Ignacio was the unlikely site of one of Mexico's biggest environmental controversies in the 1990s. One of only three gray-whale calving areas on the Pacific coast, the lagoon's inaccessibility protected it from human development, providing a primeval wintering area for thousands of whales—until 1995, when Exportadora de Sal, the company that runs the world's largest salt-producing operation near Guerrero Negro, unveiled plans to open an even larger project along the northern and eastern shores of Laguna San Ignacio. Environmentalists obtained an injunction blocking the project on the grounds that its 465-page environmental-impact statement dismissed potential effects on wildlife with a single paragraph. Activists from around the world—among them prominent figures such as lawyer Robert F. Kennedy, Jr., filmmaker Jean-Michel Cousteau and movie stars Glenn Close and Pierce Brosnan—have rallied to save the whales' lagoon.

The salt company pointed out that in the 30 years since their Guerrero Negro operation began, the whale population in Scammon's Lagoon had multiplied to its highest level in history. The recovery there had been so successful, in fact, that gray whales had been removed from the endangered-species list. Environmentalists countered that at Scammon's Lagoon, the salt was shipped from an offshore island; the plan at Laguna San Ignacio called for a shipping route through the heart of the whales' territory. They also contended that the project threatened the habitat of many other species, including the endangered black sea turtle and desert pronghorn antelope.

Most observers expected that Exportadora de Sal would win in the end by virtue of the fact that Mitsubishi Corporation had recently turned over 51 percent ownership of the salt company to the Mexican government. But in a surprise move at the end of 1999, the Mexican government bowed to environmentalist pressures and announced new regulations to permanently protect Laguna San Ignacio in its pristine state, and Exportada de Sal abandoned its salt-mining plans—one of the greatest victories in the history of Mexico's environmental movement.

GOLF   **LORETO**   The only golf course in the region is the **Loreto Golf Course,** located at the south end of the Nopoló resort area adjacent to to the Inn at Loreto Bay. The luxuriously landscaped 18-hole par-72 desert course rambles over dunelike hills close to the sea. Club rentals are available. Call before making plans, however. Following years of sporadic neglect, the course has been undergoing renovation, and only nine holes are open for limited play. It is scheduled for completion in fall 2007. ~ Boulevard Nopoló; 613-135-0788.

BIKING   **MULEGÉ**   The **Hotel Hacienda** rents mountain bikes by the hour, day or longer. The unpaved road from Mulegé to Santa Clara branches into two rugged jeep roads ideal for biking, leading to canyons that form the headwaters of the Río Mulegé. ~ 615-153-0021. **Cortez Explorers** also rents mountain bikes. ~ Calle Moctezuma 75; phone/fax 615-153-0500.

LORETO   The road to San Javier and Comondú makes for a first-rate mountain-biking adventure. Loreto has no bike rentals, though a few hotels make them available for guests' use.

CAVE TOURS   **SAN IGNACIO**   Burro trips to see the great cave murals of the Sierra de San Francisco can be arranged in San Ignacio at La Posada San Ignacio. ~ 615-154-0313. You can also arrange a trip to Cueva Palmarito at Rancho Santa Marta, or one to Gardner Cave at San Francisco de la Sierra. There are numerous other painted caves in the San Francisco de la Sierra area, and most residents of this tiny village work for archaeological expeditions that study them, so visitors with plenty of time will find limitless possibilities for exploration. All of the painted caves in the area are under government protection, and it is against the law to visit them without a guide.

MULEGÉ   Guided tours from Mulegé to see the rock art at Cañon La Trinidad or Gruta San Borjitas can be arranged with **Sal's Tours & Mountain Trips** at Hotel Las Casitas. ~ Calle Madero 50; 615-153-0232.

AUTHOR FAVORITE

My choice among the many possible backcountry trips to Indian rock art sites in this region is **Cañon La Trinidad** outside Mulegé, simply because getting there involves a beautiful canyon hike that splashes back and forth across a crystalline spring-fed river, a welcome rarity in this hot desert land. The significance of the ancient pictographs themselves is an intriguing mystery. See page 186 for more information.

All distances listed for hiking trails are one way unless otherwise noted.

HIKING

SAN IGNACIO   The best hike in the area is from Rancho Santa Marta to **Cueva Palmarito** (2.5 miles), an outstanding example of prehistoric rock art. A guide is required for the trip down a palm-lined canyon to the site. Guides from San Francisco de la Sierra can lead treks to other spectacular palm canyons in the high sierra.

SANTA ROSALÍA   The **Volcanes Tres Vírgenes**, the towering volcanos north of Santa Rosalía, have become favorite climbers' challenges in recent years. There is no clear trail to any of the summits, though a rugged four-wheel-drive road leads from kilometer 41 on the Baja Highway north into the volcano field. From there, it's a four-mile hike to the summit of the southernmost and tallest peak, which has a large crater that still fumes with noxious vapors now and then. It's a strenuous trip, and hikers usually spend the night at the summit and descend the next day.

LORETO   The old four-mile **burro trail** from the abandoned south-shore pier to the salt-filled crater of the 1600-foot volcano in the center of Isla del Carmen is one of the most spectacular hikes imaginable. Backpackers can often catch a one-way trip to the island with a sportfishing boat and arrange to be picked up the next day.

Loreto has the only commercial airport in the area covered by this chapter. **Aero California** offers daily flights between Loreto and Los Angeles, La Paz and the Mexican mainland city of Ciudad Obregón. **Alaska** and **Delta** also offer twice-a-week service from L.A., and **Continental** offers twice-a-week service from Houston. There are also flights from La Paz to Ciudad Constitución.

Transportation

AIR

Autotransportes Aguila and **Tres Estrellas de Oro** operate daily buses north to Ensenada, Tijuana and Mexicali and south as far as La Paz, with station stops at Santa Rosalía, Loreto and Ciudad Constitución. The buses will pick up passengers at the San Ignacio highway junction, in Mulegé and along Bahía Concepción, though arrival times can be erratic and there are no bus stations—you just climb aboard and pay the driver.

BUS

Santa Rosalía is one of the peninsula's two main ferry ports (the other being La Paz). A private ferry service has replaced the now-defunct SEMATUR de California, S.A. and operates small, high-speed car ferries from the mainland Mexican seaport of Santa Rosalía to the mainland port of Guaymas on Tuesday and Friday, returning on Monday and Thursday. The ferries make the 10-hour crossing at night, departing at 10 p.m. *Salón*-class re-

BOAT

clining seats can be booked on the day of departure; *turista*-class shared bunk rooms should be reserved a day in advance. Passenger fares for either class are fairly inexpensive (around US $30 *salón* or $55 *turista* one way), making the ferry such a sea-cruise bargain that you could ride to Guaymas and back just for fun. Motor vehicles cost much more: one-way fares start around US$250 for a passenger car and US$450 for a big motor home. ~ 615-152-1246; www.ferrysantarosalia.com.

CAR

All the main towns—San Ignacio, Santa Rosalía, Mulegé, Loreto, Ciudad Insurgentes and Ciudad Constitución—lie along **Route 1**, and all have large Pemex stations; Loreto and Ciudad Constitución have two apiece. Each town is about an hour's drive from the last, except Loreto, which is about two hours south of Mulegé.

Laguna San Ignacio is 68 kilometers southwest of the town of San Ignacio on an unpaved, unnumbered road. Bahía Magdalena can be reached by two paved routes—the unnumbered road from Ciudad Insurgentes to Puerto López Mateos (37 kilometers) or Route 22 from Ciudad Constitución to San Carlos (58 kilometers).

CAR RENTALS

In Loreto, the Inn at Loreto Bay has a Hertz auto rental desk, though the cars themselves often must be brought from La Paz, several hours away. Otherwise, the nearest rentals are in La Paz.

TAXIS

Mulegé and Loreto have numerous independent taxi cabs during tourist season. You can't telephone for one. Look for them around the larger hotels and in the center of town.

▼▼▼▼▼▼▼▼▼▼▼▼▼▼▼▼▼▼▼▼▼

Addresses & Phone Numbers

Hospital General ~ Santa Rosalía, 615-152-0776; Calle Salvatierra, Loreto, 613-135-0345

Cruz Rojo (Red Cross) ~ Santa Rosalia, 615-152-0604; Mulegé, 615-153-0280, after-hours 615-153-0139; Loreto, 613-135-1111

Tourist Information ~ Apdo. Postal 5, Loreto, BCS, 613-135-0411, fax 613-135-0822; San Carlos, 613-136-0253

Oficina de Migración y Aduana (immigration and customs) ~ Loreto; 613-135-0499

Camino Federales (Highway Patrol) ~ Santa Rosalía; 615-152-0839

Green Angels (roadside help) ~ Loreto; 613-135-0620

Internet access ~ San Ignacio, Internet Café and Tour Service, north side of the plaza, no phone; Mulege, Servicio Internet Minita, 615-153-0210; Loreto, Dot Com Internet Café, Calle Madero, no phone.

EIGHT

La Paz and Los Cabos

Stand on Lover's Beach looking out past El Arco, the trademark rock formation of Cabo San Lucas, and you may feel as if you have stepped into a travel poster. Gulls and pelicans wheel overhead. A cruise ship lies at anchor in the outer harbor. The Pacific Ocean rolls on and on. If you sailed due south from this, the southernmost point on the Baja Peninsula, the next land you'd see would be the coast of Antarctica.

The Cabo de Baja California, the peninsula's wide, tropical tip, extends 90 miles from La Paz to Land's End at Cabo San Lucas. Motorists who make the 300-kilometer loop around the cape discover remarkable contrasts. There's La Paz, the state capital, a fair-sized city with a dramatic history and a lovely promenade along a picture-perfect bay. A sea kayak excursion could take you to Isla Espiritu Santo, perhaps the most beautiful of all the desert islands off the Baja coast.

Heading south along the coast, you'll catch quick glimpses of the Sea of Cortez at two points near Bahía de Palmas, with its spectacular 25-mile beach, before reaching San José del Cabo. San José, the eastern half of the Los Cabos resort area, is a gentrified, historic town dating from the Spanish colonial era. With its galleries, restaurants and romantic ambience, it could be Santa Fe, New Mexico, or San Miguel de Allende but for the smell and sound of the surf breaking on the beach in front of the luxury hotel zone south of town. A half-hour's drive along a four-lane highway, the other half of Los Cabos, Cabo San Lucas, is the tourist industry epitomized, with little in the way of history or culture to interfere with the spending of money; but even here, there are hidden treasures—amazing undersea snorkeling and scuba experiences and long, secluded, almost empty beaches far removed from the big resorts.

Surfers head directly for West Cape and the spectacular Pacific waves around the expatriate artists' town of Todos Santos, which has so far escaped the explosive growth of the Los Cabos area. And then there's the cape's hidden heart, the Sierra de la Laguna. Adventurous souls willing to take a multiday backpacking trip into the sierra discover a misty highland containing one of the most diverse ecosystems in North America.

221

▼▼▼▼▼▼▼▼
La Paz

La Paz is the capital of Baja California Sur and, with a metropolitan population of about a quarter million, its largest city. It is presently one of the fastest-growing cities in Mexico and boasts the highest per-capita income of any city in the nation. A low-rise, sprawling city, it is Mexico's fourth-largest municipality in geographical area, surpassing many others with much larger populations. Baja travelers are pleasantly surprised by this clean, modern, friendly community where tourism is welcome but does not dominate the economy. The urban waterfront, skirting a picturesque bay full of sailboats and yachts, is a joy for strolling or jogging, and the downtown area has the relaxed ambience of mainland Mexico's colonial cities. With good hotels and restaurants at prices much lower than the resorts of Los Cabos, La Paz makes a great home base for exploring the deserted islands and hidden beaches nearby.

La Paz has a tumultuous history that belies its name—Spanish for "the peace." More than two centuries before the city was founded, the name was bestowed on Bahía de la Paz by explorer Sebastián Vizcaíno, who was impressed by the friendliness and hospitality of the Pericú Indians he encountered during his visit to the sheltered bay.

Such was not the experience of other Spanish conquistadores. La Paz is located on the spot where the first Spaniards set foot on the Baja Peninsula in 1533—and were immediately slaughtered by Indians. Two years later, Hernán Cortés, governor of New Spain, founded a colony near the site of present-day La Paz and struck a tentative understanding with the Indians of the area. Cortés' colony soon failed due to food and water shortages, but his negotiations with the Indians laid the foundation for Vizcaíno's peaceful visit 61 years later.

For nearly 200 years, every Spanish attempt to establish a settlement at Bahía de la Paz failed. Throughout the 17th century, English and Dutch pirates lurked in the bay's hidden rock coves, plundering the wealth of the Spanish empire from the Manila treasure galleons, which put in at San José los Cabos to replenish water supplies after crossing the Pacific, but the pirates never settled on shore. In 1720, Jesuit missionaries from Loreto tried to establish a mission in La Paz, but the mission failed after only a few years, and no trace of it remains today.

It was not until 1829, when Loreto was destroyed by a hurricane, that La Paz became a real town: the newly independent Mexican government relocated the capital of Baja California to the sheltered shoreline of Bahía de la Paz. Turmoil plagued the settlement almost from the first. During the Mexican War (1846–48), the United States Army captured La Paz and occupied it for more than two years. Five years after the war ended and La Paz was returned to Mexican control, it was again seized by gringos—this time soldiers of fortune under the leadership of General William Walker, who hoped to start his own republic in Baja and then annex it into the United States as the first pro-slavery state in the far west. Only after the Mexican Army charged to the rescue did La Paz achieve the peace that its name promised.

In the 1870s, the invention of the diving suit made large-scale harvesting of the Bahía de la Paz oyster beds possible, and La Paz was the world's largest supplier of pearls for decades. Between 1936 and 1941, however, a mysterious disease killed all the oysters,

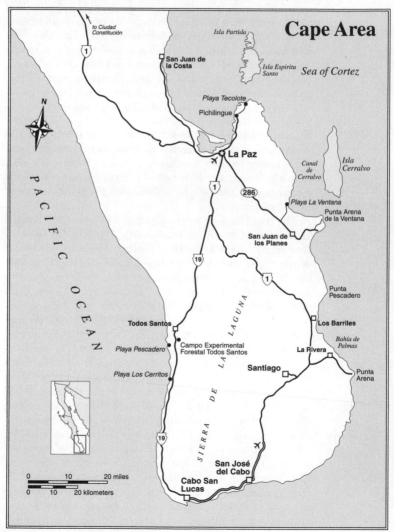

devastating the town's economy. In response, the Mexican government granted La Paz the duty-free status that all of Baja enjoys to this day, transforming it into a busy port for goods from the United States and the Pacific Rim and stimulating tourism from the Mexican mainland.

Two books by John Steinbeck—his novel *The Pearl* and his nonfiction account *The Log from the Sea of Cortez*—focused the attention of American travelers on La Paz, and by the 1950s it was a popular sportfishing destination. But the tourist boom dwindled in the 1970s as industrial fishing brought marlin, swordfish and sailfish to the brink of extinction in the Sea of Cortez and the resort development of Cabo San Lucas eclipsed La Paz as a tourist destination. Since then, gringo visitors to the city have been mostly long-term "snowbird" retirees attracted by low prices and readily available health care. Today, the game fish population is resurgent and the waters around La Paz are being discovered by growing numbers of yachters, scuba divers and sea kayakers.

SIGHTS   Much of La Paz is a gridwork of traffic-clogged streets. Residential districts sprawl across the landscape with a sameness that makes getting lost easy for those who venture far from the main route into the city center. For pleasure travelers, however, all the in-town points of interest are situated within walking distance of one another.

The Baja Highway enters suburban La Paz as Calle Rangel. Motorists who are just passing through, following the "Mex 1" signs south toward Los Cabos, turn south through a westside neighborhood, past the **Universidad Autónimo de Baja California Sur**, and back out of town without ever seeing the city center. Sightseers, however, will want to keep going straight to where Calle Rangel reaches the waterfront and merges into Paseo Alvaro Obregón, the main street that follows the water's edge through downtown and around the bay to the Pichilingue Peninsula.

The place to start a sightseeing tour of La Paz is the **malecón**, a wide walkway shaded by laurels and coconut palms that runs along the waterfront. An ambitious municipal construction project more than doubled the length of the *malecón* to five kilometers in 2005 and 2006, and it continues to grow. Along the way, it passes several fishing and excursion boat piers and stretches of white-sand beach, as well as the **Plaza Malecón**, where a gazebo-style bandstand is often the scene of municipal concerts. The friendly tourist information office is located there, too. The *malecón* is used by impressive numbers of joggers in the early morning but becomes practically deserted during the midday heat. Activity picks up in the late afternoon, and by the time the sun sets in a prolonged blaze of color that turns the bay crimson, the promenade is filled with people strolling, socializing and savoring La Paz's finest hour.

La Paz's main plaza, the **Jardín Velasco**, is four blocks south of the waterfront between Avenida Independencia and Calle Cinco de Mayo. Shaded by fig laurels, it provides a comfortable place to soak up the Mexican atmosphere. The plaza is the community's social center, and if you linger there you will inevitably find yourself drawn into conversation with local folks—even if you don't speak the same language.

On the southeast side of the plaza stands **La Catedral de Nuestra Señora de La Paz**, a rather austere brick-and-stone edifice with twin bell towers. It was built in 1860 as a "modern" revival of the architecture of the previous century's mission churches, but today the sharp edges and angles seem like a failed attempt to capture the architectural grace of the original missions. Although there is little supporting historical evidence, it is widely believed that the church stands on the spot where a short-lived Jesuit mission was built in 1720. ~ Avenida Independencia.

The **Museo de Antropología e Historia** is inconspicuously situated next to a school, eight long blocks south of downtown. Its exhibits, captioned in Spanish, provide a close look at the nomadic people who occupied Baja before the arrival of missionaries, measles and smallpox. While most of the dioramas and artifacts are about the Indians, there are also displays about missionaries, mining, U.S. invasions and the Mexican Revolution. ~ Avenida 5 de Mayo at Calle Ignacio Altamirano; 612-122-0102.

Driving east from downtown on Paseo Alvaro Obregón, you soon leave the traffic congestion behind and find yourself traversing barren, rocky hillsides on the two-lane blacktop coast road to **Pichilingue**, the terminal where the huge SEMATUR ferries from Topolobampo and Mazatlán dock. Along the way, the road passes a series of secluded coves. Some, enhanced with wide beaches of imported white sand, have been transformed into mini-resorts with palapa bars and snorkel gear rental shops. Other coves remain in their natural state—narrow strands of hard brownish beach bounded by rock cliffs and stands of tamarisk, as lonely today as three centuries ago when they served as pirate hideouts.

HIDDEN ▶ Seven miles due north of the Pichilingue Peninsula, **Isla Espiritu Santo** is one of the most fascinating islands off the Baja shore. Most of the island's coast is vertical cliffs in bright hues of red, black, white and yellow. About a dozen long, narrow coves cut into the western shore; most of them have lovely, sheltered natural beaches, making this island a favorite for sea kayaking and camping adventures. Protected (along with six other large islands) as the Islas de Golfo de California Biosphere Reserve, Isla Espiritu Santo is home to a remarkable abundance of wildlife. Visitors can expect to see ospreys, snowy egrets, great blue herons, redtailed hawks, and possibly a nocturnal great horned owl, as well as numerous species of rodents, reptiles, amphibians and elusive ring-tailed cats. A coral reef offshore attracts scuba divers.

AUTHOR FAVORITE

In a land so raw that most of it has no phone service and much of it has no human habitation, it's astonishing to discover a history that reaches back far earlier than the birth of George Washington. I found it—and you can, too—at the **Biblioteca de Historia de las Californias** in La Paz. Located on the northwest side of the plaza, opposite the church, it's housed in the former territorial government palace. This historical library contains thousands of source documents and the largest existing collection of books (in Spanish and English) about the Baja Peninsula, past and present. Sightseers may want to stop in if only for a look at the art exhibits, which include paintings of early-day missions and reproductions of Indian cave murals. Closed on weekends. ~ Calle Francisco Madero at Calle Cinco de Mayo; 612-122-2640.

Built in 1940 at the dawn of La Paz's tourism boom, the **Hotel Perla** was one of the first resort hotels on the waterfront. Its location, across the street from the *malecón* and downtown beach, is in the center of the action, close to many restaurants and shops. All of the 110 American motor inn–style rooms have air conditioning and phones, and 26 have views of the bay and sometimes a street-noise problem. There's a disco on the premises, as well as an interior courtyard with gardens and a swimming pool. ~ Paseo Obregón 1570; 612-122-0777, fax 612-125-5363, or 888-242-3757 from California and Arizona; www.hotelperlabaja.com. BUDGET TO MODERATE.

LODGING

Farther west along the waterfront, **Hotel Los Arcos** and the adjacent **Cabañas de los Arcos** offer some of the city's nicest accommodations. The three-story, Colonial-style hotel, just two blocks from the center of downtown, has 130 luxurious rooms and suites, all with air conditioning, balconies, in-room phones and cable TV. Some have bay views; others overlook the gardens and fountains of the central courtyard. The cabaña complex has 30 small individual casitas and a 22-room inn, all in a tropical garden setting, at rates slightly lower than those of the main hotel. Both the hotel and the cabañas have heated swimming pools. ~ Paseo Obregón 498; 612-122-2744, fax 612-125-4313; www.losarcos.com. DELUXE.

Room rates plummet as soon as you get away from the waterfront. The former municipal courthouse, dating back to the mid-1800s, has been restored by Swiss expatriate Esther Ammann under the supervision of the Instituto Nacional de Antropología e Historia, to create **El Ángel Azul**, a boutique bed-and-breakfast inn. Due to the law regulating national historic sites, the B&B is marked only by a small blue sign set into a blank white exterior wall, and you could walk right past it without ever noticing that it was there. This labor of love opened its doors in 1999 with just three guest rooms and has since expanded one room at a time to its present total of ten, all air-conditioned and each individually decorated in a different bright color scheme. The courtyard, filled with flowers and foliage, provides a peaceful oasis within a few blocks of downtown and the *malecón*. Rates include a sumptuous full breakfast. ~ Independencia 518; 612-125-5130; www.elangelazul.com, e-mail hotel@elangelazul.com. MODERATE TO DELUXE.

◀ HIDDEN

The **Hotel Lorimar**, a favorite of the international backpack set, is two blocks up the hill from the *malecón*, behind Hotel Los Arcos. It has 20 clean, plain, air-conditioned rooms with private baths, and an upstairs café with an over-the-rooftops view of the bay. ~ Calle Bravo 110; 612-125-3822, fax 612-125-6387. BUDGET.

An even lower-priced backpackers' hangout in a deteriorating 18th-century convent four blocks from the waterfront, the **Pensión**

California has 25 smallish blue-and-white rooms with ceiling fans. The only furnishings are mattresses on concrete platforms, and the bathrooms are aging and cramped but functional. The rooms look out over a central courtyard with a restaurant and bar, which can be noisy long into the night. Guests gather at picnic tables around the TV in the courtyard's eccentrically decorated tropical garden. A communal kitchen and laundry room are available for guests' use. The low room rate includes a double shot of tequila, morning coffee and an hour on the internet. ~ Calle Degollado 209; 612-122-2896. BUDGET.

Just a block from the plaza, the 20-unit **Hotel Yeneka** has larger, better-furnished guest rooms than most other low-budget options, though like the others its beds are mattresses on concrete platforms. It is distinguished by its crazy courtyard decor, consisting largely of painted automotive parts, including a complete though nonfunctional Model T Ford, artfully nestled in the tropical vegetation. ~ Calle Francisco Madero 1520; 612-125-4688, fax 612-122-4106. BUDGET.

All these rock-bottom budget alternatives are more appealing than the official youth hostel, the **Villa Juvinil**. Its location, in the southwest part of the city at the Universidad Autonimo de Baja California Sur sports complex, is convenient for visiting soccer teams but inconvenient for pleasure travelers. There are 72 beds, four-to-a-room in men's and women's dormitory wings, with a laundromat and grocery store nearby. ~ Calle 5 de Febrero at Boulevard Instituto de la Deporte; 612-122-4615. BUDGET.

Blending European and Mexican architectural touches, **Hotel Mediterrane** is a small lodging just a short walk away from the *malecón*. Six spacious rooms have private baths and air conditioning. The owners can provide helpful information on La Paz. Gay-friendly. ~ Calle Allende 36; phone/fax 612-125-1195; www. hotelmed.com, e-mail mail@hotelmed.com. MODERATE.

La Casa Mexicana Inn, a bed and breakfast one block inland from the *malecón*, has three individually decorated rooms (each with private bath) and two casitas. The Moorish-style house is air-conditioned, and all guest rooms have views of the bay. ~ Calle Bravo 106; 612-125-2748; www.casamex.com, e-mail inn @casamex.com. MODERATE.

Casa Jalisco, a pretty little boutique hotel eight blocks from the waterfront, has ten guest rooms decorated in warm colors with Diego Rivera–style art, contemporary handcrafted wood furnishings, and private balconies and bathtubs. Each room is equipped with wireless internet access. There's a swimming pool surrounded by palm trees. ~ Calle Jalisco at Calle Ramirez; 612-128-4311, fax 612-128-5311; www.lacasajalisco.com, e-mail casajalisco@aol.com. MODERATE.

Surrounded by a privacy wall, the **Club El Moro**, across the highway from the waterfront feels like a small, private resort, even though it's just two miles northeast of downtown. It has 18 large, attractive suites with full kitchens, private patios or balconies, and cable TV but no in-room phones. Terracotta tile floors and arched windows with wrought-iron gratings create a romantic Spanish-Moorish motif. The lush tropical landscaping conceals a heated pool and the only hotel hot tub in town. Kayaks are for rent on the premises. ~ Km. 2, Carretera a Pichilingue; phone/fax 612-122-4084, fax 612-125-2828; www.clubelmoro.com, e-mail elmoro@prodigy.net.mx. MODERATE TO DELUXE.

> On weekends in La Paz, Calle Madero and Avenida Independencia around the plaza are closed to traffic so that more than 100 vendors can set up shop in a busy flea market.

A little farther from town and a little pricier, the pink five-story **Hotel Marina**'s 70 rooms and 23 suites are light, spacious and contemporary; their sliding glass doors open onto balconies overlooking Marina Palmira, a world-class yachting haven. Facilities include a swimming pool, a jacuzzi and one tennis court. ~ Km. 2.5, Carretera a Pichilingue; 612-121-6187, fax 612-121-6277. MODERATE TO DELUXE.

Still farther northeast, **La Concha Beach Resort** is a self-contained resort built by the now-defunct El Presidente chain. Its 109 rooms feature Mexican tile floors, floral-print bedspreads and balconies overlooking a palm-lined white sand beach that curves gracefully along the bay. There are tennis courts and a heated swimming pool with poolside bar. A water sports center rents gear, and a free shuttle runs guests back and forth from downtown. ~ Km. 5, Carretera a Pichilingue; 612-121-6161, fax 612-121-6218, or 800-716-8603 in the U.S.; www.laconcha.com, e-mail laconcha@juno.com. MODERATE TO DELUXE.

A great out-of-town choice for sports enthusiasts is the family-run **Hotel Cantamar Resort & Sports Center**, located on Playa Pichilingue near the ferry terminal. Each of the 18 guest rooms and suites is air-conditioned and has a ceiling fan, a balcony and a color TV. There are a pool with a swim-up bar, a private beach with shade palapas, a marina and boat ramp, a saltwater aquarium and an exotic reptile display, as well as scuba, snorkel, kayak and wave runner rentals, a sportfishing fleet and certified dive masters. The hotel even has its own rinse tank, recompression chamber and fillet and freezing service for your day's fishing catch. ~ Calle Obregón 1665; 612-125-8644, fax 612-122-8644; www.clubcantamar.com, e-mail info@clubcantamar.com. MODERATE TO DELUXE.

La Pazlapa de Carlos 'n' Charlie's is a branch of the chain that owns rowdy restaurant/nightclubs in just about every Mexican beach resort town. This place seems more sedate than most of its

DINING

cousins, probably because La Paz attracts a more mature crowd than Puerto Vallarta or Cancún. Still, if you want to feel like you're on a real beach vacation, stop in for steak, margaritas and a fantastic view of the sunset on Bahía de la Paz. ~ Paseo Obregón at Calle 16 de Diciembre; 612-122-9290. MODERATE.

La Terraza, Hotel Perla's sidewalk café across from the *malecón* at the Hotel Perla, is an ideal spot to while away the hours with a sailboat-studded bay view at any time from the breakfast hour late into the evening. The menu is divided half-and-half between American and Mexican dishes and features catch-of-the-day seafood specials. ~ Paseo Obregón 1570; 612-122-0777. MODERATE.

Also located on the waterfront, **El Taste** serves a predictable menu of Mexican food, steaks and seafood, along with a great view. It's a perennially popular hangout for English-speaking expatriates and snowbirds. ~ Paseo Obregón at Calle Juárez; 612-122-8121. MODERATE.

Restaurante Bougainvillea offers a romantic ambience whether you choose to dine inside, out front on the wharf or in the palm-shaded rear courtyard with its fountain and mesquite-burning pizza oven. The eclectic menu features such choices as steak *au poivre*, New York–style pizza and pepper-seared tuna sashimi. ~ Malecón de Vista Coral 5; 612-122-7744. DELUXE.

Tratoria La Pazta, in the Hotel Mediterrane, is a casual Italian restaurant where fresh pasta is made to order. It features Mediterranean-style creations—linguini with squid marinated in wine sauce, spaghetti in white clam sauce—as well as fondues and other traditional Swiss dishes. The atmosphere, too, is modern European, with polished black-and-white decor and waiters wearing crisp white jackets and an air of high dignity. ~ Calle Allende 36-B; 612-125-1195. MODERATE.

El Quinto Sol, La Paz's natural food market, has a cafeteria that offers vegetable and fruit salads, yogurt smoothies, soy chorizo and a vegetarian *comida corrida*. ~ Calle Dominguez at Calle Héroes de la Independencia; 612-122-1692. MODERATE.

SLAY YOUR HUNGER

La Paz has a small Chinatown between the *malecón* and the plaza. The top restaurant in that quarter is **Restaurant El Dragón**, which serves creative versions of familiar dishes such as *chao men* and *pollo kun pau* with a special flair derived from Mexican chiles and fresh vegetables. ~ Calle 16 de Septiembre at Calle Esquerro; 612-122-1372. BUDGET TO MODERATE.

◄ HIDDEN

Restaurante Bismark II, specializing in seafood dishes and Mexican fare, is seven blocks inland and four blocks southeast of the plaza. The best way to find it is by taxi. Menu options such as *chiles rellenos con langosta* (poblano chiles stuffed with lobster) and *cochinita pibil* (Yucatán-style barbecued pork) are served at long wooden tables in a casual, smoky atmosphere. ~ Calle Degollado at Calle Altamirano; 612-122-4854. MODERATE.

The **Yeneka Restaurant**, next to the backpackers' hotel of the same name, has fish and Mexican dishes at low-budget prices. The simple restaurant is accented with artwork by three generations of the owners' family. ~ Calle Madero 1520; 612-125-4688. BUDGET.

Northeast of town on the road to Pichilingue, **Restaurant/Bar El Moro** is an indoor, air-conditioned place with dim lighting, tablecloths and uniformed waiters who are ultra-polite, though in no hurry. The menu features lobster and mainland Mexican cuisine, including an excellent *pollo en mole*. ~ Km. 2, Carretera a Pichilingue; 612-122-7010. MODERATE.

A favorite of both locals and tourists, the **Restaurante Grill Campestre** prepares Mexican and American food in a warm, inviting setting. Specialties include spare ribs with homemade barbecue sauce, hamburgers and excellent salads. ~ Km. 5.5, Carretera a Pichilingue; 612-124-0454. MODERATE TO DELUXE.

GROCERIES

La Paz's public food market, **Mercado Municipal Francisco Madero**, is four blocks inland and three blocks southeast of the plaza. Freshly caught fish and other seafood are displayed on beds of ice, and farmers from the Llano de Magdalena agricultural zone bring in truckloads of vegetables daily. Prices are posted and, although haggling is less prevalent than it once was, bargain prices can still be negotiated. ~ Calle Revolución de 1910 at Calle Degollado.

You'll find natural foods at any of **El Quinto**'s several locations, including Calles Dominguez and Independencia, Las Girasoles shopping center on Avenida Revolución de 1910, or Tonantzin shopping center at Calles 5 de Mayo and Serdan.

SHOPPING

People come from all over Baja California Sur to do their major shopping in La Paz. The leading department stores are **Perla de La Paz** (Calle Arreola at Calle Mutualismo) and **Dorian's** (Calle 16 de Septiembre at Calle Esquerro).

For fine-quality Mexican arts and crafts, visit **La Antigua California**, where you'll find everything from majolica ceramics and delicately wrought Taxco jewelry to wooden dance masks from Michoacán and lacquer boxes from Nayarit. ~ Paseo Alvaro Obregón 220; 612-125-5230.

NIGHTLIFE

The **Teatro de la Ciudad**, two miles south of the city center, presents performances by local and visiting theater and dance troupes, as well as film festivals. Call or stop by for a schedule of events. ~ Calle Legaspi at Calle Héroes de Independencia; 612-125-1917.

La Paz Lapa de Carlos 'n' Charlie's attracts an exuberant crowd, especially on weekends, when live rock bands play. Weekend cover. ~ Paseo Obregón; 612-122-9290. A popular dance club is **Super Disco**. Cover. ~ Calle Degollado; 612-125-6122. There's live rock music at **Las Varitas**. ~ Independencia 111; 612-125-2025. Look for live Mexican dance music at **La Caleta**. Cover. ~ Avenida Obregón Eipineda at Calle Juárez; 612-125-2251. **La Cabaña Club** has a mellower lounge feel. ~ Hotel Perla, Paseo Obregón; 612-122-0777.

BEACHES & PARKS

PLAYA TECOLOTE This one-and-a-half-mile-long beach on the northern end of the Pichilingue Peninsula is wide, white and backed by high dunes. There are two palapa restaurants and boat and jet ski rentals. Playa Tecolote is the departure point for sea kayak excursions to Isla Espiritu Santo, which lies a few miles to the north and can be seen clearly from the hillside behind the beach. ~ Follow the main road five miles past the Pichilingue ferry terminal. The pavement ends at the beach.

▲ Informal RV and tent camping is permitted behind the dune area. No water or hookups. There is no fee.

PLAYA LA VENTANA This remote beach stretches for ten miles along the Canal de Cerralvo. It's a favorite destination of windsurfers and adventurous surf fishermen. The wreck of the *Cedro*, a modern freighter, juts out of the water just offshore near Punta Arena de la Ventana at the west end of the beach. ~ Follow Route 286 south from La Paz toward San Juan de los Planes. A gravel road forks off to the left after 40 kilometers and leads to the east end of the beach. The main paved road continues for another 21 kilometers; shortly before it reaches the coast, another unpaved road turns off to the left and goes to the lighthouse at Punta Arena de la Ventana, on the west end of the beach.

▲ La Ventana Campground, at the small fishing village of La Ventana on the east end of the beach, has shaded tent and RV campsites with restrooms but no hookups. Punta Arena, at the west end of the beach, is great for tent camping but has no facilities. Fees for all sites are US $3 a night.

▼▼▼▼▼▼▼▼▼▼▼▼▼

Cabo del Este and Sierra de la Laguna

Cabo del Este, or East Cape, refers to the area along the shore of Bahía de Palmas, extending 20 miles from Punta Pescadero on the north to Punta Arena (not to be confused with Punta Arena de la Ventana, above) on the south and including the fair-sized fishing villages of Los Barriles and La Rivera. Fishing resorts, built by and for gringo pilots, began to spring up along the bay in the 1950s, long before the highway was paved, when the area was one of the most remote spots in Baja. The major tourism development of the Los Cabos area has not reached the East Cape; this remains a quiet, friendly, angler-oriented hideaway with a handful of small American-owned resorts—eight at last count—and limited telephone service. Virtually all fishing resorts in the Cabo del Este area have reservation phone numbers in Southern California. A few, especially those whose dining rooms are open to the public, also have answering services in San José del Cabo.

Inland from the bay, the ranching center of Santiago is a starting point for backpacking expeditions into the Sierra de la Laguna—"hidden" interior of the cape area and one of the most unique ecosystems in North America.

SIGHTS
◀ *HIDDEN*

The traditional farming village of **Santiago**, population 1000, doesn't see many tourists, even though it's located a mere half-hour's drive from Los Cabos International Airport. Of course, it's a long way from the beach and has no golf courses—in fact, no tourist infrastructure beyond a handful of restaurants and budget-basic guesthouses. What it does have is a mellow town plaza and the authenticity of real, unspoiled Mexico. It was the site of Misión Santiago el Apóstal Aiñiní, originally established by Jesuits in 1724. The bloodiest revolt of the missionary era

Cabo del Este

began here ten years later, when Guayacara and Pericú Indians killed the mission's *padre*. The revolt quickly spread to all the missions in the cape area, and several years of warfare followed before the Spanish regained control of the missions. No trace of Misión Santiago remains today.

The main sight in Santiago is **Parque Zoológico Santiago**, a small zoo containing mammals, birds and reptiles native to the Baja Peninsula as well as a lion, a tiger and a few other exotic beasts. Conditions of confinement in this zoo are less humane than they might be, though the larger animals are being moved to more spacious accommodations in response to recent animal-rights protests. This is the only zoo in Baja, and kids come from far and wide to marvel at the monkeys and big cats. Admission. ~ Santiago; no phone.

Just south of Santiago, motorists officially cross into the tropics. The **Tropic of Cancer Monument**, a simple concrete sphere beside the highway, marks the spot.

HIDDEN ►

Hikers can reach the three major canyons of the **Sierra de la Laguna**, the roadless wilderness in the center of Baja's cape region, from the small towns of Santiago, Miraflores and Caduaño, which lie between 142 and 145 kilometers south of La Paz on the way to San José del Cabo. Each of the three trails continues all the way across the cape to the vicinity of Todos Santos, and can be hiked in either direction, though the climb into the highlands is much steeper from the west side. For more information on Sierra de la Laguna, see "Islands in the Sky" on the next page.

LODGING

There are several fishing resorts along the Cabo del Este coast. The oldest one, **Rancho Buena Vista Hotel,** was built in the early 1960s with its own air strip to cater to fly-in sportsmen. After the original American owner died in a private-plane crash in the nearby mountains, subsequent owners remodeled the hotel while expanded it to its present 55 rooms. The feel is rustic, with heavy handmade furniture; some rooms are air-conditioned, while others are cooled by ceiling fans. There are no phones or TVs here, but the hotel has a swimming pool, tennis courts and its own sportfishing fleet. Meals in the dining room, included in the room rate, feature fresh-caught fish as well as meat and vegetables from the hotel's working ranch. Closed in August and September. ~ Bahía de Palmas; 613-141-0177; reservations: P.O. Box 1408, Santa Maria, CA 93456; 805-928-1719, 800-258-8200; www.ranchobuenavista.com. DELUXE.

A quarter-mile south of Rancho Buena Vista, **Hotel Buena Vista Beach Resort** occupies the former vacation home of Agustín Olachea Aviles, a famous Mexican general. Accommodations in the hotel's 60 bright, cheerful guest rooms with light wood and pastel accents are comparable to those at Rancho Buena Vista and

Islands in the Sky

The Sierra de la Laguna receives more rainfall than any other part of the Baja Peninsula; in fact, their 35 inches of precipitation annually are slightly more than the amount that falls on soggy Seattle, Washington! Most of the rain falls during the monsoon season, from July to November, though Pacific fog can shroud the sierra at any time of year.

The moisture creates a microclimate that preserves a "relic environment"—an isolated area in which rare plants have survived from a time millennia ago, before Baja became a desert. Here, amid jagged granite peaks, at least 400 tropical, desert and mountain plant species grow side by side, giving the high sierra's "islands in the sky" a biological diversity found nowhere else in North America. Palms and madrone trees, oaks and wild roses, cactuses and yucca, strawberries and wild grapes, marigolds and Spanish moss are among the lush profusion of vegetation.

The high wilderness is home to coyotes, deer, mountain lions and many smaller creatures, including a species of tree frog that is extinct except in this remote area. The higher slopes of the mountains feature areas that have been termed "hummingbird flower forests" because of the dozens of kinds of hummingbirds that winter there in large numbers.

Environmentalists are campaigning to persuade the Mexican government to declare Sierra de la Laguna a national park. Although some people fear that this would greatly increase the number of hikers and put stress on the unique and fragile ecosystem, many believe that such a declaration is necessary to block the proposed diversion of water from the sierra to Los Cabos. Any hike into the relic environments of the high sierra is a demanding multi-day trek; details are in the "Outdoor Adventures" section of this chapter. Mule trips can also be arranged in Santiago.

other resorts along this stretch of coast. Besides tennis courts and two swimming pools there is a whirlpool spa heated by mineral hot springs. Guests can rent horses at the resort's riding stables, and snorkel gear, scuba tanks or kayaks at the water sports center. Lodging is on the American plan (all meals included), with all-you-can-eat themed buffets and seating on an oceanfront terrace. ~ Carratera al Sur, Km. 105; 613-142-1962, or 2220 Otay Lakes Road, Chula Vista, CA 91915; 619-429-8079, 800-752-3555, fax 619-330-4539 in the U.S.; www.hotelbuenavista.com. DELUXE.

Farther south along the coast, the **Rancho Leonero Resort** accommodates anglers and scuba divers. The 29 large guest units have rock walls, palapa roofs, private patios and sea views. Rates are on the American plan (all meals included). ~ Camino Rancho Leonero, La Rivera; 613-141-0216 or 5671 Palmer Way, Suite E, Carlsbad, CA 92010; 760-438-2905, 800-334-2252, fax 760-438-0184 in the U.S.; www.rancholeonero.com, e-mail rancholeonero@worldnet.att.net. ULTRA-DELUXE.

Budget lodging options are few and far between in the East Cape area. Hikers bound for Sierra de la Laguna can find low-priced, no-frills rooms with private baths in Santiago at the 20-room **Hotel Palomar**. The guest rooms open out onto a tranquil courtyard garden and restaurant. Local legend has it that American crooner Bing Crosby, visiting the village during an East Cape sportfishing trip in the days when Los Cabos hardly existed, bemoaned the lack of accommodations in Santiago and urged the parents of the present owners to open this place.~ Santiago; 612-122-2604. BUDGET.

HIDDEN ►

DINING   Most East Cape resorts operate on the American plan, with all meals included as part of the lodging rate, and few independent restaurants have sprung up in the area. Several years ago, the **Rancho Leonaro Resort** opened its dining room to nonguests, and since then it has acquired a reputation as one of the best res-

FISHERMAN FRIENDLY

Within walking distance of the beach, the Hotel Los Barriles, like many in the area, caters mainly to fishermen and is busiest from May through July. The 20 guest rooms are beautifully appointed, each with two queen-sized beds featuring wooden headboards hand-carved in La Paz, and all have air conditioning and sea views. There's an inviting free-form swimming pool fringed with palm trees, as well as a large cedar hot tub. Rates include a continental breakfast. ~ Los Barriles; 613-141-0024, or 624-141-0024 in the U.S.; www.losbarrileshotel.com, e-mail relax@losbarrileshotel.com. BUDGET TO MODERATE.

taurants on the peninsula. People often drive an hour from Los Cabos just to eat here. The bill of fare, which changes daily, normally features seafood entrées. ~ Camino Rancho Leonero, La Rivera. DELUXE.

In Santiago, the **Hotel Palomar**'s restaurant specializes in seafood, offering grilled lobster, thick fish steaks and giant steamed clams at some of the best prices in Baja. ~ Santiago. BUDGET.

PLAYA DE LAS PALMAS 🏃🏇🚣⛵🎣🏄🚤🛥️⛴️🛶 This beautiful palm-lined beach extends in an unbroken arc for 25 miles along the shore of Bahía de Palmas, widening toward the south end, where an abundance of seashells makes for fun beachcombing. ~ The northern end of the beach starts two miles north of Los Barriles. A sandy unpaved road runs from there to the south end of the bay. Treacherous four-wheel-drive roads turn off toward the water's edge, but many motorists leave their vehicles near the main road and hike the quarter-mile or so. The unpaved coast road continues all the way to San José los Cabos, but the southern section of it was washed out during the mudslides of 1993; bring a high-clearance vehicle and plenty of nerve.

▲ There are several RV parks around Los Barriles. **El Cardonal Hideaway** has a restaurant, a boat ramp, restrooms with hot showers and five RV sites with full hookups as well as 20 tent sites; $8 to $11 per night (reservations: phone/fax 612-100-3382). **Juanito's Garden RV Park** also has restrooms with hot showers and 30 RV sites, all with full hookups; $11 per night. **Martin Verdugo's RV Park** has restrooms with hot showers, a swimming pool, 72 RV sites with full hookups ($12 per night) and 25 beachfront tent sites ($10 per night). **La Capilla RV Park** has palapas, restrooms with hot showers, and 20 tent and RV sites with full hookups for $7 per night.

BEACHES & PARKS

San José del Cabo

Spanning more than 30 kilometers along the southern tip of the Baja Peninsula, the metropolitan area often referred to as Los Cabos is comprised of the resort town of Cabo San Lucas, the historic Colonial town of San José del Cabo and the resort area between the two, which has grown to include several large residential developments inhabited mainly by affluent American retirees. The Los Cabos area has grown rapidly to its present population of approximately 175,000 and is expected to soon overtake La Paz as the largest "city" in Baja California Sur.

San José del Cabo is the site of the international airport and the area's banking, business and local government center. Though lacking the world-class marina facilities of its twin town, Cabo San Lucas, this rapidly growing tourist center more than compensates with the gentrified Colonial charm of its streets lined with galleries and cafés. The permanent population is around 60,000, and this figure doubles in winter with the influx of seasonal residents.

San José lies beside a freshwater estuary that was used by Spanish sea captains in the 1600s to replenish their water supplies after the long Pacific crossing from the Philippines. A Jesuit mission was established there in 1730, but was closed down by an Indian rebellion. Several years later, after the rebellion was put down, the town began to grow as a military garrison designed to control the problem of pirates preying on the Manila galleons.

SIGHTS

San José del Cabo's central historic district has evolved into an area of shops, galleries and restaurants, perfect for wandering. The main street, Boulevard Mijares, starts at the north end of town, a block from the **zócalo** (which has been split in two by the long, narrow state tourism office in its center). The plaza boasts a gazebo bandstand and shaded wrought-iron benches.

On the west side of the plaza is the **Iglesia San José**. Step inside this simple church to see a painting that memorializes the massacre of the clergy at San José's original mission church during the Indian revolt of 1734. ~ Calle Morelos.

Boulevard Mijares continues south, an attractive avenue of sidewalk cafés, art galleries and boutiques, passing the Los Cabos Club de Golf on its way to the beachfront hotel zone. This highly gringo-fied street is named after a Mexican Army lieutenant who died leading a heroic last stand against invading U.S. Marines during the Mexican War.

LODGING

Centrally located a block south of the plaza, in the heart of the Boulevard Mijares shopping and restaurant zone, the new three-story **Tropicana Inn** is built around a walled pool area and courtyard. The Tropicana Restaurant isolates the hotel from the street and provides a feeling of seclusion. The 40 guest rooms overlook the courtyard and have all the amenities of a typical U.S. motor inn—two double beds apiece, satellite TV with English-language channels, and air conditioning. It's San José's best in-town hotel, though a long way from the beach. ~ Boulevard Mijares 30; 624-142-2311, fax 624-142-1590. MODERATE TO DELUXE.

Also in a great downtown location within strolling distance of the best restaurants, galleries and shops is **El Encanto Inn**. The two-story inn has contemporary hacienda-style architecture and 26 rooms and suites (four with kitchens), plus a lush courtyard and a new swimming pool, with plans underway for 30 more poolside suites. Rates include continental breakfast. ~ Calle Morelos 133; 624-142-0388, fax 624-142-4620; www.elencanto inn.com, e-mail info@elencantoinn.com. MODERATE.

The lowest rates in town are found at the **San José Youth Hostel**, with its 25 fair-sized rooms cooled by ceiling fans. The floors and mattress platforms are concrete, the bathrooms are shared, and the decor is drab, but the location—on a dirt back street three blocks from the plaza—is fine, and the price is right. ~ Calle Obregón 2; 624-142-2464. BUDGET.

Another good low-budget bet, the **Posada Señor Mañana** has ◄ HIDDEN eight jungle lodge-style thatched-roof rooms, some with private baths, as well as open-air palapas for hammock camping. Guests are welcome to use the communal kitchen and dining room and to pick tropical fruit from the trees in the overgrown courtyard.

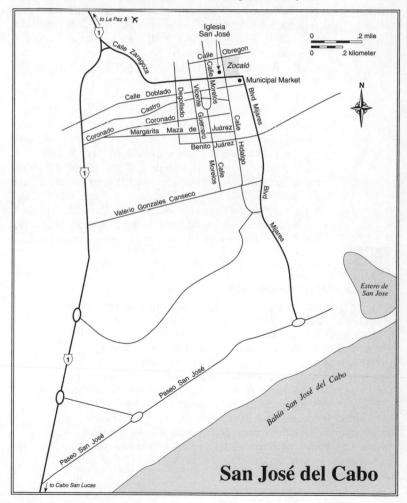

San José del Cabo

Although this funky backpackers' haven is just a block from the plaza, it seems a world apart from touristy Los Cabos because it's secluded at the end of the road beside the estuary that defines the east edge of town. ~ Calle Obregón 1; phone/fax 624-142-0462; www.srmanana.com, e-mail srmanana@1cabonet.com.mx. BUDGET.

Four blocks from the plaza and the Boulevard Mijares shopping and restaurant zone, the **Posada Terranova** is a small, modern European-style hotel. The 25 guest rooms are bright and clean; each has two double beds, color TV, modern plumbing and air conditioning. The Italian-Mexican management is friendly and personable, and the café-style tables on the front patio are ideal for lounging and getting to know other guests. ~ Calle Degollado; 624-142-0534, fax 624-142-0902; e-mail terranova@cabonet. com.mx. BUDGET TO MODERATE.

The **Presidente Inter-Continental Los Cabos Resort** has survived several changes of ownership and management since it opened in the 1970s as the first all-inclusive resort in San José's beachfront hotel zone. Location and ambience have helped it to maintain its status as the best on the beach as other resorts have sprung up to the west. The hotel's three-story, adobe-look buildings sprawl between the uncrowded end of Playa de California, the entrance to Los Cabos Club de Golf, and a natural freshwater estuary teeming with bird life. The 395 guest rooms are large and luxurious, with king-sized beds and oversized bathtubs, and most have shaded balconies overlooking Bahía de San José. Recreational facilities include the largest swimming pool in the hotel zone, plus tennis courts, rental horses and sportfishing

AUTHOR FAVORITE

In an area dominated by grand-scale resort development, I like the blend of just-like-home and Fantasyland ambience at **Huerta Verde**, a small, chic hideaway in the hills near San José del Cabo. Situated on a terraced hillside with a pastoral view, the inn is an architectural fantasy of tropical palapas, Spanish colonial domes and arches, rustic viga-and-latilla ceilings and contemporary touches. Seven air-conditioned guest suites surround a pool and walled patio nestled amid palms, vines and colorful flowering bushes that attract humming-birds and cardinals. Rooms are individually decorated with queen- and king-sized beds, *equipal* furniture and primitive art. Although the inn is three miles inland, you can still hear and smell the sea. A full breakfast is included. ~ Camino Las Animas Altas; phone/fax 624-148-0511, or in the U.S. 303-431-5162, fax 303-431-4455 ULTRA-DELUXE.

charter boats. ~ Boulevard Mijares at Paseo San José; 624-142-9229, fax 624-142-0232; www.interconti.com. ULTRA-DELUXE.

One of a cluster of international chain hotels in the center of San José's beachfront hotel zone, the **Posada Real Los Cabos** is the most modestly priced beach resort in San José's hotel zone. The modern 150-room hotel offers air-conditioned rooms with two double beds, cable TV, showers and the rest of the motor inn amenities you'd expect of a Best Western establishment; most (though not all) rooms have views of the beach and sea. There's a swimming pool and jacuzzi, bicycle rentals and fishing charters. ~ Boulevard Malecón; 624-142-0155, fax 624-142-0460, or 800-528-1234 in the U.S. MODERATE TO ULTRA-DELUXE.

The individually owned rental condos at **La Jolla de Los Cabos**, in the self-contained resort community of the same name, are some of the homiest-feeling accommodations in the hotel zone. Three- to six-story sandstone-colored buildings contain 220 studio, one-bedroom and two-bedroom suites with simple pastel furnishings. All have phones, cable TV, refrigerators and coffeemakers, and many have full kitchens. Guests have the use of four swimming pools, two lighted tennis courts, exercise rooms, saunas, steam rooms and jacuzzis. Shuttles run guests into downtown San José, five kilometers away. ~ Km. 29, Carretera Transpeninsular; 624-142-3000, fax 624-142-0546, or 800-524-5104 in the U.S. ULTRA-DELUXE.

The **Meliá Cabo Real Beach & Golf Resort** represents the state of the art in glamour tourism. It's a long way from town, almost midway between San José Los Cabos and Cabo San Lucas, but the elaborate landscaping—water surging from fountains, spilling over waterfalls, shimmering in ponds, in dramatic contrast to desert gardens of native and exotic cactuses—is designed to distract guests from any thought of leaving the hotel grounds. Boutiques, restaurants and night clubs add to the gravitational pull. Countless truckloads of white sand were imported to enhance the beach, and a stone jetty creates a sheltered area for snorkeling. One of Los Cabos' largest resorts, the Meliá has 288 air-conditioned rooms and suites with Mayan-style bas-reliefs sculpted into the stucco walls and sliding doors that open onto private garden terraces. Guests have privileges at the adjacent 18-hole Cabo Real golf course, and there are a swimming pool, one tennis court, a health club and sauna, and a dive shop that rents scuba and snorkel gear. ~ Km. 19.5, Carretera Transpeninsular; 624-144-0000, fax 624-144-0101, or 800-336-3542 in the U.S.; www.solmelia.com. ULTRA-DELUXE.

Built in 1956 by the son of Mexican president Abelardo Luis Rodriguez, the **Palmilla Resort** was the first luxury resort in the Los Cabos area. Constantly expanding and updating its resort facilities to keep ahead of the competition, it continues to reign as the premier hotel in the area. The 70 spacious guest rooms, suites and villas are individually decorated with hand-carved furniture and fine folk art, and all have balconies or terraces with ocean views. Service is extraordinarily attentive; hotel employees outnumber guests by three to one. In addition to a large swimming pool and tennis courts, the hotel has a croquet court, riding stables and its own sportfishing fleet, as well as a complete health spa and a 27-hole golf course designed by Jack Nicklaus. ~ Km. 27.5, Carretera Transpeninsular; 624-144-5000, fax 624-144-5100, or 800-637-2226 in the U.S.; www.palmillaresort.com. ULTRA-DELUXE.

Affluent surfers will find the best surfing beach in Los Cabos right outside their rooms at **Cabo Surf Hotel**, a 22-room resort secluded from the public eye. The air-conditioned rooms, which range from cozy ocean-view units with one king-sized or two double beds to spacious villas with full beachfront terraces, feature solid-feeling handcrafted furniture and contemporary Mexican artwork. All rooms have private phones and satellite TV, and some have wireless internet access for an extra fee. The resort has a full spa, as well as a surf school and surf shop owned by former world champion Mike Doyle. ~ Playa Acapulquito, Km. 28; 624-172-6188, fax 624-142-2676 or 858-964-5117 in the U.S.; www.cabosurfhotel, e-mail info@cabosurfhotel.com. ULTRA-DELUXE.

DINING

Damiana, a steak and seafood restaurant in a renovated 18th-century hacienda on the east side of the plaza, has outdoor seating on a romantic patio shaded by pines and shrouded in bougainvillea. It offers the finest candlelight dining in San José del Cabo, including such house specialties as charcoal-broiled lobster in achiote sauce and grilled abalone in *salsa ajillo* (garlic and chile *guajillo* sauce). ~ Boulevard Mijares; 624-142-0499. DELUXE.

Morgan's, a signature restaurant by renowned international designer Morgan MacLeod, serves catch-of-the-day fish and other continental cuisine prepared in the styles of Tuscany and Provence. Bread and pastries are baked fresh daily. Elaborate wall murals and hand-carved furniture create a rustic-elegant ambience. Dinner only. ~ Calles Manuel Doblado and Hidalgo; 624-142-3825. DELUXE.

Ms. MacLeod has a second location, **Morgan's Encore**, also in the downtown historic district. ~ Calles Morelos and Obregón; 624-142-4737. DELUXE.

HIDDEN ►

A homey little Mexican restaurant with brightly painted walls, *papel picado* (cut paper) ceiling banners, posters of flamenco dancers and an English-language paperback book exchange, **Restaurant Jasmin's** offers traditional dishes such as *pollo en molcajete* (stuffed chicken breast roasted and served in

a lava rock mortar) and tequila shrimp, as well as more international fare such as sea bass Florentine and barbecued baby back
ribs. There are also cheesy vegetarian options. ~ Calle Morelos
(behind the church); 624-142-1760. MODERATE.

One of the classiest restaurants in town, **La Panga Antigua**
features imaginative nouveau seafood. A typical dinner might
begin with an heirloom tomato soup with salmon tartar, move on
to an entrée such as snook filet with mango ratatouille, prawns
sautéed in chardonnay, or a poblano chile filled with mixed
seafood and served over fettuccine primavera, topped off with a
chocolate dessert tamale. ~ Calle Zaragosa 20; 624-142-4041.
DELUXE.

Nearby, beef lovers flock to the shady outdoor patio at **La
Bodega Steak and Wine House**, where the menu highlights are
ribeye, New York–cut steaks and filet mignon, grilled in your
choice of marinades and rubs, including salsa *borracha* (beer,
chile ancho and herbs) and *chimichurri* (guajillo chile, garlic,
cilantro, onion and olive oil). For diners who prefer seafood,
there are unusual selections such as octopus with mushrooms in
garlic sauce and whole squids stuffed with *huitacochtle*. ~ Calle
Zaragoza, one block from Plaza Mijares; 624-142-6619. MOD-
ERATE TO DELUXE.

Asian stir-fry dishes and Mediterranean pastas are prepared
at the **Tequila Restaurante**. Guests can dine in a lush courtyard garden with attentive service and strolling musicians. Closed Wednesday. ~ Calle Doblado 1011; 624-142-1155. DELUXE.

For a dining experience that may change your idea of
Mexican food, leave the historic district to visit **Zuomo**, where
you can sample outstanding presentations of "pre-Columbian
fusion" cuisine. The minimalist decor reflects chef-owner Sergio
Figueroa's early culinary training in a Japanese Zen monastery;
the menu reflects the years he spent in Oaxacan Indian villages.
You might (but don't have to) start your dinner with *tlayuda
Oaxaqueña*, a quesadilla made with baked *gusano* moth larvae
and fried grasshoppers. For a main course, how about *pato en*

ITCHIN' FOR A SMOKE

Just off Route 1 on the road into town, **Pescadería Sea Food Market** has
just seven tables in a dining area beside the smokehouse. It offers one of the
widest choices of seafood *antojitos* and entrées in Los Cabos, from marinated raw oysters to smoked marlin steaks. They will also cook and
serve fish you've caught, or smoke them so you can take them home. ~
Calle Castro at Carretera Transpeninsular; 624-142-3266. MODERATE.

mole negro (duck in Oaxacan black mole sauce) or a tortilla-laered "lasagna" made with *requesón* (a ricotta-like cheese), *flor de calabaza* (squash blossoms) and *huitlacoche* (corn truffles)? And for dessert, perhaps mamay fruit and Oaxacan cheese ice cream. ~ Plaza Las Velas 1, 624-105-0808. MODERATE TO DELUXE.

The **Mercado Municipal,** located toward the west end of town, has an eating area where eight *comedores* serve inexpensive meals ranging from fish tacos to roast chicken, plus soft drinks, fresh fruit juices and *licuados* (fruit smoothies). ~ Between Calles Castro and Coronado. BUDGET.

Zipper's Bar & Grill on Playa Costa Azul is a big beachfront palapa long known as a surfers' hangout. In simpler times it was a basic hamburger joint, but as the surrounding resort area has grown, it has added mesquite-grilled steaks and barbecued ribs to the menu. The restaurant uses only imported U.S. beef, which is more tender and juicy than the free-range Mexican beef served in many Baja steakhouses. ~ Km. 28.5, Carretera Transpeninsular; 624-172-6162. MODERATE.

SHOPPING   San José's **Mercado Municipal** is located between Calles Coronado and Castro a few blocks south and west of the main plaza. While locals still come to this market to buy produce, much of it is given over to arts and crafts.

Part gallery and part museum, **Antigua Los Cabos** is just off the main plaza and features quality tequilas and a wide range of fine Mexican *artesanía*, including pre-Columbian reproductions in gold, silver and clay certified authentic by the National Museum of Anthropology in Mexico City. ~ Calle Mijares 5; 624-146-9933.

San Jose's burgeoning art gallery district runs along Calle Obregón and its cross streets for two blocks just off the main plaza. Here, **Amber Gallery** exhibits sculpture and jewelry fashioned by hand from Chiapas amber. ~ Calle Obregón 18; 624-105-2332. Impressionist painter Dennis Wentworth Porter founded the first art gallery in San José los Cabos, **Wentworth Porter Gallery,** where he shows his own works and those of other

FOLK ART FIXINS'

One of the most interesting folk art galleries in San José del Cabo is **Huichol Collection Galeria Museo,** one of a nationwide chain of shops that sell the intricate beadwork, embroidery and decorated lacquer trays and boxes made by the deeply traditional Huichol Indians of Nayarit. ~ Boulevard Mijares at Calle Zaragoza.

internationally known artists. ~ Calle Obregón 20; 624-142-3141. Works by about 40 local artists are exhibited across the street at **Pez Gordo**. ~ Calle Obregón 19; 624-142-5788. Local artists are also exhibited at **Old Town Gallery**. ~ Calle Obregon 20-A; 624-142-3662.

Copal has a selection of folk art from the Mexican mainland, including dance masks, furniture and ceramics. ~ Calle Zaragoza 20; 620-142-3070. An art walk of these and other galleries in the district, with wine and hors d'oeuvres, is held every Thursday evening from November through May, 5:00–9:00 p.m.

San José lacks the rowdy night life scene of neighboring Cabo San Lucas. This is a town for romantic moonlight strolling. If you just gotta dance, there's live music most nights at the **Tropicana Bar and Grill** in the Tropicana Inn. ~ Boulevard Mijares 30; 624-142-1580. There's live rock-and-roll most weekends at the **Iguana Bar**. ~ Boulevard Mijares; 624-142-0266. **Cactus Jack's** has it all—dancing, live music, giant-screen sports TV and karaoke. ~ Boulevard Mijares. Live Latin jazz can be found Wednesday through Friday nights at **Havana's**. ~ Route 1, Km. 29; no phone.

NIGHTLIFE

PLAYA COSTA AZUL 🐎 🏄 🚣 🚤 🛥 🍹 Sections of this long, straight beach in front of the San José hotel zone are sometimes known by various names, including Playa de California and Playa del Nuevo Sol, but it's all one wide, straight beach. Sometimes it's idyllic. At other times, waves crash against it with the force of dynamite blasts. ~ Southeast of San José del Cabo.

BEACHES & PARKS

▲ Sharing the beach with resort hotels, **Brisa del Mar RV Resort** has 70 tent and RV sites, all with water (but don't drink it) and electricity and most with sewer hookups. Facilities include restrooms with hot showers, a swimming pool, a laundry room, a volleyball court, and a game room with pool and ping-pong tables. Sites cost $11 a night for tents and $18.50 to $30 per night for RVs. ~ 624-142-3999.

Welcome to the least "hidden" place in Baja. As recently as 1970, Cabo San Lucas was a tiny fishing village of 500 people, both smaller and more remote than such hidden destinations as Bahía de los Angeles or Bahía Tortugas. Most residents worked for an American corporation that operated an industrial tuna fishing platform offshore. All that changed when the Mexican government, flush with new-found wealth from skyrocketing crude-oil prices in the mid-1970s, set plans in motion to create a series of beachfront mega-resorts: Cancún, Zihuatanejo, Puerto Vallarta—and Cabo San Lucas. Building a marina and installing an ambitious infrastruc-

Cabo San Lucas

ture of public utilities and paved roads, the government soon enticed a number of major resort chains to build hotels, and the flood of development began as sport fishermen, scuba divers and sun worshippers from the United States and Canada poured into the little village.

Today, any semblance of the sleepy hideaway of years past has been obliterated by what old-timers perceive as construction run amok. Anchoring the west end of the Los Cabos resort corridor, Cabo San Lucas itself now boasts a population of over 60,000. For many, the symbol of excessive growth was the construction of the five-story Plaza Las Glorias shopping mall and condominium development, which created a solid four-block-long wall between the marina and the main street, blocking not only the view but also the sea breezes that used to cool the town.

SIGHTS   Cabo San Lucas is self-explanatory. The center of the action is **Marina Cabo San Lucas**, a 380-slip facility that can accommodate yachts up to 150 feet in length. The marina fills the inner harbor, which has been dredged and carved into a perfect square. High-rise shopping malls, hotels, restaurants and condominiums box the marina on three sides, isolating it from the rest of the town. ~ 624-143-1251; e-mail normaf@cabomarina.com.mx.

The small, rocky cape of land that gives the town its name extends southward, forming the west shore of the outer harbor. These days, it is often called Land's End to distinguish it from the town. No road reaches the tip of the cape, so you have to take a water taxi or hike to get there. **El Arco**, the distinctive natural rock arch at the tip of the cape, is perhaps Baja's most familiar landmark and the southernmost point of land on the peninsula. Beyond El Arco, two rock pillars known as **Los Frailes** rise from the sea and are frequented by seals and sea lions.

The main street of Cabo San Lucas, **Calle Lázaro Cárdenas** is lined with bars, galleries and shops. The town plaza, at Calles Lázaro Cárdenas and Zaragoza, has recently been refurbished with picturesque wrought-iron benches and lampposts, and the buildings surrounding it are undergoing beautification and gentrification. To the north of the main street, the town's residential district comprises small houses and unpaved streets that form a stark contrast with the luxury resorts south of the marina.

LODGING   Travelers heading west along the corridor from San José to Cabo San Lucas pass one resort complex after another. Probably the most striking, though far from the largest, is the **Twin Dolphin Hotel**, a small luxury hotel on a private beach. . . . Well, legally speaking it's public like all Baja beaches, but gawkers have to walk through the hotel under the scrutiny of the staff to get there. The resort enjoys a reputation as a celebrity hideout and takes care to protect guests' privacy, but sightseers often wander in for a look at the replicas of ancient Indian cave murals that decorate the lobby walls. The 50 rooms and suites are in fourplex cabañas scattered throughout the property; all have private patios or terraces with sunset views. Recreation facilities include a riding stable, a putting green, a swimming pool and a charter fishing fleet. ~ Km. 11.5, Carretera Transpeninsular; 624-145-8190, fax 624-145-8196, or 800-421-8925 in the U.S.; www.twindolphin.com. ULTRA-DELUXE.

A small, affordable hideaway five minutes from the beach by bus or taxi, the thatched-roof **Club Cabo Motel & Campground** ◄ HIDDEN has ten modern suites, studios and cabañas, all air-conditioned, most with kitchenettes. It's secluded and well-removed from traffic noise; the loudest sounds around are those of the birds that congregate in the adjacent dense stand of large mesquite and palm trees. There's a swimming pool, as well as hiking and biking trails. RV sites are also available. ~ Route 19 at Route 1; phone/fax 624-143-3348; e-mail clubcabo@cabonet.net.mx. MODERATE.

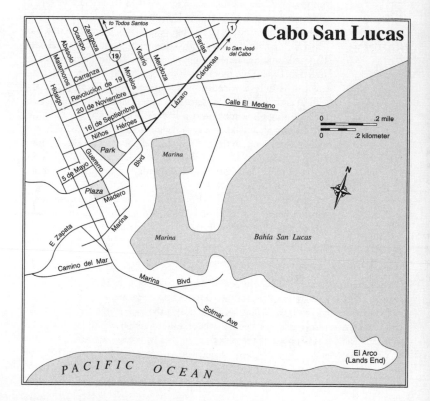

Cabo San Lucas' biggest resorts are located along Playa El Medano, the sheltered swimming beach east of town. The reigning queen of the beach is the **Meliá San Lucas.** All of its 151 spacious, air-conditioned rooms and suites, decorated in cool blue hues and furnished in wicker, share a perfect view of El Arco across the water. Palm trees shade a free-form swimming pool and outdoor hot tub. Watersports equipment rentals and fishing charters are available. ~ Playa El Medano; 624-143-4444, fax 624-143-0418, or 800-336-3542 in the U.S.; www.solmelia.com, e-mail ventas.melia.loscabos@solmelia.com. ULTRA-DELUXE.

Located on the point between the east side of the marina and Playa El Medano, the **Hotel Hacienda Beach Resort** is an elegant manifestation of Spanish colonial charm—replete with fountains, aqueducts, bell towers and pseudo-ancient statuary accented by bright tropical flowering vines. Its guest units include 23 Colonial rooms with ocean views, 30 beach cabañas with refrigerators and separate sitting areas, 12 deluxe suites and six townhouses. There's a putting green, a swimming pool, tennis courts and a beachfront water sports center that rents everything from snorkels to Waverunners. ~ Calle Gomez Farias; 624-143-0122, fax 624-143-0666, or 800-733-2226 in the U.S. ULTRA-DELUXE.

HIDDEN ▶

In striking contrast to the big resort hotels that line much of Playa El Medano, friendly little **Casa Rafael's** has just 10 rooms. This pink boutique hotel, originally a single-family home, was converted in 1994. One block from the beach and a short walk from town, it is fully air-conditioned and has a pool, sun decks and jacuzzi amid lush tropical gardens, as well as a small gym, a pool table, a ping-pong table and a library. The rooms are individually decorated, and some have private jacuzzis. Rates, which vary widely depending on the view, include a gourmet breakfast; other meals are also served. ~ Calle Medano at Camino de Pescadores; 624-143-0739, fax 624-143-1679; e-mail casarafa@cabonet.net. mx. MODERATE TO DELUXE.

If you want to be in the center of the action, consider the **Marina Fiesta Resort & Spa**—that seven-story wall of balconies and sliding glass doors along the east side of the marina. Rooms

FUN, SUN 'N' SEWAGE

Cabo San Lucas' year-round population has grown to more than 5000, virtually all of whom are employed in the construction, hotel and restaurant industries, and swells to 30,000 residents during the winter months. The rapid growth has outstripped public utilities and sanitation facilities, and Cabo San Lucas has become the only place in Baja where tap water is not safe to drink.

have the upscale severity often associated with time-share condos. All of the 155 air-conditioned rooms and suites have microwaves and refrigerators, and half of them have full kitchens. There's a swimming pool, and taxis shuttle guests to the beaches. ~ Marina 37; 624-145-6020, fax 624-145-6021, or 800-745-2226 in the U.S.; www.marina-fiesta.com, e-mail reservations@marinafiesta resort.com. ULTRA-DELUXE.

The **Hotel Finisterra**, the old-timer among Cabo resorts, stands on a hilltop; a steep driveway winds up from Boulevard Marina. The original hotel was built in the 1950s of sandstone blocks quarried nearby, and it blended perfectly into the natural surroundings until a recent expansion multiplied the number of rooms to 197 by adding two eight-story towers that overshadow the old lodge. Rooms in the new section are brighter and more spacious, with one king-sized or two queen-sized beds and balconies overlooking the water. Prices are slightly higher for rooms facing the ocean than those facing the bay, because they provide the best vantage in the area for whale watching right from your room, especially on the higher floors. The resort has three swimming pools, charter fishing boats, and a dive shop that rents snorkeling and scuba gear. ~ Boulevard Marina; 624-143-3333, fax 624-143-0590. ULTRA-DELUXE.

The **Hotel Solmar Suites**, a white, modern, two-story complex located on the far side of the sandstone ridge south of the marina, stands alone on Playa Solmar. The wide beach is dangerous for swimming, and the waves swelling in from the open ocean often strike shore with explosive crashes, drowning out the noise from town. There are 190 guest rooms and suites decorated in Southwestern adobe style, each with a separate sitting area, a king-sized bed or two double beds, and a patio or balcony with a view of the Pacific. The hotel grounds have three heated swimming pools, tennis courts and a dive shop, but the biggest draw is its sportfishing charter fleet. ~ Avenida Solmar; 624-146-7700, fax 624-143-0410, or 310-359-9861 in the U.S.; www.solmar.com. ULTRA-DELUXE.

Cabo San Lucas has few mid-range accommodations. Lodging rates drop astonishingly as you get away from the water. **Hotel Marina Cabo San Lucas**, centrally located on a busy shopping street just a block from the marina, has 21 clean, air-conditioned suites around a courtyard swimming pool and hot tub. The decor consists of flowers handpainted on otherwise bare white walls. Avoid the rooms on the street side of the hotel: they can be noisy. ~ Calle Vicente Guerrero at Boulevard Marina; 624-143-0030; e-mail hotelmarinainn@hotmail.com. MODERATE TO DELUXE.

Built in 1994, the three-story **Siesta Suites Hotel** has 20 plain but spacious efficiency units, most with kitchens. Some have cable TV and air conditioning, and others have only ceiling fans. The friendly folks who run the hotel have quickly built up a steady, year-after-year clientele, so reservations are essential in the winter months. ~ Calle Emiliano Zapata; phone/fax 624-143-2773, or 866-271-2733 in the U.S.; www.cabosiestasuites, e-mail siesta @cabonet.net.mx. MODERATE.

Resembling an American-style motor inn, the **Hotel Santa Fe** is located within easy walking distance of downtown Cabo San Lucas and the marina, and a short trip by bus or water taxi from the beaches. Each of the 46 air-conditioned guest rooms has a queen-sized bed, a fold-out sofa bed and a kitchenette. There's a purple swimming pool and a protected parking lot, and a deli, laundromat and convenience store occupy the side of the hotel that faces the street. ~ Calles Zaragoza and Obregón; 624-143-4401, fax 624-143-4402; www.hotelsantafeloscabos.com, e-mail hotelsantafe@loscabos.com. MODERATE.

The Bungalows Breakfast Inn, located in a quiet residential neighborhood five blocks from "downtown" Cabo San Lucas, offers 16 contemporary studio suites and two-bedroom casitas, all with air-conditioning, refrigerators, TVs and VCRs. There's a heated pool and a free video library. A gourmet breakfast featuring tropical fruits and freshly ground coffee is included in the room rate. ~ Boulevard Miguel Angel Herrera; phone/fax 624-143-5035, or 888-424-2226 in the U.S.; www.cabobungalows. com, e-mail bungalow@cabonet.net.mx. DELUXE.

A longtime fishermen's favorite, the **Hotel Mar de Cortés** is located along lively Calle Lázaro Cárdenas a block from the marina. All 90 air-conditioned rooms and suites surround a garden courtyard with a swimming pool and a palapa bar with a fireplace. The older section of the hotel has small, dim rooms with twin beds or one double bed, and plenty of historic character. Those in the newer part are larger, though more ordinary, with two double beds. Some units have kitchens. ~ Calle Lázaro Cárdenas 40; 624-143-0032, fax 624-143-0032, or 800-347-8821 in the U.S.; www.mardecortez.com, e-mail info@mardecortez.com. BUDGET TO MODERATE.

HIDDEN ► You'll find something completely different from the run-of-the-mill beach resort scene at the improbably named **Blarney Castle Inn**, set high on a desert hillside behind the town. The whimsical architecture is vaguely castlelike, though there's an un-Irish lack of greenery. The sea views over Cabo San Lucas and Playa Medano are incomparable. The nine guest suites range from compact studios to a palatial multilevel penthouse with three and a half baths and five fireplaces, and appropriately there is a wide spread in room rates. All units are air-conditioned and have fully equipped kitchens and patios or private decks. There's a small swimming pool and a large outdoor jacuzzi. ~ Upper end of Calle Libertad, Colonia Lienzo Charro; 624-143-2160 or 866-470-

3868 in the U.S.; www.blarneycastleinn.com, e-mail reservations@ blarneycastleinn.com. MODERATE TO ULTRA-DELUXE.

Cabo San Lucas has more than 100 restaurants, nearly all of them clustered around the marina, on Calle Lázaro Cárdenas or along Playa El Medano. Some have signs so familiar you may feel as if you're back home—KFC, Domino's Pizza, Subway, Dairy Queen. . . .

You can pretend you're anywhere on earth as you scarf down a cheeseburger and fries or barbecued chicken at the windowless **Hard Rock Café**, with a view of Tom Petty's old guitar. ~ Plaza Bonita Mall; 624-143-3779. MODERATE.

Nearby you'll find more all-Americana at the **Harley Davidson Bar & Grill**, where you can dine on burgers and fries to the accompaniment of TV sets blaring sports events via satellite. You can also rent motorcycles here. ~ Marina; 624-143-3337. MODERATE.

For a splurge meal that you'll remember as wonderful instead of just overpriced, dine at **El Galeón Italian Ristorante**, the hillside restaurant at the turnoff to the Hotel Solmar Suites. Make reservations for seating on the terrace after dark for a dazzling view of the marina's lights under a starry sky. The international menu highlights Italian gourmet cuisine—antipasti, seafood and veal. ~ Boulevard Marina; 624-143-0443. DELUXE.

A new entry in the fiercely competitive Los Cabos restaurant scene, **Pericos in the Lighthouse** is the second restaurant location for the Rebolledo Castelan family, who have been operating the famed Pericos restaurant in Cancún since 1976. Meals are quite

MEXICAN HAUTE CUISINE

If you thought you knew what Mexican food was all about, a fine dinner at **Mi Casa Restaurante** may be an eye-opener. Fresh, high-quality ingredients are used in making regional specialties from the Mexican mainland. Sea bass comes smothered in your choice of sauces, rubs and marinades such as *tikin xic*, a Yucatecan achiote marinade, or *mojillo*, a garlic and *guajillo* chile rub, and served with warm homemade tortillas. The *pollo en mole* shows why the Aztecs considered this chocolate-and-chile delicacy the food of the gods. Another specialty is tamales bandera, one each in the three colors of the Mexican flag—*pollo en mole* (red), shredded pork with tomatillo salsa (green) and ranch cheese with chile (white). Most seating is on a romantic, secluded patio behind the restaurant. The table service uses handmade Mexican ceramics, glassware and silverware and bright handwoven tablecloths and napkins. ~ Avenida Cabo San Lucas; 624-143-1933. DELUXE.

generous and feature such typical Mexican restaurant fare as *pollo en mole* and beef fajitas, but the real draw here is the colorfully over-the-top decor, with its life-size dancing Day of the Dead skeletons, and the restaurant's trademark "forever fiesta" atmosphere. Marimba bands and mariachis play as exuberant waiters encourage patrons to dance around the room wearing sombreros to get a free shot of tequila. ~ Boulevard Cantina-Marina; 624-144-4219. MODERATE TO DELUXE.

The most extensive wine list in Los Cabos (120 wines from throughout Latin America and around the world) is the claim to fame at **Casa Rafael's Restaurant,** located in a former family home converted into a small boutique hotel. The restaurant offers service poolside in a lush garden room or in the Ocean Room, where the centerpiece is a large saltwater aquarium. The fare includes medallions of lobster with black bean sauce, as well as filet mignon smothered with morel mushrooms. ~ Next to Marina Sol; 624-143-0739. DELUXE.

Pancho's Restaurant prepares more than 80 traditional regional dishes from Sonora, Puebla and Oaxaca on a big mesquite grill and serves them in a traditional Mexican atmosphere, complete with local musicians six nights a week. While the food is exceptional, Pancho's is better known for having the world's largest tequila collection—more than 400 varieties. Bet you can't sample them all. . . . but you *can* make advance reservations for a tequila tasting—four large shots of tequila demonstrating the four stages of aging, plus one shot of Pancho's homemade mezcal and an hour-long explanation of the fine points of tequila appreciation and a souvenir "Master of Tequilas" diploma. ~ Calle Hidalgo at Calle Zapata; 624-143-0973. BUDGET TO MODERATE.

Mocambo, another longtime local favorite, specializes in seafood and *ceviche*. Whole fried *huachinango* (red snapper) are sold by weight. Other specialties include *congrejo al mojo de ajo* (crab in garlic sauce) and grilled lobster. A mariachi band plays

MEXICAN SUSHI?

Locally caught seafood including dorado, tuna and sea bass gets the sushi treatment with a Mexican fusion flair at **Tsuki Sushi and Tepan Grill**. Among the specialties are the moonlight roll (salmon, tuna and squid with a peanut sauce) and currican sashimi (crab and tuna in orange sauce). There are also shrimp chiles rellenos, tempura seafood and meat, seafood or vegetable tepanyaki grilled at your table, not to mention five kinds of sake. ~ Plaza Puerto Paraiso 277, 2nd floor; 624-105-1023. MODERATE TO DELUXE.

while you eat. ~ Calle Leona Viario at 20 de Noviembre; 624-143-6070. BUDGET TO MODERATE.

As the name suggests, the specialty at **O Mole Mio** is chicken in any of a variety of rich sauces including chocolatey *mole poblano* and a *mole verde* made with pumpkin seeds. There are also seafood dishes such as a tuna steak in mango-papaya salsa. The decor features spectacular artistry in handcrafted wood, metal and colored glass. ~ Boulevard Marina at Plaza del Sol; 624-143-7577. MODERATE TO DELUXE.

Amid its trendy restaurants, Cabo San Lucas does have some traditional open-air *comedores*. They don't come any more authentic than **El Palacio del Taco**. Besides *tacos al pastor* (sliced pork), *suadero* (rib meat), *longaniza* (Yucatecan sausage) or *cabeza* (brain), the stand also makes tortas, the grilled *bolillo* bun sandwiches that are the most popular fast food among Mexicans. ~ Calle 16 de Septiembre between Morelos and Leona Vicario; cell 624-147-6894. BUDGET.

Despite its out-of-the-way location, **La Golondrina Restaurant and Trading Post** has been serving some of the best barbecued meats and seafood in town for more than 30 years. The restaurant occupies the oldest building in Cabo San Lucas, established as a remote trading post in 1896. Guests at Cabo's most exclusive resorts find their way here through the back streets for dinner and margaritas in the patio garden with its wrought-iron benches and dragon lampposts. The menu, which changes often, lists more than 100 entrées ranging from Mexican standards, pastas and steaks to lobsters and vegetable stir-fries; portions are large, and the seafood combo is nothing less than gigantic. There is an extensive wine list. Dinner only. Reservations are essential. ~ Calle Mijares between Calles Matamoros and Abasolo; 624-143-0542. DELUXE.

The mesquite-grilled steaks and lobsters at **Edith's Restaurant** are great, and the exotic drinks and elaborate desserts are even better. There's live music nightly by a mellow jazz trio. But the best thing about this restaurant is its hillside location with a spectacular view of the harbor and El Arco. Dinner only. ~ Playa El Medano at Paseo del Pescador; 624-143-0801. DELUXE.

GROCERIES Stock up for a beach picnic with imported meats and cheeses, organic produce, homemade salads and wine from **La Europea**. ~ Puerto Paraiso Plaza 39-B, Marina; 624-105-1818. Another good Cabo San Lucas deli, natural food and wine shop is **Tutto Bene**. ~ Boulevard Marina at Camino del Cerro (near the traffic circle); 624-144-3300.

SHOPPING Most Cabo San Lucas shopping is located around the Marina in several big shopping malls, **El Tesoro Los Cabos** (formerly Plaza

Las Glorias) and **Puerto Paraiso Plaza**. The shops, which sell sportswear, silver jewelry and upscale Mexican folk art, change constantly and seem designed for cruise ship passengers ashore for a few hours with nothing to do but shop. **Libros, Libros** has one of the most extensive selections of English-language books in Baja. ~ Boulevard Marina (next to Carlos 'n' Charlies); 624-143-3172.

There is also a tourist-oriented **Public Market** at the municipal pier near the Hotel Finisterra. Bargaining is expected, asking prices are quite high, and many "Mexican folk art" items are knockoffs from China, but if you know what you're looking for, you might find it here. ~ Municipal Pier, Boulevard Marina.

For metal sculpture, handmade furniture and pre-Columbian reproductions by local artists, check out **Galería El Dorado**. ~ Boulevard Marina; 624-143-4670.

A wonderful array of masks, dolls and figurines from all over mainland Mexico is found at **Faces of Mexico**. ~ Calle Lázaro Cárdenas; no phone. Amazing handicrafts from the Huichol Indians of Nayarit are exhibited at **Huichol Collection Galería Museo**. ~ Boulevard Marina; 624-143-4055. Ceramics from the famous arts and crafts districts around Guadalajara are sold at **Artesanías Tonala y Tlaquepaque**. ~ Calle Zaragosa at Avenida de la Juventud; 624-143-2814.

Los Cabos's famous, long-established blown glass factory, **Vitrofusion**, offers tours and sells an array of glass gift items from unique, elaborately worked sculptures to the heavy, virtually unbreakable drinking glasses you'll see in many of the better restaurants around town. Look for the sign on the left just past the hospital. ~ Route 19 west of town; 624-143-0255.

NIGHTLIFE   Cabo San Lucas is party central, not only for the Los Cabos area but for the entire Baja Peninsula. Among the liveliest saloons are **Squid Roe** (Boulevard Marina; 624-143-0655), the pricier **Giggling Marlin** (Calle Lázaro Cárdenas; 624-143-4144) and the **Río Grill** (Boulevard Marina 31-A; 624-143-3475). None of these places charges a cover, and revelers stumble up and down the street from one to the next.

One club that does charge a cover—and often a stiff one—is the **Cabo Wabo Cantina**, owned by Van Halen veteran Sammy Hagar, which presents big-name rock bands on many weekends. ~ Calle Guerrero; 624-143-1188. Then there's **Zoo Bar & Dance**, a newish dance club with life-size animal sculptures and African decor. ~ Boulevard Marina; 624-143-5500.

If your preference is for someplace mellow, cool out at **Sancho Panza's Wine Bistro**. Located in the alley behind the lighthouse tower, it features blues on Sundays and Latin jazz or mellow jazz the rest of the week. ~ Plaza Las Glorias; 624-143-3212. Soothingly ultra-hip characterizes the ambience at **Barometro,** a purple-and-aqua neon-lit club that features deejay acid jazz and big-screen projections of arty un-derwater photos, plus mimes, fire dancers and other offbeat live performers. ~ Marina board-walk; 624-143-1466.

Everything happens at once at the **Caliente Casino Real** in the Plaza Nautica: music videos, dancing, karaoke and as many as 12 games playing on the 43 TV monitors in the sports bar, as well as a "fan-tasy casino"—no money bets. ~ Boulevard Marina; 624-143-1934.

> Sammy Hagar lent his club's name to his award-winning tequila, Cabo Wabo tequila. If you can't visit the cantina for a shot, you can get a bottle online.

And for men whose idea of a great vacation includes lap dances, **Lord Black,** a *club caballero* (that's Mexican for "strip joint") is centrally located right behind Plaza Nautica, just a few steps from the marina. ~ Boulevard Marina 1; 624-143-6344.

Foremost among the few gay and lesbian clubs in Los Cabos the **Rainbow Bar** has mango margaritas, techno dance music and late hours; nothing happens until after midnight. ~ Marina Cabo Plaza; no phone.

PLAYA DEL AMANTE "Lover's Beach" lies just north of the famous, photogenic rock arch at the tip of the prom-ontory southeast of town, with good swimming and great snor-keling and scuba diving. Despite the fact that no road goes near it, it's by far the most popular and crowded beach around. Flo-tillas of water taxis and glass-bottom boats run back and forth from the marina constantly, carrying visitors to and from this beach. It is also possible to reach it by a 15-minute hike over the ridge from the end of Playa Solmar.

BEACHES & PARKS

PLAYA SOLMAR This beach on the Pacific side of Land's End is unprotected from the crashing waves; it's dangerous to swim there. For this reason, resort development along the beach has been minimal, and it's a great place for solitary hiking. ~ Take the road that leads from Boulevard Marina to the Hotel Solmar streets and hike down to the beach from there.

PLAYA EL MEDANO Also known as Playa Las Palmas, this is Cabo's resort beach, lined with big hotels and pa-lapa restaurants. Nearly every day, you'll find thousands of peo-ple sunbathing and swimming here. All kinds of water sports equipment, including snorkels, kayaks and jet skis, are for rent along the beach. ~ Take Paseo El Pescador south from Calle Lá-zaro Cárdenas to Paseo El Medano.

Todos Santos

▼▼▼▼▼▼▼▼▼

Sixty-seven kilometers north of Cabo San Lucas on Route 19, Todos Santos is the Shangri-La of the Baja cape. This small town has so far averted the kind of resort development that has transformed Los Cabos into a tourist industry icon. Like San José del Cabo, Todos Santos is protected as a national historic district. Unlike San José, no one has yet poured millions of dollars into gentrifying it, though a gradual increase in real estate development aimed at American baby-boomer retirees has multiplied the population of permanent residents to approximately 4500. The unpredictable weather along the Pacific coast has discouraged large-scale investment. Precisely for this reason, hundreds of expatriate artists from the United States have chosen to make their homes in Todos Santos, and it is experiencing a commercial renaissance in the form of proliferating galleries and bed and breakfasts, though unlike Los Cabos, it's still surrounded by farms instead of highrise condos and golf courses. Largely through word-of-mouth the town is being "discovered" by more and more snowbirds each year.

In 2006, Todos Santos became the first town in Baja to be selected as a "Pueblo Magico," a designation awarded by SECTUR, the Mexican secretariat of tourism, to fewer than two dozen communities throughout the country with unique historical, cultural or religious significance. (Others include San Cristóbal de las Casas, Chiapas; San Miguel de Allende, Guanajuato; Tequila, Jalisco; and Izamal, Yucatán.)

SIGHTS

Todos Santos is a Mexican national historic district, and all rebuilding and new construction in the town center must be approved by the Instituto Nacional de Antropología e Historia. In 1723, missionaries set up an outpost here to convert the indigenous people in the nearby mountains, but they were driven away in less than two years when the locals rebelled against the church and its requirements of modest clothing and monogamy. A permanent mission, the Misión Santa Rosa de Todos Santos, was built in 1733 on the site where the town church still stands. Around it grew a trading center that served the farms which were springing up in the area. Beginning in 1848 when the Mexican War with the United States ended, Todos Santos became a sugarcane growing and processing area, and most of the buildings in the historic district date to that era. The chimneys of several abandoned sugar mills still tower over the surrounding area. Todos Santos and its farmlands were trampled and burned during a major battle for control of Baja California during the 1910 Mexican Revolution. Prosperity returned and lasted until the 1950s, when a long drought spelled the end of the sugarcane plantations.

Almost a ghost town, with most of its historic buildings abandoned and crumbling, Todos Santos came back to life in 1984, when the highway from Cabo San Lucas was paved, bringing the first wave of artists and tourists.

The heart of the historic district is the small zócalo, flanked by stuccoed brick buildings, many of which date back to the mid-19th century. The plaza is watched over by the **Iglesia de Nuestra Señora de la Paz**, a picturesque church with a multitiered bell tower and a vestibule from the original mission church. You'll also find early artworks by missionaries in Baja as well as a statue of the church's namesake, the Virgin of Pilar, which was made in Spain and brought here via La Paz in the 1740s. The statue represents the miraculous appearance of the Virgin Mary in Zaragoza, Spain, which—according to legend—enabled the apostle James the Elder to convert many Romans in Spain to Christianity around A.D. 40. ~ 612-143-4180.

Also fronting on the zócalo is the vaguely Moorish-style **Teatro–Cine General Manuel Márquez de León**. Originally built as a motion picture theater in 1944, it fell into disrepair but has now been restored and is used for concerts, plays and other community special events.

A block east, the **Centro Cultural Profesor Néstor Agúndez Martínez** (usually referred to by the Anglo citizenry as the "cultural center" or "museum") occupies the town's former schoolhouse. A small collection of Indian artifacts is exhibited here, along with paintings from the Mexican Revolution era, including one of La Coronela, a local woman who became a revolutionary hero. The showpiece of the museum are large, faded murals depicting the history and culture of Mexico, dating back to the 1930s. Restoration is underway, and some murals are now as bright as new. The cultural center also exhibits the works of present-day local painters. ~ Corner of Calles Topete and Obregón.

◆◆◆

SAINTS AND SLAVES

Todos Santos, a town of 4000, dates back to 1723. One of the longest-lived Jesuit missions, it hosted survivors from several other southern Baja missions that had been abandoned because of catastrophic epidemics. Misión Santa Rosa de Todos Santos lasted until 1840, and as soon as the missionaries left, plantation owners put the local people to work in cane fields that produced much of the West Coast's sugar during the 19th century.

The local "haunted house," a two-story sugar baron's mansion built of stone with tall, pointed Gothic windows, is known as **Casa Dracula**. To take a peek at it, follow Calle Topete north from the plaza for two blocks, turn left at the T intersection and go one block. It's on your right. ~ Calle Nicolas Bravo.

The **Campo Experimental Forestal Todos Santos**, a botanical garden containing virtually all native cactuses, trees and shrubs of the Baja peninsula along with examples of other tropical desert vegetation from around the world, is seven kilometers south of town.

LODGING   Todos Santos' Spanish Colonial–style **Hotel California** was built long before the first paved road reached the west side of the cape. After standing closed for several years, the historic hotel was totally renovated inside and out in 2004 and 2005 and reopened its doors with 11 playfully decorated rooms and suites, which have folk art decor and bright paint jobs but no air conditioning, phones or TVs. Visitors can't spend more than an hour in Todos Santos without hearing how The Eagles vacationed here while Don Henley composed the classic rock song "Hotel California." Henley himself denies it, claims they never set foot in Todos Santos, and says the hotel of the song was purely metaphoric. One investigative journalist from *Rolling Stone* learned that the hotel had a different name when the album was released, and that the manager renamed it Hotel California to attract more tourists to Todos Santos. Believe what you want; you'll find a curio shop selling what must be the world's largest selection of Eagles and Hotel California paraphernalia right across the street. ~ Calle Benito Juárez; 612-145-0525. MODERATE.

Across the street and down the block from the Hotel California, the **Motel Guluarte** has eight clean, very plain rooms cooled by table fans. There's a small swimming pool and a shaded second-floor balcony. Room rates are less than half those at Hotel California. ~ Calle Benito Juárez; 612-145-0006. BUDGET.

The elegant **Todos Santos Inn** occupies the restored brick home built by a 19th-century sugar baron. Eight guest rooms and suites, individually furnished in Colonial style, open onto a classic courtyard garden complete with a fountain, classic archways, a small swimming pool and wine bar. The inn offers personalized Spanish-language instruction packages. Closed August and September. ~ Calle Legaspi 33; phone/fax 612-145-0040; www.todossantosinn.com. ULTRA-DELUXE.

One of the most luxurious lodgings in Todos Santos, and the only beachfront lodging in town, the **Posada la Poza** has just seven spacious, air-conditioned suites, each overlooking either the ocean or the adjacent desert park. In-room amenities include fine Swiss bed linens, CD players and binoculars for birdwatching. There is no television on the premises, but high-speed internet access is available, and several guest units have private hot tubs or jacuzzis. There's also a swimming pool. Breakfast is included in the room rate. ~ On the beach; 612-145-0400, fax 612-145-0453; www.lapoza.com. ULTRA-DELUXE.

Small, intimate bed-and-breakfast casita compounds comprise the largest number of lodging possibilities in Todos Santos. Representative of the breed is the **Hacienda Todos Los Santos Guest House Inn,** situated on a hilltop overlooking town. The three individual guest units are individually decorated with contemporary flair, and big potted plants echo the lush flowering gardens, tropical fruit trees and lofty date palms that fill the grounds. There's a swimming pool. ~ Todos Santos; 612-145-0547; e-mail haciendadelossantos@prodigy.net.mx. MODERATE TO DELUXE.

Located about a mile from the town center, **Casa Bentley Suites** is one of the of the most stylish new lodgings in town. It incorporates a historic adobe house dating back to 1850, along with two modern houses built of stone by the owner, Oregon geology professor Bob Bentley, whose collection of mineral specimens is displayed throughout the inn. Secluded in a walled compound within a two-acre mango orchard, the inn offers a swimming pool, fountain and lush tropical landscaping. The six guest suites are individually decorated with eclectic mixes of furnishings. Some are air-conditioned, and all have king- or queen-sized beds. ~ Calle Pilar 38; phone/fax 612-145-0276; www.casa bentleybaja.com, e-mail casa.bentley@yahoo.com. DELUXE TO ULTRA-DELUXE.

◀ *HIDDEN*

Alegria, a beautiful owner-designed inn, is a modern rendition of a Colonial-style hacienda. Sweeping curves blend with traditional elements like *nichos* and Saltillo tiles to create an ambience of timeless graciousness. The seven guest rooms and suites feature handcrafted furniture and original art. Most units are air-

◀ *HIDDEN*

RAINBOW ROOMS

Another of the newest lodgings in Todos Santos—and certainly the most colorful—is the four-casita **Hotelito.** The inn is owned and managed by world-class British designer Jenny Armit, who has created this ultramodern inn around a palm-filled courtyard and painted it in the widest possible range of brilliant hues. Individually decorated with remarkable attention to detail, the suites have outdoor terraces or private gated gardens with hammocks and lounge chairs. ~ Rancho de la Cachora; 612-145-0099; www.thehotelito.com, e-mail elhotelito@mac.com. MODERATE TO ULTRA-DELUXE.

conditioned, and all have satellite TV, phones and wireless internet access. The pool area is surrounded by a stonework deck, palm trees and gardens. Rates include a full hacienda breakfast. ~ Carretera La Cachora; 612-145-0700, fax 612-145-0368; www. alegriainn.net, e-mail alegriats@prodigy.net. DELUXE TO ULTRA-DELUXE.

The lowest rates in the Todos Santos area can be found at **Eco-Surf Camp** south of town. There's a palapa surf shop, a makeshift bar, and accommodations in a cluster of thatched-roof cabanas and old travel trailers that look as if they were abandoned long ago by snowbirds who didn't trust them to make it back to the border without falling apart, as well as campsites for surfing enthusiasts to pitch their tents or hang their hammocks while waiting for the perfect wave. (This is also the place to watch for a perfect sunset.) The "eco-" part of the name indicates that the management is into solar power, composting toilets, water reclamation and garbage recycling. Surfboards, snorkeling equipment and bikes are available for rent. Inquire ahead, as lodging may be unavailable during five-day surf camps; some surfing programs are for women only, and male guests aren't accepted at those times. ~ Eight kilometers south of Todos Santos; 612-145-0882; e-mail teampaty1@hotmail.com. BUDGET TO MODERATE.

DINING

The central gringo hangout in town is the **Caffe Todos Santos**, where you can sip an espresso, cappuccino or latte in the 19th-century hacienda courtyard or indoors surrounded by local artists' paintings. The menu includes Mexican dishes, French pastries, sandwiches of imported deli meats and cheeses on home-baked multigrain bread, and all-organic fresh fruit plates. ~ Calle Centenario 33; 612-145-0300. MODERATE.

AUTHOR FAVORITE

One of the best reasons I can think of to drive out to the ultra-mellow surfers and artists community of Todos Santos is the seafood and pasta with homegrown salad served at the **Café Santa Fe**. The premier restaurant in Todos Santos, this historic hacienda attracts diners all the way from Los Cabos with its sensational Italian cuisine. The interior has been beautifully renovated, and there is additional seating on the garden patio. Salads are made with locally grown organic vegetables. House specialties include a unique version of lasagna, gourmet pizza, and shrimp-and-lobster ravioli. There's tiramisu for dessert. ~ Calle Centenario; 612-145-0340. MODERATE TO DELUXE.

Another of the longest-established restaurants in town, the **Café Santa Fe** serves authentic northern Italian food in a historic 1850s landmark building facing the town plaza. Because of signage restrictions, it is identified only by a discreet "Restaurant" sign over the grandiose doorway. Indoor and outdoor dining areas center on a shady garden courtyard. The menu focuses on fresh local seafood and locally grown organic produce. It's reputed to be the finest Italian restaurant on the Cape, so day-trippers from Los Cabos often come to Todos Santos just to eat here; accordingly, reservations are essential. Closed Tuesday. ~ Calle Centenario; 612-145-0340. MODERATE TO DELUXE.

If you're weary of the gringo-pleasing array of chicken, cheeseburger, pizza and shrimp dishes that seem to be standard fare at more and more full-service restaurants throughout Los Cabos, one unlikely option is **Suki's**, a contemporary Asian restaurant in a tropical courtyard setting as exotic as the selection of stir-fries, spicy soups, spring rolls and tempura on its Japanese-Korean-Thai menu. If you're a vegetarian, this is your best bet. No reservations, it's first-come, first-served. So plan to dine there when no tour buses from Los Cabos are in town. ~ Calle Hidalgo between Rangel and Cuauhtémoc; 612-145-0847. MODERATE.

Todos Santos has even more restaurants than art galleries, and they appear and disappear with alarming swiftness. But there's one thing you can always count on: dozens of local street vendors, food stands and holes-in-the-wall that serve everything from shrimp tacos to American-style turkey hot dogs. Stroll along any commercial street in town to find vendors of such Mexican specialties as *machaca* (shredded beef—or, in these parts, sometimes fish), *birria* (goat stew), *menudo* (tripe) and *tacos de cabeza* (literally, head tacos—made from cow brains and tongue). Easily grossed out? Then opt for more familiar fish tacos, burritos and quesadillas—a sidewalk feast for very little *dinero*. Try the fish and shrimp tacos at **Carnitas Barajas** (Calle Degollado at Cuauhtémoc), the beef tacos and *papas rellenas* (stuffed potatoes) at **Tacos Chalako's** (Calle Juarez at Hidalgo) or the *torta de pierna*—grilled pork leg sandwich—at **Tres Hermanos** (Calle Marquez de León at Juarez). BUDGET.

For a sit-down Mexican meal, the place to go is **Restaurant Bar Las Fuentes**, an open-air palapa restaurant just off Route 19 at Todos Santos's only stoplight. Tables are set amid lush gardens by a fountain, and the bill of fare features house specialties such as *langosto al mojo de ajo* (lobster in garlic sauce) and *nopales rellenos con queso* (cheese-filled nopal cactus paddles), as well as the weekend favorite, *pollo en mole*. ~ Calle Degollado at Militar; 612-145-0257. MODERATE.

Though it may not look like much from the front, **Los Adobos de Todos Santos** serves outstanding Mexican gourmet fare in a surprising garden terrace setting behind a historic sug-arcane warehouse. Menu items you're not likely to encounter elsewhere include *sopa Tarasca* (chipotle bean soup) and *huitacochtle* beef tenderloin (cooked with the tasty corn fungus often called "Mexican truffles"). There's also *chile en nogada*, a wonderful national dish rarely served north of the border, con-sisting of a poblano chile stuffed with a blend of ground pork and fruit and topped with a creamy white sauce of ground wal-nuts and pomegranate seeds, traditionally eaten on Mexico's Día de la Independencia because its colors are those of the Mexican flag. ~ Calle Hidalgo between Juárez and Militar; 612-145-0203. MODERATE TO DELUXE.

The only restaurant on the beach in Todos Santos is the ele-gant little **El Gusto!** in the Posada la Poza. The gourmet fare changes seasonally and ranges from seafood dishes merging con-tinental and Mexican influences to vegetarian cuisine using or-ganic produce locally grown exclusively for the restaurant. For lighter dining, *tapas* are served in the hotel bar overlooking the ocean. The sunset view is unbeatable. ~ On the beach; 612-145-0400. DELUXE.

GROCERIES There are three small grocery stores in town, located at the cor-ner of Calles Juárez and Marquez de León, Calles Juárez and Zaragoza, and Calles Morelos and Colegio Militar.

SHOPPING About 20 galleries and studios exhibit the works of the local artists' colony. Don't miss **Charles Stewart Gallery** (Calle Cen-tenario at Calle Obregón; 612-145-0265), **Galería de Todos Santos** (Calle Legaspi 33; 612-145-0514), **Galería Indigo** (Calle Juárez at Hidalgo; 612-137-3473), **Galería Logan** (Calle Juárez at Morelos; 612-145-0151), **Galería Wall** (Calle Juárez 3; 612-145-0527) or **Girasoles Galería de Susan Diaz Rivera** (Calle Juárez; 612-145-0480).

El Tecolote carries a good selection of English-language books, American magazines and newspapers. In fact, El Tecolote is one of only two English-language bookstores on the Baja Peninsula. ~ Calle Juárez at Calle Morelos; 612-145-0372.

BEACHES & PARKS

PLAYA SAN PEDRO This small beach bordered by palm trees is a surfer's dream and a motor-home driver's nightmare. ~ Seven kilometers south of Todos Santos and two kilometers west of the highway.

▲ Tent camping is permitted on the beach. No fee or facilities.

PLAYA PESCADERO Another surfers' favorite, this beach is covered with round boulders at the north end but becomes smooth and wide as it sweeps southward for about four miles. ~ Eight kilometers south of Todos Santos.

▲ San Pedrito RV Park has restrooms with [...]
swimming pool, a laundry room and a restaurant [...]
are 72 RV sites with full hookups ($15 per night).
dozen beachfront tent sites ($3 per night plus $2 p[...]

PLAYA LOS CERRITOS 🏃 🏊 🎣 The most specta[...]
beaches around Todos Santos, this broad, white [...]
curves gracefully over an expanse of six miles. Surfer[...]
combers love it. ~ Twelve kilometers south of Todo[...]
three kilometers west of the highway.

▲ There was once a large *ejido* campground at the north end
of this beach, but it was destroyed by a storm and abandoned.
Today, RV travelers can camp without hookups or restrooms in
the forlorn ruins, and tenters can camp on the beach beyond.
Somebody from the *ejido* may come around to collect a $3 fee.

▼▼▼▼▼▼▼▼▼▼▼▼▼▼
Outdoor Adventures

FISHING

LA PAZ Isla Cerralvo, southeast of the Pichilingue Peninsula, is renowned for its 70- to 80-pound amberjack and grouper and for *pargo*,
a giant red snapper that has been called the strongest and most
difficult of all fighting fish. Fishing trips to Cerralvo are operated
by **Fisherman's Fleet** (612-122-1313; www.fishermansfleet.com,
e-mail fishermansfleet@hotmail.com) at the Club El Moro.
Other fishing charter services operating out of La Paz marinas
include the **Dorado Velez Fleet** (Los Arcos Hotel; 612-122-2744); and **Jonathan Roldan's Tailhunter Store & FUBAR
Cantina** (Cortez Club—relocating soon; 612-121-6120).

CABO DEL ESTE Sportfishing, including casting for roosterfish
and deep-sea fishing for marlin, sailfish and swordfish, is the
mainstay of the East Cape. Many resorts in the area operate their
own fishing fleets, and many organize all-inclusive fishing tours
from the U.S. One such service is **Neptune Tours**, affiliated with
the Fiesta Inn. ~ In the U.S.: 209-223-5680, 888-875-4700;
www.neptunetours.com. The **Rancho Buena Vista Hotel** also
operates its own fishing fleet. ~ P.O. Box 1408, Santa Maria, CA
93456; 805-928-1719, 800-258-8200; www.ranchobuenavista.
com. **Cass Fishing Tours** arranges sportfishing vacations at sev-

◆◆

KAYAKING IN LA PAZ

Isla Espiritu Santo has recently begun to rival Bahía Concepción as Baja's
most popular sea-kayaking destination. Multiday guided trips along the
island's west coast, with its sea canyons, hidden beaches and resident
sea lions, can be arranged through **California Seafaris**. ~ Marina
de La Paz; 612-111-7335.

ral hotels in the area. ~ In the U.S.: 800-593-6510, 800-593-6510; www.casstours.com. Locally, you'll find fishing *pangas* for hire with guides in Los Fraıles. Contact **Cabo Pulmo Tours**. ~ 624-147-5149.

LOS CABOS The waters off Los Cabos are famous worldwide for marlin, sailfish and swordfish. Sport fishermen catch some 10,000 of them each year. Other game fish common to the area are wahoo, dorado and yellowfin tuna.

Keenly aware of the decline of big-game fisheries farther north in the Sea of Cortez, and the economic devastation that would follow if the same thing happened around Los Cabos, all fishing fleets promote catch-and-release sport fishing, and a growing number insist on it. A fishing trip can be arranged through any resort hotel. Reputable companies include **Palmilla Sportfishing Fleet** (Hotel Palmilla, San José Los Cabos; 624-142-0582, or 800-637-2226 in the U.S.), **ABY Sport Fishing Charters** (tourist dock, Cabo San Lucas; 624-144-4203), **Pisces Sportfishing Fleet** (Marina Cabo San Lucas; 624-143-1288, or 800-946-5599 in the U.S.) and **Minerva's** (Marina Cabo San Lucas; 624-143-1282).

SURFING & WIND-SURFING

LA PAZ Windsurfers head for Playa La Ventana in the winter, when strong winds blow on the channel between the beach and Isla Cerralvo.

CABO DEL ESTE Bahía de Palmas is gaining a reputation for great windsurfing, and Los Barriles is the site of the annual Vela-O'Neill Baja Championships sailboard races. Sailboards are available for rent at several East Cape hotels. At the south end of the bay, Punta Arena has a point break that makes for good board surfing during the August-to-October *chubasco* winds. It is virtually the only place on the Sea of Cortez that attracts surfers.

LOS CABOS The best surfing spot in the area is a small cove known locally as **The Monuments**, reached via the Mirador del Medano turnoff five kilometers east of Cabo San Lucas. This cove is perfectly situated to catch the swells deflected from Land's End. Boards can be rented at **Killer Hook Surf Shop** (Avenida Hidalgo, San José del Cabo; 624-142-2430) or **Pisces Water Sports Center** (Marina Cabo San Lucas; 624-143-1288).

TODOS SANTOS The Pacific side of the cape is considered one of Baja's best surfing areas during the winter months, with many and varied point and beach breaks. Great surfer beaches include Playa El Pescadero, Playa los Cerritos, Punta Gasparino and Playa Migriño. Bring your own board or rent one in Los Cabos. You'll find a surf shop and camaraderie at the **Pescadero Surf Camp** (Km. 64, Barrio Las Palmas; 624-130-3032) or **Eco Surf Camp** (south of Todos Santos). The latter hosts week-long **Teampaty Surf Camps** for women. ~ e-mail teampaty1@hotmail.com.

LA PAZ Popular dive destinations from La Paz include the wreck of the ferry *Salvatierra* and the white coral reef off the coast of **Isla Espiritu Santo**. The ultimate dive in Baja, however, lies nine miles north of the island. **El Bajo** (also called the Marisla Seamount) is a group of three underwater mountain peaks, the tallest of which reaches to within 60 feet of the surface. The seamount attracts large fish, including 16- to 20-foot manta rays and hammerhead sharks. Though guides insist that both are harmless, this is not a dive for the faint of heart. You might even encounter a whale shark, the largest fish on earth. Trips can be arranged at **Kimbaja Adventures** (Marina Palmira, Km. 2.5, Carretera Pichilingue; 612-121-5874); **Scuba Baja Joe** (Malecón at Calle Ocampo; 612-122-4006, fax 612-122-4000); **La Paz Diving Service** (Calle Nayarit 10; 612-122-3761) or **Scuba Aguilar** (Avenida Independencia 107; 612-142-1826, fax 612-142-8644).

CABO DEL ESTE The Mexican government officially established **Cabo Pulmo** as a marine park in 1995 and prohibited fishing there. The 11-mile-long underwater park contains eight living coral reefs that divers rarely visit. There is also a wreck of a fishing boat, which lies in 18 feet of water. Complete information on scuba and snorkeling sites is available at the park activities center.

LOS CABOS The best spot for snorkeling is the vicinity of **Playa del Amante**. The cliffs that isolate the beach on both sides drop about ten feet below the water's surface to a sandy bottom with coral and colorful fish.

Cabo San Lucas' famous dive zone is between the inner harbor and Land's End, where several underwater canyons descend into an enormous gorge, 3000 feet deep, that lies off Playa del Amante. "Rivers" of sand flow down the bottoms of these canyons and spill over cliffs in spectacular sandfalls.

Expert divers head for **Banco Gorda Primero**, which lies at a depth of 110 feet. On this bank of rare black coral, divers are often rewarded by a close encounter with a large billfish, a whale

AUTHOR FAVORITE

I've explored the James Bond wrecks in the Bahamas and swum with predators in the Cave of the Sleeping Sharks near Isla Mujeres, but I've never seen an underwater sight quite as strange as the sandfalls that spill into the submerged 3000-foot gorge off Cabo San Lucas' **Playa del Amante**. This ultimate snorkeling experience is situated between the inner harbor and Land's End. See page 255 for more information.

shark or even a gray whale. Los Cabos dive shops include **Killer Hook Surf Shop** (Avenida Hidalgo, San José del Cabo; 624-142-2430), **Land's End Divers** (624-143-2200) and **Amigos del Mar** (Cabo San Lucas Marina; 624-143-0505; www.amigos delmar.com).

WHALE WATCHING

LA PAZ Baja California Seafaris offers whale-watching excursions in winter. ~ Marina de La Paz; 612-111-7335. Two-hour sunset cruises on the Bahía de la Paz are offered by the **Hotel Marina**. ~ Km. 2.5, Carretera Pichilingue; 612-121-6254.

LOS CABOS Panchito Tours operates whale-watching trips from Cabo San Lucas during the winter months. ~ 624-143-8532. **Aero Califia** offers one-day fly-in whale-watching tours to Bahía Magdalena for up to 12 passengers. ~ Boulevard Marina 4-A (Costa Real Cabo Hotel); 624-143-4302. Another, though not necessarily a less expensive, option is to spot passing whales from the **Whalewatchers' Bar** in the Hotel Finisterra.

TENNIS

LOS CABOS Eight lighted, hard-surfaced tennis courts are open to the public for a fee at **Los Cabos Club de Golf**. ~ 624-142-0905. While this is the only public tennis complex in Los Cabos, several beach resort hotels have courts for guests' use.

GOLF

Although La Paz, the state capital and largest city in Baja California Sur, does not have a single golf course, Los Cabos has no fewer than 11 public and private courses, with more in the planning stages. The public **Campo de Golf–San Jose del Cabo** (624-142-0905), located between the town and hotel zone in San José, has nine holes. Jack Nicklaus designed the 18-hole par 71 **Club Campestre San José Golf Course** (Km. 119, Libramiento Aeropuerto; 624-144-1200, or 877-795-8727 in the U.S.; www.questro.com.mx), as well as the 27-hole course at the **Palmilla Golf Club** (624-142-0708, or 800-637-2226 in the U.S.; www.palmillaresort.com/golf/index.asp, e-mail ourclub@palmillaresort.com), the 18-hole **El Dorado Golf Club** (Route 1, Km. 21; 624-144-5451, or 877-795-8727 in the U.S.), the new 18-hole **Puerto Los Cabos Golf Club** (Paseo de los Pescadores; 624-144-1200, or 877-795-8727 in the U.S.; www.questro.com.mx) and the 18-hole **Cabo del Sol–Ocean Course**, while Tom Seiskopf designed the 18-hole **Cabo del Sol–Desert Course** (both Route 1, Km. 10.3; 624-145-8200; www.cabodelsol.com) and Robert Trent Jones designed the 18-hole **Cabo Real Golf Club** (624-144-1200, or 877-795-8727 in the U.S.; www.caboreal.com) at the Meliá Cabo Real. Rounding out the field are the 18-hole **Cabo San Lucas Country Club** golf course (624-143-4654, or 888-328-8501 in the U.S.;

Los Cabos boasts five golf courses designed by renowned golfer Jack Nicklaus.

www.golfincabo.com), the nine-hole **Mayan Palace Golf Los Cabos** (Route 1, Km. 30; 624-142-0905; www.mayanresorts-golf.com). These courses are open to the public, and all have carts and clubs for rent.

If your idea of a good time encompasses the popular Mexican sport of riding a horse in the crashing surf, head for **Marcos' Horse Rentals**. The stable also offers four-hour, very scenic guided rides to Faro Viejo. ~ Hacienda Beach Resort, Playa El Medano, Cabo San Lucas; 624-143-0123. You can also rent horses for one hour, two hours or longer, or arrange a trail ride or lesson, at **Cabo Real Cuadra San Francisco** at the Meliá Cabo Real Hotel. ~ 624-144-0160.

RIDING STABLES

The **Sierra de la Laguna** is probably the most fascinating destination in Baja for trekkers, and one of the most difficult. Dense vegetation and extremely rugged terrain make north–south travel virtually impossible in the sierra, but three major east–west trails provide access to the high country. All three trails were often used by local residents to travel across the cape in the days before the coastal highway was built. Then they faded into obscurity and were confused by animal trails, but with increased use by hikers in the 1990s, they are becoming clearly defined again. None of the sierra's most interesting areas can be reached on a day hike. Trekkers should be prepared for near-freezing nights in the high country in winter, and fog or rain at other times of year.

HIKING

The most spectacular and popular of the sierra trails is **Cañon San Dionisio**. It runs 18 miles between Rancho San Dionisio on the east end (19 kilometers up an unpaved road from Santiago) to La Burrera on the west end (18 kilometers up another unpaved road from the highway, a few kilometers south of Todos Santos). The eastern half of the trail runs through the canyon, with pools and waterfalls, before climbing through a boulder field to La Laguna, the heart of the sierra. La Laguna was a mountain lake more than a mile across until about 1870, when erosion ruptured it and sent its water pouring down Cañon San Dionisio. Today it is a broad meadow about 5500 feet above sea level, flanked on the north and south by the sierra's two tallest mountains—Picacho La Laguna (6507 feet) and Cerro Las Casitas (6855 feet). Allow three or four days to hike to La Laguna and back from the east, two or three days from the west, or three to five days to go from one end of the trail to the other. Guides and pack animals are often available at Rancho San Dionisio.

The other two trails go through canyons on the north and south sides of 6002-foot Cerro Blanco, a steep granite peak that lies ten impassable miles south of La Laguna. Both are easier than the San Dionisio route, reaching maximum elevations of less than 4000 feet, but the climb is more demanding from these trails up the mountainsides to the hummingbird flower forests on the high slopes. The 14-mile **Cañon San Bernardo** trail goes between the tiny villages of Boca de la Sierra on the east (8 kilometers on an unpaved road from Miraflores) and Santo Domingo on the west (15 kilometers along a maze of dirt roads that branches off the road from Todos Santos to San Juan del Asseradero). Watch for signs and, when in doubt, ask locals for directions to Santo Domingo. The ten-mile **Cañon San Pablo** trail goes from Rancho El Salto on the east (6.5 kilometers on an unpaved road from Caduaño) to the village of El Guerigo on the west (35 kilometers on a tricky maze of unpaved roads from El Pescadero off Route 19).

▼▼▼▼▼▼▼▼▼▼▼
Transportation

AIR

In La Paz, **Aeropuerto General Manuel Márquez de León** has daily flights to and from Los Angeles, Phoenix and Tijuana on Aero California.

Los Cabos International Airport, north of San José del Cabo, serves both San José and Cabo San Lucas, landing more than two dozen flights daily from the United States. Aero California flies in from Los Angeles, Phoenix and Denver. Mexicana also has flights from Denver, as well as San Francisco, Los Angeles, San Diego, Tokyo and many Mexican cities. Strangely enough, one of the leading carriers to Los Cabos is Alaska Airlines, with service from San Diego, Los Angeles, Portland, Seattle, Victoria and Anchorage.

BOAT

Ferries operate between the Pichilingue ferry terminal east of La Paz and the mainland cities of Topolobampo (10 hours, daily except Sunday, 10 p.m.) and Mazatlán (18 hours, daily except Saturday, 3 p.m.) Fares are very reasonable for foot passengers, but expensive for vehicles—over US$100 for a car and several hundred dollars for a motor home. ~ 612-125-3833.

Cabo San Lucas is a port of call for cruise ships operated by **Royal Caribbean** (888-313-8883), **Carnival** (888-227-6492) and **Princess** (888-774-6237). All three lines offer seven-day cruises from Los Angeles to the "Mexican Riviera"—meaning Cabo San Lucas, Puerto Vallarta and either Mazatlán or Acapulco. Passengers' day in Cabo is a cursory visit, almost incidental to the cruise experience itself, with its shipboard casino, dancing, lounge entertainment, nonstop organized activities and food, food, food!

BUS

Autotransportes Aguila runs 13 buses a day from the U.S. border to Los Cabos. All of them stop in La Paz en route. From there, seven of them travel clockwise around the cape, by way of Santiago, and six go counterclockwise by way of Todos Santos.

Route 19 branches off from Route 1, 26 kilometers south of La Paz. The two highways meet again in Cabo San Lucas, forming a 299-kilometer loop around the cape and linking all the towns mentioned in this chapter.

CAR

In La Paz, **Hertz** (612-122-5300), **Avis** (612-122-1813), **Budget** (612-125-9696) and **Thrifty** (612-125-9696) have offices downtown and at the international airport.

CAR RENTALS

In Los Cabos, the many car rental agencies that have airport desks include **Avis** (624-142-0680), **Budget** (624-143-0241), **Dollar** (624-142-6071), **National** (624-143-6000) and **Thrifty** (624-142-1671).

Taxis are the only mode of public ground transportation serving both the La Paz and Los Cabos airports. In La Paz, the cab fares set by the government for the short trip into the city are so expensive that you might as well rent a car.

PUBLIC TRANSIT

In Los Cabos, where the taxis are government-owned, fares depend on the number of passengers. They are fairly reasonable to San José del Cabo, more expensive to the Los Cabos Corridor resorts and Cabo San Lucas. Many Los Cabos resorts have free airport shuttles.

La Paz has an extensive local bus system. Most buses run to and from the Mercado Municipal at Calles Revolución and Degollado, where passengers transfer to reach other parts of the city.

Fares are very low. Los Cabos has no local buses, but ten **Autotransportes Aguila** intercity buses stop in San José every day, on their way between Cabo San Lucas and La Paz.

Water taxis are a key mode of public transportation in Cabo San Lucas, where a major visitor destination, Playa del Amante, cannot be reached by road.

▼▼▼▼▼▼▼▼▼▼▼▼▼▼▼▼▼▼▼▼▼▼

Addresses & Phone Numbers

Tourist Information Center ~ La Paz; 612-122-5939

Green Angels (roadside help) ~ 624-125-9677

Tourist Office ~ San José del Cabo; 624-142-1199

Migración (Immigration) ~ La Paz, 612-125-3493; Cabo San Lucas, 624-143-0135

American Consular Agency ~ Cabo San Lucas; 624-143-3566; 24-hour emergency number 619-692-2154

Canadian Consul ~ San José del Cabo; 624-142-4333

Cruz Roja (Red Cross) ~ La Paz, 612-122-1111; Cabo San Lucas, 624-143-3300; San José del Cabo, 624-142-0316

General Hospital ~ La Paz, 612-142-7377; San José del Cabo, 624-142-3713; Cabo San Lucas, 624-142-0013

Policia ~ La Paz, 612-122-0393; Cabo San Lucas, 624-143-0057; San José del Cabo, 624-142-0361

Patrulla de Caminos (Highway Patrol) ~ La Paz, 612-122-3235; Los Cabos, 624-146-0573

Emergency number: 066

Los Cabos International Airport ~ 624-146-5111

Internet access ~ Baja Net Internet Café, Calle Madero 430, La Paz, 612-125-9380; Club Internet, Avenida Zaragoza, San José del Cabo, Los Cabos Online, Boulevard Mijares #26, San Jose del Cabo, 624-142-5282; Dr. Z's Internet Café Bar, Boulevard Lázaro Cárdenas, Cabo San Lucas, 624-143-5390, Internet Café, Plaza Arambulo, Calle Zaragoza at Boulevard Lázaro Cárdenas, Cabo San Lucas; Los Adobes de Todos Santos Internet Cafe, Calle Hidalgo, Todos Santos, 612-145-0203

▼▼▼▼▼▼▼▼▼▼

Glossary

CUISINE

almejas—clams

atún—tuna

birria—goat stew

cabrilla—sea bass

calamar—squid

callos—scallops

camarones—shrimp

cangrejo—crab

carne asada—barbecued beef strips marinated in a red-chile sauce

ceviche—uncooked seafood marinated in lime juice, vinegar, oil, cilantro and spices

chilaquiles—tortilla strips, chicken and cheese scrambled together

chiles rellenos—stuffed chile peppers

cochinita pibil—pork barbecued in an orange marinade

cocteles—cocktails

comedor—an open-air, fast-food eatery

comida corrida—daily special

dorado—mahimahi

elotes—corn on the cob served with chili powder, lime and cream

gambas—prawns

huachinango—snapper

jurel—yellowtail

langosta—lobster

lenguado—halibut

pescado—fish

pez espada—swordfish

pollo en mole—chicken in a chile-and-chocolate sauce

pulpo—octopus

sabalo—tarpon

sierra—mackerel

tiburón—shark

MÁS PALABRAS (MORE WORDS)

abarrotes—groceries

abierto—open

aceite—motor oil

acumulador—vehicle battery

agua—water

angeles verdes—Green Angels

bahía—bay

ballena—whale

banda de ventilador—fan belt

baño—bath; restroom
bolsa de dormir—sleeping bag
calambre—sunburn
camino—road
campar—to camp
caña de pescar—fishing rod
carretera—highway
casita de campaña—tent
cerrado—closed
cuota—toll
chubasco—tropical storm
delfin—dolphin
ejército—army
ejido—agricultural commune
equipo de bucear—diving gear
estacionar—to park
farmacia—pharmacy
foco de mano—flashlight
gemelos—binoculars
gringo—person from the United States or Canada
gruta—cave
guía—guide
isla—island
licencia de manejar—driver's license
llanta—tire
magna sin—unleaded gasoline
malecón—waterfront promenade
maquiladora—border factory
mecánico—mechanic
mochila—backpack
pájaro—bird
palapa—thatched-roof shelter
panadería—bakery
panga—open wooden fishing boat
peligroso—dangerous
Pemex—gas station
picacho—peak
pinturas rupestres—rock art
playa—beach
punta—point
refaccionería—auto-parts store
seguros—insurance
sierra—mountain range; mackerel
supermercado—supermarket
tienda—store
velocidad maxima—speed limit
zopilote—vulture

Index

Addresses & phone numbers. *See* Addresses & phone numbers *in regional chapters*

Aeropuerto General Manuel Márquez de León, 268

Agua Blanca: sights, 157

AIDS, 15

Air travel, 29–30. *See also* Transportation *in regional chapters*

Algodones, 100–102; border crossing, 76; dining, 101; groceries, 101–102; lodging, 101; sights, 101

Algodones Dune Field, 101

Andador Costero (Santa Rosalía), 194

Animals: pets, 19–20; wildlife, 40–45

Avenida Revolución (Tijuana), 78–80; dining, 82–83; groceries, 86; lodging, 81; nightlife, 88–89; shopping, 86–87

Bahía Concepción, 197, 198

Bahía de los Angeles area, 164–71; beaches & parks, 170–71; camping, 170, 171; dining, 168–69; driving tour, 168–69; groceries, 169; lodging, 166–68; map, 167; nightlife, 169; sights, 165–66

Bahía de los Angeles (bay), 166; beaches, 170

Bahía de Palmas area: lodging, 234, 236

Bahía de Todos Santos, 129

Bahía Magdalena area, 211–14; beaches & parks, 214; camping, 214; dining, 214; groceries, 214; lodging, 213–14; sights, 211–13

Bahía San Luís Gonzaga, 136

Bahía Tortugas (town): dining, 179; lodging, 179; sights, 178

Baja (overview), 1–71; animals, 40–45; culture, 65–71; driving, 30–32; events, 7–10; food, 66–68; geology, 35–36; history, 50–65; itinerary, suggested, 4–5; language, 68–70, 271–72; map, 3; music, 70–71; outdoor adventures, 45–49; people, 65–66; plants, 36–40; regions, 2, 6; time zones, 173; transportation, 29–34; visitor information, 10–11; weather, 6–7, 235. *See also specific areas and towns*

Beaches & parks. *See* Beaches & parks *in area and town entries; see also* Playa *entries*

Biblioteca de Historia de las Californias, 226

Biblioteca Mahatma Gandhi, 194

Biking, 103, 218

Birds, 43–45

Boat tours, 181, 184

Boat travel, 30. *See also* Transportation *in regional chapters*

Bodegas de Santo Tomás (winery), 127

Border crossings, 22–24, 72–76

Border region, 2, 72–105; addresses & phone numbers, 105; map, 77; outdoor adventures, 102–103; transportation, 103–105. *See also specific border towns*

Boulevard Agua Caliente (Tijuana), 80; dining, 84; groceries, 86; lodging, 81; nightlife, 89–90

Boulevard Mijares area (San José del Cabo), 238; dining, 242; lodging, 238, 240–41; nightlife, 245; shopping, 244

Bullfighting, 85

Bus travel. *See* Transportation *in regional chapters*

Cabo del Este and Sierra de la Laguna, 232–37; beaches & parks, 237; camping, 237; dining, 236–37; lodging, 234, 236; map, 233; sights, 233–34

Cabo San Lucas, 245–55; beaches & parks, 255; dining, 251–53; groceries, 253; lodging, 246–51; map, 247; nightlife, 254–55; shopping, 253–54; sights, 246

Cactuses, 36, 37–38

Calendar of events, 7–10

Caliente Race Track, 80; nightlife, 89–90

Calle Lázaro Cárdenas (Cabo San Lucas), 246; lodging, 250; nightlife, 254; shopping, 254

Calmallí: sights, 177

Camping, 48–49. *See also* Camping *in area and town entries*

Campo Experimental Forestal Todos Santos, 258

Canal de Ballenas, 166

Cañon de Guadalupe, 93

Cañon del Diablo, 134

Cañon La Trinidad, 199

Cape region (La Paz and Los Cabos), 6, 221–70; addresses & phone numbers, 269–70; map, 223; outdoor

Lodging Index

Dining Index

HIDDEN GUIDES

Adventure travel or a relaxing vacation?—"Hidden" guidebooks are the only travel books in the business to provide detailed information on both. Aimed at environmentally aware travelers, our motto is "Where Vacations Meet Adventures." These books combine details on unique hotels, restaurants and sightseeing with information on camping, sports and hiking for the outdoor enthusiast.

THE NEW KEY GUIDES

Based on the concept of ecotourism, The New Key Guides are dedicated to the preservation of Central America's rare and endangered species, architecture and archaeology. Filled with helpful tips, they give travelers everything they need to know about these exotic destinations.

PARADISE FAMILY GUIDES

Ideal for families traveling with kids of any age—toddlers to teenagers—Paradise Family Guides offer a blend of travel information unlike any other guides to the Hawaiian islands. With vacation ideas and tropical adventures that are sure to satisfy both action-hungry youngsters and relaxation-seeking parents, these guides meet the specific needs of each and every family member.

Ulysses Press books are available at bookstores everywhere. If any of the following titles are unavailable at your local bookstore, ask the bookseller to order them.

You can also order books directly from Ulysses Press
P.O. Box 3440, Berkeley, CA 94703
800-377-2542 or 510-601-8301
fax: 510-601-8307
www.ulyssespress.com
e-mail: ulysses@ulyssespress.com

HIDDEN GUIDEBOOKS

____ Hidden Arizona, $16.95
____ Hidden Baja, $14.95
____ Hidden Belize, $15.95
____ Hidden Big Island of Hawaii, $13.95
____ Hidden Boston & Cape Cod, $14.95
____ Hidden British Columbia, $18.95
____ Hidden Cancún & the Yucatán, $16.95
____ Hidden Carolinas, $17.95
____ Hidden Coast of California, $19.95
____ Hidden Colorado, $15.95
____ Hidden Disneyland, $13.95
____ Hidden Florida, $19.95
____ Hidden Florida Keys & Everglades, $13.95
____ Hidden Georgia, $16.95
____ Hidden Hawaii, $19.95
____ Hidden Idaho, $14.95
____ Hidden Kauai, $13.95
____ Hidden Los Angeles, $15.95
____ Hidden Maine, $15.95
____ Hidden Maui, $14.95
____ Hidden Miami, $14.95

____ Hidden Montana, $15.95
____ Hidden New England, $19.95
____ Hidden New Mexico, $15.95
____ Hidden Oahu, $14.95
____ Hidden Oregon, $15.95
____ Hidden Pacific Northwest, $19.95
____ Hidden Philadelphia, $14.95
____ Hidden Puerto Vallarta, $14.95
____ Hidden Salt Lake City, $14.95
____ Hidden San Diego, $14.95
____ Hidden San Francisco & Northern California, $19.95
____ Hidden Seattle, $14.95
____ Hidden Southern California, $19.95
____ Hidden Southwest, $19.95
____ Hidden Tahiti, $18.95
____ Hidden Tennessee, $16.95
____ Hidden Utah, $16.95
____ Hidden Walt Disney World, $13.95
____ Hidden Washington, $15.95
____ Hidden Wine Country, $14.95
____ Hidden Wyoming, $15.95

PARADISE FAMILY GUIDES

____ Paradise Family Guides: Kaua'i, $17.95
____ Paradise Family Guides: Maui, $17.95
____ Paradise Family Guides: Big Island of Hawai'i, $17.95

Mark the book(s) you're ordering and enter the total cost here ⇨

California residents add 8.75% sales tax here ⇨

Shipping, check box for your preferred method and enter cost here ⇨

❏ BOOK RATE   FREE! FREE! FREE!

❏ PRIORITY MAIL/UPS GROUND   cost of postage

❏ UPS OVERNIGHT OR 2-DAY AIR   cost of postage

Billing, enter total amount due here and check method of payment ⇨

❏ CHECK   ❏ MONEY ORDER

❏ VISA/MASTERCARD _____EXP. DATE_____

NAME _____PHONE_____

ADDRESS _____

CITY_____ STATE _____ ZIP_____

MONEY-BACK GUARANTEE ON DIRECT ORDERS PLACED THROUGH ULYSSES PRESS.

ABOUT THE AUTHOR

RICHARD HARRIS has written or co-written 35 other guidebooks including Ulysses' *Hidden Cancún & the Yucatán*, *Hidden Belize*, *Hidden Highways Arizona*, *Weekend Adventure Getaways: Yosemite Tahoe* and the bestselling *Hidden Southwest*. He has also served as contributing editor on guides to Mexico, New Mexico, and other ports of call for John Muir Publications, Fodor's, Birnbaum and Access guides. He is a past president of PEN New Mexico and currently president of the New Mexico Book Association. When not traveling, Richard writes and lives in Santa Fe, New Mexico.

ABOUT THE ILLUSTRATOR

GLENN KIM is a freelance illustrator residing in the San Francisco Bay area. His work appears in many Ulysses Press titles, including *Hidden Southwest*, *Hidden Tahiti* and *Hidden Belize*. He has also illustrated for the National Forest Service, several Bay Area magazines, book covers and greeting cards. He is now working with computer graphics and having lots of fun.